KH607

LINKING

Developmental Assessment and Early Intervention:
Curriculum-Based Prescriptions

Second Edition

Stephen J. Bagnato, Ed.D.
University of Pittsburgh School of Medicine
Children's Hospital of Pittsburgh
Pittsburgh, Pennsylvania

John T. Neisworth, Ph.D.
Penn State University
University Park, Pennsylvania

Susan M. Munson, Ph.D.
Duquesne University
Pittsburgh, Pennsylvania

AN ASPEN PUBLICATION®
Aspen Publishers, Inc.
Rockville, Maryland
1989

Library of Congress Cataloging-in-Publication Data

Bagnato, Stephen J.
Linking developmental assessment and early intervention:
curriculum-based prescriptions/Stephen J. Bagnato,
John T. Neisworth, Susan M. Munson.--2nd ed.
p. cm.
Rev. ed. of: Linking developmental assessment and curricula. 1981.
Bibliography: p.
Includes index.
ISBN: 0-8342-0063-5
1. Education, Preschool--Curricula.
2. Child development--Evaluation.
3. Special Education--Curricula. I.Neisworth, John T.
II. Munson, Susan M. III. Bagnato Stephen J.
Linking developmental assessment and curricula. IV. Title.
LB1140.4.B33   1989   371.9--dc20   89-6777
CIP

Editorial Services: Jane Coyle Garwood

Library of Congress Catalog Card Number: 89-6777
ISBN: 0-8342-0063-5

Printed in the United States of America

1 2 3 4 5

Contents

Foreword

The authors, Drs. Stephen Bagnato, John Neisworth, and Susan Munson have once again made a much-needed contribution to the field of early childhood handicapped education. This scholarly yet practical book thoroughly covers what is central to the education of young handicapped children, the linking of developmental assessment with curriculum. Professionals will find that this book gives them the information necessary for linking assessment and programming efficiently and effectively using "best practices."

In 1981 Bagnato and Neisworth published a widely used book focusing on systematic preschool assessment linked with curriculum, which was the first book ever to address this important concept. Since that time strides have been made in both the conceptualization and application of this concept that have necessitated not just a revision of the first book, but an entirely new book.

The passage of PL 99-457 calls for the use of best practices in meeting its intent. These practices are addressed in detail and with clarity in this book. It is particularly noteworthy that this book is dedicated to bridging the gap between two disciplines, those of the developmental school psychologist and the early childhood special educator. Exemplary curriculum-based assessment methods emphasize the importance of synthesizing information from the various members of the interdisciplinary team. A functional approach to assessment and programming is stressed.

It is evident that the authors had the practitioner in mind when they developed this book. The format of the chapters is particularly helpful to the reader. At the beginning of each chapter there is an outline of the chapter contents. Headings and subheadings within the chapter follow this logical outline. The authors have anticipated practitioners' questions and answered them clearly and comprehensively. The writing style makes the material enjoyable to read and informative.

Linking Developmental Assessment and Early Intervention covers a number of themes and issues that professionals in the field should find beneficial. One such issue, presented in Chapter 1, are the factors that contribute to the gap between assessment and intervention; another concerns the developments that have led to the closing of these gaps.

Those of us who have been in special education for a long time recall the days when the school psychologist at a staff meeting presented scores on tests, labeled a child, and gave general recommendations that were difficult to implement and were often meaningless to the teacher who was charged with creating a program for the child. In those days teachers had no instrument for ongoing assessment. It is little wonder that the resulting curriculum for the child was often hit or miss.

We laud the content of this book, which is dedicated to the integration of testing and teaching. It is a valuable resource to teacher trainers, students in training, and practitioners in the field. Books currently available do not go into depth in covering this most important aspect of early childhood education for the handicapped. In practice, preschools often have not closed the gap between assessment and intervention. This book should help them accomplish this goal.

The authors have demonstrated that they have a wealth of knowledge and experience that enables them to bring us up to date on the latest thinking, research, and status on the linking of assessment with curriculum. However, they point out the need for further research in this area.

In Chapter 2 a section of particular significance contrasts the contemporary and the traditional views of assessment. The reader should be convinced that there are better methods of assessment than those we have used in the past. No longer is it permissible for a single discipline to determine assessment and programming. Models supporting the linking of assessment with programming are described in support of this interdisciplinary approach.

The description of the assessment topology presented in Chapter 3 provides the reader with a way to organize the types of assessment used in early intervention programs. Practitioners will find the adaptive strategies to enhance prescriptive assessment invaluable when modifying assessment to meet the individual needs of children.

A detailed review of curriculum-compatible developmental scales is provided in Chapter 4. The practitioner seeking an assessment instrument will have a wide variety from which to choose.

Chapter 5 is one of the chapters most valuable to direct service personnel. The authors stress that curriculum is contingent not only on the needs of children but on the professional and personal characteristics of teachers. Models of curricular content are covered in this chapter. Especially helpful is the section focusing on considerations in curriculum evaluation.

In Chapter 6 the authors once again demonstrate their sensitivity to the needs of practitioners by providing examples of developmental curricula to illuminate the complimentary roles of assessment and programming. The authors readily admit that in curriculum there is no Holy Grail as there is in assessment; therefore, they provide the reader with guidelines for matching curriculum with the unique needs of a given child.

Chapters 7 and 8 conclude the text and provide true-to-life, step-by-step descriptions of the LINK model using preschoolers with various disabilities. These chapters illustrate the following four phases using forms, tables, and easy-to-read case reports: (1) screening/identification, (2) prescriptive developmental assessment/ curriculum linkage, (3) programming intervention, and (4) progress evaluation/ monitoring.

The practitioner will appreciate the content of the book's appendixes. Among the materials included in Appendix A are outlines of developmental scales, including information regarding publishers and dates of publication, appropriate age range, assessment type, domains or contents, adaptive options, and other pertinent information. Appendix B, which is similar in format to Appendix A, contains a description of developmental curricula. Appendix C, which gives samples of developmentally based assessment reports, provides culminating reinforcement for information contained throughout the text. The appendixes also contain LINK forms that can be ordered separately to allow the practitioner to readily apply the model.

In closing, the linking of assessment with curriculum is perhaps the most important consideration in guaranteeing appropriate services for young children with special needs. Bagnato, Neisworth, and Munson are to be commended for producing a landmark book that provides a solid framework for understanding and applying the linkage between assessment and programming. This book will prove to be an invaluable resource for practitioners, teacher trainers, and researchers.

Merle B. Karnes, Ed.D.
Professor of Special Education
and Early Childhood/Elementary Education
Director, Colonel Wolfe School
for Special Children
University of Illinois
at Urbana-Champaign

Preface

The best practices in developmental assessment are now a part of PL 99-457: team approaches, multidomain measures, multiple sources of information, parent participation, program prescriptions, and handicap adaptations. The LINK system described in this book enables professionals to employ these best practices in practical and economical ways.

In the 1981 edition of this work, we first proposed the concept of systematic assessment/curriculum linkage; since then, the procedure has gained greater clarity and practicality through the increasing prominence of criterion- or curriculum-based evaluation (CBA). The linkage procedure and related content in this edition are dedicated to bridging the gap between the work of two primary early childhood specialists: the developmental school psychologist and the early childhood special educator. However, the curriculum-based methods advocated here synchronize the assessment of all interdisciplinary team members, including physical and occupational therapists, speech/language clinicians, social workers, parents, and consulting personnel.

This second edition is grounded in the practical developmental concepts introduced in the earlier edition; yet it is an entirely new book. In Chapters 1 and 2, we provide a much clearer description of the developmental concepts that distinguish this approach, which is both functional and handicap-sensitive. Chapter 2 presents support for the prescriptive linkage model by describing compatible models and research. Chapter 3 offers the reader a practical picture of the multidimensional assessment model and a four-phase developmental assessment/curriculum linkage system entitled **LINK:** *A Developmental Assessment Curriculum System for Special Needs Preschoolers*. We introduce the new concept of a prescriptive developmental assessment battery (PDA) selected for each child's handicaps and yielding curriculum entry points for individualized intervention. Chapter 5 parallels Chapter 3 and discusses the attributes, uses, and models for early childhood curricula. Chapters 4 and 6, also parallel chapters, provide close-ups of developmental scales and developmental curricula that facilitate prescriptive linkage. A new dimension in these chapters involves the use of synopses of each instrument, publisher, cost, and other factors, followed by a more detailed close-up of the unique features of each exemplary measure. We believe this will help the reader to examine and select compatible combinations of scales and curricula more efficiently. Chapter 7 illustrates the LINK system in step-by-step detail, using a case vignette on a cerebral palsied child. (A special feature is the illustration of five LINK forms available under separate order from the authors to help the reader use the LINK system in professional practice. See Appendix F.)

Finally, Chapter 8 offers six case vignettes and an applied exercise to demonstrate the selection of assessment batteries and the application of LINK for preschoolers with various developmental disabilities: premature infant birth, autism, visual impairment, hearing impairment, Down syndrome, traumatic brain injury, and language/learning disabilities. We believe these handicap-sensitive portraits of children provide a practical, "real-life" dimension to make clear the use of the LINK system.

Family assessment is also a mandate that should and must be addressed by early childhood specialists. New instruments and approaches are being developed that will interrelate professionals and parents in the interests of the child. Given the importance of family empowerment and appraisal, this book nevertheless focuses on useful and necessary child-focused assessment, with recognition of the participation of parents in their child's assessment and education. Another whole volume would be necessary to address properly the rationale, methods, and instruments for family-focused assessment. Several other authors offer works devoted to this topic, encouraging the reader to give equal emphasis to the issues and practices related to family appraisal. (Several sources on family assessment are provided in Chapter 2.)

We are grateful to the practitioners, professors, and students whose enthusiasm for the first edition made this second edition possible. We appreciate the many suggestions we received from professionals in the field and the critiques from valued colleagues that helped us sharpen the focus of the book and retain its practical content. Special appreciation is extended to Dr. Merle Karnes, who graciously agreed to write the foreword for this text. Dr. Karnes' name and career are synonymous with early intervention; we value her comments on our work. We would be remiss not to mention the prolonged and skillful efforts of Pat Dintaman, whose assistance on several phases of the book speeded its completion. Glenda Carelas performed word processing miracles with the several manuscript drafts, eventually providing the hard copy that went to the publisher. And, many thanks to Angela Capone, Carol Sue Bernardo, Mary Smith, and the dozens of students who coped their way through preliminary drafts of the book; they had the rare opportunity to criticize openly their professors (!) and to shape many changes.

The urgent need for useful, practical assessment—assessment that helps to design, guide, and evaluate treatment—cannot be overemphasized. We concur with Hayes, Nelson, and Jarrett (1987) that "the time now seems ripe for a vigorous expansion of research on the contribution of assessment to treatment outcomes. Because treatment utility provides the practical basis for a concern with clinical assessment, it seems important to proceed rapidly to its demonstration" (p. 973). We trust the procedures discussed in this volume will contribute to treatment by bringing assessment and intervention together.

SJB
JTN
SMM

1

The Gap between Assessment and Intervention

Parents ask three basic questions when they suspect that their child may have a problem: "What's wrong with my child? What will my child be like later? What can be done to help?" As professionals, we know that answers to these questions are not easy. Each question, in fact, requires a different set of considerations and different assessment procedures and instruments.

"What's wrong with my child?" asks for a diagnosis—what syndrome or clinical category does the child best fit? This decision requires comparing the child's characteristics and performance with the typical or normative performance for children of the same age. This comparison can provide useful information for purposes of placement and perhaps preliminary program direction. Thus, norm-based assessment plays a primary role in diagnosis or categorization of childhood disorders.

"What will my child be like later?" is a question of prognosis or prediction. Such a question can have no definitive answer; developmental progress does not depend exclusively on diagnostic category or "what's wrong." To a great extent, prognosis depends on the quality of subsequent experiences and the impact of intervention. Accordingly, predictions or best guesses depend on results from norm-based assessment and best estimates about the probable efficacy of intervention.

"What can be done to help my child?" is the ultimate aim, for answers to this question may guide the planning and kind of developmental program that is offered.

1

The question of program planning and treatment recommendations for instruction and therapy poses different demands upon assessment and is, of course, the most important concern of parents. Answers to this question can guide the planning and delivery of effective early education services. Careful and sensible assessment can produce a blueprint or framework for child developmental programs. But "many's the slip twixt cup and lip"; traditional diagnostic assessment reports can be shared with teachers and parents, but they are usually examined in vain for practical program recommendations. Indeed, many diagnostic reports are "dead ends" that offer little more than scores, clinical labels, and (perhaps) vague recommendations for programming. This gap between assessment and programming need not exist. This book presents the reasons, procedures, and materials for the two fundamental approaches that can bring assessment and programming together: (1) convert traditional diagnostic instruments and reports to program-relevant information (linkage), and (2) employ assessment materials that are deliberately designed to link to program objectives (criterion- or curriculum-based assessment). The book's content is dedicated to the integration of "testing and teaching."

FACTORS CREATING THE GAP

A "gap" exists when assessment results and reports fall short of providing specific information for program planning. A number of factors have contributed to the distancing of assessment from intervention; we discuss three major factors in this section: (1) confusion or lack of assessment purpose, (2) traditional assessment standards and practices, and (3) professional boundaries.

Conflicts in Assessment Purpose

Recent literature shows clear agreement among assessment specialists that the purpose of the assessment must be the fundamental criterion for selecting, using, and reporting assessment instruments. From child development research we find proponents of purpose: "different decisions require different types of instruments and different types of assessment strategies . . . it is the *purpose* and not the population that defines the instrument chosen" (Wachs & Sheehan, 1988, p. 401). And from counseling and clinical psychology, Hayes, Nelson, and Jarrett (1987) presented a compelling case for evaluating assessment according to its *utility,* which hinges on how well it fulfills its purpose. Identification of the purpose of the assessment is so crucial that the present authors have offered a preliminary typology of measures categorized by purpose (J.T. Neisworth & Bagnato, 1988). As detailed later in this text, the purposes of assessment include comparing child status with peers (norm-based), appraising the quality of the child's environment (ecological), analyzing social exchange (interactive), detecting the perceptions or impressions about a child (clinical or judgment-based), identifying feasible educational/ therapeutic objectives, and monitoring child progress (curriculum-based).

"Assessment for instructional purposes can be viewed as the bottom line for assessment. . . . When the semantics and theoretical disputes are set aside, it becomes clear that the real purpose of assessment is to develop hypotheses about, give direction to, or make plans for individual and group programming" (J.T. Neisworth, 1982, p. vi). On this theme there is considerable interprofessional agreement. Thirty years ago, Meehl (1959) asserted that the ultimate role of assessment is that of providing useful treatment information. Through several decades, professionals have complained of the lack of equivalence of purpose between testing and treatment (Adams, 1972; Cronbach & Gleser, 1965; Korchin & Schuldberg, 1981). Recently, McReynolds (1985) has pointed out that the usefulness of assessment becomes a crucial issue as clinicians spend more time in treatment efforts. The admonitions can be summed up: Recognize that there are multiple purposes for assessment; identify the assessment purpose before selecting instruments and procedures; carry out assessment and reporting that fulfills the mission or purpose. The ultimate mission for assessment is its active and continuing role in intervention.

Characteristics of Traditional Assessment

There are at least five characteristics of conventional child assessment that make it irrelevant or minimally useful for instruction. First, traditional clinical assessment usually employs global measures of theorized traits or capacities (e.g., intelligence, aptitude, motivation). Such measures lack the specificity and the program or curricular relevance needed to identify objectives. The measurement of inferred conditions or traits is an attempt to describe what the child *is* (retarded, disturbed, brain damaged), rather than what the child *does* (gets along with peers, dresses and grooms self, recognizes letters). Thus, traditional global assessment does not play much of a role in changing diagnoses arrived at through clinical judgment or in directing treatment (Adams, 1972).

Second, norm-based assessment has been predominant. Yet, while norm-based measures may be useful for comparing the child's status with a referent group, they have not yielded prescriptions for action. This issue is, of course, one of confused purpose, as already discussed. "Proving" a child is retarded (meets standardized syndrome criteria) does not produce an individualized educational program (IEP).

Third, psychometric considerations have been the primary criteria for evaluating assessment devices. The bases for acceptance or rejection of an instrument are content, construct, concurrent, and predictive validities; internal consistency; and test-retest reliabilities. Validity concerns the relationships among scores on a given instrument with those of other instruments; reliability has to do with relationships among scores on the same device (Campbell & Fiske, 1959). The preoccupation with psychometric criteria focuses on the structure rather than the function or treatment utility of assessment (Hayes, Nelson, & Jarrett, 1987). For purposes of early intervention, what is needed is utility or use validity, that is, estimates of the degree to which an instrument or assessment procedure contributes to the conduct or effect of intervention. Methods to estimate treatment utility are being developed, but certainly teacher/therapist judgment in this regard should be sought and respected. If a teacher gets little or no help from the assessment tools, they are essentially useless from the interventionist's point of view, even though the instruments may meet psychometric criteria. Giving the teacher the child's height, weight, head circumference, and foot size would be instructionally useless (and ludicrous!), although such measurements are highly reliable and valid.

A fourth problem related to traditional assessment is the nature of the reports prepared and given to teachers and therapists. Such reports are often vague, confusing, and loaded with jargon. Usually test-centered, they organize results around each instrument given rather than around developmental needs or presenting problems (Bagnato, J.T. Neisworth, & DeSaunier, in press).

Finally, there is little or no common content base between traditional assessment materials and early childhood curricula. Even when norm-based instruments and curricula do share content (e.g., Gesell Developmental Schedules and developmental curricula), until recently such equivalence has not been recognized and exploited. The linkage process described in this book makes possible the use of norm-based developmental assessment for prescribing developmental objectives.

Professional Boundaries

Until recently, the several professions concerned with early childhood have been separate, with role descriptions peculiar to each. The division of labor between psychologist and therapist or teacher has been distinct and even legalized. Teachers have not been permitted to give and interpret certain "tests," and school psychologists have been prevented from offering treatment or consultation. Professional jargon has distanced psychologists from teachers, teachers from social workers, and everybody from parents. Such a professional Tower of Babel does little to promote useful communication for designing and delivering education. Rather than being partners in program planning, teachers and psychologists have carried out separate, nonoverlapping duties, each knowing little about the potential for integrating or sharing roles. Although handicapped children have been integrated with nonhandicapped children, little professional integration has occurred. Professional insulation curtails the valuable "cross-talk" that can bring specialists together in the child's and family's interest.

Within regular early childhood education, there are distinct schools of thought that erect barriers and sometimes confuse parents and other professionals. Three main theoretical/philosophical approaches can be identified: maturationist, cognitive-developmental, and behavioral. Each of these has distinct do's and don'ts with regard to child care and instruction (Peters, J.T. Neisworth, & Yawkey, 1986). Some of these differences add to the problems encountered when, for example, inservice training is provided to regular early childhood staff who are preparing to integrate developmentally delayed children into their programs. Structured curricula, direct instruction, assessment and monitoring, and individualized education plans may seem antithetical to child maturationist views. Likewise, "canned lessons" (e.g., DISTAR) leave little room for spontaneous teaching and are controversial.

Finally, even within special education, the separate categorical approach has created further conceptual, treatment, and assessment differences. The use of special education categories has encouraged and even required reliance on diagnostic, dead-end assessment—assessment that does not lead anywhere beyond assignment to a clinical category. Thus, diagnostic assessment contributes to placement, but not to practice.

FACTORS CLOSING THE GAP

Fortunately, this is a time of rapid change within early intervention. Federal incentives to states, funding for demonstration and research, and the convergence of social philosophies and professional forces are unifying assessment and intervention. We can identify four directions that result in intervention-based assessment; here we discuss them only briefly, since they relate to material addressed elsewhere in the book.

Legal Changes

Anyone working within early intervention is aware of the landmark legislation and litigation over the past 15 years. Taken together, PL 94-142 and PL 99-457 are promoting changes that help to integrate assessment/intervention enterprises.

Handicapped infants, preschoolers, and their families must receive assessment, specification of services, IEPs, and individualized family service plans (IFSP). Assessment must identify the child's present developmental status (based on objective criteria), strengths and needs of the family, and major expected program outcomes for infant and family (Garwood, Fewell, & J.T. Neisworth, 1988). Note that the law requires *multidisciplinary* team assessment and specific, objective assessment information to formulate major expected outcomes. As noted previously, global measures do not lead to specific therapeutic objectives; the requirement of specific measures that generate more specific educational objectives forcibly pushes assessment toward a curricular or intervention-based model.

Team approaches bring with them the need for some common base and language. The use of developmental scales and curricula provides the common denominator to permit cross-disciplinary communication. When child needs are identified in terms of specific developmental objectives, testing and teaching are unified (Duffy & Fedner, 1977; Salvia & Ysseldyke, 1978). Some authors

(Simeonson & Bailey, 1988) recommend transdisciplinary training so that each professional can appreciate and at least minimally function in another professional role. Others have suggested that multiprofessional teams work together during the assessment process. Instead of the psychologist independently assessing cognition, the physical therapist evaluating neuromotor status, and the speech and language therapist assessing communication, all would work together to arrive at integrated and mutually useful information. Certainly, blending professional efforts will go a long way toward closing the assessment gap.

Changes in Professional Preparation

College preparation programs for school psychologists and special educators are equipping these professionals to work together in assessment. To be sure, professional boundaries are formidable, but both school psychology and special education now have early childhood specialties. The developmental school psychologist (Bagnato, J.T. Neisworth, Paget, & Kovaleski, 1987) focuses on assessment, program planning, treatment recommendation, and program evaluation for handicapped and at-risk infants and preschoolers. Noteworthy is the recent position statement of the National Association of School Psychologists (Schakel, 1987). The statement on early intervention services encourages school psychologists to

- ensure that programs for young children are built on a recognition of the needs and developmental characteristics of preschoolers that make them different from older children
- work with school administrators, teachers, and parents to develop programs that attend to all important aspects of the development of young children, including cognitive, motor, self-help, socioemotional, and communication development
- promote programs that provide reliable and valid means of screening young children for possible handicapping and "at-risk" conditions as early as possible
- encourage the use of flexible team assessment approaches that take into account the unique attributes and variability of young children and the influence of home and family factors on their development
- support the provision of necessary individualized services without attempting to assign labels for specific handicapping conditions
- work toward establishing programs that provide a broad spectrum of options for intervention, opportunities for parents to receive support and assistance, and mainstreaming opportunities wherever possible
- encourage university programs, professional associations, public schools, and other continuing education providers to provide opportunities for prac-

titioners to receive professional development experiences that adequately prepare them to serve the needs of young children and their families

- help establish networks of communication and collaboration among the many agencies that provide services to infants, toddlers, and preschool children, setting aside "turf" issues and sharing resources and expertise

- advocate for the provision of state and federal funding to ensure that appropriate programs for infants, toddlers, and preschoolers are provided.

The early childhood specialization within special education has also grown rapidly (see Figure 1-1). Only a few years ago, specialized training was rare; it was usually accomplished by patching together components of special education, regular early childhood education, and child development. Now dozens of specialized training programs are available, and the number is expanding along with enrollments. Although the programs vary considerably, they include multidisciplinary awareness and (perhaps) training, courses in developmental assessment, and the writing of IEPs based on developmental objectives.

Curriculum-Based Assessment

One of the strongest factors closing the gap between assessment and intervention has been the adoption of curriculum-based assessment (CBA) practices. CBA is clearly the form of assessment preferred by the educator and therapist. Its relevance to the child's program cannot be denied; it is the most direct way to portray child needs and to monitor progress. Many curriculum-based devices are now available to the psychologist and special educator. The specificity of curriculum-based assessment permits school psychologists to go beyond diagnosis; it permits prescriptive assessment for developmental programming. CBA is a type of assessment that uses curricular objectives as assessment items (see Chapter 3). This methodology directly links assessment with the program, leaving little doubt about content validity.

Two types of CBA can be identified: curriculum-embedded scales and curriculum-referenced scales. Curriculum-embedded scales are composed of items taken directly from the program's curriculum. Essentially, the assessor locates entry points within the curriculum. Tracking child progress through the curriculum involves noting when mastery of specific objectives is achieved. School psychologists increase their credibility with teachers by using "gapless" CBA as one major form of program-relevant assessment. Of course, this form of assessment is clearly "testing to the teaching" and yields little information beyond curricular progress.

Curriculum-referenced scales contain items generic to many developmental curricula and, thus, can be used to place a child in various programs. While the assessment and curricular items may not be identical, they are usually similar enough for

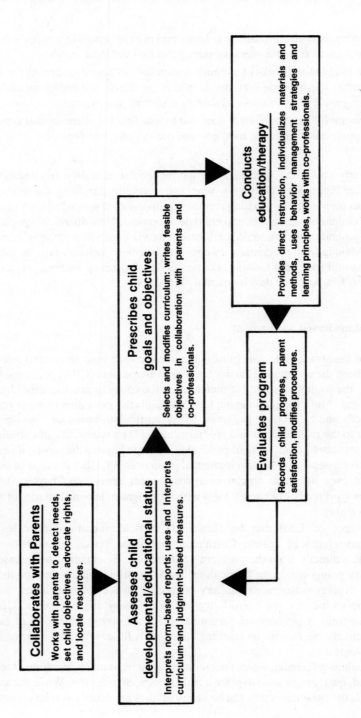

Figure 1-1 Professional Responsibilities of the Early Childhood Special Educator

the purpose of entering a child into the curriculum. Since these scales are not curriculum-specific, they have wider use and may be preferred in districts or regions where programs may use different developmental curricula.

Closely allied to the CBA movement is the already-mentioned increasing attention to the treatment utility of assessment (Hayes, Nelson, & Jarrett, 1987). When the basic justification for assessment is that it provides information of value to the planning, execution, and evaluation of treatment (Korchin & Schuldberg, 1981), assessment does not fall short in providing a program framework.

Program Accountability

Along with public law and professional research, program accountability encourages multidimensional assessment. When program administrators wish to maximize detection of progress, it makes sense to assess multiple dimensions of child development through multiple instruments. Not only does the multidimensional battery assist in program evaluation, it also becomes the key to planning specific objectives and interdisciplinary treatment.

It seems apparent that the demand to detect program effects, including child progress, requires assessment that is sensitive to change. The global measures yielded by traditional norm-referenced devices (e.g., IQ) are not capable of detecting the many changes effected by a program. Equally clear is that the pressure of "accountability" tends to force an over-reliance on easily measurable objectives and to avoid teaching important but less measurable goals. Teaching to the test is an oft-cited problem, especially when accountability demands are present. It can be argued, however, that teaching to the test or testing to the teaching is appropriate if the "test" (curriculum) contains developmentally important items and sequences.

In sum, useful assessment encompasses the following six attributes:

1. *The assessment should be intervention- or program-based.* This means that either curriculum-based scales or other measures that are readily "linkable" to potential program objectives should be used.
2. *The assessment must be child-relevant.* Even though a program may have a good curriculum in place, results from the several forms of assessment may indicate a profile of strengths and needs not accommodated by the program. In this case, another program or another curriculum should be sought.
3. *The assessment should be sensitive to child progress.* Many instruments can be linked to curricula, but a number of them do not have sufficient specificity to detect sometimes small, but still functional, increases in child or parent competencies. Likewise, some curricula do not contain enough objectives to permit more continuous progress (formative) assessment.
4. *The assessment should be adaptive.* Anyone who has worked with handicapped youngsters knows that inflexible, robot-like administration of instru-

ments almost always underestimates child functioning. Obvious stimulus and response limitations must be recognized and accommodated. Many new instruments are designed for, or are easily adapted to, various handicaps or employ functional items that stress whether a child can get something done, rather than how it is done.

5. *The assessment reports should be informative to responsible individuals.* Even sensible assessment is of little value when the report is poorly organized or contains confusing terminology. Generally, reports that are developmental and program-based are clear and readily put into action. Such reports are organized around curricular objectives, that is, they are curriculum-based rather than test-based.

6. *The assessment devices should be multiple and complementary.* This refers to the use of several instruments that examine different settings (e.g., preschool, home) or different sources (e.g., parent, teacher, other professionals) and that are revised over a period of time.

The following chapters address each of these assessment attributes. Early childhood assessment findings need not be filed away and looked at only when required; rather, developmental assessment can and must provide the blueprint or map for ongoing developmental intervention.

2

Foundations for Assessment/Curriculum Linkage

Contemporary versus Traditional Viewpoints on Assessment
    Functional versus Categorical Orientation
    Assessment versus Testing
    Developmental versus Psychometric Approach
    Criterion versus Norm Referencing
    Task Analysis and Training versus Ability Training
    Longitudinal versus One-Time Samples
    Multiple versus Single Variable
    Prescriptive versus Diagnostic Purposes
    Ecological versus Child-Only View

Purposes and Practices of Prescriptive Assessment
    The Multidimensional Perspective
        Multimeasure
        Multisource
        Multidomain
        Multipurpose

Linking Developmental Assessment and Intervention
    Phase 1: Screen/Identify
    Phase 2: Assess/LINK
    Phase 3: Program/Intervene
    Phase 4: Evaluate/Monitor

Supporting Models and Research for LINK

Prescriptive Approaches
    Functional Educational Evaluation
    Developmental Scales As Curricula
    Assessment As Intervention
    Competency Assessment Battery
    Adaptive Process Assessment

Linked Assessment/Intervention/Evaluation
System To Plan Early Childhood Services (SPECS)

Applied Research
  Validity and Efficacy of Prescriptive Multidimensional Assessment
  Reliability and Validity of Developmental Assessment/Curriculum Linkages

Practical child assessment and program planning are two major missions of early-intervention specialists. Many scales, measures, and approaches are available for the developmental assessment effort. Likewise, many materials and activities are available for developmental instruction and therapy. Unfortunately, the assessment tools and instructional programs have not often meshed (Bagnato, 1981a; Bagnato & J.T. Neisworth, 1981). Assessment of a child's intelligence, for example, is of little value to a teacher who is concerned with planning a program for that child's motor or social development, or even for concept development. Since many early educators use curricula that include hierarchies of developmental skills or objectives, they receive the most help when those who assess a child can report what developmental skills the child has mastered, what ones ought to be taught next, and what instructional/therapeutic strategies might prove most effective. In brief, early educators need blueprints or plans that can be used to construct developmental programs for children. However, few field-tested materials have been available to fulfill these needs and to link or synchronize developmental assessment and early intervention.

Fortunately, in the last decade new perspectives and practices have been developed to begin to close the gap between assessment and intervention. Yet, though these recent advances are important, many preschool programs have not incorporated them systematically into their services to young exceptional children and their families. We now turn to a discussion of each of these advances.

CONTEMPORARY VERSUS TRADITIONAL VIEWPOINTS ON ASSESSMENT

Nine major factors distinguish contemporary views on assessment and intervention from older perspectives that view assessment and treatment as separate operations. In this section, we summarize the major features and advantages of these factors as they shape assessment/curriculum linkage viewpoint and approach.

Functional versus Categorical Orientation

Previous approaches to assessing developmentally disabled children emphasized a categorical or diagnostic approach. Diagnosis refers to the labeling of a child, that is, the assignment to a clinical category, such as mental retardation, cerebral palsy, or autism. Diagnosis of the child's "condition" is assumed to provide direction to instruction and therapy. Such diagnosis may also be termed a genotypic appraisal because it presumes to identify a general, underlying condition; it describes what a particular child allegedly *is* (e.g., mentally retarded, emotionally disturbed, language delayed, neurologically impaired).

There are two major limitations to the genotypic, diagnostic approach: (1) various exceptionalities are not distinct or pure, in that different handicap groups share disability characteristics; and (2) identification of disability does not automatically suggest preferred individualized treatment. Assignment to a clinical category (diagnostic assessment) is particularly difficult and unproductive at the infant and preschool levels. The young exceptional child has not yet developed a stable repertoire of skills, changes rapidly, and has not experienced the organizing and enhancing effects of structured play and therapy.

In contrast, functional appraisal is a more practical and clinically proven approach. A functional approach or phenotypic appraisal describes what a child *does* or *does not do* under specified conditions; it describes and operationally defines the observable skills and deficits that the child typically exhibits. Functional or phenotypic assessment provides a framework for goal-planning; it conveys the notion that progress is to be expected and that such progress can be charted and described so that goals can be revised.

Assessment versus Testing

Testing and assessment are related but not identical activities. Each of us has had our capabilities tested in our school experience, but few of us have had our skills assessed. The critical differences between these two operations are magnified when serving handicapped infants and preschoolers. The prime distinctions concern the quality, scope, and usefulness of the information obtained during the appraisal process. Essentially, the end point of testing is merely quantitative; the child is described by a number. On the other hand, assessment integrates both quantitative and qualitative data that are translated into treatment-based terms. As Salvia and Ysseldyke (1987) point out,

> *Testing,* then, means exposing a person to a particular set of questions in order to obtain a score. That score is the end product of testing. . . . *Assessment* in educational settings is a multifaceted process that involves far more than the administration of a test. When we assess students, we consider the way they perform a variety of tasks in a variety of settings and contexts, the meaning of their performance in terms of the total functioning of the individual, and likely explanations for those performances. . . . It provides information that can enable teachers and other school personnel to make decisions regarding the children they serve. (pp. 3-4)

Assessment must be a comprehensive process of collecting information about the child across all developmental areas. Information must be gathered that permits analysis of status in language, personal-social, motor, cognitive, and interactive areas. Seldom are developmental problems "pure" and specific. An infant with motor problems may not be able to move around the environment or initiate social interactions as much as another child. As a result of restricted mobility, other areas of development may suffer, for example, cognitive development. Often, also, language and social growth are stunted when mobility problems are severe. It should be clear, therefore, that problems in one area of functioning may be related to problems in others. Assessment, accordingly, must cover all areas of development in order to provide the whole picture of the child's functional development.

Comprehensive assessment is often prescriptive as well as descriptive; it describes a child's strengths and weaknesses with a practical end result—the creation of an Individual Education Program (IEP) or individual plan of therapy and instruction. The school psychologist and the teacher are generally the pivotal individuals in this assessment process. The critical difference is that prescriptive assessment, unlike diagnostic assessment, results in recommendations that focus intervention and promote progress. The school psychologist who conducts child assessments and adheres to a prescriptive orientation maintains credibility with the early childhood special educator, other team members, and parents. Assessment conducted with a focus on attainable objectives is most justifiable because it is most useful. This orientation ensures the appropriate match between scales and purpose and synchronizes the assessment-intervention-evaluation sequence.

Developmental versus Psychometric Approach

With young handicapped children, developmental theory provides the underlying research base and developmental-behavioral strategies provide the content and methods. Thus, clinical research clearly demonstrates that developmental sequences and expectancies offer a viable bridge between assessment and early intervention. With this underpinning in theory and practice, the content validity of assessment and treatment is unquestioned. Yet, while normal developmental sequences may not apply strictly to all exceptionalities in terms of the purposefulness of some behaviors (e.g., block stacking for cerebral palsied children), the functional sequence does provide a reference point for practical goal planning and determination of the degree of developmental dysfunction. The developmental approach to assessment is structured, yet it offers the advantage of a flexible clinical strategy for assessing young handicapped children.

While developmental assessment examines the child's developmental skills or functional strengths and weaknesses, psychometric assessment is designed to measure psychological traits or alleged processes and to express the results numerically. Intelligence, personality, motivation, creativity, and other traits are assessed with psychometric instruments to produce scores (e.g., IQs). These scores usually summarize how well the child did and "how much" of the trait the child presumably has, usually relative to age peers. Note that the traits measured are not specific things the child does or does not do; they are qualities the child supposedly has or does not have.

A strictly psychometric approach offers neither a developmental sequence of expectancies nor a bond between assessment and intervention. Moreover, the psychometric approach demands rigid adherence to standardization procedures. Regardless of the child's handicap, the items and demands used are the same as those used with the nonhandicapped child on which the test was standardized and normed. Such an approach does not allow the use of alternative or adaptive strategies, such as altering the stimulus characteristics of tasks or permitting alternative response modes for the child to circumvent impairments and demonstrate intact skills. The psychometric approach does allow comparison with a norm group and thus permits diagnosis. It does not, however, provide an accurate picture of the child's actual capabilities, nor does it identify developmental strengths and weaknesses important in program planning.

Criterion versus Norm Referencing

Norm-referenced assessment has been overused in the early-intervention field (J.T. Neisworth & Bagnato, 1988; Shonkoff, 1981). Norm-based evaluation has clear and important applications, namely, screening and differential diagnosis. However, reliance on this method for prescriptive and progress evaluation purposes is unwarranted; moreover, the method has led to insensitive measurement of child change in early-intervention programs. The preeminent form of assessment in the field will become, perhaps already is, curriculum-based assessment—a form of criterion-referenced evaluation.

Criterion-referenced assessment refers to measurement of a performance relative to a stated standard. Curriculum-based assessment evaluates a child's attainment of developmental (curricular) objectives. But *attainment, mastery,* and *learning* are terms that must be qualified with stated criteria. When has a child "learned" how to print his name? When has the preschooler learned to share her toys? Most objectives must be accompanied by known criteria to permit them to be considered as accomplished. Hasty IEP writers often state after each objective: "90 percent of the time." Yet this criterion frequently makes no sense and simply cannot be verified. What does "prints his name correctly 90 percent of the time" really mean? Many teachers prefer to use a more discrete criterion, such as "correctly five consecutive times"; or they refer to maintenance and generalization by using "correctly nine out of ten times for the next week at home as well as at the center." Whatever standards are chosen, they should be clear enough to permit agreement among observers. Of course, criteria can be shifted to higher standards, as capabilities are refined. (Spiral curricula use a shifting-criterion approach by including objectives that become more elaborate and demanding as they are reintroduced at higher age, stage, or repertoire levels.) The use of reasonable criteria with curriculum-based assessment allows relative certitude that children are indeed learning and using what they learn. The criteria should not be so cumbersome and time-consuming that they are not really used; sometimes a simple rating scale or parent report can verify that a child has mastered a set of objectives and is ready to move on.

Task Analysis and Training versus Ability Training

Special education and allied professions have a long history of experimenting with ineffective therapeutic approaches. However, in the last decade, special education in general and early intervention in particular have demonstrated that combined developmental and behavioral approaches have the best track record. Yet outdated methods still abound. In particular, methods that purport to improve a child's abilities have received considerable criticism and have no substantial record of success. Neuropsychological, cognitive retraining, and dynamic approaches represent only the most recent versions of the ability-training faith.

Effective education for young exceptional children relies upon research-based strategies that emphasize a developmental task analysis of skills and behavioral methods of instruction and treatment. Rather than nebulous "abilities," developmental task analysis involves the sequential breakdown of measurable skills, allowing a child's current range of primitive-to-advanced capabilities to be assessed and framed as instructional objectives. An approach that stresses task-analytic methods naturally blends developmental and behavioral dimensions, stresses adaptive and functional techniques, and, thus, links assessment and intervention.

Longitudinal versus One-Time Samples

Young exceptional children present special problems for both assessment and treatment. Infants and preschool children with sensorimotor and social deficits have limited behavioral repertoires and variable patterns of arousal and responses, owing to their lack of experiences with their environment, the disabilities themselves, and their young ages. Traditional approaches that emphasize single-session and single-source assessments of these children, especially when diagnosis is the issue, are unethical and unjustifiable.

Serial assessments are the key to accurate description, prescription, and prediction in early intervention. School psychologists and other diagnostic specialists must advocate for longitudinal procedures for assessing status and outcome. Longitudinal techniques using both norm- and curriculum-based methods most effectively link assessment and intervention and offer valid strategies for monitoring progress and establishing accurate individual predictions of school-age needs. Predictions regarding individual outcome and potential can be made only after a child's response to structured intervention has been appraised. Longitudinal assessment-intervention strategies permit such analysis. The developmental school psychologist and preschool administrator must arrange program priorities to allow for longitudinal procedures.

Multiple versus Single Variable

Gone are the days when diagnostic specialists could "test" only intelligence and believe that the child's behavior and skills were sampled representatively. The infant's and preschool child's lack of integration in developmental competencies makes this approach ludicrous. Nevertheless, many preschool programs and the traditionally trained psychologists employed by them continue to use this unidimensional perspective and approach. They attempt to extend downward limited school-age practices and apply them to a preschool population. Preschool programs that fail to employ a developmental curriculum and that provide services in an unsystematic and intuitive manner are accomplices in promoting outmoded and unethical practices.

Broad and integrated services can be delivered only when programs target multiple dimensions of child and family needs. Multidimensional assessment addresses the child's complex of developmental and behavioral needs within and across several domains of functioning and detects the impact of disabilities on development. These multiple domains include cognitive, language, perceptual fine motor, socioemotional, gross motor, and self-care domains. In addition, various behavioral response classes must be targeted: self-regulation, reactivity, activity, normalcy, endurance, attention, and others.

Prescriptive versus Diagnostic Purposes

Many linkage-related concepts overlap, yet each has unique features. Thus, diagnosis is to categorical placement as prescription is to intervention. The distinction between diagnosis and prescription underscores the most important aspect of assessment: purpose. Testing, the attainment of a score or index on a child, is conducted primarily to categorize the child's problem and to apply a label. In contrast, a child is assessed in a functional manner by combining both quantitative and qualitative information. Although this may seem to involve superficial semantic play, the distinction is central to effective service delivery for preschool children. The school psychologist who conducts most child assessments must adhere to a functional-prescription orientation in order to maintain credibility with the early childhood special educator, other team members, and parents.

Ecological versus Child-Only View

It is not surprising that assessment has been focused almost exclusively on the child. After all, it is the child who develops or does not develop, who has problems, needs, and potential. It is the child whose IEP we design through use of assessment findings. Assessment may look at the child only when diagnosis, or sheer description, is the sole purpose of the assessment. As emphasized throughout this chapter, however, while contemporary assessment can include diagnosis, it stresses program planning. When developmental objectives are identified, a curriculum is entered, intervention strategies are considered, and parents become involved.

Thus, assessment must include appraisal of relevant settings and circumstances. Certainly, the home environment should be considered, as well as parenting skills and other domestic circumstances. Additionally, the quality of the preschool, day care, or other facilities should be evaluated. The people and circumstances that form the child's developmental context contribute heavily to both the status and future of the child. Proper, albeit minimal, assessment of this ecosystem permits better program placement, instructional prescriptions, parent participation, and progress across settings.

This book stresses the importance of multisource assessment (i.e., preschool, day care, home, clinic) in order to obtain the best estimates of child functioning. Thus, parent/family judgment or ratings, anecdotes, and other measures of the child's functioning at home provide crucial perspectives in the child assessment picture.

We emphasize, however, that family assessment is yet another matter. New instruments and procedures are being developed to permit families to identify their needs and priorities (Dunst, Jenkins, & Trivette, 1984; Dunst & Trivette, in press). Most of these instruments use family self-report, since it is the family members' own perceptions that must be ascertained, not the pronouncements of an outside professional regarding family status. This phenomenological approach also avoids much of the concerns about intrusiveness into the family's affairs. A family ecosystems approach helps to assess the family's own estimate of needs with regard to information, support, explanations to others, community services, and family functioning (Bailey & Simeonson, in press). Description of these emerging instruments and methods is beyond the scope of this book, yet their recognition of the importance of family participation in the child assessment process must be stressed. To exclude parent participation in child assessment is misleading, unethical, and also against the law. The judgment-based measures discussed in Chapters 3 and 4 provide means for professionals to seek parent ratings of a child's developmental status and progress. Development of instruments to assess family strengths and needs is a strong new direction in early intervention that recognizes the primacy of the family context for child and, especially, infant development. Perhaps in the near future there will be available an array of family instruments that can be useful in concert with the child assessment tools reviewed in this book.

PURPOSES AND PRACTICES OF PRESCRIPTIVE ASSESSMENT

Early screening and assessment of special-needs preschoolers are critical operations, but such appraisals must be prescriptive. Assessment is purposeless and indefensible unless it provides information that is relevant for instructional and therapeutic purposes. Early intervention demands that assessment strategies generate functional targets for individualized curriculum goal planning. Unlike global diagnostic efforts that focus upon identifying the child's "fit" within a particular disability category, prescriptive assessment proceeds "beyond diagnosis to prescriptions for developmental progress" (J.T. Neisworth & Bagnato, 1986, p. 180).

Previously, this approach was referred to as the diagnostic-prescriptive model. While more relevant to early intervention, prescriptive developmental assessment retains the same procedural strengths of the old diagnostic-prescriptive model in special education and avoids the connotations of diagnosis, labeling, and categorization while incorporating more refined features. Prescriptive assessment synchronizes each step in the assessment-intervention-evaluation sequence. Once again, the unifying bridge is the sequence of developmental skills and/or processes—the focus of the developmental task analysis that underlies the content of traditional developmental scales and commercially available developmental curricula. A developmental task analysis generates a common base for each of the assessment and curricular functions or purposes. Whether this is seen as "teaching to the test" or "testing-to-the-teaching," it is a model in which assessment tasks and curricular tasks are highly similar. Thus, entry of a child within various domains of a curriculum and evaluation of both progress and treatment effectiveness can be readily accomplished by using these curricular "targets" or goals as benchmarks. Because of the common developmental base, there is little doubt about the content validity of curriculum-based prescriptive assessment.

The Multidimensional Perspective

Public Law 94-142 and its recent amendment, PL 99-457, mandate multivariate appraisal for all handicapped children. Multidimensional assessment produces a comprehensive survey of the child's present levels of physical, cognitive, communication, social development, and self-help skills based on acceptable, objective criteria. It provides the "big picture" of functioning rather than the limited glimpse produced by traditional "one-test, one-score" approaches. "Multidimensional assessment refers to a comprehensive and integrated evaluation approach that employs *multiple measures,* derives data from *multiple sources,* surveys *multiple domains,* and fulfills *multiple purposes*" (J.T. Neisworth & Bagnato, 1988, p. 24). In this section, we examine these four aspects of multidimensional assessment.

Multimeasure

Multimeasurement refers to the use of several measures, that is, a battery of developmental scales, to appraise child/parent capabilities and needs. Recent research demonstrates that accurate and prescriptive assessments are provided when the batteries are composed of several different types of measures (norm-based, adaptive curriculum-based, judgment-based, and ecological) that examine various child and environmental dimensions and the interactions among them (these various types of measures are discussed in Chapter 3). Such multimeasure batteries may include not only traditional cognitive scales and criterion-referenced instruments but also measures of play skills, information-processing, attention, coping, and parent-child interaction.

Multisource

Diagnostic specialists must not rely on only one source of information (e.g., only the psychologist or only the parent). The use of several independent sources of information provides a truer estimate of the child's status. For example, low-incidence handicaps and situation-specific behaviors require multisource appraisals across environments (clinic, home, and classroom) and people (parents and team professionals) to produce representative assessments. Multisource assessment increases the likelihood of parent and professional agreement, integrates team decision making, and enhances the external validity of both assessment and treatment (McGongiel & Garland, 1988). The practice of removing a child from the home or preschool for assessment in the "testing room" does not provide multisource assessment and produces limited and biased estimates of a child's capabilities and needs.

Multidomain

Assessment must be comprehensive. This means examining the several interrelated developmental and behavioral areas that describe a young child's total profile. This profile includes the traditional areas of development, such as cognitive, language, perceptual-fine motor, socioemotional, language, gross motor, and self-care. However, with younger and more severely disabled children, additional areas need to be appraised, such as self-regulation, social competence, reactivity, habituation, emotional expression, endurance, normalcy, and self-stimulation. Ecological and interactive areas should also be appraised, for example, the impact of chaotic settings, parent sensitivity to behavioral cues, and child-versus-parent-initiated activities. Multidomain, then, refers to the appraisal of not only one or two areas, but a range of important developmental functions. Note, too, that these important developmental functions are skills that can be taught or promoted.

Multipurpose

Finally, multidimensional assessment must serve several major purposes and link these purposes. The several assessment operations and purposes are screening/identification, comprehensive assessment/curriculum linkage, programming/intervention, and progress monitoring/program evaluation. Within this sequence, each purpose is a prerequisite for a succeeding one, as the assessment becomes more finely focused. The first purpose, screening, provides only a gross estimate of the child's status; it merely sorts children into two categories, for example, a problem that should be further examined versus no problem. Screening instruments are refined to minimize false negatives (failure to detect a problem when, upon further inspection, one is found) and false positives (detecting a possible problem when there is none). False negatives are of special concern because they involve children who are experiencing developmental difficulties but are not identified for early intervention. The new legislation (PL 99-447) provides for an "at-risk" diagnosis, permitting much more latitude in early screening and identification. For example, although not yet established as practice, it is possible that properly assessed family circumstances related to problems in child development may provide the basis for "at-risk" status.

Developmental assessment, the second purpose, yields a close-up, fine grain analysis. Measures are chosen that are compatible with a developmental approach and with the curriculum employed in the program. This permits estimates of child developmental status and yields direction and content for curriculum linkage and program planning.

The third purpose of assessment is to guide actual day-to-day program content changes and intervention methods. The links established through developmental assessment enable professionals to design goals and objectives that are feasible within the program's available curriculum, techniques, and materials.

Finally, child progress and program efficacy are assessed in terms of the developmental-behavioral goals within the curriculum. This purpose is met through essentially the same procedures, but the assessment may be both formative and summative.

In summary, multipurpose assessment describes a child's development and may be used to place the child in an appropriate setting, plan a developmental program, monitor progress, and evaluate the program's impact. Since the child's development is the major concern, the assessment must employ a developmental base that is similar to the content of the developmental program in which the child is enrolled.

LINKING DEVELOPMENTAL ASSESSMENT
AND INTERVENTION

The four primary purposes for assessment in early childhood special education are (1) screen/identify, (2) assess/link, (3) program/intervene, and (4) monitor/ evaluate. A variety of appraisal measures are used to accomplish these functions. However, it is important to view these purposes as interrelated. **LINK:** *A Developmental Assessment/Curriculum Linkage System for Special Needs Preschoolers* (Bagnato, 1981a, 1984; Bagnato & J.T. Neisworth, 1981; see Appendix F) operationalizes a prescriptive assessment strategy that guides instrument selection and synchronizes each of the sequential assessment-intervention operations and purposes. The linkage system, in essence, formalizes the trial-and-error clinical procedures that diagnostic specialists often use when attempting to assess and plan programs for young children with complex disabilities. The major premise of the linkage procedure is that assessment and treatment are inseparable components of the same larger process: developmental intervention. The hierarchy of developmental skills and stages that have been identified through research is the unifying bridge between assessment and intervention. This bridge is often called the developmental task analysis. The linkage system, therefore, offers a procedure to blend philosophy, purpose, and practice in developmental assessment and early intervention.

As Figures 2-1 and 2-2 illustrate, the four overlapping phases of the assessment/ curriculum linkage model occur in sequence. Each phase is a prerequisite for a subsequent phase; also, each phase matches operations and purposes that are increasingly fine-focused in their functions. At the prescriptive assessment/ curriculum linkage phase, assessment *is* intervention. The four-phase sequence can be viewed conceptually as a series of wide- to narrow-angle sighting lenses. One would choose a wide-angle lens to survey a landscape broadly while overlooking small details (i.e., screening). Conversely, one would select a narrow-angle lens in order to increase magnification and, thus, attention to detail (i.e., comprehensive prescriptive assessment). An explanation of each phase and its matched assessment-intervention operation and purpose follows.

Phase 1: Screen/Identify

Developmental screening, the first linkage phase, is a sorting operation that compares the "landmark" skills demonstrated by an individual child with expectations for the child's age. If the child's general capabilities fall below those normative expectations, the child is identified as "at risk." Thus, developmental screening is designed to identify or detect possible areas of developmental dysfunction. In order to accomplish this operation, we select global norm-based or even judgment-based developmental measures that estimate development in multiple

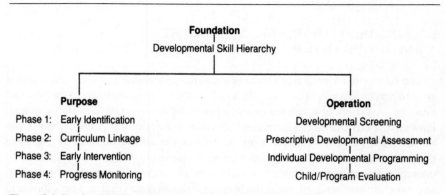

Foundation
Developmental Skill Hierarchy

Purpose	**Operation**
Phase 1: Early Identification	Developmental Screening
Phase 2: Curriculum Linkage	Prescriptive Developmental Assessment
Phase 3: Early Intervention	Individual Developmental Programming
Phase 4: Progress Monitoring	Child/Program Evaluation

Figure 2-1 Synchronized Theory, Purposes, and Operations in the LINK System.

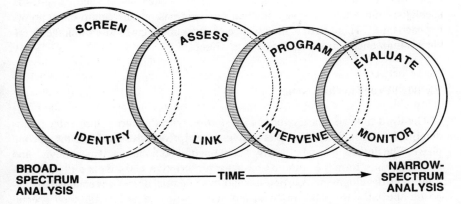

BROAD-SPECTRUM ANALYSIS ——————————TIME——————————▶ NARROW-SPECTRUM ANALYSIS

Figure 2-2 Linking Assessment-Intervention Goals. *Source:* From Psychological Evaluation of the Developmentally and Physically Disabled (p. 183) by V.B. Van Hassett and M. Hersen (Eds.), 1987, New York: Plenum Publishing Corporation. Copyright 1987 by Plenum Publishing Corporation. Reprinted by permission.

---

domains, including cognitive, language, motor, personal-social, and sensory areas. The screening merely identifies or highlights potential problem areas, that is, it provides only an indication of normal or at-risk functioning; few specifics emerge from the screening. This screening overlaps with the next phase of developmental assessment. It provides a guide or starting point for a narrower, more precise analysis of identified areas.

Phase 2: Assess/LINK

The second phase involves comprehensive developmental assessment for the purpose of prescribing curriculum objectives or developmental linkages. Again, some overlap is evident with the screening operation, in that this more precise assessment phase targets the problem area(s) identified through screening and confirms or refutes the screening results. Like the screening phase, comprehensive developmental assessment describes child functioning across multiple domains. Curriculum-based, norm-based, and clinical judgment scales (to be discussed in Chapter 3) are used for this more precise analysis. However, the curriculum-based instrument is central to the evaluation. It samples more functional behaviors in these areas (e.g., cognitive, language, perceptual-fine motor, gross motor, socio-emotional, self-care) and generates a more accurate appraisal of specific skills and deficits. The results identifying the child's developmental difficulties place the child within a diagnostic category and then can be used to diagnose (e.g., cerebral palsy, mental retardation). More importantly, the prescriptive developmental assessment offers a precise description of the child's range of functioning. The identified functional range encompasses a sequence of fully acquired (+), emerging

($\pm$), and absent ($-$) skills. Once the range has been determined, diagnostic specialists can establish developmental prescriptions or curriculum entry points for each child. This phase is the essence of assessment/curriculum linkage; it ensures congruence between testing and teaching.

Phase 3: Program/Intervene

The third linkage phase overlaps by starting with the curriculum entry points determined through the comprehensive prescriptive assessment in the second phase. The developmental objectives contained in both the assessment device and the curriculum form the common basis for prescriptive assessment and programming. The developmental curriculum and its sequential objectives enable the diagnostic specialist to "talk" in consistent terms with the early childhood special educator. The curriculum entry points identified during comprehensive assessment now are translated into individualized objectives within the curriculum. With these entry points, early interventionists can proceed to lower or higher levels within the developmental hierarchy of objectives in order to frame purposeful goals and objectives that match the child's instructional and therapeutic needs. These curricular objectives provide criteria for teaching and mastery and, therefore, offer one dimension of the young handicapped child's IEP. Clinical or diagnostic teaching helps the early interventionist identify the most effective instructional and behavioral strategies to promote learning for a particular child and to complete the IEP.

Phase 4: Evaluate/Monitor

The final linkage phase encompasses elements of each of the previous phases. The evaluation process involves methods for documenting both child progress and program effectiveness. The overlap with the third phase occurs insofar as program evaluation must relate to some criteria. The criteria for evaluation are the objectives that were established as an outcome of prescriptive developmental assessment and curriculum linkage. Evaluation enables the early-intervention team to fulfill the purpose of monitoring child progress and treatment efficacy.

Another overlap with the operations in previous phases concerns the repeated use of the battery of norm-based, curriculum-based, judgment-based, and ecological scales for description and prescription. Serial assessments in a longitudinal manner are the primary methodology of developmental evaluation. Summative evaluation usually involves pretest-posttest global comparisons of progress, usually after a year or perhaps after 6 months; for example, developmental ages (DA) and developmental quotients (DQ) generated by the norm-, curriculum-, and judgment-based measures might be assessed each quarter. Formative evaluation uses the developmental curriculum on a daily/weekly/monthly basis to document measurable changes in learning with respect to the curricular objectives as benchmarks of progress. Formative evaluation enables the interventionist to detect inappropriate goals and ineffective therapeutic strategies for a particular child and to modify them within the context of treatment. Evaluation and monitoring, often neglected by many preschool programs, are critical functions within the LINK model. Such evaluation and monitoring justify our programs for children and advertise our expertise to parents, administrators, and funding sources; they bring the assessment-intervention process full cycle. As Brooks-Gunn and Lewis (1982) assert, "Assessment and intervention are linked through the evaluation of child progress" (p. 42).

SUPPORTING MODELS AND RESEARCH FOR LINK

Clearly, there is an urgent need for useful, practical assessment—assessment that helps to design, guide, and evaluate treatment. We concur with Hayes, Nelson, and Jarrett (1987) that "the time now seems ripe for a vigorous expansion of research on the contribution of assessment to treatment outcome. Because treatment utility provides the practical basis for a concern with clinical assessment, it seems important to proceed rapidly to its demonstration" (p. 973).

Since the 1981 version of this book, in which we first proposed the concept of systematic assessment/curriculum linkage, the construct has gained greater practical clarity, primarily through the increasing prominence of criterion- or curriculum-based evaluation (CBA). Still, few studies or alternative versions of either the concept itself or of CBA have been completed. As services to special-needs infants, preschoolers, and their families are broadened, linkages between program philosophy, purposes, and practices will become even more important. This final section reviews conceptual models, approaches, and supporting research that serve to validate the linkage concept and approach. We trust the procedures discussed will contribute to the advances we must make to bring assessment and treatment together.

PRESCRIPTIVE APPROACHES

Functional Educational Evaluation

Haeussermann (1958) and Jedrysek, Klapper, Pope, and Wortis (1972) developed a functional educational evaluation format that permits assessment that is adaptive to the young child's impairments, particularly those of cerebral palsied children. It yields estimates of developmental functioning across several sensory and cognitive areas. The results of this "adaptive-capacity" evaluation then serve as a curriculum guide, a developmental profile that displays strengths and weaknesses and suggests instructional goals and strategies. Tasks are arranged sequentially along a developmental continuum. A child's performance is evaluated both upward and downward along the sequence until a level is reached that represents the child's current level of maturity or operation, given the disabilities. This level then establishes a target for curriculum planning and instruction. The educational evaluation is "a systematic sampling strategy across the child's functional skills and problem areas with the primary objective of . . . determining the kinds of training and experience that will best promote his own adaptive functional abilities . . . and . . . the special circumstances which are needed to create conditions for learning in the handicapped child" (Haeussermann, 1958, p. ix). Simply put, the functional evaluation determines the instructional plan.

Developmental Scales As Curricula

Meier (1976) has suggested a practical format for analyzing and sequencing the tasks included in the Bayley Scales of Infant Development or the Gesell Developmental Schedules. Landmark or global tasks along the sequence are viewed as entry, intermediate, or terminal objectives. Teachers can add developmental behaviors between the entry or terminal objectives to extend the task analysis. This method assumes that traditional norm-referenced scales like those of Bayley and Gesell can serve as a "profile and base for curriculum planning" (Meier, 1976, p. 190). Thus, the series of developmental behaviors included in traditional scales function as both a scale (to profile strengths and weaknesses) and as a curriculum framework. Meier's infant assessment-curriculum linkage concept has been operationalized in many commercially available developmental curricula, such as the Early Learning Accomplishment Profile (Sanford, 1978) and Developmental Programming for Infants and Young Children (Schafer & Moersch, 1981).

Assessment As Intervention

Brazelton (1982) advocates an approach that views assessment as a vehicle for enhancing infant development. The assessment experience is perceived as providing infants with a series of structured opportunities to act and react to stimulation and to learn to integrate their competencies in several areas. Additionally, infant assessment is a teaching opportunity for parents. The assessment accomplishes the following four major purposes: (1) it defines developmental capabilities; (2) it enhances communication between parent and professional; (3) it evaluates progress; and (4) it promotes learning not only for the infant but also for the parents, by highlighting the infant's strengths and limitations.

Competency Assessment Battery

Brooks-Gunn and Lewis (1981) designed the Competency Assessment Battery (CAB) to assess the abilities and describe the progress of handicapped infants and preschoolers (birth to 48 months). The CAB combines the advantages of several norm, criterion, and adaptive methods within a multisource battery to increase the sensitivity and comprehensiveness of evaluation. Assessments are focused within four major domains: linguistic, cognitive, social-affective, and environmental. Quantitative and qualitative measures also survey such areas as mother-child interaction, self-recognition, object permanence, expressive language, and attention/information processing style. The CAB consists of the Bayley Scales of Infant Development, the Uzgiris-Hunt Infant Psychological Development Scale, and measures of attention, language use, temperament, and interaction. Assessment results from this battery are used to design computer-generated individual interventions for young handicapped children.

Adaptive Process Assessment

Some have advocated a process-oriented approach to assessment that appraises several dimensions, including the match between the child and the child's learning situation, rapport with others, understanding of task expectations, mode of responding, and manner of learning new skills. This approach to assessing severely handicapped children (1) describes the attributes of the handicapping condition, (2) determines the conditions that promote or hinder the acquisition of skills, (3) offers a foundation for designing adaptable and modified instructional programs, and (4) guides the evaluation of child progress and program effectiveness.

Linked Assessment/Intervention/Evaluation

Bricker (1987) has offered a framework designed to relate the activities of assessment, intervention, and evaluation, building upon the procedure first detailed by Bagnato and J.T. Neisworth (1981). Bricker's model provides narrower detail regarding the formative evaluation of child progress on a session/daily/weekly/monthly/quarterly basis. Bricker also promotes the appropriate use of norm-referenced and curriculum-referenced instruments, as well as direct observation of behavior, for linking assessment and program planning and for monitoring learning and developmental progress.

System To Plan Early Childhood Services

The System To Plan Early Childhood Services (SPECS) (Bagnato & J.T. Neisworth, 1989b) is a planning system that structures team member decision making regarding child and family assessment and intervention. SPECS synthesizes assessment data from norm-, curricular-, and judgment-based sources into a common rating. It is a clinical judgment assessment system that integrates assessment and permits comprehensive service planning and progress efficacy evaluation in an economical and efficient manner. The system includes five components: (1) Perceptions of Developmental Status (PODS), (2) Child Services Indicator, (3) Perceptions of Family Status (POFS), (4) Family Services Indicator, and (5) Team Record of Education and Therapy (TREAT). All members of the interdisciplinary team, including parents, cooperate in the assessment, service delivery planning, and evaluation sequence.

APPLIED RESEARCH

Validity and Efficacy of Prescriptive Multidimensional Assessment

Bagnato (1984) used an interdisciplinary multidimensional assessment battery to monitor the status, curricular needs, and progress of 54 multihandicapped, brain-injured infants and preschoolers aged 6 to 60 months. The study had two objectives: (1) to determine the level of team congruence on curriculum- and judgment-based assessment measures and (2) to analyze their concurrent validity on norm- and curriculum-based developmental scales. The battery included the following specific measures: Bayley Scales of Infant Development (BSID), Gesell Developmental Schedules—Revised (GDS-R), Early Intervention Developmental Profile (EIDP), Carolina Record of Individual Behavior (CRIB), Developmental Profile-II (DP-II), and Perceptions of Developmental Status (PODS). In terms of the concurrent validity of curriculum-based assessment, the results demonstrated that the BSID, GDS-R, and EIDP measures were consistent in pinpointing the skill acquisition of the group of children, although the measures were completed by different team members. Maternal skill assessments on the DP-II measure overestimated the children's stable level of skill development.

Regarding interdisciplinary team agreement, the congruence of seven team members, including the parents, was studied. Strong agreement emerged among team members' curricular assessments involving physical and occupational therapists, speech/language therapists, psychologists, teachers, pediatric nurses, and parents on the EIDP subscales over a 6-month period. No significant differences among professional evaluations and curricular entry points were evident, except for dramatic underestimations by the child psychiatrist in identifying the children's socioemotional capabilities. The results also showed that clinical judgments on the PODS and CRIB measures, including those of the parents, were congruent and matched the children's actual performances on curriculum-based measures.

LeLaurin (1985) used neurodevelopmental/prescriptive and ecobehavioral assessment and treatment approaches to teach normal, at-risk, and handicapped infants (birth to 3 years). The assessment/treatment battery included the Griffiths Mental Development Scale and the criterion-referenced Vulpe Assessment Battery. The results showed that a prescriptive, curriculum-based approach within a response-contingent program of 40-weeks' duration promoted the developmental progress of children beyond expected maturational levels.

A diagnostic-prescriptive model was employed to plan intervention for infants and preschoolers with congenital and acquired brain injuries (Bagnato & J.T. Neisworth, 1985a). Longitudinal results over a 6-month period of intensive pediatric rehabilitation showed dramatic results for children with either type of brain injury. Although patterns of progress differed (related to the kind of insult), both groups showed gains in all developmental curricular domains that generally exceeded the progress expected based on maturation alone. The intensive treatment approach had similar impacts for both brain injury groups.

Two studies specifically addressed the technical adequacy of curriculum-based scales compared with selected norm-based criterion measures. Bagnato and J.T. Neisworth (1985b) conducted a study with 58 developmentally disabled preschoolers with mild-severe deficits. The level of diagnostic agreement among four developmental measures—Gesell Developmental Schedules (GDS), HICOMP Track Record, Preschool Attainment Record, and Perceptions of Developmental Status—was compared. The strongest intercorrelations were evident between the GDS and HICOMP measures.

In the second study, 50 neurologically impaired infants and preschoolers were evaluated concurrently and independently by a multidisciplinary team, using eight developmental scales (Bagnato & Murphy, 1989). The separate measures included the Bayley Scales of Infant Development (BSID), Gesell Developmental Schedules (GDS), Early Intervention Developmental Profile (EIDP), Hawaii Early Learning Profile (HELP), Learning Accomplishment Profile (LAP), Memphis Comprehensive Developmental Scale (MCDS), HICOMP Preschool Curriculum (HICOMP), and Portage Curriculum Guide. The "criterion indexes" were the DA and DQs of the BSID and GDS measures. The HELP, EIDP, and HICOMP curriculum-based instruments showed the greatest match in both developmental age and developmental quotient indexes, using multiple correlation techniques and repeated-measure ANOVAs.

The SPECS system described earlier was piloted with a group of infants and preschoolers with acquired brain injuries to evaluate its economy and usefulness for a pediatric rehabilitation team (Bagnato, Mayes, & Nichter, 1988). The multidimensional battery consisted of two levels of administrative and clinical appraisal that had three objectives: (1) diagnosing the degree of neurodevelopmental deficit, (2) prescribing treatment goals, and (3) monitoring child progress and treatment efficacy. Results with 12 children showed promising results for SPECS as a program-based measure that is sensitive to child change from the acute care to rehabilitation setting.

Reliability and Validity of Developmental Assessment/Curriculum Linkages

MacTurk and J.T. Neisworth (1978) analyzed the differential utility of norm-referenced and curriculum-based measures in a mainstreamed preschool setting over 6 months. Intercorrelations between Gesell diagnostic results from a psychologist and teacher-evaluated curriculum progress ranged from $R = .61$ to $.93$ for both groups, with a mean correlation of $R = .91$ for the handicapped group. The results reflected a developmental similarity between Gesell test behaviors and HICOMP Preschool Curriculum objectives and supported the usefulness of traditional developmental scales as reliable criterion-based measures of individual child progress and intervention effectiveness. They also demonstrated that a curriculum built on the same developmental landmarks as the assessment device could be used to track normative progress.

The efficacy of a method to match diagnostic data from traditional developmental measures with goals in developmental curricula was evaluated using teachers of handicapped preschool children (Bagnato, 1981a). Results supported the utility of the assessment/curriculum linkage method by demonstrating that teachers showed a high level of internal consistency in identifying curricular goals for individual children based on diagnostic data from traditional developmental scales. Matches were completed among data from the Gesell Developmental Schedules (GDS) with goals on the HICOMP Preschool Curriculum and the Project Memphis Curriculum.

Bagnato (1980, 1981b) compared the differential effectiveness of traditional-versus-translated school psychological reports in providing functional information to preschool teachers about individual child functioning. Specifically, the research demonstrated that the format for reporting results measurably influenced how well teachers could construct IEP goals for individual children. With traditional reports, teachers disagreed over 50 percent of the time regarding individualized goals but agreed nearly 90 percent of the time using the "translated" format. To facilitate prescriptive curriculum linkage, the translated format used subheadings that matched the domains of the curriculum, descriptions of a child's skills in functional terms, and lists of "developmental ceilings" and "emerging skills" for each child (see translated reports in Appendix C).

Developmental assessment/curriculum linkages were empirically established and published by Bagnato and Llewellyn (1982) for developmental tasks on the HICOMP Preschool Curriculum and tasks contained in other commercially available instruments, including the Early Intervention Developmental Profile, Learning Accomplishment Profile, Gesell schedules, Bayley scales, and Uniform Performance Assessment System (see Appendix D).

The utility of the assessment/curriculum linkage procedure and multiple measures was evaluated within the context of a public school special early education program in Pennsylvania (Devenney, 1983). The format for children with mild-to-severe developmental deficits used Perceptions of Developmental Status (PODS), the BRIGANCE Diagnostic Inventory of Early Development (BDIED), the HICOMP Preschool Curriculum, and the Portage Guide to Early Education to assess child status, plan individualized programs, and monitor progress. The system proved important in systematizing the assessment-intervention-evaluation process and in fostering both administrative and clinical accountability. Each instrument in the program format proved compatible with treatment objectives.

LEAP is a federally funded integrated preschool program for autistic preschoolers at the Early Childhood Institute, University of Pittsburgh. A description of the LEAP approach (Hoyson, Jamieson, & Strain, 1984) showed that the assessment/curriculum linkage concept was integrated in their developmentally and behaviorally based intervention model. The scope and sequence of instruction with each normal and disabled child were dictated by objectives derived from initial assessments translated on the Learning Accomplishment Profile (LAP). Initial selected objectives on the LAP were within the child's traditional or "functioning" range. The program emphasized frequent progress checks to monitor gain over time due to treatment. Efficiency indexes were also used to document degree of gain during treatment and instruction. The results on 13 normal and 6 autistic preschoolers ($N = 19$) over a 2-year period demonstrated significant gains concurrently on the McCarthy Scales of Children's Abilities and the LAP instruments. Gains were also evident in terms of the numbers of curriculum objectives achieved compared with those of normal preschoolers. The linkage format proved compatible with a data-based, behaviorally oriented approach.

3

Developmental Assessment: Principles and Procedures

Stimulus Changes
Response Options
Alternative Scoring Systems
Adaptive Toys
  Developmental Toys
  Toys with Handicap-Sensitive Qualities
  Electromechanical Toys
Norms for Handicapped Preschoolers

Summary

Early childhood assessment has been redefined within the past decade. Advances have made possible more accurate and useful descriptions and prescriptions for handicapped and at-risk children. This chapter provides an overview of these advances and offers a set of organizing principles and procedures for prescriptive developmental assessment. Specifically, it (1) defines prescriptive developmental assessment and principles, (2) details selection criteria for optimal measures, (3) categorizes available early childhood assessment instruments, (4) advocates multidimensional batteries, and (5) reviews alternative assessment strategies.

DEFINITION AND FEATURES OF PRESCRIPTIVE
DEVELOPMENTAL ASSESSMENT

Before providing a formal definition, it will be helpful to examine each of the concepts in the term *prescriptive developmental assessment*. *Prescriptive* indicates that the purpose of the assessment process is to determine a set of recommendations that specifies or guides selection of instructional/therapeutic objectives and strategies; the result is a blueprint for intervention. *Developmental* denotes the content basis of the assessment: not psychological, biological, or theoretical processes, but appraisal of present and emerging actual capabilities. The domains of development, as previously discussed, include cognitive, motor, affective, language, and interrelated competencies. Our knowledge of typical child development sequences helps us to describe the capabilities of children at different ages and the variations in development that are to be expected. When children perform below age expectations, the results may alert us to developmental dysfunctions— or, of course, to inaccurate child appraisal. Developmental milestones and progressions act as the major referents for prescriptive developmental assessment. Finally, *assessment* refers to procedures for describing child status that are flexible, comprehensive, and designed to accommodate the realities of developmentally disabled children. Assessment includes interview and observation, in addition to testing, and involves multiple instruments, sources, and occasions. It departs dramatically from sheer "testing."

Developmental "testing" is an outmoded practice of historical interest only. Testing is a simple and limiting activity that fails to capture the complexity, variability, and richness of child characteristics. Traditional psychometric or developmental testing was based on a kind of physical measurement analog: simply measure traits with the testing instrument, record the numbers, convert them to some common measure, and report the results. Testing usually involved one administration by a single tester, often in a special testing room. From our contemporary perspectives, this one-shot crude approach is laden with problems of validity, reliability, and common sense! Clearly, the robot-like use of measurement devices ignores consideration of the facts of life: children can have a bad day, the situation can be unfamiliar and distracting, the tester may not know the ways to foster a particular child's responses, and the test items may demand ways of responding that are difficult or impossible for a handicapped child. Thus, very often, mere testing has yielded distorted descriptions and gross underestimates of child/family status.

In summary, then, prescriptive developmental assessment is a flexible and comprehensive approach to child appraisal that is systematic and practical in its outcome. It is the basis for unifying assessment and programming, and it provides a common language between the psychologist and teacher/therapist. It synchronizes each overlapping phase in the linkage model.

Phases in LINK:
A Developmental Assessment/Curriculum Linkage System

Phase 1: Screen/Identify

This refers to a global process of surveying the behavior and characteristics of children, families, and their environments in order to detect general problem areas that require focused appraisal. Identification is the outcome of the screening process in which presumed problem domains are detected to guide more precise analysis.

Phase 2: Assess/LINK

This involves comprehensive developmental assessment, that is, an increasingly fine-focused process of analyzing, describing, and profiling each child's range of current developmental and behavioral characteristics and needs across multiple areas of functioning, thereby providing a practical basis for individualized treatment planning. Prescriptive linkage refers to the outcome of the comprehensive assessment process: a document that prescribes matches between child needs and curriculum and program goals and service delivery options. Prescriptions are expressed in the form of IEPs and IFSPs. Developmental task analysis is the common denominator of assessment results and IEP curricular goals. It involves a procedure for analyzing the child's range of fully acquired (+), emerging (±), and absent (−) capabilities as revealed through assessment, in order to select congruent curricular activities at appropriate levels.

Phase 3: Program/Intervene

This involves developmental programming, that is, a mix of developmental, behavioral, ecological, and adaptive methods that facilitate the acquisition of IEP and IFSP goals. Developmental task analysis bridges the assessment-programming gap and highlights goals to be matched with appropriate strategies. Developmental intervention refers to instructional and therapeutic action based on the goals and methods suggested by prescriptive developmental assessment.

Phase 4: Evaluate/Monitor

This involves evaluation, the process of appraising the progress of children as well as the efficacy of the total intervention program. The process uses sensitive multidimensional measures in the PDA. Both periodic change on a daily/weekly/monthly basis (formative) as well as overall gains at the end of a longer period of intervention (summative) are important. Formative evaluation permits the monitoring that allows programs to chart change and readily detect when program modifications are necessary.

PRESCHOOL MEASURES USED BY TEACHERS AND PSYCHOLOGISTS

A variety of assessment measures are used in early childhood special education. Those available vary widely in quality and usefulness. Since assessment is such a vital component of the intervention process, it is important to understand the scales most frequently used and the criteria employed to select them.

A survey of 105 preschool programs for handicapped children across 34 states (Johnson & Beauchamp, 1987) employed three major sections: a rating of frequency of use of an array of common preschool measures, a narrative description of test selection factors they used, and a rating of 30 characteristics of methods that influence test selection and use. The results demonstrated and implied several considerations concerning preschool measure selection and use. The three most frequently used instruments were the BRIGANCE Diagnostic Inventory of Early Development (Brigance, 1978) (46 percent), the Learning Accomplishment Profile: Diagnostic Edition (LeMay & Griffin, 1981) (39 percent), and an array of other scales (4 to 12 percent), including locally developed measures, the Portage Guide to Early Education (Shearer et al., 1976), the Minnesota Child Development Inventory (Ireton & Thwing, 1979), and the McCarthy Scales of Children's Abilities (McCarthy, 1972). It is important to note that nearly half the respondents reported dissatisfaction with existing scales, necessitating the use of locally designed instruments to meet "unique" local needs. The most frequently used curriculum (11 percent) was the Hawaii Early Learning Profile (Furuno et al., 1979). Thus, though a curriculum-referenced scale (i.e., BRIGANCE) was the most commonly employed device, almost half of the teachers were still using either norm-referenced or informal, locally developed scales for assessment and programming. In terms of the factors that prompted scale selection, the most discouraging finding was that 46 percent used a test primarily because it was already in place or presumably because program administrators mandated its use within a program. However, other factors were of considerable significance. The most important selection factors were broad scope structure, developmental base, inclusion of several areas, profiling of strengths and weaknesses, easy adaptation for program planning, easy interpretation to parents, and ease of use by both teachers and paraprofessionals.

Several conclusions are apparent from the survey data. First, teachers evidently have limited choices in selecting assessment measures for program use. Changes in administrative decision making are needed to overcome this limitation. Relatedly, perhaps teachers need greater guidance in how to select instruments for appropriate purposes. Training programs need to stress assessment and instrument selection and recommendations for specific types of measures based on purpose. Even after a decade or more, programs still fail to use a framework for assessment that leads directly to intervention. Curriculum-based systems are widely used; and norm-referenced measures still are used inappropriately for programming purposes, for example, the Denver Developmental Screening Test (20 percent!). However, criterion- or curriculum-referenced instruments showed the highest usage. Finally, it is apparent from the survey that teachers view assessment and intervention as "linked" but believe that the quality of available materials is poor as a basis for accomplishing this purpose. It is clear also that preschool teachers are generally unaware of recently developed systems that have linkage-to-programming qualities.

Many of the same problems that arise for preschool teachers in scale selection are also apparent for school psychologists who provide services in preschool settings. Preschool psychologists (NASP/APA Special Interest Preschool Group, 1987) were surveyed regarding many aspects of preschool service delivery, including training needs, range of role responsibilities, research, intervention strategies, and assessment tools and techniques. Among the 105 psychologists responding to the survey, the most frequently cited measures were norm-referenced scales: Stanford-Binet, Vineland, McCarthy, WPPSI, Bayley, and K-ABC (33 to 64 percent). The second most frequently cited types of scales were criterion- or curriculum-based systems: BRIGANCE (18 percent), Battelle (6 percent), Early Intervention Developmental Profile, DASI-II, Portage, HELP, and LAP (3 to 4 percent). No test selection factors were included in the survey, but analysis of the psychologists' expressed needs indicated that they require (1) greater knowledge of preschool assessment techniques, for example, nonverbal, informal, play, observation (91 percent); and (2) knowledge and skills useful in intervention, especially curriculum planning in early education (27 percent). Forty-two percent of the respondents believed that their available preschool assessment techniques were inadequate and indicated that they desired information on current and new procedures.

The following implications can be drawn from the survey results regarding assessment in early childhood special education:

- Both teachers and preschool psychologists have outdated knowledge of available assessment techniques and have a pressing need for knowledge of curriculum-referenced instruments.
- There is a general awareness among teachers, more so than among psychologists, of the primary purpose of preschool assessment, namely, program planning.
- Compared with psychologists, teachers have a much clearer appreciation of the importance of program-relevant assessment selection factors, such as developmental base, multiple domains, translation to parents, and adaptation for programming.
- School psychologists need greater preservice and inservice training in appropriate intervention-based preschool techniques, with a reduced emphasis on limited norm-referenced assessment. Wider conceptualizations of their now-specialized roles as "Developmental School Psychologists" (Bagnato, J.T. Neisworth, Paget, & Kovaleski, 1987) are necessary to prevent a downward extension of a model from school-age to preschool.
- Both groups have little appreciation of the importance of using in a program a uniform developmental curriculum system to which other instruments can be linked. There is too much reliance on technically inadequate, locally designed techniques.
- Neither group emphasizes the sequential nature of assessment, programming, and progress evaluation nor the integral involvement of several team members and parents in the assessment process.
- Neither group comprehends the necessity and advantages of using multiple measures to accomplish several related purposes. Psychologists and teachers alike still engage in the "search for the Holy Grail of assessment instruments"—the hope that one instrument will do all things!
- Generally, assessment is still conducted apart from intervention, although considerable lip service is paid to assessment/curriculum linkage.

Clearly, theory and practice must not continue to be treated as unrelated efforts. Contemporary early childhood education must be developmentally based, in order to assess what is taught and to teach what is assessed.

CRITERIA FOR SELECTING DEVELOPMENTAL SCALES

Assessment measures vary considerably in their capability to offer useful information to describe and prescribe for young exceptional children. Limitations of infant and early childhood assessment measures commonly involve the following problems: clusters of unrelated tasks and abilities, lack of sequencing, inadequate ranges of simple-to-difficult skills (i.e., floors and ceilings), emphasis on only one domain of functioning (e.g., cognition or motor), handicap biasing factors, absence of a theoretical base, limited behavior samples, lack of adequate reliability and validity, and little or no relationship to program curriculum.

Early-intervention specialists and preschool psychologists must recognize that no single measure is adequate alone to accomplish the job. The special needs of young handicapped children are so complex that a multimeasure approach is crucial for comprehensive assessment and individualized intervention planning. Research in early intervention over the past decade supports the use of multidimensional, interdisciplinary, and curriculum-based strategies to address the needs of children.

Seven criteria must be observed when analyzing and selecting scales to be incorporated within an individually tailored prescriptive assessment battery: (1) developmental base, (2) multidomain profile, (3) multisource sample, (4) curricular links, (5) adaptive options, (6) ecological emphasis, and (7) technical support. The following subsections provide detail on these research-based criteria as a basis for guiding scale selection and promoting assessment/curriculum linkage. Psychologists, teachers, and other team members can use the form in Exhibit 3-1 to evaluate, in terms of these criteria, the appropriateness of developmental measures for their programs.

Developmental Base

- Are the activities within the assessment measure hierarchically structured and sequenced according to a developmental task analysis or developmental process format?
- Is the design of the scale based upon some reputable developmental orientation?

In general, it is important that assessment measures be constructed to reflect some underlying developmental philosophy. The most common and useful mergers between theory and content are the developmental task model exemplified by the Gesell or Bayley scales and the developmental process model illustrated by the Uzgiris-Hunt Piagetian measure. With this developmental base in theory and content, the process of assessment has greater content and construct validity. By using the same underlying foundation, developmental curricula can better accommodate assessment results. Hierarchical organization and developmental task analysis provide the lattice of developmental skills and competencies to be assessed and mastered. In this developmental task analysis, skills are sequenced along a continuum according to age expectancy, level of difficulty, and/or adaptive stage. The smaller the increments between prerequisite items in the task analysis, the more sensitive the measure, a characteristic clearly needed for assessment and curriculum goal planning for handicapped infants and preschoolers. The developmental base and

Exhibit 3-1 Evaluation and Selection Criteria Rating Form for Prescriptive Developmental
Assessment Measures

Scale _____   Publisher _____

Address _____   Phone _____

Ratings: 0 = Does not meet criterion
1 = Partially meets criterion
2 = Fulfills criterion

Developmental Base
_____ 1. Are the activities within the assessment measure hierarchically structured and
sequenced according to a developmental task analysis or developmental process
format?
_____ 2. Is the design of the scale based upon some reputable developmental orientation?

Multidomain Profile
_____ 3. Does the assessment measure organize items into several distinct yet interrelated
subdomains?
_____ 4. Does the multidomain organization of competencies allow the detection of fully
acquired (+), emerging (±), and absent (−) capabilities?
_____ 5. Does the scale offer separate scores/indexes for each subdomain?

Multisource Sample
_____ 6. Does the assessment measure integrate information obtained from several people (parent, professional) and methods (observation, ratings, performance,
interview)?
_____ 7. Can several different team members independently contribute information to complete the scale?

Curricular Links
_____ 8. Is the assessment measure organized into developmental domains similar to those
surveyed in the early intervention program's curriculum?
_____ 9. Does the scale contain tasks/items similar in content and behavioral demands to
those included in the program's developmental curriculum?

Adaptive Options
_____ 10. Does the scale provide structured modifications of tasks to accommodate the sensory and response limitations of young children with sensory, motor, and adaptive deficits?
_____ 11. Can a professional "clinically" alter the tasks within the scale to accommodate
children with various handicaps?
_____ 12. Does the scale provide or allow modifications for scoring the performances of
young handicapped children?

Ecological Emphasis
_____ 13. Does the scale provide information on the child's interaction with the physical
and social environment (e.g., attention to tasks, peer interaction, need for
prompts and limits, ability to cope with new situations)?
_____ 14. Does the scale integrate information from both home and school?

Exhibit 3-1 continued

Technical Support

_____ 15. Has research established the reliability, validity, and diagnostic utility of the assessment measure?

_____ 16. Has the scale been adequately standardized and/or field-tested in general?

_____ 17. Has the scale been field-tested and/or standardized on any handicap group?

_____ 18. Does the scale contain separate norms or any comparative data for young handicapped children?

_____ Total Evaluation Score

_____ /36 (total possible score) =_____ %

task analysis generate mutual behavioral criteria that link assessment, intervention, and progress evaluation.

Multidomain Profile

- Does the assessment measure organize items into several distinct yet interrelated subdomains?
- Does the multidomain organization of competencies allow the detection of fully acquired ($+$), emerging ($\pm$), and absent ($-$), capabilities and of separate age and functional levels for each domain?

Assessment must sample a broad array of developmental and behavioral skills and response classes. Moreover, it is important that assessment measures and curricula have similar samples at both the domain and skill/task levels. Typical groupings of developmental skills include cognitive, language, perceptual-fine motor, socioemotional, gross motor, and self-care. Furthermore, subtle behavioral dimensions must often be appraised, particularly for more severely disabled children (e.g., temperament, endurance, normalcy, goal-directed behavior, attention, reactivity, and self-stimulation). Since no single measure taps this array, multiple measures are required in an individually tailored diagnostic battery. A broad analysis enables early-intervention specialists to identify different functional levels in each area of concern, to analyze competencies within the task analysis, and to isolate curricular goals to guide intervention. Such an analysis also detects intact abilities that are often obscured by sensorimotor impairments when the instruments include a wider sample of behaviors beyond "landmark" skills. Admittedly, a "separate" domain organization is somewhat artificial, since capabilities are intertwined and young children must be viewed holistically, such as in the emergent relationship among language, social competency, self-control, and thinking. Nevertheless, multidomain analysis provides important information as a basis for linking assessment and individualized intervention.

Multisource Sample

- Does the assessment measure or battery integrate information from several professionals and the parent?

The assessment scales or battery must include the findings of several persons who have observed the child's behavior across different settings. Multisource procedures enable one to monitor both the capabilities that are inconsistent, emerging, and situation- or person-specific and the generalization of skills. Multisource assessment adjusts for and challenges the limitations of rigidly formalized norm-referenced assessments. The reliability of our assessment increases as the number of sources or behavior samples rises. In turn, this raises the level of confidence in our assessment of competencies and identification of curriculum goals. For young handicapped children, interdisciplinary/multisource assessment procedures are, in fact, mandatory. With assessments derived from a team of professionals (e.g., psychologist, teacher, speech/language therapist, occupational and/or physical therapist, nurse, pediatrician, social worker), paraprofessionals (e.g., aides, family friends), and the parents, we can more accurately design programs and gauge the developmental status and progress of young handicapped children.

Curricular Links

- Are the assessment measures compatible in structure and content with the curriculum used in the program?

Curriculum linkage and prescriptive assessment are pragmatic methods for increasing the usefulness of traditional developmental scales in the initial phases of individualized curriculum goal planning. As previously discussed, the tasks contained in most curricula are similar to those contained in well-known developmental scales; thus, a natural bridge is available for criterion-referenced assessment. Actually, whether good or bad, most curricula were developed by surveying and incorporating the content of scales, such as the Gesell and Bayley. Fortunately, this creates the congruence between sampled and predicted behaviors—between testing and teaching—that is required. Curricular links are most obvious in the similarity between domains assessed and programmed (e.g., cognitive, play, motor) and the specific behaviors targeted (e.g., uncovering hidden objects, matching shapes, sharing, and turn taking). Someone familiar with traditional developmental scales and developmental curricula can readily see similarities in content, coverage, domains, and even specific items.

Adaptive Options

- Does the scale provide alternative strategies for modifying assessment tasks with young children displaying sensory, motor, and adaptive deficits?

- Does the scale provide or allow modifications for scoring the performances of young handicapped children?

Prescriptive developmental assessment must be flexible and adaptive. Only a few instruments have those capabilities, and they are predominantly criterion- or curriculum-based systems.

It is important that assessment measures have standardized procedures for adapting tasks or, at least, can be modified for this purpose. Two kinds of adaptations are critical: (1) modifying the stimulus properties of objects and materials, and (2) permitting alternative child response options. Common examples of stimulus modifications include handles on formboards for cerebral palsied children and magnification or textured designs for the visually impaired. Alternative response modes often involve head pointers, light beams, and eye localization for preschoolers with dual neuromotor and language deficits and signing and pantomime directions for the hearing impaired. Some recently published scales and curricula contain adaptive options; for example, the Battelle Developmental Inventory, the Uniform Performance Assessment System, and Developmental Programming for Infants and Young Children. Alternative scoring procedures are also available, such as the multidimensional scoring system proposed by Cole, Swisher, Thompson, and Fewell (1985). Diagnosticians use adaptive strategies when they exclude biasing items, prompt behaviors on a task, retest, and substitute objects that are within the child's experiences.

Ecological Emphasis

- Does the instrument or battery provide information on the physical and social environment in which the child interacts?

The child does not behave or progress in isolation. The recent legislative trends regarding IFSPs are tangible evidence of the emphasis on the family context for child development. Effective assessment and programming depend upon skill in analyzing environmental conditions in home and preschool that promote development. Thus evaluative measures must be selected based upon their sensitivity in pinpointing such dimensions as classroom arrangements (e.g., zone vs. individual), qualities of toys, style of approaching a child (e.g., gradual vs. abrupt), effect of noise and other stimulation, and factors that influence stress and coping (e.g., lack of finances, chronic illness, learned helplessness, maternal depression). Contextual factors—including home, preschool, and interpersonal competencies and needs—must be part of the comprehensive assessment.

Technical Support

- Does the assessment measure have demonstrated reliability and validity data to justify its use?
- Is adequate field-test information available to support the instrument?

Assessment measures must consistently describe (reliability) the behaviors that they actually measure (validity). Different forms of technical support are required. For example, repeated testings by the same or different persons on a child must result in similar findings. Measures must discriminate between an impaired child and a nonhandicapped one. Measures must adequately sample various constructs (e.g., attention, primitive reflexes, preacademic concepts) and show results that match those of similarly designed measures. Finally, the scales must have diagnostic and treatment validity, in that they serve a practical assessment function; even anecdotal records have some technical base. Early-intervention specialists must also evaluate scales in terms of their normative or field-test base. For example, do they have separate norms for various handicap groups? Have they been field tested with the target population and met performance criteria (e.g., evaluate progress, facilitate parent involvement in the process)? All measures must justify their use; this is also true for program tools designed locally.

AN ASSESSMENT TYPOLOGY IN EARLY INTERVENTION

Choosing the appropriate tool for a specific clinical and/or research purpose is vital. Instruments designed for nonhandicapped youngsters have been force-fitted to fulfill functions not originally intended. Creative advances in the technology of early childhood assessment now enable us to appraise with greater validity and instructional utility. The available assessment instruments and purposes can be categorized into several classes. Our categorization or typology of assessment devices encompasses eight distinct categories of instruments, as shown in Table 3-1. In this section, we examine each of these types of instrument. In each case, introductory descriptive citations are drawn from a comprehensive review of the assessment typology in J.T. Neisworth and Bagnato (1988).

Curriculum-Based (CB)

"Curriculum-based (CB) assessment traces a child's achievement along a continuum of objectives, especially within a developmentally sequenced curriculum" (pp. 26-27). Curriculum-based assessment is the predominant form of child skill appraisal in most infant stimulation and preschool programs for at-risk and handicapped children. Two types of CB measures are evident: curriculum-embedded and curriculum-referenced scales. Curriculum-embedded scales *are* the curriculum; thus, the assessment and instructional tasks are identical. In contrast, curriculum-referenced scales contain tasks and criteria that are similar to those in frequently used developmental curricula but more generic and "landmark" in nature. The primary purposes of curriculum-based scales are to identify a child's unique treatment needs and objectives and to monitor progress through a developmental task analysis of increasingly sophisticated competencies.

Table 3-1   Assessment Typology in Early Childhood Special Education

Scale Type	Definition/Purpose	Example
Curriculum-based (CB)	Monitors treatment needs and progress	Learning Accomplishment Profile
Adaptive-to-handicap (AH)	Circumvents disabilities via adaptations	Developmental Programming for Infants and Young Children
Process (PR)	Detects competencies via interpretations of qualitative behavior changes	Information-Processing Approach
Norm-based (NB)	Compares and diagnoses child functioning via norms	Bayley Scales of Infant Development Battelle Developmental Inventory
Judgment-based (JB)	Organizes multisource perceptions about child/family	Perceptions of Developmental Status
Ecological/environmental (EE)	Examines features of child's total environment	Home Observation for Measurement of the Environment
Interactive (INT)	Analyzes social interchanges	Parent Behavior Progression
Direct observation of behavior (DOB)	Records contingent relationships among ongoing behavior and events	PLA-Check

Adaptive-to-Handicap (AH)

"Adaptive-to-Handicap (AH) scales include or permit the use of alternative sensory or response modes to minimize false item failure" (p. 30). Sensorimotor (e.g., cerebral palsy) and affective/behavioral (e.g., autism) impairments often obscure the young exceptional child's "true" capabilities. AH scales circumvent the child's disability by offering systematic procedures to modify the stimulus features of materials and the response modes employed in order to isolate evidence of intact cognitive and adaptive/coping capabilities. Adaptive scales also facilitate diagnostic teaching; they allow the early interventionist to isolate the types of environmental arrangements, task modifications, and instructional strategies to permit optimal child learning.

Process (PR)

"Process (PR) assessment examines changes in child reactions (e.g., smiling, vocalizing, heart rate, surprise, glee) as a function of changes in stimulus events, and qualitative advancements in the child's cognitive abilities" (p. 32). A PR type of adaptive assessment can also be used to detect possible underlying intellectual capacities when biological impairments or limited behavioral repertoires make more objective approaches difficult. Typically, PR methods rely upon affective reactions as indicators of the child's comprehension and memory. Assessment strategies that gauge advancements in the child's *stage* of cognitive competence are also considered PR measures.

Norm-Based (NB)

"Norm-based (NB) assessment compares a child's developmental skills and characteristics to those of a referent group (normative) comparable in terms of important child and demographic dimensions" (p. 33). Norm-based measures use standard scores (e.g., DQ/IQ, DA/MA, percentiles, T-scores) for three primary purposes: (1) to describe a child's functioning in terms of developmental expectancies for the child's age, (2) to place the child within some diagnostic category, and (3) to predict the child's eventual outcome status. Norm-based measures are overused in early intervention. They are particularly insensitive in registering the impact of treatment.

Judgment-Based (JB)

Judgment-based (JB) measures *"collect, structure, and usually quantify the impressions of professionals and caregivers about a child's developmental and be-*

havioral status or the characteristics of the child's environment" (p. 36). Judgment-based measures are valuable additions to comprehensive developmental assessment batteries. Primarily, they broaden the sample of behaviors and provide a more representative picture of the child's typical pattern of functioning and generalization of learning. By collecting perceptions from teachers, parents, and other professionals about child, family, and environmental attributes, early interventionists can check the accuracy or congruence among judgments. Thus, JB scales enable a team to monitor internal agreement. Team congruence results in consistent programming tailored to the child's and family's needs. Such judgments also provide some social validity (Wolf, 1978) by relying on the diverse perceptions of several people who have worked with the child over time and in various settings. Another important use of JB scales for program linkage is in describing subtle traits and response classes that influence functioning but are difficult to assess formally. Some of the traits that can be judged include attention, participation, motivation, appearance, self-regulation, and play style.

Ecological/Environmental (EE)

Environmental or "ecological (EE) assessment refers to the examination and recording of the physical, social and psychological features of a child's developmental context" (p. 39). Prescriptive assessment requires that the interaction between child and environmental characteristics be accurately and functionally determined. Ecological measures broaden the context of developmental assessment beyond the child and enable team members to screen the impact of various external factors—antecedent, contemporaneous, and consequent events—on the child's progress. For example, physical features—such as lighting, room arrangement, number of people present, and toy qualities—can be assessed. Social and psychological dimensions that can be estimated include rewards and limits, emotional responsivity of the mother, and peer interaction.

Interactive (INT)

"Interactive (INT) assessment examines the social capabilities of the infant and caregiver and the content and extent of synchrony between them" (p. 41). Often, it is important to evaluate the dyadic interaction between parent and child and teacher and child. Such an evaluation provides detail on verbal and nonverbal interchanges and how these influence child behavior. Interactive assessment is a narrow form of ecological appraisal that focuses upon such exchanges as the mother's ability to read and respond to the handicapped child's cues and body gestures and the child's ability to respond and reinforce the caregiver's initiations. Such aspects as the timing, content, initiation, and reinforcement of behavior are analyzed in order to establish goals for parent training and classroom programming.

Direct Observation of Behavior (DOB)

Direct observation of behavior (DOB) "refers to structured procedures for collecting objective and qualifiable data on ongoing behavior" (p. 43). Structured observation is used in all aspects of child and environmental assessment to provide greater detail on discrete instances of behavior and the contingencies among events. Structured programs to map child interactions within the classroom are available; these serve to fine-tune the comprehensive assessment of the preschooler and the relevant environment and to guide decision making about behavior management and total programming. Although beyond the scope of this text, DOB is a crucial skill for school psychologists and master teachers. When a child is having difficulty in specific skills or evidences behavior disorders, "close-up" assessment through direct observation seems mandatory.

THE PRESCRIPTIVE DEVELOPMENTAL ASSESSMENT BATTERY (PDA)

Infants and preschoolers with neurodevelopmental disabilities share characteristics that complicate both assessment and intervention. These characteristics include highly variable states of arousal, varying degrees of neuromotor impairment, sensory dysfunctions, absence of clear response modes, stereotyped self-stimulatory patterns, seizures, labile temperaments, absence of well-defined social communication capabilities, and primitive object play patterns (J.T. Neisworth & Bagnato, 1987). A paradox exists in that accurate assessment is the key for individualized treatment. Yet limitations of the child and limitations of the assessment strategies in themselves make accurate appraisal difficult; this is especially true when one strives to isolate among such young children certain intact cognitive/adaptive skills from sensory and neuromotor disabilities. Researchers have worked hard to resolve these problems and have made recommendations for useful collections or batteries of instruments.

Early intervention research over the past decade is consistent in indicating that effective assessment schemes for young handicapped children should encompass seven attributes. They should (1) reflect a developmental structure; (2) survey multiple developmental and behavioral dimensions; (3) employ a battery of several matched norm-based, curriculum-based, judgment-based, and ecological measures; (4) blend the assessments of several team members and the parents; (5) prescribe or link assessment and curricular goals; (6) adapt procedures for diverse disabilities, and (7) monitor child progress and program efficacy. In short, prescriptive developmental assessment (PDA) is interdisciplinary (i.e., involves team members and the parents), multidimensional (i.e., covers numerous child/family/environmental attributes), and curriculum-based (i.e., emphasizes individual treatment planning based upon identification of needs).

A "core" prescriptive developmental assessment battery includes, at a minimum, four types of scales: (1) norm-based (NB), (2) adaptive curriculum-based

(CB), (3) judgment-based (JB), and (4) ecological (E). As highlighted in the previous discussion, each type performs a specific function and ensures precise prescriptions for intervention planning. Interdisciplinary prescriptive developmental assessment batteries designed in this manner make sense from both clinical and research standpoints. To review, PDA batteries synthesize data from several different people across different situations, use a variety of measures, and survey multiple developmental and behavioral areas. Specifically, for purposes of developmental diagnosis, the NB scale in the battery provides a technically adequate comparison of the child's levels of functioning with those of peers. The CB instrument in the battery is selected to be functionally appropriate for a child with a particular handicap (i.e., by design and field testing or by inclusion of adaptive options), accommodates linkage of tasks from the NB scale, and generates developmental and behavioral objectives for planning IEPs and IFSPs and monitoring progress. The JB scale enables team members to detect subtle and easily overlooked aspects of behavior and to identify areas of agreement/disagreement about child needs. Finally, the ecological (E) scale influences treatment by enabling the team to sample relationships among child/family and environmental variables so as to broaden the focus of intervention.

Chapter 8 is devoted to detailed case studies of children and families that illustrate individualized prescriptive assessment batteries and program linkages. At this point, it is helpful to offer concrete examples of individual batteries (based on disability) to illustrate the concept. Table 3-2 profiles two different prescriptive assessment batteries with the same purpose: individualized intervention planning. Battery 1 was chosen for a visually impaired toddler, while Battery 2 was selected for a 4-year-old autistic preschooler. Note that each includes the "core" battery (NB, CB, JB, and E scales). In each battery, the predominant measure is the curriculum-based instrument, chosen for its handicap-sensitive qualities.

ADAPTIVE STRATEGIES TO ENHANCE PRESCRIPTIVE ASSESSMENT

"Precision prescriptive teaching demands better performance of the evaluator which frequently results in the criterion-referenced use of instruments that were originally developed on a norm-referenced basis" (Chinn, Drew, & Logan, 1975, p. 75). Often, available instruments used in a standard fashion are not appropriate for handicapped children. However, when those instruments are *adapted* and used in a flexible manner, emphasizing modifications that fit the child, they reveal a more useful side. One must remember that assessment, unlike testing, provides a broad, rich base of qualitative and quantitative information about child functioning. For example, by using a flexible clinical approach, norm-referenced measures can be modified so that they release criterion- or curriculum-referenced data to guide program planning. To accomplish this end, clinical modifications in assessment procedures must frequently be dictated by the degree of functional deficit presented by the young handicapped child.

Table 3-2 Prescriptive Developmental Assessment Batteries

Type	Visually Impaired (CA = 24 mo)	Autistic (CA = 48 mo)	High-Risk LD (CA = 66 mo)
Norm-based	Reynell-Zinkin Scales (1979)	Battelle Developmental Inventory (1984)	McCarthy Scales (1972), Stanford-Binet IV (1986)
Curriculum-based	Oregon Project Curriculum (1979)	Individualized Assessment and Treatment: PEP (1979)	HICOMP Curriculum (1982), Beginning Milestones (1985)
Judgment-based	Maxfield-Buchholz Scale (1958)	Childhood Autism Rating Scale (1986)	Perceptions (1988), Child BCL (1983)
Ecological	Parent Behavior Progression (1979)	Parenting Stress Index (1983)	HOME (1979)

Adaptive Modifications

The early-intervention specialist must be adept at adaptive assessment techniques. Even though newly developed materials make assessment more nondiscriminatory and handicap-sensitive, the early interventionist must be knowledgeable about "common sense" techniques for assessing the functional capabilities of children, particularly infants and preschoolers with such low-incidence disabilities as cerebral palsy, moderate-severe retardation, autism, and visual and hearing impairments. Common solutions involve the following four distinct approaches: (1) designing specially normed tests for a specific handicap group, (2) excluding biasing items or tasks from traditional scales, (3) altering the stimulus properties of objects and tasks within traditional measures, and (4) modifying the response modes required to complete tasks. Exhibit 3-2 summarizes prominent adaptive options.

Perhaps the best overall examples of the adaptive assessment strategy are offered by Haeussermann (1958) and Dubose et al. (1979). These clinicians advocate a process-oriented approach that enables the assessor to evaluate upper and lower limits of the handicapped child's capabilities in various cognitive, behavioral, language, and social/affective areas. This is accomplished by sequencing from primitive to advanced the skills required in these areas and then modifying the properties of objects and toys and the responses required to enable the handicapped preschooler to demonstrate competence. The process allows one to determine functional developmental ranges and levels while also identifying treatment goals and effective instructional strategies. (See Appendix A for a fuller explanation of the

Exhibit 3-2 Some Adaptive Assessment Strategies for the Young Exceptional Child

- Modify the stimulus properties of objects and materials.
- Alter or broaden the response modes available.
- Exclude tasks that bias performance and prorate scoring.
- Use multidimensional scoring methods (0,1,2) to tap performance'quality.
- Rearrange the order of presentation of assessment items.
- Combine tasks from various scales that sample specific functions ("smorgasbord approach").
- Combine multiple measures of the same abilities and check congruence.
- Use the test-teach-test procedure to determine learning rate.

Haeussermann Educational Evaluation technique.) Stimulus changes and the use of response options are two strategies that can be used in adapting assessment.

Stimulus Changes

The use of stimulus changes involves changing the objects and materials in a particular task so that they are more stimulating and motivating. Noteworthy examples are changes in the physical attributes of toys, such as color, shape, texture, movement, and sound. Such modifications are typically required for children with visual, hearing, language, motor, and behavioral deficits. Common stimulus modifications include the use of knobs on formboard shapes, larger blocks, enlarged pictures, raised dots on counting tasks, different textures on three-choice discrimination matching tasks, microswitches on a Jack-in-the-Box toy, and concrete-versus-pictured objects.

Kiernan and Dubose (1974) attempted to assess the intellectual performance of deaf-blind children on the Cattell Infant Intelligence Scale. Concurrently, items were selected from other infant scales and adapted to accommodate the children's sensory deficits. Tasks were modified by increasing the size of some items, altering textures, and changing some items from two to three dimensions. In general, stimulus characteristics, such as increased brightness and color, were emphasized. Other physical attributes were also altered, for example, by changing the size of blocks and puzzle pieces to facilitate manipulation. The study demonstrated that children performed significantly better with the adapted scale compared with their own concurrent performances on the traditional Cattell scale.

Hoffman (1982) has proposed a procedure for modifying administration of the Bayley Scales of Infant Development (BSID) to accommodate the limitations of children with sensorimotor impairments. The modifications are called "optimizing techniques." In general, the procedure calls for standardized administration of the BSID in the typical manner. Then, an analysis is made of those items that were failed, probably due to the impact of the handicapping condition. Two scoring systems are used to quantify and qualify ranges of functional skills. The systematic procedure relies upon positioning techniques by a physical therapist and the use of alternative equipment, mostly involving stimulus modifications. Descriptions of alternative toys are listed for selected assessment items. Examples of object changes include a larger blue ring with red braided wool string, nesting boxes, larger pegs, variously sized books, fatter crayons, a large metal spoon, and other modifications in the size of materials.

Response Options

The use of response options requires an analysis of the most consistent and easily accessible way available for the young handicapped child to complete a task. Response options consist of head pointers and light beams, eye localization, signing and pantomime, magnets to steady upper limb tremors, yes-no eye blinks, multiple-choice answer formats, naturalistic play with associated toys, augmentative computer communication systems, response-contingent toys, and affective reactions to unexpected events.

Perhaps the best recent example of an alternative response strategy for children with neuromotor impairments is Kanor's use and modification of toys (Kanor, 1988). This involves adapting toys, such as the Drumming Bear and Penguin Roller Coaster (both from Fisher-Price), with pressure-sensitive microswitches so that the young child can demonstrate knowledge of cause-effect. In another approach, Kearsley (1981) analyzed a young child's awareness of discrepancies among a series of visual events (e.g., a car on an inclined plane topples a clown at the bottom unexpectedly after repeated trials) by affective reactions of surprise, glee, fear, smiling, or increased body rhythm. These reactions were judged to be "replacement" reactions for the child's impaired sensory and neuromotor disabilities. Kearsley's research indicates that such approaches may have better predictive validity for severely impaired children.

It must be remembered that assessment of young multiply handicapped children is further confounded by the fact that their disabilities often prevent or limit access to stimulating learning experiences during "critical" developmental periods. Their receptivity to stimulation is blunted; therefore critical cognitive, language, and personal-social skills necessary for later complex learning are not intact. For example, the physically impaired and blind infant has significant sensorimotor dysfunctions that tend to blunt the development of a conception of object permanence.

Because so many handicapped youngsters have had restricted sensory and motor experiences, adaptive developmental assessment must be viewed as a continuous stimulation/learning activity. The process not only determines current levels of operation but also teaches the young child the critical features of novel problems and situations. This facilitates the development of selective attention, orientation to the task, interpersonal skills, and basic problem solving. In this manner, testing and teaching are interdependent phases of the same diagnostic process.

The primary outcome of adaptive-process assessment is to effect a "match" between a child's capabilities and the instructional environment. Developmental skills must be assessed within different situational contexts, that is, home versus preschool and teacher/specialist versus parent. In this way, the influences of different people and different environments in eliciting behavior can be appraised. Also, the virtues of certain adults and helpful situational factors, such as low distraction and secure surroundings, can be incorporated in the intervention program. Evidence of generalization and learning is provided if a child demonstrates a skill consistently across situations and across teachers. Thus, children should experience a variety of professionals who work with them; this will increase skill generalization and result in more stable performance.

Finally, behavior should be assessed within a known context so that the interaction between situational demands and child capabilities can be monitored. For example, a planned play situation within the preschool setting using a variety of materials can provide valuable diagnostic data. Observing how a severely involved child attempts to obtain and handle a toy or object, searches for a spoon dropped during feeding, or inserts a spoon in a cup provides evidence of object constancy, skill in the use of tools and utensils, comprehension of object functions, and understanding of interpersonal relationships.

Representative measures in this expanding area are the Developmental Activities Screening Inventory II (Dubose & Langley, 1982), the Callier-Azusa Scale for the assessment of deaf-blind children (Stillman, 1974), the Evaluation and Programming System (Bricker et al., in press), and the Battelle Developmental Inventory (Guidubaldi, Newborg, Stock, & Wnek, 1984). As yet, few commercially available developmental scales use the adaptive-process assessment approach. Most often, the evaluator must put together and adapt a variety of measures that provide functional estimates of capabilities. This tends to increase the reliability of the results, their comprehensiveness, and, ultimately, the instructional confidence we can place in them.

Alternative Scoring Systems

Scores and developmental indexes (e.g., those for age and rate) affect judgments and expectations about a child's current status and potential for progress. Precise numerical profiles of the young handicapped child's range of abilities are, nonetheless, important and useful for communicating among professionals. Normative data based on nonhandicapped populations do not always provide an appropriate comparison with the handicapped preschooler. Sensorimotor impairments limit optimal performance on items, even though the child may understand the concepts involved and the intent of the task. Scores derived from such a biased sample of behaviors can result in erroneous descriptions of levels of functioning.

Alternative scoring procedures can remedy this discriminatory assessment practice to some extent. Various authors have proposed more meaningful scoring systems that can incorporate both quantitative and qualitative evidence of functional capabilities. Some researchers (Bagnato & J.T. Neisworth, 1981; Cole et al., 1985; Naglieri, 1981; Simeonsson, Huntington, & Parse, 1980) suggest that indexes based on developmental age ranges, ceiling scores, continuum scoring procedures, and comparisons between normative and adaptive scores provide more meaningful descriptions of current functional levels and progress. Naglieri (1981) reported extrapolated scores for young children functioning at a developmental rate below 50 on the MDI of the Bayley Scales of Infant Development.

Bagnato and Murphy (1989) have proposed a procedure for adaptive scoring of the Bayley Scales of Infant Development (BSID). The procedure involves several aspects: excluding the biasing items within the task analysis (e.g., fine motor items for cerebral palsied infants, expressive language items for infants with communication delays/deficits); determining the proportion of a month that each item is worth in the task analysis; and multiplying this proportion by the number of passes, including emerging skills ($\pm$). The result is an adapted developmental age estimate. A ratio developmental quotient is then calculated and compared with the estimate gained from the BSID normative tables. The procedure is supported by longitudinal research over 2 to 3 years that predicted later functioning and later developmental deficit on 100 brain-injured preschoolers.

The Kent scoring adaptation of the Bayley Scales of Infant Development offers a commercially available procedure for rescoring the BSID into five rather than two domains. The procedure provides descriptions of a strategy for deriving developmental ages and for reorganizing various tasks by a clinical sorting procedure into cognitive, language, social, fine motor, and gross motor domains.

One of the most promising clinical adaptive scoring procedures for severely handicapped children is the multidimensional technique of Cole et al. (1985). The strategy increases the sensitivity of assessment instruments to the handicapped child's level of proficiency in completing tasks. Thus, it allows one to rate or score qualitative evidence of competence through a continuum scoring system. Rather than provide merely a binary (i.e., correct vs. incorrect) or Likert (i.e., single-continuum) scoring system, the multidimensional format empowers the assessor to quantify several qualitative dimensions of a child's response to each task. For example, each response to a particular task (e.g., finding hidden objects) is scored for frequency of response, generalization, initiation, and fluency—each scored on a continuum of 0 points (no response) to 3 points. Results of studies with this graded scoring system suggest that it can enhance the sensitivity of most developmental assessment measures employed with severely handicapped children.

Continuum or functional scoring systems are also prevalent in many of the judgment-based assessment devices now becoming available. Two of the most prominent are the Perceptions of Developmental Status (PODS) (Bagnato & J.T. Neisworth, 1987) and the Carolina Record of Individual Behavior (CRIB) (Simeonsson, 1985). The PODS rates judgments about developmental competencies on a Likert scale of 1 (severe) to 5 (normal/above average) in 20 areas. The CRIB provides scores on a scale of 1 to 9 in 22 different domains, including ratings of the severity of self-stimulatory behaviors.

Adaptive Toys

Specialists recognize that typical toys are not always appropriate for children with sensory, neuromotor, and behavioral disabilities; hence, young handicapped children need special toys. Such toys must be chosen on the basis of their capacity to motivate and invite cognitive, social communication, and perceptual-motor behavior. Many of the objects and toys included in tests or curriculum packages lack the qualities required for the young exceptional child. For example, diagnosticians often mistakenly assume that an infant or toddler has not acquired the ability to uncover hidden objects when the child fails to complete the rubber-rabbit-and-cup task on the BSID. However, the rabbit is so small, so lacking in prominent features, and so unappealing and the cup is so difficult for disabled children to manipulate that failure is nearly guaranteed, even for some nonhandicapped children. Substituting more colorful and movable toys, like windup shoes or animals and a textured, easily grasped washcloth for the cup, peaks interest and often results in successful completion of the object-constancy task. In response to such needs, toy companies and some special materials manufacturers have researched and developed toys for special populations. The advent of microcomputer technology has given, perhaps, the greatest impetus to the design of handicap-appropriate play materials and alternative modes of response. Developmental school psychologists and other early-intervention specialists should now use these nondiscriminatory toys as a regular part of their formats for assessing and teaching developmentally disabled and at-risk infants and preschoolers.

Developmental Toys

Langley (1985) and Capone, J.T. Neisworth, Bagnato, and R. Neisworth (1988) have discussed various dimensions of the appropriate selection and adaptation of toys for use with both normal and disabled infants and preschoolers. Several aspects must be considered when matching the toy with the child. Exhibit 3-3 summarizes important toy selection criteria in terms of developmental applications (e.g., does the toy facilitate both social and communicative interactions?) and stimulus-response qualities (e.g., can the toy be adapted for the child's visual limitations and fine motor impairments?). Some prime considerations concern whether the toy matches the child's ability level, whether it can simultaneously elicit several purposeful behaviors, whether it taps capabilities in related developmental domains, and whether it promotes interactions with people. Obviously, many toys are inappropriate for the disabled child and require adaptations. Toys with pressure-sensitive switches are one of the more recent modifications.

Developmental toys have important uses in both assessment and teaching/ therapy. Response-contingent toys (e.g., those that produce big effects and reinforce small actions) help clinicians to refine their assessment results. An array of toys offers a valuable rapport-building means and a natural context in which to observe a child's style of play and stage of exploratory, social problem-solving and symbolic competence. Assessment of play skills is such a crucial activity that some specialists have designed specific instruments and diagnostic procedures for this purpose. The Play Assessment Scale (Fewell, 1987) may be the best available example of a play appraisal technique that serves diagnostic and program planning purposes.

Exhibit 3-3 Selection Criteria for Developmental Toys

Developmental Application:

- Will the toy be appropriate for the developmental abilities of the child?
- Will the toy be capable of eliciting a range of developmental skills so as to encourage the child to acquire more progressive behaviors while reinforcing targeted skills?
- Will the toy afford the child experiences that are otherwise unattainable?
- Will the toy enable the child to adapt to his or her everyday surroundings (i.e., will it elicit behaviors that will facilitate the child's control over his or her environment)?
- Will the toy have the potential to elicit a variety of behaviors across a wide developmental spectrum?
- Will the toy be used to elicit behaviors across developmental domains (i.e., cognitive, sensory motor, social)?
- Will the toy be an effective agent for facilitating social and communicative interactions?
- Will the toy facilitate concomitant and collateral developmental skills (i.e., will the toy develop head rotation although its primary function is to enhance visual awareness and localization)?
- How much potential does the toy have for eliciting a variety of play behaviors?
- Will the toy accommodate to a variety of chronological and developmental levels?
- Will the toy have potential to be enjoyed simultaneously by more than one child or in a turn-taking situation?
- Will the toy be effective across a variety of handicapping conditions?
- In the selection of toys for a classroom or for specific instructional purposes, will there be a range and variety of toys available for eliciting targeted behaviors and for simultaneously matching the current cognitive, sensory, physical, and arousal level of the child or children?

Processing and Response Qualities:

- Can the toy afford the child independent play experiences, or must a peer or adult always assist in toy play?
- Is the activation mode appropriate for the motoric grading potential of the child (i.e., is the child sufficiently strong, flexible, or coordinated to operate the toy)?
- Can the toy be adapted to better accommodate the child's auditory and visual acuity/efficiency, movement possibilities, postural control, and level of tactile/proprioceptive integration?
- Can the toy enable the child to adjust his or her level of arousal and attending (i.e., can the toy be used to calm and organize an excitable or hyperirritable child or to alert the nonresponsive, lethargic child)?
- Can the toy be adapted or positioned to allow the child to explore it and to obtain different tactual, visual, or auditory perspectives?
- Will the toy allow for cognitive mastery or success in physical control (i.e., will the toy challenge but not frustrate)?
- Will the child have to maintain contact (visual, physical, or auditory) with the toy in order for it to operate or for it to be enjoyed?

Source: From "Selecting, Adapting, and Applying Toys as Learning Tools for Handicapped Children" by M.B. Langley, 1985, *Topics in Early Childhood Special Education, 5*(3), pp. 105-106. Copyright 1985 by PRO-ED. Reprinted by permission.

Toys with Handicap-Sensitive Qualities

Some American and European toy companies have created toys and play materials with features that make them appropriate for the handicapped child. Johnson & Johnson (1982) and European toy makers Ambi and Kouvalias market a line of toys that are constructed of various plastic and wood materials and are colorful, movable, sound-producing, and multisensory. The toys are designed so that special preschoolers are stimulated and can activate the toys by small movements. Johnson & Johnson's line of toys are exemplary in that developmental research guided their design and helped establish the validity and age-appropriateness of each toy in terms of color, shape, sensory attributes, motivational quality, and prerequisite skills. The Stand-up Man is a disjointed man figure that is colored bright red and blue; each part of the man is connected by a string attached to a ring that can be gently pulled to make the man rise. The Tracking Tube was created to foster eye-hand coordination skills in reaching and in focusing attention to a bright red ball suspended in a liquid encased in the clear plastic center of the rattle. In addition, the tube has a squeaker and bell enclosed in a squeezable rubber ball at either end.

European toy makers like Ambi and Kouvalias have designed creative toys that are easily activated by cerebral palsied children. Autistic youngsters also show better attention skills and exploratory play with some of these toys. For example, Kouvalias produces a music box base with "slinky" arms and small colorful wooden balls attached; small movements activate the music box and also make the balls clack loudly. Ambi has created a clown on a roller ball base that can be swatted with minimal effort so that the clown bobs like a weighted Bozo doll and rolls across the floor or table.

Electromechanical Toys

Microchip and other electronic technology is being used in producing and adapting toys for assessment and teaching. The electromechanical toys allow alternative methods for a child to respond to a learning task. Battery-operated toys with pressure- and temperature-sensitive switches enable cerebral palsied infants and preschoolers to learn discriminations and to show that they possess cause-effect and means-end developmental skills. Kanor (1988) has adapted many commercially available toys with special switches, particularly those produced by Fisher-Price. Electromechanical toys have many vital qualities. They provide immediate task-embedded reinforcement for the child who is typically unresponsive, possibly due to a sense of "learned helplessness" imposed by motor or sensory limitations (Zuromski, 1984). Thus, these toys can provide powerful reinforcement of initially weak adaptive behaviors. They can provide functional interactions with the environment and teach prerequisite behaviors that may be needed in the future to control the environment. They can teach contingencies between the child's behavior and purposeful environmental consequences. Finally, such toys can be used to detect subtle changes in functional behaviors and to establish baseline and progress checks within a program.

Electromechanical toys are increasingly used for diverse purposes, for example, to prevent or blunt the disabling behavioral effects of chronic illness and failure-to-thrive (Watson, Hayes, & Vietze, 1982) and to create an optimal learning environment for severely handicapped children (Warren, Alpert, & Kaiser, 1986). Preschool psychologists and teachers should incorporate response-contingent toys into their assessment and therapy routines for all children. These toys help the young disabled child to learn adaptive competencies that may be generalized to new settings, materials, and people—the criterion of ultimate functioning (Brown, Nietupski, & Hamre-Nietupski, 1976).

Norms for Handicapped Preschoolers

Psychologists and early interventionists often have little understanding of the extent to which developmental disabilities distort the emergence of skills in various behavioral areas. They lack sense of the typical or "normative" function (or rather, dysfunction) expected of handicapped preschoolers. Assessment can be neither accurate nor prescriptive unless appropriate comparisons are made with both handicapped and nonhandicapped peers. Unique language deficits are common among children with Down syndrome. Blind infants will not use available motor skills to reach or crawl toward objects or people until they learn to respond to sound cues (Fraiberg, Siegal, & Gibson, 1966). Many cerebral palsied children lack the ability to express clear facial expressions or emotional states because of their poor control of facial-oral-motor muscles.

Mastery motivation is considered a naturally occurring ability among young children. They are said to be neurologically programmed to explore their environments and to experience "co-occurrences" or stimulus-response opportunities that encourage further exploration and discovery learning (Brinker & Lewis, 1982). Thus mastery motivation is considered to be a natural and critical aspect of learning. Some studies, however, demonstrate clearly that physically handicapped infants and preschoolers lack mastery motivation because of their overdependence on caregivers who structure and direct their learning (Jennings, Connors, Stegman, Sankaranarayan, & Mendelsohn, 1985). This finding has implications regarding both the typical distortions in development caused by physical impairments and the changes required for assessing and teaching in such cases. Knowing what to expect is the first step. Clinicians need a firm knowledge base in atypical development before their prescriptive assessment efforts can be credible. In this relatively uncharted area, various resources that describe "handicap norms" are becoming available (Wachs & Sheehan, 1988). Admittedly, empirical research is needed to confirm these clinical descriptions (Bagnato & J.T. Neisworth, 1987; Dunst & Rheingrover, 1981, 1983; Fewell, 1981; Hanson, 1984; Langley, 1980). Table 3-3 offers a brief list showing how cognitive and affective processes are delayed and distorted in their emergence by visual and motor impairments, compared with normal expectancies.

Table 3-3   Functional Impact of Developmental Disabilities on Dual Cognitive-Affective Processes

Process	Normal (months)	Blind (months)	Cerebral Palsy (months)
Reaches and grasps	3-5	10	14
Repeats purposeful actions	4-8	14	18
Extends arms to mother	3-5	8-12	18
Smiles spontaneously	1-2	12	4
Uncovers hidden objectives	6-8	15-20	18
Shows separation anxiety	8-12	24-36	24
Engages in reciprocal social games (i.e., Peek-a-Boo)	6-8	14	12-14

Source: From *Teachable Moment and the Handicapped Infant* by B. Langley, 1980, Reston, VA: The Council for Exceptional Children. Copyright 1980 by The Council for Exceptional Children. Adapted by permission.

SUMMARY

Prescriptive developmental assessment is essential for individualized developmental intervention. New strategies and procedures must be combined in a creative manner to accomplish useful assessment. Working within the framework of a developmental-behavioral approach, the psychologist and teacher, through assessment, can determine *where* the child stands in the developmental sequence, *what* the child's present capabilities and deficits are, and *how* and *under what conditions* the child learns best.

4

Close-ups of Curriculum-Compatible Developmental Scales

Definitions

Organization and Content

Child Measures
  Newborn-Infant
    Normal Developmental
    Kent Infant Development Scale (KIDS)
    Infant Psychological Development Scale (IPDS): Dunst Revision
    Brazelton Neonatal Behavioral Assessment Scale (BNBAS) (Revised)

    Handicap-Sensitive
    Early Coping Inventory (ECI)
    Carolina Record of Individual Behavior (CRIB)

  Infant-Preschool
    Normal Developmental
    BRIGANCE Diagnostic Inventory of Early Development (BDIED)
    Griffiths Mental Development Scales (GMDS)
    Learning Accomplishment Profile—Diagnostic Edition (LAP-D)
    Developmental Profile II (DP-II)

    Handicap-Sensitive
    Battelle Developmental Inventory (BDI)
    Scales of Early Communication Skills (SECS) for Hearing-Impaired Children
    Reynell-Zinkin Developmental Scales for Young Visually Handicapped Children
      (RZS)
    Uniform Performance Assessment System (UPAS)
    Autism Screening Instrument for Educational Planning (ASIEP)
    Perceptions of Developmental Status (PODS)

  Kindergarten Transition
    Normal Developmental

Woodcock-Johnson Psychoeducational Battery-Preschool Cluster (WJPEB)
Cognitive Skills Assessment Battery (CSAB)
Bracken Basic Concept Scale (BBCS)
McCarthy Scales of Children's Abilities (MSCA)

Handicap-Sensitive
Pictorial Test of Intelligence (PTI)

Contextual Measures
   Home
      Home Observations for Measurement of the Environment (HOME)
      Parenting Stress Index (PSI)
      Family Needs Survey (FNS)

   Program
      Early Childhood Environment Rating Scale (ECERS)
      Teaching Skills Inventory (TSI)

An array of classic and newly developed measures exist for early-intervention specialists to assess young exceptional children and the contexts in which they develop. However, only a few of these instruments have features that enable them to link effectively to commonly used developmental curricula. Instruments that facilitate assessment/curriculum linkage are curriculum-compatible.

This chapter reviews and critiques 25 measures that are most compatible with curricula used in infant and preschool programs for handicapped children. In order to accomplish program linkage, measures should be chosen based upon their appropriateness to the child's disabilities and their match with the content and sequence of skills in the program's curriculum.

DEFINITIONS

Curriculum-compatible scales are developmentally based assessment instruments that reference or sample tasks typically stressed in infant and preschool developmental curricula but are not integral to any particular curriculum. In short, they are curriculum-referenced rather than curriculum-embedded measures (to be discussed in Chapter 6). As noted in Chapter 3, curriculum-compatible scales are chosen according to seven criteria: (1) developmental base, (2) multidomain profile, (3) multisource sample, (4) curricular links, (5) adaptive options, (6) ecological emphasis, and (7) technical support. The selected review in this chapter profiles and critiques scales that meet, at a minimum, these seven linkage criteria.

Prescriptive linkages or task matches between assessment measures and curricula can occur at several levels. *Domains* are the broadest level of organization; they refer to the major developmental areas targeted. These usually include cognitive, language, perceptual/fine motor, socioemotional, gross motor, and self-care domains. Assessment instruments that are organized by these domains are immediately compatible with most developmental curricula. The *subdomain* level is the next narrower level of organization; it refers to important subdivisions within the major domains. Examples of these are memory, reasoning, and concepts in the cognitive domain; social competence, emotional expression, and coping skills in the socioemotional domain; and primitive reflexes, trunk control, and movement patterns in the gross motor domain. *Developmental tasks* represent the narrowest level of organization; they include also the sequence by which the tasks or skill competencies are ordered from primitive to advanced. Uncovering a completely hidden object, following a light through a circular path, matching three shapes, sitting with support, and identifying another child's emotional distress are all examples of developmental tasks within domains and subdomains.

Linkages between instruments and curricula should occur ideally at each of the above levels; matches at the task level, of course, identify prescriptive linkages most precisely. Of the available assessment instruments, the Battelle Developmental Inventory and the BRIGANCE Diagnostic Inventory of Early Development seem to provide the broadest range of prescriptive linkages with commercially available curricula at the domain, subdomain, and developmental task levels. However, in terms of our seven selection criteria, important dimensions distinguish these two instruments and must also be considered in choice and use. The close-ups of curriculum-compatible scales in this chapter review those special features that best promote prescriptive linkage (see Table 4-1). Despite inherent limitations, the close-ups represent in our opinion the best examples of matches between scales and curricula that currently exist. Appendix A reviews other scales that are useful for clinical purposes but are not exemplary for comprehensive prescriptions.

ORGANIZATION AND CONTENT

The close-ups are organized under two major headings: child measures and contextual measures. The child measures are divided into three major areas (newborn-infant, infant-preschool, and kindergarten-transition) and two subareas (normal developmental and handicap-sensitive). *Newborn-infant* scales cover only the birth to 36-month age range. *Infant-preschool* measures survey the entire birth to 84-month span. *Kindergarten-transition* refers to scales that emphasize skills important for success in kindergarten and for the preschool-to-school transition in the approximate ages of 4 to 6 years, although a wider age range may be sampled by individual measures. As to the two subareas, *normal developmental* refers to measures that include expected developmental sequences, may contain norms, and do not have clear handicap adaptations. *Handicap-sensitive* measures include or permit stimulus and response modifications and sometimes include norms for selected disabilities.

Contextual measures are scales that appraise the social and physical aspects of the child's interactive environment. *Home measures* are instruments that sample

Table 4-1 Curriculum-Based Scale Summary Form

Curriculum-Based Scales	Author/Year	Publisher	Type/Features
Newborn-Infant			
Kent Infant Development Scale (KIDS)	Reuter & Bickett, 1985	Developmental Metrics Kent, OH	Norm-based – parent report – 252 infant behaviors
Infant Psychological Development Scale (IPDS): Dunst Revision	Dunst, 1980	PRO-ED Austin, TX	Norm-based – matches with curriculum – 7 scoring categories
Brazelton Neonatal Behavioral Assessment Scale (BNBAS)	Brazelton, 1984	Lippincott Philadelphia, PA	Interactive/judgment – n = 20+ norms – response to social and physical stimulation
Early Coping Inventory (ECI)	Zeitlin, Williamson, & Szczepanski, 1984	COPING Edison, NJ	Judgment-based – norms = 1,040 H; 227 N – scores coping efficacy – handicap-sensitive
Carolina Record of Individual Behavior (CRIB)	Simeonsson, 1985	University of North Carolina Chapel Hill, NC	Judgment-based – 1-9 rating scale – rates stereotypies – handicap-sensitive
BRIGANCE Diagnostic Inventory of Early Development (BDIED)	Brigance, 1978	Curriculum Associates North Billerica, MA	Curriculum-based – allows adaptations – computer scoring
Griffiths Mental Development Scale (GMDS)	Griffiths, 1970	Test Agency, England	Norm-based – largest standardization – sample handicap profiles

Instrument	Authors, year	Publisher, location	Characteristics
Learning Accomplishment Profile–Diagnostic Edition (LAP-D)	LeMay, Griffin, & Sanford, 1978	Kaplan School Supply, Lewisville, NC	Norm/criterion-based – compatible with LAP – motivating toys
Developmental Profile II (DP II)	Alpern, Boll, Shearer, 1986	Western Psychological Services, Los Angeles, CA	Judgment-based norms – best preschool interviews – clear questions
Battelle Developmental Inventory (BDI)	Newborg, Stock, Wnek, Guidubaldi, & Svinicki, 1984	DLM/Teaching Resources, Allen, TX	Norm/curriculum-based – standardized adaptations – $n = 800$ – handicap-sensitive
Scales of Early Communication Skills for Hearing Impaired (SECS)	Moog & Geers, 1975	Central Institute, St. Louis, MO	Norm-based – nonverbal samples – field test in oral programs – handicap-sensitive
Reynell-Zinkin Developmental Scales-Visually Impaired (RZS)	Reynell & Zinkin, 1979	Stoelting Co., Chicago, IL	Norm-based – functional skill analysis – 3 group norms – handicap-sensitive
Uniform Performance Assessment System (UPAS)	Haring, White, Edgar, Affleck, & Hayden, 1981	Psychological Corporation, San Antonio, TX	Criterion-referenced – "learning curve" – adaptations – handicap-sensitive
Autism Screening Instrument for Educational Planning (ASIEP)	Krug, Arick, & Almond, 1980	ASIEP, Portland, OR	Norm-based – 5-component system – handicap-sensitive

Table 4-1 continued

Curriculum-Based Scales	Author/Year	Publisher	Type/Features
Perceptions of Developmental Status (PODS)	Bagnato & J.T. Neisworth, 1989a	American Guidance Service Circle Pines, MN	Judgment-based – functional ratings – team organizers – handicap-sensitive
Kindergarten Transition			
Woodcock-Johnson Psychoeducational Battery-Preschool Cluster (WJPEB)	Woodcock & Johnson, 1977	DLM/Teaching Resources Allen, TX	Norm-based – excellent norms – samples preacademic competencies
Cognitive Skills Assessment Battery (CSAB)	Boehm & Stater, 1974	Teachers College Press Columbia University, New York, NY	Criterion-referenced – samples K content – motivating pictures/easel format
Bracken Basic Concept Scales (BBCS)	Bracken, 1984	Psychological Corporation San Antonio, TX	Norm/criterion-based – links with concept program – research with deaf
McCarthy Scales of Children's Abilities (MSCA)	McCarthy, 1972	Psychological Corporation San Antonio, TX	Norm-based – neurodevelopmental – 18 subdomains – highly motivating

Pictorial Test of Intelligence (PTI)	French, 1964	Riverside Publishing Chicago, IL	Norm-based – process/product abilities – MA/DQ – handicap-sensitive for cerebral palsied

Home Measures

Home Observation for Measurement of the Environment (HOME)	Caldwell & Bradley, 1978	University of Arkansas	Judgment-based/ecological – parent/home variables – 0-72 months – identifies interactive needs
Parenting Stress Index (PSI)	Abidin, 1983	CPPC Brandon, VT	Norm/judgment/interactive – handicap norms – parent "self-statements" – pathology cut-off – handicap-sensitive
Family Needs Survey (FNS)	Bailey & Simeonsson, 1985	University of North Carolina Chapel Hill, NC	Judgment-based – parent self-report – coping factors – identifies "social work" goals

Program Measures

Early Childhood Environment Rating Scale (ECERS)	Harms & Clifford, 1980	Teachers College Press Columbia University, New York, NY	Judgment-based/ecological – samples physical setting – version for special preschoolers
Teaching Skills Inventory (TSI)	Robinson & Rosenberg, 1985	University of Nebraska Omaha, NE	Judgment-based/interactive – observes parent teaching – field tested with disabilities – highlights goals

parent and family characteristics and the physical environment within the home. *Program measures* are instruments that sample the physical setting within a preschool program and tap the teaching and/or therapeutic competencies of caregivers.

For each close-up, a concise outline is followed by narrative analysis and an exhibit or table that illustrate the unique content of the measure. Each scale is reviewed according to specific dimensions. First, identifying information—including publisher, year, authors, cost, and address/phone—is provided. Next, eight content features, including selection criteria, are addressed: assessment type, age range, domains/contexts, handicap options, curricular links, scoring/sample, technical support, and training needed. Finally, each review concludes with a list of unique factors, considerations, and concerns, followed by specific research reference citations.

We believe that this organization will enable the early-intervention specialist to analyze and select instruments more efficiently in addressing their child programs' goals and needs. In turn, this will promote the linkage between assessment, curriculum-planning, and progress/program evaluation.

NEWBORN-INFANT

The *Kent Infant Development Scale* (KIDS) (Reuter & Bickett, 1985) contains the most complete sample of competencies of infant behavior in the first year of life of any available norm-based measure (252 skills) (see Exhibit 4-1). Despite the fact that it is primarily a parent/caregiver report instrument, the KIDS's structure and content make it highly curriculum-compatible and therefore prescriptive.

The KIDS surveys the infant's behavioral repertoire in five domains: cognitive, language, motor, self-help, and social (see Exhibit 4-2). Within these domains, the scale taps many nontraditional characteristics and competencies, such as "gets startled by sudden voices or noises," "remembers where things are kept in the house," "imitates an action of an adult long after it occurred," and "shows jealousy." Care was taken to phrase items simply and to select colloquial terms so that parents and laypersons could reliably judge the behavior. In scoring, the KIDS offers several categories of scoring but unfortunately does not allow the recording of emerging skills.

While no truly adaptive features are included in the scale, the KIDS has been field-tested with severely brain-damaged children functioning within the infant developmental range. The authors advocate direct observation as an important supplement to caregiver information covering such areas as rumination, temperamental style, attention, and motivational level for program planning. An important and valuable feature of the KIDS is computer scoring of the scale, including the response given for each item, the developmental age level for each domain, and the total raw score of behaviors within each of the five areas. In addition, a computer-generated report is offered.

The manual for the KIDS shows care in design and development. The norms, while not national, are clearly representative of infant expectancies. Spanish ver-

Kent Infant Development Scale (KIDS) (Second Edition)

Author(s):   J. Reuter, L. Bickett
Year: 1985
Publisher: Developmental Metrics
Address: 126 West College Avenue, PO Box 3178, Kent, OH 44240
Phone: (216) 678-3589
Cost: $10 +

Assessment type: Norm-based; judgment-based determination of developmental age status.
Age range: Chronological or developmental ages 0–12 months.
Domains/Contexts: 5 domains: cognitive, motor, language, self-help, social; encompassing 252 behavioral descriptions.
Handicap options: Relies on parent report; focuses on clear behavioral characteristics by age level; some items emphasize emotions and visual recognition rather than motor responses.
Curricular links: Multidomain profile of developmental capabilities; emerging behaviors offer gross prescriptive objectives.
Scoring/Sample: A (yes), B (did but outgrew), C (no longer able), D (can't do yet); parent report; developmental ages, percentiles, delays.
Technical support: Norms: $N = 480$ infants, N.E. Ohio in well-baby clinics and pediatricians' offices; test-retest .88 +, concurrent validity with Bayley .70 +; reliability with severely handicapped .96 +.
Training needed: Comprehensive knowledge of the scale and strong parent interview skills.

Critique:
- Specialized and comprehensive measure for the first year of life.
- Couples technical adequacy with economy and practicality.
- Offers few adaptive qualities.
- Should not be considered an infant curriculum, but can be prescriptive.

Citations:
Stancin, S., Reuter, J., Bickett, T. (1984). Validity of caregiver information on the developmental status of severely brain-damaged young children. *American Journal of Mental Deficiency, 88*(4), 388–395.
Feiring, L. (1985). Review of the Kent Infant Development Scale. In J. Mitchell (Ed.), *Ninth mental measurements yearbook* (Vol. 1) (pp. 786–787). Omaha, NE: University of Nebraska Press.
Tlucak, S. (1987). The Kent Infant Development Scale: Concurrent and predictive validity of a modified administration. *Psychological Reports, 60,* 887–894.

Exhibit 4–1   Selected Task Samples from the KIDS

---

181. gets startled by sudden voices or noises
182. makes sounds when smiled at or tickled by an adult
183. walks holding onto furniture
184. crawls up stairs
185. smiles if an adult makes a funny face
186. plays with hands
187. smiles at the sight of a favorite toy
188. plays with two toys at the same time
189. shakes head "no"
190. picks up small objects the size of a pea
191. throws or flings a ball
192. sits up alone for a long time
193. walks, if both hands are held for balance
194. holds and drinks from a cup
195. pulls off socks
196. drinks from a cup held by an adult
197. holds spoon for a second when it's placed on his/her hand
198. laughs if an adult makes a funny face
199. reaches and pats image in mirror
200. plays with feet

Source: From *The Kent Infant Development Scale Test Booklet* (p. 13) by J. Reuter and L. Bickett, 1985, Kent, OH: Kent Developmental Metrics. Copyright 1985 by Kent Developmental Metrics. Reprinted by permission.

---

sions of the scale are available; and normative efforts are under way in Germany, the Netherlands, Spain, and Chile. The KIDS has been studied concurrently with the Bayley Scales of Infant Development. At this time, no studies are available to compare its use with early developmental curricula. Nevertheless, the KIDS has the compatibility in structure, content, and sampling that makes it very valuable for infant programming. Its field testing with severely impaired children adds a possible handicap-sensitive dimension.

Despite its norm-base, the KIDS is still a judgment-based type of assessment measure and, given the limitations of reported-versus-observed behaviors, should not be used as a sole program instrument. However, we believe that the KIDS can be a valuable component in a prescriptive assessment battery for the at-risk and handicapped infant. Its careful developmental base, its active, clear item descriptions, and its broad analysis of developmental competencies support its use as an initial prescriptive instrument. For example, the KIDS could be paired with the Carolina Curriculum for At-Risk and Handicapped Infants or the Early Learning Accomplishment Profile to offer an exemplary assessment/curriculum linkage.

In the field of child development, Piagetian scales have been used extensively for research purposes. Recently, diagnostic specialists have attempted to use such instruments as the *Infant Psychological Development Scale* (IPDS) (Uzgiris & Hunt, 1975a) for assessing the competencies of handicapped infants. However, one of the shortcomings of the IPDS and similar instruments has been the lack of a

Exhibit 4–2 KIDS Profile Sheet

Name: _____ Sex: _____

Birthdate: _____ Chronological Age in Months _____

Date of Testing: _____

DA IN MONTHS	FULL SCALE	COGNITIVE DOMAIN	MOTOR DOMAIN	LANGUAGE DOMAIN	SELF-HELP DOMAIN	SOCIAL DOMAIN	DA IN MONTHS
	252	52	78	38	39	51	
≥14.0	229	46	73	33	36	45	≥14.0
13.5							13.5
13.0	224	45	72		34	44	13.0
12.5	214						12.5
12.0	205	41	65	31		42	12.0
11.5							11.5
11.0	202	40		29	30	41	11.0
10.5	194						10.5
10.0	186	38	59	26	28	37	10.0
9.5	180						9.5
9.0	174	35	54	24	26	35	9.0
8.5	163						8.5
8.0	151	31	48	20	23	30	8.0
7.5	140						7.5
7.0	128	27	39	16	20		7.0
6.5	123						6.5
6.0	118	24	35		17	25	6.0
5.5	103						5.5
5.0	88	18	24	14	12	19	5.0
4.5	76						4.5
4.0	65	13	16	11	9	14	4.0
3.5	57						3.5
3.0	50	9	12	9		11	3.0
2.5	42						2.5
≤2.0	33	6	7	6	7	6	≤2.0

	FULL SCALE	COGNITIVE DOMAIN	MOTOR DOMAIN	LANGUAGE DOMAIN	SELF-HELP DOMAIN	SOCIAL DOMAIN
Raw Score:	____	____	____	____	____	____
Developmental Age:	____	____	____	____	____	____

Source: From *The Kent Infant Development Scale Manual* (p. 34) by J. Reuter and L. Bickett, 1985, Kent, OH: Kent Developmental Metrics. Copyright 1985 by Kent Developmental Metrics. Reprinted by permission.

Uzgiris and Hunt Infant Psychological Development Scale (IPDS): Dunst Revision

Author(s):   C.S. Dunst
Year: 1980
Publisher: PRO-ED
Address: 5341 Industrial Oaks Boulevard, Austin, TX 78735
Phone: (512) 892-3142
Cost: $30+

Assessment type: Norm-based/process; description of stage of cognitive competence or sensorimotor development.

Age range: 0–30 months.

Domains/Contexts: Sensorimotor abilities in seven subscales: object permanence, means-end, vocal imitation, gestural imitation, operational causality, spatial relationships, scheme actions.

Handicap options: Qualitative scoring procedures and flexible tasks accommodate the behavior patterns of various handicaps.

Curricular links: Developmental programming accomplished when linked with *Infant Learning* (Dunst, 1982), a program matching assessed levels with goals and intervention strategies (see Chapter 6).

Scoring/Sample: Seven scoring categories for DAs: +(elicited behavior), √ (demonstration needed), ± (emerging), − (absent), O (omitted), R (reported), M (mistrial); age placements and concurrent validity in a sample of N = 36 handicapped and at-risk infants/toddlers in Washington, D.C.

Technical support: Concurrent and construct validity data adequate; wide field-testing with various handicaps, but with small samples.

Training needed: Supervised administration by infant diagnostic specialist.

Critique:
- Detects qualitative features of infant's interaction with the environment.
- Provides flexible procedures to accommodate some handicaps.
- Offers intervention linkages when used with parallel curriculum.
- Norm group is limited.
- Requires more concurrent and predictive validity studies.

Citations:

Hefferman, T., & Black, P. (1984). Use of the U-H scales with handicapped infants: Concurrent validity of Dunst age norms. *Journal of Psychoeducational Assessment, 2,* 159–168.

Dunst, C.J., Brassell, R.R., & Rheingrover, R.M. (1981). Structural and organizational features of sensorimotor intelligence among retarded infants and toddlers. *British Journal of Educational Psychology, 51,* 133–143.

Dunst, C.J., & Rheingrover, R.M. (1983). Structural characteristics of sensorimotor development among Down's syndrome infants. *Journal of Mental Deficiency Research, 27,* 11–22.

structured scoring manual, profile forms, and procedures that would foster precision. Also, the IPDS is not organized to release prescriptive information for treatment-planning. *A Clinical and Educational Manual for Use with the Uzgiris and Hunt Scales of Infant Psychological Development,* designed by Dunst (1980), superbly eliminates these shortcomings and strengthens the IPDS for prescriptive assessment purposes.

The revised IPDS has numerous features that support its use with handicapped infants from birth to 30 months of age. Although inadequate, the IPDS was normed on $N = 36$ infants. Thus, the derived developmental ages have both a theoretical and research base. In addition, the IPDS is one of the few instruments that has been field tested with infants and toddlers of varying developmental disabilities, including severe retardation, Down syndrome, and cerebral palsy.

The IPDS uses a flexible multidimensional scoring system to determine the nature of the infant's interaction with people and objects in the environment. For example, not only are emerging skills recorded, but also whether demonstrations or prompting was needed to elicit a behavior. This feature adds to its program relevancy.

Developmental competencies across several developmental processes in cognition, social communication, and motor exploration are sampled by the IPDS (see Exhibit 4-3). Flexible scoring, administration procedures, and multidomain coverage highlight the scale's adaptive use for young handicapped children. This broad survey, while Piagetian in orientation, appraises competencies that are targeted in most infant intervention programs. For prescriptive curriculum-based practices, the revised IPDS can be linked with its treatment package, *Infant Learning: A Cognitive-Linguistic Intervention Strategy* (Dunst, 1981) (see Chapter 6). The IPDS can be used with other curricula as well.

Dunst's revision of the IPDS effectively systematizes the assessment process. The accompanying forms allow diagnosticians to profile discrepancies in levels of functioning between processes, derive developmental ages, and determine important behaviors for intervention. The forms operationally define the critical behaviors that exemplify each task.

The Dunst revision of the IPDS is a much-needed and very pragmatic tool. Its clinical application of a Piagetian approach is a model for other instruments, and its linkage to an existing curriculum with the same theoretical base greatly enhances its worth to practitioners. The IPDS's potential can be fully realized if the inadequate normative base for the instrument is expanded to make it truly a hybrid measure, that is, a norm, curricular, and adaptive/process measure.

Structurally, the *Brazelton Neonatal Behavioral Assessment Scale* (BNBAS) (Brazelton, 1984) is actually a clinical judgment measure that allows infant specialists to rate the quality of the behavior that their actions have elicited from the infant. Practically, the BNBAS is an ingenious tool that couples norm, curricular, and judgment features to appraise the interactive behavior of infants.

The BNBAS has been used traditionally with normal newborns until approximately 3 months of age. However, the needs of premature infants and newborns

Exhibit 4–3 Example of the Visual Pursuit/Object Permanence Sequence from the IPDS

Child's Name _____   Date of Birth _____   Date of Test _____

I: VISUAL PURSUIT AND THE PERMANENCE OF OBJECTS

SCALE STEP	AGE PLACEMENT (Months)	DEVELOPMENTAL STAGE	ELICITING CONTEXT	CRITICAL ACTION CODE	CRITICAL BEHAVIORS	SCORING 1	2	3	4	5	OBSERVATIONS
E₁	1	I	Visual Fixation	—	Fixates on object held 8 to 10 inches above the eyes						
1	2	II	Visual Tracking	1d	Tracks object through a 180° arc						
2	3	II	Visual Tracking	2c	Lingers at point of object's disappearance—child in supine position or in an infant seat						
E₂	4	III	Visual Tracking	—	Searches for object at point of disappearance—child seated on parent's lap						
3	5	III	Visible Displacement	3c	Secures partially hidden object						
4	6	III	Visual Tracking	2d	Returns glance to position above the head after object moves out of visual field						
E₃	7	IV	Visual Tracking	—	Reverses searching for object in anticipation of reappearance—child seated on parent's lap						
E₄	7	IV	Visible Displacement	—	Withdraws object held in hand following covering of hand and object with cloth						
5	8	IV	Visible Displacement	4d	Secures object hidden under a single screen						
E₅	9	IV	Visible Displacement	5b	Secures object hidden with two screens (A & B)—hidden under A twice then B—searches under A only						
6	9	V	Visible Displacement	6c	Secures object hidden under one of two screens—hidden alternately						
7	9	V	Visible Displacement	7c	Secures object hidden under one of three screens—hidden alternately						
E₆	10	V	Successive Visible Displacement	8e	Secures object hidden through a series of successive visible displacements with three screens						
8	10	V	Superimposed Screens	9c	Secures object under three superimposed screens						
9	13	V	Invisible Displacement	10d 10e	Secures object hidden with a single screen						
10	14	VI	Invisible Displacement	11c	Secures object hidden with two screens (A & B)—hidden under A twice then B						
11	14	VI	Invisible Displacement	12c	Secures object hidden under one of two screens—hidden alternately						
12	15	VI	Invisible Displacement	13c	Secures object hidden under one of three screens—hidden alternately						
13	18	VI	Successive Invisible Displacement	14c	Secures object hidden with three screens—object left under last screen—child searches along pathway						
E₇	22	VI	Successive Invisible Displacement	14d	Secures object hidden with three screens—object left under last screen—child searches directly under last screen						
14	23	VI	Successive Invisible Displacement	15c	Secures object hidden with three screens—object left under first screen—child searches in reverse order						

Source: From *A Clinical and Educational Manual for Use with the Uzgiris and Hunt Scales of Infant Psychological Development* by C.J. Dunst, 1980, Austin, TX: PRO-ED. Copyright 1980 by PRO-ED. Reprinted by permission.

Brazelton Neonatal Behavioral Assessment Scale (BNBAS) (Revised)

Author(s): T.B. Brazelton
Year: 1984
Publisher: Spastics International Medical Publications
(J.B. Lippincott, Philadelphia, PA)
Address: 50 Netherhall Gardens, London, England NW3 5RN
Cost: $40+

Assessment type: Interactive; appraisal of infant's response and self-regulation to physical and social stimulation.

Age range: Newborn to 1 month

Domains/Contexts: 28 items and 9 supplementary items organized into 6 research-based factors or clusters: habituation, orientation, motor, state variation, state regulation, physiological stability.

Handicap options: Describes neurophysiological processes appropriate for infants and severely handicapped and traumatically brain-injured preschoolers: continuum scoring and natural and elicited observations are handicap-appropriate.

Curricular links: Focus on infant X environment matches and such strategy-oriented tasks as consolability (e.g., degree of effort required to calm) offers natural translations to intervention; "assessment as intervention"

Scoring/Sample: 1-9 point scoring continuum; 10 years of clinical research on large samples of mostly normal infants; recent use with handicapped infants; sample normative samples $N=20$ yielding gestational age comparisons (GA).

Technical support: Research based on reliability, stability, and predictive validity available; test-retest and inter-rate reliabilities are quite variable.

Training needed: Supervised training required by qualified examiner with BNBAS credentials.

Critique:

- Superb early interactive assessment measure.
- Important blend of developmental and neurophysiological dimensions.
- Offers intervention implications.
- Scoring format greatly needs revision for consistency across items and domains.

Citations:

Brazelton, T.B. (1982). Assessment as a method for enhancing infant development. *Zero to Three, 2*(1), 1–8.

Leijon, E.R. (1982). Assessment of behavior on the Brazelton scale in healthy preterm infants from 32 conceptional weeks until full-term age. *Early Human Development, 7,* 109–118.

Bagnato, S.J., Mayes, S.D., & Nichter, C. (1988). An interdisciplinary neurodevelopmental assessment model for brain-injured infants and preschoolers. *Journal of Head Trauma Rehabilitation, 3*(2), 75–86.

Worobey, J., & Belsky, J. (1982). Employing the Brazelton Scale to influence mothering: An experimental comparison of three strategies. *Developmental Psychology, 18,* 736–743.

with developmental difficulties have spurred use of the instrument by infant interventionists (e.g., Kansas revision, Als instrument). In fact, clinicians have advocated the use of the BNBAS for severely impaired children because of the important, functionally appropriate behavior patterns that it samples (Bagnato et al., 1988; Simeonsson et al., 1980).

Brazelton (1982) has promoted an "assessment as intervention" orientation for use of the scale by interventionists. This approach extends the value of the instrument primarily for the purpose of conveying to parents the capabilities that their vulnerable infants exhibit. The assessment sessions reveal an intervention-based character, as the assessor demonstrates methods of handling and interaction that promote optimal behaviors from fragile infants. For example, the scale samples such behaviors as consolability, which effectively task-analyzes the sequence of infant self-quieting behaviors, from adult-managed to self-managed, that can quickly be converted to guidelines for arranging treatment (see Exhibit 4-4).

The BNBAS samples such crucial neurophysiological, neurobehavioral, and interactive patterns as habituation, orientation, motor, state variation, state regulation, and physiological stability. The nine-point Likert scoring scales offer an effective way to quantify and qualify an infant's functioning in each of these clusters. Thus, the scale does project some adaptive qualities, since it relies on naturalistic and contrived situations for observation. Unfortunately, the scales are not all compatible; in some, the 1 and 9 ratings represent a developmental continuum; in others, 1 and 9 are extremes, in which 5 is the midpoint. This shortcoming makes cross-item comparisons difficult, even though procedures exist for rescoring items. The recent revision of the BNBAS has overlooked this limitation.

The BNBAS is currently the best available measure of infant interactive behavior with a prescriptive focus. The advantages of its use with handicapped infants are just beginning to be recognized. Gestational norms for the six clusters (Leijon, 1982) provide a diagnostic element to complement the scale's unique clini-

Exhibit 4-4 Subtest Example from the BNBAS

---

17. Consolability with intervention (6 to 5, 4, 3, or 2 for at least 15 secs.)
    1 Not consolable.
    2 Pacifier or finger in addition to dressing, holding, and rocking.
    3 Dressing, holding in arms, and rocking.
    4 Holding and rocking.
    5 Picking up and holding.
    6 Hand on belly and restraining one or both arms.
    7 Hand on belly steadily.
    8 Examiner's voice and face alone.
    9 Examiner's face alone.

Source: From *Neonatal Behavioral Assessment Scale* (p. 17) by T.B. Brazelton, 1984, London, England: Spastics International Medical Publications. Copyright 1984 by Spastics International Medical Publications. Reprinted by permission.

Early Coping Inventory (ECI)

Author(s):	S. Zeitlin, G. Williamson, M. Szczepanski
Year:	1988
Publisher:	Scholastic Testing Service, Inc.
	480 Meyer Road, P.O. Box 1056, Bensenville, IL 60106
Phone:	1 (800) 642-6787
Cost:	$25 +

Assessment type: Judgment-based; observation and rating of the infant's capability to respond to, adapt, and control environment.

Age range: 4 to 36 months.

Domains/Contexts: 3 coping clusters: sensorimotor organization, reactive behaviors, self-initiated; multiple ratings across several situations.

Handicap options: Functional ratings focus on competence in coping with the environment, using compensations for sensorimotor impairments.

Curricular links: Ratings highlight specific coping strategies used by each child; these are hierarchically arranged as to maturity level and thus guide the planning of goals and environmental arrangements.

Scoring/Sample: Adaptive behavior index, coping effectiveness scores, coping profile based on conversion tables relying on the 1–5-point rating scale: 1 (not effective) → 5 (consistently effective across situation).

Technical support: Based on coping theory research on infants and the transactional model; field-test data on 1,040 handicapped and 227 nonhandicapped infants/toddlers in early intervention and day care settings.

Training needed: Thorough knowledge of infant development and practice in reading manual and using scale; appropriate for use by paraprofessionals.

Critique:
- Unique clinical judgment scale.
- Specialized focus on coping competencies.
- "Task analysis" of coping patterns.
- Clear functional interpretation.
- Derived scores lack normative meaning.
- Should be interpreted and used only with multiple assessors.

Citation:
Zeitlin, S., & Williamson, G. (unpublished manuscript). Coping behaviors characteristic of handicapped and nonhandicapped young children.

cal character. Wider use of the BNBAS with handicapped infants and toddlers is needed to research systematically its diagnostic utility.

Refinement in the goals of early intervention are apparent in the increasing emphasis on adaptive style, rather than specific developmental skills, of young handicapped children. Infant specialists are interested in helping the child to learn and use more independent self-initiated behaviors to manage the environment. The

Early Coping Inventory (ECI) (Zeitlin, Williamson, & Szczepanski, 1988) is an exemplar of this trend in adaptive behavior measures. The ECI is a judgment-based observational scale that samples infant adaptive or coping patterns across three dimensions: (1) sensorimotor organization, (2) reactive behaviors, and (3) self-initiated behaviors (see Table 4-2). The 5-point Likert rating scale offers a multi-dimensional scoring system to quantify and qualify the "effectiveness" of inter-action with the child's environment. Effectiveness has three criteria: the behavior must be (1) appropriate for the situation, (2) appropriate for the child's develop-mental level, and (3) successfully used by the child (the behavior results in a consequence).

The coping behaviors in each cluster are not truly task-analyzed, yet they do represent a loose functional hierarchy in which less mature competencies (e.g., child tolerates different intensities of touch) are precursors to more mature com-petencies (e.g., child demonstrates ability to comfort self). Thus, although the scale is not a curriculum, the ratings do alert a program's team members to the "what" and "how" of the infant's interaction with the environment. This knowl-edge is important for arranging the home or classroom/therapy environment to pro-mote more adaptive patterns.

At this point, field-test and technical-adequacy research has been conducted only by the authors. Yet, the authors must be commended on their commitment to studying the scale with its intended population. The ECI has been field tested on $N = 1,040$ handicapped and 227 nonhandicapped infants, one of the largest handi-capped samples for any available measure. Means and standard deviations allow individual comparisons with nondisabled and disabled samples.

Despite the ECI's strengths, users must be aware that the measure should not be used by itself but rather grouped as part of a larger diagnostic battery. Because it is a clinical judgment measure, the inconsistent item definitions can be interpreted differently by lay people and professionals. Care should be exercised in using mul-

---

Table 4–2 Sample Coping Competencies from the ECI

Sensorimotor organization

Child responds to a variety of sounds (e.g., voices, toys, soft-to-loud noises).	1	2	3	4	5
Child adjusts to irrelevant sounds in the environment.	1	2	3	4	5

Reactive behavior

Child accepts warmth and support from familiar persons.	1	2	3	4	5
Child reacts to feelings and moods of other people.	1	2	3	4	5

Self-initiated behavior

Child expresses likes and dislikes.	1	2	3	4	5
Child initiates action to communicate a need.	1	2	3	4	5

Source: From *Early Coping Inventory: A Measure of Adaptive Behavior* (pp. 2, 4, 6) by S. Zeitlin, G.G. Williamson, and M. Szczepanski, 1988, Bensenville, IL: Scholastic Testing Service, Inc. Copyright 1988 by Scholastic Testing Service, Inc. Adapted by permission.

Carolina Record of Individual Behavior (CRIB)

Author(s):	R.J. Simeonsson
Year:	1985
Publisher:	Author
Address:	School of Education, CIREEH, Peabody Hall 037A, University of North Carolina Chapel Hill, NC 27514
Phone:	(919) 962-5579
Cost:	NA

Assessment type: Judgment-based; clinical assessment of subtle response classes that characterize a child's response to the environment; particularly useful for young severely handicapped children.

Age range: Developmental range 0-48 months.

Domains/Contexts: 22 developmental (i.e., object orientation, receptive communication) and behavioral (i.e., reactivity, attention) domains and numerous rhythmic habit patterns (RHP) (i.e., head bang, hand flap).

Handicap options: Structures observational assessment of severely handicapped; based on observation and impressions across people and situations.

Curricular links: Describes child dimensions that influence the content, intensity, and organization of treatment; identifies general functional levels within important domains.

Scoring/Sample: 1-9 Likert scale (1 = primitive/9 advanced or 5 = normal/1 and 9 extremes); 0, 1, 2 assesses RHP severity; uses multiple ratings across situations.

Technical support: Based on Bayley IBR and Brazelton scales; comparative data with norm and curricular instruments and temperament scales; descriptive "norms" on $N = 600$ by handicap group.

Training needed: Familiarity with operational definitions in scales.

Critique:
- Provides valuable structure to clinical judgment data.
- Assesses crucial child adaptive processes.
- Operationalizes hard-to-observe, subtle response classes.
- Item wording may be too difficult for parents and paraprofessionals.

Citations:

Simeonsson, R.J., Huntington, G.S., Short, R., & Ware, T. (1982). The Carolina Record of Individual Behavior: Characteristics of handicapped infants and children. *Topics in Early Childhood Special Education, 2*(2), 43–55.

Blacher-Dixon, J., & Simeonsson, R. (1981). Consistency and correspondence of mother's and teacher's assessments of young handicapped children. *Journal of the Division for Early Childhood, 3*, 64–71.

Bagnato, S.J., & Mayes, S.D. (1986). Patterns of developmental and behavioral progress for young brain-injured children during interdisciplinary intervention. *Developmental Neuropsychology, 2*(3), 213–240.

tiple raters of a child and determining congruence among them—a point not stressed enough in the manual.

The ECI has numerous strengths that support its wide use in pediatric rehabilitation and early-intervention programs, particularly for severely impaired children. As curricula are developed to emphasize the infant's transactions with the environment and generalization of behavior across situations, the ECI will be a complementary clinical and diagnostic instrument for prescriptive purposes.

In the search for precision in assessment, professionals are becoming increasingly sterile and too test-based in their approaches for evaluating children. Professionals often assess children without an underlying conceptual framework to guide their observations and thus tend to put their often valuable clinical judgments and expertise on hold. The *Carolina Record of Individual Behavior* (CRIB) (Simeonsson, Huntington, Short, & Ware, 1982) offers a framework by which observers can record their clinical impressions about a child's behavior in structured and naturalistic contexts. Its expanded content is based on the Bayley Infant Behavior Record.

Focusing on the severely handicapped preschooler functioning in the birth to 3-year age range, the CRIB provides an effective method of describing a child's developmental and behavioral competencies in noncategorical terms. It uses a 9-point rating scale to appraise such subtle response classes as motivation, reactivity, endurance, body tone/tension, attention, social orientation, and consolability (see Exhibits 4-5 and 4-6). In addition, the CRIB enables the clinician to rate the severity of various stereotypies, such as head banging, hand flapping, body rocking, rumination, and tongue thrusting. The CRIB describes the child's characteristics in such a way that intervention programs can be developed that tailor the level of intensity of stimulation and the organization of the environment to the child's capacity to adjust to and benefit from the program. The CRIB can be a valuable addition to any prescriptive assessment battery. Descriptive norms on approximately 600 severely impaired preschoolers generate a base for individual comparisons. Because of its sometimes difficult wording, the CRIB is judged to be more effectively used by professionals than by parents or nonprofessional aides. The CRIB represents an important and creative advance in alternative forms of assessment that are adaptive to the child's needs and thus are handicap-sensitive.

INFANT-PRESCHOOL

Constructed by a school psychologist, the *BRIGANCE Diagnostic Inventory of Early Development* (BDIED) (Brigance, 1978) is based on a developmental task-analytic model, combines norm- and criterion-based features, and integrates assessment with curriculum goal planning. The BDIED surveys the birth to 7-year age range while analyzing child performance across 98 skill sequences within 11 major developmental domains, including prespeech behaviors, general knowledge and comprehension, fine motor skills, and preambulatory motor skills (see Exhibit

Exhibit 4–5 Object Orientation

A7 Responsiveness to objects, toys or test materials: Score behavior which is spontaneous rather than in direct response to demonstration or elicitation. (Circle One)

1 Does not look at, show interest and/or seem aware of objects.

2 Looks at and/or turns toward only if object attracts attention (e.g., makes noise, flashes light, etc. (high stimulus items only).

3 When presented with materials, turns to or looks at briefly but does not attempt to approach, reach for, or manipulate any object.

4 Sustained interest in objects as they are presented (e.g., turns to, looks at, smiles at, etc.).

5 Does attempt to approach or manipulate objects: uses in same manner regardless of form or function (e.g., bangs all objects, mouths all objects).

6 Reaches for and manipulates objects in a variety of exploratory ways—holding, feeling, visual examination, shaking, etc.

7 Manipulates object with some regard to form (e.g., puts block in cup, peers into box, sticks finger in hole, etc.).

8 Manipulates object with appropriate regard to form or function (e.g., rocks doll, pushes car, stacks blocks).

9 Plays imaginatively with materials, uses objects several ways.

X Not applicable.

Source: From *The Carolina Record of Individual Behavior* by R.J. Simeonsson, 1985, Chapel Hill, NC: University of North Carolina. Copyright 1985 by University of North Carolina. Reprinted by permission.

Exhibit 4–6 Reactivity

B2 The ease with which the child is stimulated to react in general; his sensitivity or excitability; reactivity may be positive or negative. (Circle One)

1 Only responds to physically intrusive and/or aversive stimuli (e.g., sudden change of position, pin prick, ice).

2 Reactive to strong and repeated nonintrusive stimulation (e.g., loud noises, bright lights; does not habituate).

3 Periodic reaction to strong stimulation; habituates rapidly.

4 Some tendency to be underreactive to usual testing stimuli and/or changes in environment.

5 Shows appropriate awareness to usual testing stimuli and/or changes in environment.

6 Some tendency to be overreactive to changes in environment and/or testing stimuli.

7 Overreactive to changes in immediate environment; alerts, startles.

8 Overreactive to selected stimuli enough to cry and/or withdraw (e.g., noises, lights, people).

9 Very reactive—every little thing causes child to startle, cry, and/or withdraw; reacts quickly.

X Not applicable.

Source: From *The Carolina Record of Individual Behavior* by R.J. Simeonsson, 1985, Chapel Hill, NC: University of North Carolina. Copyright 1985 by University of North Carolina. Reprinted by permission.

BRIGANCE Diagnostic Inventory of Early Development (BDIED)

Author(s): A. Brigance
Year: 1978
Publisher: Curriculum Associates, Inc.
Address: 5 Esquire Road, North Billerica, MA 01862
Phone: (617) 667-8000
Cost: $80+

Assessment type: Curriculum-based; criterion-referenced analysis of developmental and preacademic readiness skills.

Age range: Birth to 84 months.

Domains/Contexts: 98 skill sequences in 5 major domains: motor, speech, general knowledge and comprehension, written language, math.

Handicap options: Any adaptation that allows the child to perform optimally, including stimulus and response changes, is encouraged; common household objects can be used; qualitative scoring strategies are included.

Curricular links: Hierarchical arrangement, developmental task analysis, and similarity of item content ensure a compatibility with commonly available curricula.

Scoring/Sample: Data gathered from multiple sources: observational, performance, interview, clinical teaching; scoring involves circling completed tasks, underlining target objectives and color coding, with S = satisfactory, N = needs improvement.

Technical support: Age placement of items by reviewing traditional scales, such as Gesell, Bayley, etc.; specific research references are cited as criteria.

Training needed: Knowledge of child development and thorough familiarity with procedures in the manual.

Critique:
- One of the best and most frequently used criterion/curriculum-referenced developmental measures.
- Easy to use, motivating, flexible, and adaptive.
- Procedures blend assessment, selecting objectives, and evaluating progress.
- Appropriateness with severely handicapped is questionable.
- Needs more technical-adequacy studies.

Citations:
Johnson, L.J., & Beauchamp, K.D. (1987). Preschool assessment measures: What are teachers using? *Journal of the Division for Early Childhood, 12*(1), 70–76.
Bagnato, S.J. (1985). Critical review of the BRIGANCE BDIED (invited test review). In O.K. Buros (Ed.), *Ninth mental measurements yearbook* (pp. 1109–1121). Lincoln, NE: Buros Institute, University of Nebraska Press.

Exhibit 4–7 Selected Visual-Motor Tasks from the BRIGANCE Diagnostic Inventory of Early Development

C-7 78-81
C-7C

Cutting With Scissors
2-0 1. Places scissors on fingers and holds correctly.
2. Opens and closes scissors.
2-6 3. Snips or makes small cuts in paper.
4. Holds paper for cutting.
3-0 5. Cuts 13 cm paper in two.
6. Cuts 13 mm line within 12 mm in 15 seconds.
4-0 7. Cuts triangle with 5 cm sides within 12 mm in 35 seconds.
8. Moves paper while cutting.
5-0 9. Cuts 13 cm circle within 12 mm in 35 seconds.
10. Cuts 13 cm circle within 6 mm in 35 seconds.
11. Cuts 13 cm curving line within 6 mm in 35 seconds.
6-0 12. Cuts cardboard and cloth.
13. Cuts out items such as paper dolls. 7-0

Developmental Age: 2-0

Notes:

C-8 82-3
C-8B

Painting With Brush:
1-6 1. Makes whole arm strokes which may form arc and go off page.
2-0 2. Some wrist/scrubbing action.
3. Regards process as more important than end product.
4. Experiments with vertical and horizontal lines, dots or circular movements.
3-0 5. Gives name to picture not readily understandable to others.
4-0 6. Objects and designs are crude or imperfect in size and space relationships, but usually recognizable.
7. Concerned more with end product than with process.
5-0 8. Evaluates and criticizes own painting.
9. Selects colors with care. 6-0

Developmental Age: 1-6

Notes:

C-9 84
C-9

Clay:
2-0 1. Manipulates clay.
2. Pounds.
3. Squeezes.
4. Pulls apart.
3-0 5. Makes flat round cakes.
6. Makes rolled ropes.
7. Makes balls.
4-0 8. Makes crude objects not always recognizable by others.
5-0 9. Makes refined objects which are recognizable by others. 6-0

Developmental Age: 2-0

Notes:

Source: BRIGANCE® *Diagnostic Inventory of Early Development*, Copyright © 1978 Curriculum Associates, Inc. Reprinted by permission.

4-7). Item placement and skill sequencing were accomplished by reviewing the organization of items in traditional developmental scales; the BDIED uniquely references the source of these placements for each item. Multisource procedures for scoring child performance are provided (interview, observation, diagnostic teaching, and pragmatic task modifications). The BDIED also accommodates different response styles so that adaptations for various handicaps are possible, although not specifically indicated. Developmental ages are indicated for each sequence of developmental skills; the scale links assessment with intervention by arranging tasks in a hierarchical manner and by matching appropriate objectives to these tasks in each subdomain. Computer-based programs are available to translate child assessment data directly into BDIED plans.

BRIGANCE Prescriptive Readiness: Strategies and Practice (Brigance, 1985) is a curriculum-based package of instructional activities that are appropriate for preschool, kindergarten, and early first-grade levels and that match with assessment tasks on the BDIED (see Chapter 6). These activities detail objectives, rationale, instructional sequences, teaching recommendations, and indicators of learning difficulties for 400 developmental and behavioral skills.

Although the BDIED is one of the best available criterion-based measures of developmental functioning in a noncurricular format, many of its skill sequences lack the detail to provide assessments sufficiently precise for severely handicapped preschoolers (auditory, visual, language, perceptual, and fine motor areas). Thus, the BDIED is judged to be most effectively used for children with mild-to-moderate disabilities.

Many professionals have used the *Griffiths Mental Development Scales* (GMDS) (Griffiths, 1970) as their primary instrument to conduct research and to diagnose and plan programs for handicapped infants and young children. Despite the cautions in using content designed for and standardized on British children, the GMDS have many practical and technical advantages over other similar measures.

The GMDS cover the birth to 96-month age range, which solves the problem of using a different status and outcome measure for infant and preschool programs. Surveying six separate developmental areas (see Table 4-3), the scales offer independent developmental ages and quotients for each subscale to generate a differential profile of capabilities (Mott et al., 1986).

The content of the scales are curriculum-compatible and, because of the functional task basis, can be readily linked with most developmental curricula for goal planning. The GMDS show some adaptive options in that the order of item administration can be modified to accommodate the child's interest and responsiveness. The manual includes a series of sample profiles of young children with various disabilities so that individual children can be compared with a handicapped peer, offering a type of disability "norm."

The GMDS are well-standardized and technically adequate compared with other similar measures that are much less adequate, namely, the dated Gesell Developmental Schedules (4 weeks to 72 months). In fact, the norms of the GMDS have been drawn on the largest group of infants of any comprehensive norm-based scale

Griffiths Mental Development Scales (GMDS)

Author(s): R. Griffiths
Year: 1954; 1970
Publisher: Association for Research in Infant & Child Development;
            Distributor: The Test Agency
Address: Cournswood House, North Wycombe, Bucks, England
Phone: Naphill (024 024) 3384
Cost: $250 +

Assessment type: Norm-based; diagnoses degree of developmental deficit.

Age range: 0-8 years (separate infant scale); the abilities of babies (birth to 24 months); the abilities of young children (24 to 96 months).

Domains/Contexts: 5 independent subscales: locomotor, personal-social, hearing and speech, eye and hand coordination, and performance; practical reasoning at 36 + months; 498 items.

Handicap options: Manual includes chapter and "template profiles" on infants and children with severe communication, cognitive, and sensorimotor deficits for handicap comparison purposes; allows altered order-of-item administration and response to child's interest.

Curricular links: Multiple domains and traditional developmental task content matches with most curricula.

Scoring/Sample: Separate developmental ages/rates for each subscale and overall developmental quotient and age for entire test.

Technical support: Norms = 2,263 British children, age stratified; test-retest: infant scale = .87, overall = .77; well-standardized and technically adequate; Griffiths & old Binet = .79-.81; Griffiths exceeds Bayley by 10 pts.

Training needed: Should be given by a psychologist with thorough grounding in infant and handicap assessment.

Critique:
- Very comprehensive measure covering wide age range.
- Largest standardization of any infant/preschool scale.
- Caution with representativeness of British norms.
- Unique use of sample handicap profiles for comparisons.
- Large item pool (498 items) facilitates linkage.
- Dated standardization suggests prime use for qualitative prescriptive vs. diagnostic purposes.

Citations:
Ramsay, C., & Fitzhardinge, P.M. (1977). A comparative study of two developmental scales: The Bayley and the Griffiths. *Early Human Development, 1*(2), 151–157.
Hindley, C.B. (1965). The GMDS. In O.K. Buros (Ed.), *The Sixth Mental Measurements Yearbook* (pp. 523–524). Highland Park, N.J.: Gryphon Press.

Table 4–3   Selected Tasks from the GMDS Subdomains for Ages 12 to 36 Months

Age	Locomotor	Personal-Social	Hearing and Speech	Eye and Hand	Performance	Practical Reasoning (36 + Only)
12 mo.	Creeps on hands and knees	Obeys "Give me the cup"	Reacts to music vocally	Interested in motor car	Accepts third cube without dropping	——
	Side-steps around play pen	Plays "pat-a-cake"	Babbles monologue when alone	Holds pencil as if to mark paper	Removes both cubes from box	——
36 mo.	Rises from kneeling w/o using hands	Gives first name on request	Names 12 of 18 objects in box	Threads six beads	Reassembles screw toy	Knows "big" and "little"
	Crosses both feet and knees when seated	Gives family name on request	Uses two descriptive words	Handles scissors, tries to cut paper	Completes six-hole board	Repeats three digits

Source: Adapted from *Griffiths Mental Development Scales* by R. Griffiths, 1970, Bucks, England: Association for Research in Infant & Child Development. Copyright 1970 by Association for Research in Infant & Child Development. Reprinted by permission.

(N = 2,263). The overall test-retest reliability of the scale is somewhat problematic (R = .77), but predictive comparisons with some measures like the Binet are quite good. Comparisons with the Bayley scales suggest that the GMDS systematically offer higher levels on both the mental and motor subscales.

Generally, the GMDS are little known among typical community-based, infant-preschool programs. However, it is strongly recommended that programs review the GMDS content and match it with their own program's curriculum, especially in view of the GMDS' wide age range and multiple domains. The emphasis on "practical reasoning" skills at 36 months and above helps to bridge the gap between preschool and preacademic emphases, while still retaining the developmental approach. The GMDS can be a valuable addition to a program's assessment pool if appropriate caution is maintained in the use of British norms and some GMDS content. Using it in a battery with other measures for corroboration of levels is strongly advised. More studies are needed to compare the utility of the GMDS with other similar measures, such as the Gesell schedules and the Battelle Developmental Inventory, particularly in view of the recurring questions about the adequacy of the latter two instruments for diagnostic purposes.

The *Learning Accomplishment Profile—Diagnostic Edition* (revised) (LAP-D) (LeMay, Griffin, & Sanford, 1978) and its associated curriculum materials—products of the Chapel Hill, North Carolina, Outreach Project—represent one of the most frequently used criterion-referenced curriculum scales covering the 0- to 5½-year range. The LAP-D is an expanded compilation of a variety of developmental tasks culled from such traditional instruments as the Bayley scale and placed at similar age levels, as determined by norm-referenced measures. The LAP-D scale combines the advantages of normed sequencing of developmental skills with precise targets for initiating individualized program planning.

The LAP-D is considered a developmental task-analysis diagnostic instrument that details functioning in five distinct areas: (1) fine motor, (2) gross motor, (3) language, (4) cognition, and (5) self-help. Unlike narrower-scope, norm-based scales, it divides its major domains into subareas, including manipulation, writing, matching, object movement, counting, comprehension, and grooming (see Exhibit 4-8). The detailed scale covers the age range of birth to 6 years across these functional areas and helps generate a diagnostic profile of the child's range of fully acquired (+), absent (−), and emerging (±) developmental capabilities. The profile forms the diagnostic basis for individualized goal planning by establishing developmental "targets" and age reference points, rather than comparative statistical quotients.

The LAP-D has several features that make it unique among the newer criterion-based measures. First, it is one of the most colorful and interesting of the curriculum scales. The large red carrying case contains a rich variety of tasks—involving formboard, peg placement, drawing, beanbag, color matching, puzzles, block building, bead stringing, octopus dressing toy, and lacing—that are inherently appealing to young children and provide a motivational support for obtaining the child's maximum level of performance. Also, the variety of tasks allows some

---

Learning Accomplishment Profile—Diagnostic Edition (LAP-D)

Author(s):   D. LeMay, P.M. Griffin, A. Sanford
Year: 1978
Publisher: Kaplan School Supply Corporation
Address: 1310 Lewisville-Clemmons Road, Lewisville, NC 27023
Phone: 1 (800) 334-2014
Cost: $325+

Assessment type: Norm-based/criterion-referenced; provides a diagnostic sample of current developmental skills compatible with the LAP curriculum.
Age range: 30-73 months.
Domains/Contexts: 5 domains: fine motor, gross motor, language, cognition, self-help; 13 subdomains, including manipulation, writing, matching.
Handicap options: Minimal; toys are colorful and motivating.
Curricular links: Compatible with LAP curriculum tasks; generates a developmental task analysis for individualized prescriptive goal planning.
Scoring/Sample: +, −, ±; direct performance, observation, and report.
Technical support: $N = 35$ children (preliminary version sample $N = 239$); test-retest = .98.
Training needed: Teacher administered; thorough knowledge of manual and curricula.

Critique:
- Motivating materials.
- Provides a developmental task analysis and is curriculum-compatible.
- Confusion between the LAP curriculum and LAP-D needs clarification with professionals.
- Lack of norms as a "diagnostic" measure brings its use into question in comparison with the Battelle.

Citation:
Sexton, D., Hall, J., & Thomas, J.P. (1984b). Correlates of parent-professional congruency scores in the assessment of young handicapped children. *Journal of the Division for Early Childhood, 8*(2), 99–106.

---

adaptive accommodations to be made. Second, because of the colorful, high-interest tasks and flip-card administration format, the scale can be given by the teacher in approximately 1½ hours, providing relevant educational goals and qualitative descriptions of the child's developmental and instructional needs. Finally, the LAP-D is based upon continuing research efforts to establish a normative and technical basis in terms of reliability and validity, although the technical manual cites current data on only 35 children. Total scale test-retest reliability is reportedly .98, with subscale correlations of .91-.97.

As part of a total assessment-intervention process, the LAP-D helps to formulate an adaptive and individualized program for prescriptive teaching. In brief, the

Exhibit 4–8 Sample Goal Sequence on Comprehension Skills from the LAP-D

Language/Cognitive: Comprehension

Developmental Age	Item	Behavior	1st +/−	2nd +/−	Comments
6	LC1	Responds to name			
15	LC2	Looks toward object			
15	LC3	Responds to "look"			
15	LC4	Points to objects			
18	LC5	Points to 3 body parts			
24	LC6	Follows 3 commands			
24	LC7	Hands objects to examiner			
24	LC8	Points to 6 body parts			
24	LC9	Follows 8 commands			
30	LC10	Responds to 2 prepositions			
30	LC11	Follows 2-step command			
33	LC12	Shows use of objects			
33	LC13	Points to objects by use			
36	LC14	Points to 5 actions			
36	LC15	Points to 10 objects			
42	LC16	Points to 15 objects			
42	LC17	Points to 9 actions			
48	LC18	Responds to 4 prepositions			
48	LC19	Relates pictures to story			
48	LC20	Points to numerals 1 - 10			
54	LC21	Matches picture and verbal description			
60	LC22	Selects items in category			
66	LC23	Responds to "who, what, where"			
72	LC24	Follows 3-step command			
72	LC25	Shows left/right			
72	LC26	Points to letters A - Z			
72	LC27	Points to words			

Last Item Administered

Less Errors — —

Comprehension Score

Add LN and LC to derive Language total score.

Source: From *Learning Accomplishment Profile: Diagnostic Edition* (Revised edition) by D.W. LeMay, P.M. Griffin, and A.R. Sanford, 1978, Winston-Salem, NC: Kaplan School Supply. Copyright 1978 by Kaplan School Supply. Reprinted by permission.

LAP-D (together with the total curriculum program to be discussed in Chapter 6) accomplishes six major objectives in early special education: (1) provides a record of functional skills, (2) establishes an initial developmental task analysis to guide teaching in multiple areas, (3) allows for creative additions to the goal sequence, (4) provides a means for measuring progress, (5) highlights individual strengths and weaknesses, and (6) enables the teacher to initiate curriculum-embedded assessment within the classroom environment.

Developmental Profile II (DP II)

Author(s):   G. Alpern, T. Boll, M. Shearer
Year: 1980; 1986
Publisher: Western Psychological Services
Address: 12031 Wilshire Boulevard, Los Angeles, CA 90025
Phone: (213) 478-2061
Cost: $30 +

Assessment type: Judgment-based, norm-based appraisal of a child's developmental capabilities, based on interview of parent/caregiver.
Age range: 0-108 months.
Domains/Contexts: 5 domains: physical, self-help, social, academic, communication (217 tasks).
Handicap options: Caregiver judgments provide observational data; combined report and observational data can facilitate assessment of autistic children.
Curricular links: Domains and "landmark" skills are comparable with those included in typical preschool curricula.
Scoring/Sample: Pass-fail, yes/no scaling; DAs, DRs, and significant difference cut-offs for deficits; observation, interview/report samples.
Technical support: Norms = 3,008 children; validity and reliability are adequate for general screening purposes; concurrent validity with Binet, LAP, IPDS.
Training needed: Thorough reading of the manual, knowledge of child development, and practice and experience in interviewing parents.

Critique:
- Structures caregiver perceptions about developmental skills.
- Remains the best available early childhood interview scale.
- "Does" and "can do" question stems are clear for parents.
- Tasks are instructionally relevant and developmentally sequenced.
- Exceeds the VABS in clinical usefulness for young exceptional children.

Citations:

Harris, S.L., & Fagley, N.S. (1987). The Developmental Profile as a predictor of status for autistic children: Four to seven year follow-up. *School Psychology Review, 16*(1), 89–93.

Sexton, D., Hall, J., & Thomas, J.P. (1984a). Multisource assessment of young handicapped children: A comparison. *Exceptional Children, 50,* 556–558.

Parent reports of child capabilities are often considered unreliable. Their accuracy depends on many factors, including the clarity of the skills and how the question is asked. Many parents systematically overestimate child capabilities. Parents of severely impaired children, however, tend to portray their children's status more accurately. For these reasons, tests like the *Developmental Profile II* (DP II) (Alpern, Boll, & Shearer, 1986) are considered indispensable in comprehensive diagnosis.

The DP II is a norm-referenced developmental screening measure that relies on a structured interview with the parents to estimate a child's current levels of functioning. The DP II is unique among screening measures in that it is multidimensional, reliable, valid, and well-standardized.

Surveying the age range from birth to 12 years, the DP contains 217 developmental tasks ordered within five functional domains: (1) physical, (2) self-help, (3) social, (4) academic, and (5) communication. The tasks are presented as questions that tap the developing child's level of competence in each area. The DP II is probably the best standardized interview screening measure currently available, since it is standardized on 3,008 children.

Scoring is done by either circling a zero for a failure or the "month number" opposite an item to indicate a pass. Basal and double-ceiling levels are established, as on other measures, to represent the upper and lower limits of functioning. The total number of passes is utilized to determine developmental age scores for each functional domain. Questions are asked in terms of whether the child "does" and "can" perform a particular activity, to obtain notions of actual functioning and capability (see Exhibit 4-9). Scores representing functioning are interpreted in terms of the degree of "developmental lag" between chronological age and current levels of functioning and the discrepancies between developmental levels across the multiple domains. The significance of lags is determined from the norm tables.

The Developmental Profile II presents certain unique characteristics and is invaluable as part of a larger diagnostic battery. It facilitates the use of parent judgments in formulating interventions and aids in standardizing the diverse perceptions of significant adults who know and serve the child. As an interview measure, it is adaptive in accurately portraying the perceived needs of handicapped children and providing a potential basis for counseling and parent training. Finally, it provides a valid and reliable basis for multisource assessment and establishes initial targets for curriculum prescriptions by highlighting perceived capabilities and deficits.

The *Battelle Developmental Inventory* (BDI) (Newborg, Stock, Wnek, Guidubaldi, & Svinicki, 1984), a standardized developmental scale, is the only current example of a norm-referenced diagnostic measure that also integrates criterion- or curriculum-referenced features into its structure (although it is not a curriculum). The BDI analyzes the acquisition of 341 critical developmental skills from birth to 8 years and within five functional domains and 22 subdomains. Functional capabilities are assessed in the following major domains: personal-social, adaptive, motor, communication, and cognitive. Unique clusters of subdomain

Exhibit 4–9 Sample Communication Subscale Questions from the DP II

Newborn: 0-6 months
  1. Does the child use vocal noises for play? The child must PLAY with sounds (not just cry, gurgle, or laugh when something happens).

Infant I: 7-12 months
  4. Does the child sometimes imitate spoken "words" such as "da-da" or "ma-ma"? The child may not know what these words mean.

Infant II: 13-18 months
  8. Does the child say the names of at least five things (not in imitation and not including names of people)? The words must be said well enough to be understood by a stranger.

Toddler I: 19-24 months
  12. Does the child put two or more words together to form sentences? "Me, go," "You give," "Tom want," are all examples of passes. But, if the child ALWAYS uses the same two words together (so that they are really one word to the child), that does not rate a pass.

Toddler II: 25-30 months
  13. Does the child either repeat parts of nursery rhymes or join in when others say them?

Source: Reprinted from the *Developmental Profile II* Scoring/Profile Form, by Gerald D. Alpern, Thomas J. Boll, and Marsha S. Shearer. Copyright ©1984 by Western Psychological Services, and reprinted by permission of the publisher, Western Psychological Services, 12031 Wilshire Boulevard, Los Angeles, California 90025.

---

skills are sampled in such areas as adult interaction, expression of feelings/affect, coping, attention, and reasoning (see Exhibit 4-10). The authors have incorporated recommendations from recent early-intervention research into the design and construction of the BDI.

The BDI assessment battery consists of components that follow the LINK model by fulfilling four interrelated purposes linking assessment and intervention: (1) screening and identification, (2) comprehensive assessment and goal planning, (3) programming and intervention, and (4) evaluation of child progress and program effectiveness. The BDI ensures norm-referenced identification of young children who are exceptional and highlights those developmental areas that require more comprehensive appraisal. The battery's multidimensional structure allows a comprehensive analysis of functional capabilities, incorporating diagnostic data from multiple people and sources (teachers, therapists, parents, observation, interviews, and child performance). A unique adaptive feature of the BDI is its inclusion of assessment adaptations for specific sensorimotor impairments and general guidelines on presenting testing tasks for various categories of young handicapped children (see Exhibit 4-11). In addition, the developmental and behavioral content of the BDI is congruent with the goals and tasks of frequently used infant and preschool curricula. Finally, the organization of the BDI enables interdisciplinary team members to assess children independently, so that formative and summative evaluations of progress and program efficacy can be accomplished.

Normative and technical data on the BDI support its use. However, some questions have been raised as to whether its DQs might "overestimate" the rates for

---

Battelle Developmental Inventory (BDI)

Author(s):	J. Newborg, J. Stock, L. Wnek, J. Guildubaldi, J.S. Svinicki
Year:	1984
Publisher:	DLM/Teaching Resources
Address:	PO Box 4000, One DLM Park, Allen, TX 75002
Phone:	1 (800) 442-4711
Cost:	$160+

Assessment type: Norm-based/curriculum-referenced; diagnosis, linkage, and progress evaluation purposes.

Age range: 0-95 months.

Domains/Contexts: 5 domains: personal-social, adaptive, motor, communication, cognitive; 22 subdomains (e.g., coping, peer interaction, attention, memory, expression of feelings); 341 items.

Handicap options: General adaptations for various handicaps; standardized stimulus/response options for visual, hearing, neuromotor, and behavioral/emotional disorders with most items.

Curricular links: Compatibility of domain and items with commonly used preschool curricula by programs; developmental task sequences by age within each subdomain. Battelle curriculum development in progress.

Scoring/Sample: Domain scores (DA, Z, T, DR, NCE, percentile); structured assessment, observation, interview data; norm group, $N = 800$, national sample continuum scoring 0, 1, 2 of items. Recalibrated norms available as of 1989.

Technical support: Limited, but emerging; reliability and validity based on pre-publication version; research supports concurrent validity, inter-rater reliability, and internal consistency; program efficacy research is limited.

Training needed: Although appropriate for nonpsychologists, supervised practice in administration for handicapped preschoolers across the entire age span is critical.

Critique:
- Matches spirit of PL 94-142/99-457.
- Merges norm-, adaptive-, curriculum-based features (á la LINK system).
- Needs technical evaluation in field-test settings.
- Exemplifies the best current example of curriculum referencing and assessment/intervention/evaluation linkage beyond a curriculum.

Citations:
McLean, M.A., McCormick, P.A., Bruder, M.B., & Burdg, L.D. (1987). An investigation of the validity and reliability of the Battelle with a population of children younger than 30 months with identified handicapping conditions. *Journal of the Division for Early Childhood, 11*(3), 238–246.

Bailey, D., Vandivieve, L., Dellinger, T.B., & Munn, G.A. (1987). The Battelle Developmental Inventory: Teacher perceptions and implementation data. *Journal of Psychoeducational Assessment, 3,* 217–226.

Bracken, B.A. (1987). Limitations of preschool instruments and standards for minimal levels of technical adequacy. *Journal of Psychoeducational Assessment, 4,* 313–326.

Exhibit 4–10 Attention Tasks from the BDI

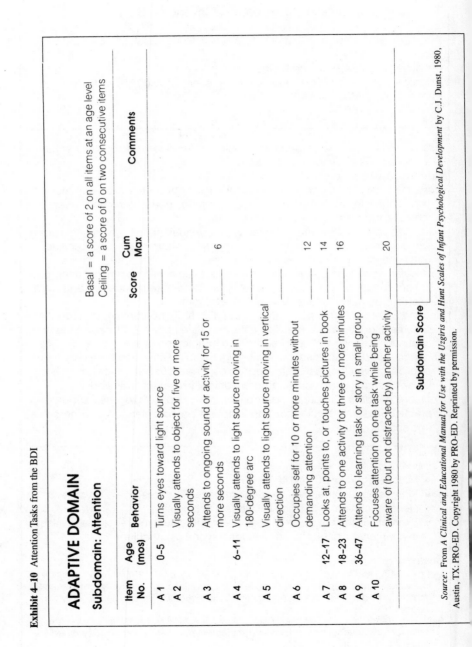

ADAPTIVE DOMAIN
Subdomain: Attention

Basal = a score of 2 on all items at an age level
Ceiling = a score of 0 on two consecutive items

Item No.	Age (mos)	Behavior	Score	Cum Max	Comments
A 1	0–5	Turns eyes toward light source			
A 2		Visually attends to object for five or more seconds			
A 3		Attends to ongoing sound or activity for 15 or more seconds		6	
A 4	6–11	Visually attends to light source moving in 180-degree arc			
A 5		Visually attends to light source moving in vertical direction			
A 6		Occupies self for 10 or more minutes without demanding attention		12	
A 7	12–17	Looks at, points to, or touches pictures in book		14	
A 8	18–23	Attends to one activity for three or more minutes		16	
A 9	36–47	Attends to learning task or story in small group			
A 10		Focuses attention on one task while being aware of (but not distracted by) another activity		20	

Subdomain Score [ ]

Source: From *A Clinical and Educational Manual for Use with the Uzgiris and Hunt Scales of Infant Psychological Development* by C.J. Dunst, 1980, Austin, TX: PRO-ED. Copyright 1980 by PRO-ED. Reprinted by permission.

DOMAIN Cognitive **AGE** 4 to 5 years **CG 25**
(48 through 59 months)

SUBDOMAIN Reasoning and Academic Skills

BEHAVIOR The child gives three objects on request.

MATERIALS Six cubes (other available objects)

STANDARD PROCEDURES

PROCEDURE

Structured. Place the six cubes in a row on the table before the child. Say to the child, **"Give me three blocks."** If the child does not respond, repeat one request. After the child has given you the three cubes, do not consider the response complete until the child has had time to give you another cube if he or she wishes. Consider the response complete when the child draws his or her hand back from the table and looks up at you as though waiting for your approval.

SCORING

Credit is given if the child gives or separates **three and only three** cubes from the six cubes on the table.

2 points = as above
1 point = 2 or 4 cubes
0 points = anything else

ADAPTATIONS FOR THE HANDICAPPED

Severe Motor Impairment—Arm or Hand. Credit is given if the child is able to push the three cubes to you. Place the cubes slightly further apart than they would be normally placed. If the child cannot physically move the cubes, pick up one cube at a time (while retaining all cubes previously picked up) and ask, **"Do I have three now?"** Do this for all six cubes.

Severe Visual Impairment. After the cubes are placed on the table, take the child's hand and place it on each of the six cubes individually. Do not count them. Say, **"Give me three blocks."** Allow the child to feel the cubes, using both hands if he or she wishes, before giving them to you.

Severe Hearing Impairment or Emotional Disturbance. Hold up three fingers to indicate the number three but discontinue this sign before the child responds.

Source: From *Battelle Developmental Inventory* by J. Newborg et al., 1984, Allen, TX: DLM/Teaching Resources Corporation. Copyright 1984 by DLM/Teaching Resources Corporation. Reprinted by permission.

developmentally disabled preschoolers. In early 1989 the publisher issued a re-calibrated normative manual for the BDI that may resolve these problems. How-ever, further research is needed on this question. The inventory was standardized on 800 infants, preschoolers, and early school-age children across the birth to 8-year age range, using a national norming sample stratified according to age, race, and sex. Reliability (test-retest, inter-rater) and validity (content, construct, and criterion-rated) data reported in the manuals seem to support the stability of the battery, its factorial validity, and its relation with other developmental and intel-lectual measures. Child diagnostic data are reported in three forms for each major domain and subdomain: age equivalents (DA), percentiles, and standard scores (developmental quotients, z/t-scores, and normal curve equivalents).

The BDI is an excellent example of a multidimensional assessment battery that blends norm- and criterion-referenced features to link assessment and interven-tion. Its inclusion of adaptive evaluation strategies ensures the collection of more accurate and functional diagnostic and instructional data.

Finally, the publisher reportedly plans to develop a curriculum based on the con-tent of the BDI. A unique feature of this curriculum will be goals based on clusters of items rather than on each individual item in the test.

Few adequate measures are available for young hearing-impaired children. The *Scales of Early Communication Skills for Hearing Impaired Children* (SECS) (Moog & Geers, 1975) are often used to assess the young disabled child's range of verbal and nonverbal abilities in order to pinpoint goals for programming. The SECS are a norm-based instrument that appraises prerequisite communication skills in four major areas. The skills are arranged in hierarchical sequences to en-able the clinician to screen functional capabilities and to highlight starting points for instruction and therapy (see Exhibit 4-12).

The SECS are solidly based on data from 14 programs in the United States that have emphasized oral methods with hearing-impaired preschoolers. However, the scales cover a wide age range (24-96 months) and survey only 34, albeit critical, communication skills. Thus, the SECS must be considered an interim screening measure. They are nevertheless, very useful for initial program goal planning. For novices working with hearing-impaired children, the scales provide important structure to the assessment. Moreover, the SECS can be easily linked with other scales, such as the Battelle Developmental Inventory, in a battery. In addition, they are generally compatible with the few available curricula for young hearing-impaired children, such as the Clark Early Language Program and Developmental Communication Curriculum (see Chapter 6).

There is a need to design assessment instruments that are both functionally ap-propriate for and normed upon children with a particular disability. The *Reynell-Zinkin Developmental Scales for Young Visually Handicapped Children* (RZS) (Reynell & Zinkin, 1979) are one of the few such handicap-specific tools; they are also one of the most unique.

The RZS promote a functional assessment procedure that shuns prediction and classification and advocates for prescriptive and progress assessment objectives.

Scales of Early Communication Skills (SECS)
for Hearing-Impaired Children

Author(s):	J.S. Moog, A.V. Geers
Year:	1975
Publisher:	Central Institute for the Deaf
Address:	818 South Euclid Avenue, St. Louis, MO 63110
Phone:	(314) 652-3200
Cost:	$20+

Assessment type: Norm-based; hierarchical sequences of critical language/communication skills.

Age range: 24-96 months.

Domains/Contexts: 4 subscales: receptive language skills, expressive language skills, nonverbal receptive skills, and nonverbal expressive skills.

Handicap options: Includes nonverbal skill samples and criteria about use of prompts and demonstrations to observe learning.

Curricular links: Developmental sequencing guides identification of functional communication levels and, thus, instructional/therapeutic goals.

Scoring/Sample: Observation of elicited behavior in naturalistic and structured settings; +, −, ± ratings.

Technical support: Field testing in 14 oral programs for the hearing impaired in U.S. N = 372 children; percentile ranks and standard scores $\underline{x}$, SD = 10 for each age, scale, and total.

Training needed: Thorough knowledge of the manual, critical skills, and typical behavior of young hearing-impaired children.

Critique:
- One of the few developmental measures for the hearing impaired.
- Adequate field testing and norms for the deaf.
- Important nonverbal subscales.
- Better as a screening than a criterion/prescriptive measure.

For this reason, the child's performance on the scales do not yield an IQ or DQ estimate; rather the scales characterize functioning in terms of a developmental age "range." Similarly, the child's observed completion of tasks reveals current competencies that, within the developmental progression, provide goals for developmental intervention and support (see Exhibit 4-13). The administration procedures are flexible, so that different child response modes can be accommodated and the stimulus features of objects and activities can be altered, as long as the intent and process requirements of the task remain intact.

The norms on the RZS are also unique and valuable, since they enable one to distinguish a child's capabilities in reference to those of blind, partially sighted, and normal-sighted children. The norm sample is realistic and natural as well, since some children with multiple handicaps were included (e.g., children with

Exhibit 4–12 Item Examples from Subscales of the Scales of Early Communication Skills

---

I. Receptive language skills
  A. Demonstrates awareness that the mouth and/or voice convey information.
    1. Responds to a verbal stimulus.
    2. Watches and/or listens to the speaker spontaneously.
  B. Demonstrates comprehension of a few words or expressions.
    1. Identifies at least one word or expression from a choice of 2 or 3.
    2. Demonstrates comprehension of at least one word or expression in a natural situation.

II. Expressive language skills
  A. Demonstrates awareness that vocalizations are used to communicate.
    1. Vocalizes when expected to imitate speech.
    2. Vocalizes spontaneously while looking at another person or to get someone's attention.
  B. Demonstrates the ability to use a few syllables, words, or expressions.
    1. Imitates at least one phoneme, syllable, or word.
    2. Uses at least one syllable, word, or expression consistently and meaningfully.

III. Nonverbal receptive skills
  A. Demonstrates the ability to respond appropriately to a simple gesture.
  B. Demonstrates the ability to respond to subtle or elaborate gestures when the situation does not make the meaning obvious.

IV. Nonverbal expressive skills
  A. Communicates by using simple gestures.
  B. Communicates by using elaborate gestures.

Source: From *Scales of Early Communication Skills* by J.S. Moog and A.V. Geers, 1975, St. Louis, MO: Central Institute for the Deaf at Washington University Medical Center. Copyright 1975 by Central Institute for the Deaf at Washington University Medical Center. Reprinted by permission.

---

mild cerebral palsy and hearing impairment). While limited in technical terms, this sample offers a valuable comparative framework with which to characterize the status and needs of individual children using three different points of reference. The authors of the RZS admonish clinicians, especially psychologists and pediatricians, to conduct an assessment rather than a testing of a child's capabilities.

The RZS are compatible with a curriculum-based approach that strives to discover a child's current competencies and programming needs. The items themselves place a weighted emphasis on auditory and tactile modes of experiencing and learning, rather than on vision. Performance assessments should be supplemented by naturalistic observations of the child's interaction with the environment, using different people, objects, and settings to obtain the most representative results. However, assessors should be already familiar with the behaviors of visually impaired young children before attempting to use and interpret the scales. It is obvious that the RZS need greater refinement in design and technical adequacy. For example, no reliability studies are reported in the manual; these can and should be conducted, despite the authors' contention that profile analysis does not lend itself to statistical evaluation.

Reynell-Zinkin Developmental Scales (RZS)
for Young Visually Handicapped Children

Author(s):	J. Reynell, K. Zinkin
Year:	1979
Publisher:	Stoelting Company
Address:	1350 South Kostner Avenue, Chicago, IL 60623
Phone:	(312) 522-4500
Cost:	$40

Assessment type: Norm-based; provides a detailed flexible assessment procedure for visually impaired infants and young children and a basis for program planning; shuns prediction, advocates profiles of current abilities.

Age range: 0-60+ months.

Domains/Contexts: 7 domains: social adaptation, sensorimotor understanding, exploration of environment, response to sound and verbal comprehension, vocalization and expressive language (structure), expressive language (vocabulary and content), and communication.

Handicap options: Focuses upon functional assessments for blind children who may have additional handicaps; norms for blind and partially sighted groups, which also include those with cerebral palsy and hearing impairments; premium on tactile/auditory tasks.

Curricular links: Tasks within domains hierarchically arranged but not task-analyzed; developmental tasks and processes congruent with most curricula; items have adaptive and instructional features; assesses serial progress.

Scoring/Sample: 1 (+), 0 (−); raw scores, subtest totals generate developmental age equivalents for blind, partially sighted, and sighted children; based on performance assessment, report, and naturalistic observation.

Technical support: N = 203 "recordings" for 109 children in three diagnostic groups: blind (97), partial (86), borderline (20); little technical adequacy data available.

Training needed: Direct experience with blind children about typical stages and behaviors; supervised administration of the scale; primary use by psychologists.

Critique:
- Promotes assessment versus testing.
- One of the few measures to include normal and handicap "norms."
- Includes tasks sensitive to multiple impairments.
- Enables profiling of functional status.
- Developmental progressions typical of blind children (e.g., later sensory coordination).
- Needs "true" norming on normal children as well.

Citation:
Reynell, J., & Zinkin, K. (1975). New procedures for the developmental assessment of young children with severe visual handicaps. *Child Care, Health and Development, 1,* 61–69.

Exhibit 4-13 Sensorimotor Understanding Subscale from the RZS

Item No.	Item Description	Score
1	Active grasp of object put into hand	
2	Orientation of hand for grasping, e.g. turning over	
3	Bimanual exploration of objects	
4	Hand-mouth exploration of objects	
5	Explorative manipulation of shape	
6	Explorative manipulation of texture	
7	Searching momentarily for something lost from grasp	
8	Extensive search for lost object	
9	Relating 2 objects. Stage (i) Taking objects out of container	
10	Relating 2 objects. Stage (ii) Putting things into container or any other creative relationship (e. g. building)	
11	Exploration of moveable parts of objects, e.g. box with lid	
12	Getting small object out of simple round box with lid	
13	Replacing toy and lid	
14	Getting sweet out of screw-capped bottle	
15	Replacing screw-cap	
16	Large and small round boxes. Putting correct lids on	
17	Same for 3 boxes	
18	Sorting beads into big and small	
19	Sorting beads into round and square	
20	Sorting 'different' one out of four:— a) size b) shape	
	SCORE (Max. 20)	

Source: From *Reynell-Zinkin Scales: Developmental Scales for Young Visually Handicapped Children* by J. Reynell and K. Zinkin, 1979, Berkshire, England: NFER-Nelson. Copyright 1979 by NFER-Nelson. Reprinted by permission.

The RZS are unique and much needed as a hybrid norm-criterion-adaptive measure for young blind children. All early interventionists should be familiar with the content, design, and appropriate use of the RZS when matched to the child's functional limitations and needs.

The *Uniform Performance Assessment System* (UPAS) (Haring, White, Edgar, Affleck, & Hayden, 1981) is perhaps the first of the new breed of criterion-referenced instruments that is adaptable to a young child's functional disabilities. The UPAS was designed to accomplish effectively three objectives: (1) provide an instructional focus, (2) monitor small increments of change, and (3) modify tasks to meet the child's impairments. The UPAS makes clear distinctions between items that have instructional value and implications and those that are merely "diagnostic" in character. Thus, the selection of instructional objectives is dictated by the adaptive purpose of a particular cluster of behaviors for the child's real-life functioning (see Table 4-4).

Practically, the UPAS is cumbersome and time-consuming to use. Consumers need to understand, however, that the needs of children with multiple impairments and moderate-to-severe retardation require greater precision in measurement, which is necessarily time-consuming. The UPAS is clearly not a measure for fledgling programs.

The UPAS is creatively adaptive in its design. It operationalizes progress evaluations by offering a method for longitudinal appraisal involving the establishment of a "learning curve." This allows the program to chart percentage of items achieved within a particular period of time that matches, exceeds, or departs from preintervention expectancies. The UPAS is also flexible, in that it allows one to modify items in numerous ways. For example, assessors can exclude items, break-

---

Table 4-4 Sample Preacademic and Self-Social Tasks from the UPAS

Preacademic	Self-Social
Discrimination	*Play*
46. ©match objects	31. interact appropriately with materials
47. ©match lottos	⊚ a. in group activities
48. ©sort pegs/blocks	⊚ b. in 1:1 or small group
49. ©sort on 2 dimensions	⊚ c. during free choice
50. ©match colors	32. interact with peers
51. ©# COLORS SELECTED (of 6)	⊚ a. low social behavior
	⊚ b. high social behavior
	33. claim and defend possessions
	⊚ a. physically
	⊚ b. verbally

Uniform Performance Assessment System (UPAS)

Author(s):   N.G. Haring, O.R. White, E.B. Edgar, J.Q. Affleck, A.H. Hayden
Year: 1981
Publisher: The Psychological Corporation
Address: 555 Academic Court, San Antonio, TX 78204
Phone: 1 (800) 228-0752
Cost: $100+

Assessment type: Criterion-referenced; functional, curriculum-based analysis of adaptive skills, instructional needs, and atypical behaviors of moderately and severely handicapped.
Age range: 0-72 months.
Domains/Contexts: 5 domains (250 items): preacademic/fine motor, communication, social/self-help, gross motor, and behavior management; wheelchair needs, atypical behavior patterns, developmental reinforcement levels.
Handicap options: Functional emphasis incorporates any handicap modification in stimulus dimensions and/or response modes; "learning curve" facilitates intraindividual comparisons.
Curricular links: Functional sequences generate IEP goals directly; instructional needs assessed and strategies rated (e.g., prompting, shaping); assessment-programming-evaluation linked.
Scoring/Sample: +, −; differential scoring for percentage of items adapted or nonadapted; notations for types of item modifications used.
Technical support: Reliability and validity are excellent, using methods appropriate for criterion-referenced scales.
Training needed: Extensive clinical and/or teaching experience with moderately and severely handicapped children and practice with UPAS.

Critique:
- Sensitive to small increments of change.
- Separates "diagnostic" tasks from purposeful, instructional behaviors.
- Exemplary as a formative child progress/program evaluation measure.
- Complex to use except in well-established programs.
- Protocol forms are poorly designed and complicated.

Citation:
Hanson, M.J. (1985). Analysis of the effects of early intervention services for infants and toddlers with moderate to severe handicaps. *Topics in Early Childhood Special Education, 5*(2), 36–51.

Autism Screening Instrument for Educational Planning (ASIEP)

Author(s): D.A. Krug, J.R. Arick, P.J. Almond
Year: 1980
Publisher: PRO-ED
Address: 5341 Industrial Oak Blvd., Austin, TX 78735
Phone: (512) 451-3246
Cost: $194

Assessment type: Norm-based multidimensional battery; multisource data on child functioning: atypical behavior, language interaction, skills, and learning rate.

Age range: 18 months to 35 years.

Domains/Contexts: Consists of 5 instruments: Autism Behavior Checklist, sample of vocal behavior, interaction assessment, Educational Assessment of Functional Skills, and prognosis of learning rate; surveys multiple domains, including language, body concept, imitation, in-seat behavior, sensory, relating, body/objectives, social, and self-help.

Handicap options: Multisource assessment using naturalistic observation, elicited performance, clinical judgment ratings, and trial teaching.

Curricular links: Educational Assessment of Functional Skills is a criterion-referenced probe to screen and identify acquisition of early developmental skills that suggest entry points for more comprehensive developmental curricular evaluation.

Scoring/Sample: Percentile ranks and cut-off scores.

Technical support: Normed on 1,049 individuals: 172 = autistic, 423 = severe mental retardation, 254 = emotionally disturbed, 100 = deaf/blind, 100 = normal (ABC scale only).

Training needed: Thorough familiarity with the different scales and criteria; can be used by many team professionals.

Critique:
- The only comprehensive assessment battery for autistic children.
- Contains treatment-based elements but not a curriculum.
- Excellent comparative norms and standardizations for scales.
- Compatible with curriculum for atypical children.
- Needs wider marketing and distribution to the field.

Citation:
Volkmar, F.R., Cicchetti, D.V., Dykens, E., Sparrow, S.S., Leckman, J.F., & Cohen, D.J. (1988). An evaluation of the Autism Behavior Checklist. *Journal of Autism and Developmental Disorders, 18*(1), 81–97.

ing tasks down into smaller parts, using prosthetic devices to foster optimal performance, and adding new items to subscales to reflect nontargeted skills that are important to an individual child's development. These adapted items can also be used to measure progress if the child at a later time no longer needs to use the adaptation to complete a task.

Poor or nonexistent field testing and research bases are the failings of most new handicap-specific devices. In contrast, in design and development, the UPAS is a model for other similar measures. It has excellent reliability and validity, determined through procedures appropriate for criterion-referenced instruments. Analyses of stability and predictive validity that have been conducted support the scale's confident use with moderately and severely impaired children. Moreover, the authors offer suggestions regarding the incorporation of the UPAS into various natural field-based program evaluation arrangements (e.g., multiple baseline, matched subjects, control-contrast group).

The UPAS is curriculum-based and adaptive. Its construction and content embody the best of handicap-sensitive assessments with a program planning focus. Professionals are advised to evaluate the UPAS for use in their programs, given its clear link between prescriptive and progress evaluation aims.

The *Autism Screening Instrument for Educational Planning* (ASIEP) (Krug, Arick, & Almond, 1980) is the only comprehensive noncurricular assessment bat-

---

Table 4-5   Selected Items from the Autism Behavior Checklist and the Educational Assessment of Functional Skills

Autism Behavior Checklist	Educational Assessment of Functional Skills
1. Whirls self for long periods of time.	Receptive Language Subscale:
2. Strong reactions to changes in routine.	1. Turns to vocalize when cellophane is crinkled nearby.
3. Flaps hands.	2. Comes when called.
4. Covers ears at many sounds.	3. Gives object on request.
5. Echoes questions or statements.	Body Concept Subscales:
6. Stares into space for long periods.	1. Claps to imitate.
7. Developmental delay identified prior to 30 months of age.	2. Touches body parts named.
	3. Imitates hopping.
8. Actively avoids eye contact.	Expressive Language Subscale:
	1. Says "cookie" to get desired object.
9. Has no social smile.	2. Gives own name when asked.
10. Has "special abilities" in one area.	3. Gives age when asked.

Source: Reprinted from *Autism Screening Instrument for Educational Planning* by D.A. Krug, J.R. Arick, P.J. Almond, 1980, Austin, TX: PRO-ED. Copyright 1980 by PRO-ED. Reprinted by permission.

tery for young autistic children. It fills a great need in the field for an integrated system that is flexible, yet technically adequate in providing a multidimensional appraisal of the functional competencies of autistic preschoolers (see Table 4-5). While not a curriculum itself, the ASIEP provides a clear probing of curricular domains in its component for the educational assessment of functional skills; furthermore, it is compatible with the Individualized Assessment and Treatment curriculum of Schopler and Reichler (1979) (see Chapter 6).

The ASIEP is a system that is both technically and clinically solid. Most of the relevant studies have been conducted on the Autism Behavior Checklist component, which has been standardized on 1,049 individuals, including autistic, severely mentally retarded, emotionally disturbed, and deaf/blind individuals. The standardization shows a clear clinical distinction between the autistic children and the other diagnostic groups. The ASIEP enables the clinician to assess children through a variety of means, including structured performance assessments, naturalistic observations, clinical judgment ratings, and trial teaching, using prompts and demonstrations to evaluate learning rate. Its flexible but standardized multisource format provides an important adaptive feature, enabling the diagnostic specialist to obtain as accurate assessment of the "untestable" atypical child as possible.

The authors are to be commended for developing a highly useful yet technically sound system that integrates several critical assessment components. While clinically useful, some of the components are judged to be cumbersome to use and score (i.e., interaction assessment). On balance, however, the ASIEP will be an invaluable addition to those programs that enroll young atypical children for diagnostic and programming purposes.

Adaptive procedures include the sources from which information is collected about children and families. Clinical judgment methods gather the impressions of several adults across several settings about the functional capabilities of young handicapped children. This provides social input regarding the real-life capacity for children to interact with people and objects in their world, despite their disabilities. In this way, clinical impressions can supplement and even challenge the results of narrower and less flexible forms of assessment. Thus, judgment-based assessments are another form of handicap-sensitive assessment.

Perceptions of Developmental Status (PODS) (Bagnato & J.T. Neisworth, 1989) is a clinical judgment-based assessment instrument that allows each member of an interdisciplinary early-intervention team, including the parents and medical and educational professionals, to "cross-talk" and negotiate decisions, through a common denominator, about the developmental and behavioral competencies and service delivery needs of handicapped infants, preschoolers, and families. PODS provides a series of functional rating scales that enables team members to synthesize results from various measures and people, to appraise status and progress over time, and to detect subtle changes in important, yet difficult-to-assess, domains of functioning. In short, the PODS and its related product, the Child Services Indicator, synchronizes team assessment, service delivery decision making, and progress/program evaluation.

Perceptions of Developmental Status (PODS)

Author(s):	S.J. Bagnato, J.T. Neisworth
Year:	·1989
Publisher:	American Guidance Service
Address:	Publisher's Building, PO Box 99, Circle Pines, MN 55014
Phone:	1 (800) 328-2560
Cost:	$40 +

Assessment type: Judgment-based; contrasts multiple perceptions of a child's functional capabilities to promote interdisciplinary team decision making about program and to service delivery goals and options.

Age range: 12 to 72 months.

Domains/Contexts: 5 domains and 19 subdomains: communication, sensorimotor, physical, self-regulation, cognitive, self-social, general development; observations in natural settings.

Handicap options: Reliance on clinical judgment and naturalistic observation of adaptive behaviors; focuses upon functional responses to the environment; functional ratings versus age-level comparisons for mild-to-severe problems.

Curricular links: Multidomain organization compatible with curriculum structure; direct translation of assessment levels to service delivery/programming needs.

Scoring/Sample: Likert ratings on 5-point scales for each subdomain: 5 (normal), 4 (borderline), 3 (mild), 2 (moderate), 1 (severe)—subdomain and $\bar{x}$ domain scores; team member ratings across several situations; indexes of percentage of typical functioning.

Technical support: Test-retest and inter-rater reliability for various diagnoses and concurrent validity data on $N = 300+$ preschoolers in preschool, special education, day care, and hospital clinic settings.

Training needed: Thorough reading of manual and direct knowledge of the child through observation.

Critique:

- Synchronizes noncategorical team assessment and program planning.
- Detects discrepancies among raters across settings.
- Documents generalization of skills beyond training context.
- Facilitates the synthesis of all forms of assessment on same continuum.
- Structures subjective impressions about child status and needs.
- One component of System to Plan Early Childhood Services (SPECS).

Citations:

Bagnato, S.J., Kontos, S., & Neisworth, J.T. (1987). Integrated day care as special education: Profiles of programs and children. *Topics in Early Childhood Special Education,* 7(1), 28–47.

Bagnato, S.J. (1984). Team congruence in developmental diagnosis and intervention: Comparing clinical judgment and child performance measures. *School Psychology Review, 13,* 7–16.

Bagnato, S.J., & Neisworth, J.T. (1985b). Assessing young handicapped children: Clinical judgment versus developmental performance scales. *International Journal of Partial Hospitalization. 3*(1), 13–21.

The PODS is the primary child appraisal instrument in a complete package called the System to Plan Early Childhood Services (SPECS). It surveys status and capabilities in six domains and 19 subdomains, including a global rating of "general development" (see Exhibit 4-14). Professionals often use data from norm-referenced and curriculum-referenced infant and preschool instruments, observations, and questionnaires to estimate child functional levels; the PODS thus translates diverse data into terms that are common with those of other team members. The rating items are presented in Likert format, with a 1 (severe) to 3 (mild) to 5 (normal) functional ratings. Each point on the Likert scale coincides with an operational definition that serves as a referent for the rater. The rater need only match one of the given descriptors on each item to the child's behavior to determine the functional level. The scores for each item can be summed for a total score, or mean subscores for the six developmental domains can be created in order to provide a profile of the child's perceived functional status. Comparative profiles about children from each team member can be created on a PODS profile sheet in order to evaluate team congruence in assessment.

The original edition of the PODS (Bagnato, J.T. Neisworth, & Eaves, 1977) was studied to establish its utility as a monitor of perceived child status and progress and to appraise the reliability of the rating scale with preschool children (Bag-

Exhibit 4–14 Self-Control and Normalcy Subdomains from the PODS

Self-Control: Capability to regulate own behavior involving understanding of what is required in social situations, to comply with directions, and, eventually, to start and stop own behavior without constant guidance or control from adults.

- Typically controls own behavior as well as or better than children of the same age. 5
- Usually, but inconsistently, shows self-control skills expected of similar-age children. 4
- Sometimes is able to control own behavior, but shows observable problems in how to act in social situations, comply with adult commands, and regulate behavior without guidance/discipline. 3
- Only occasionally can control own behavior; others must constantly supervise and discipline the child. 2
- Constant supervision and control are necessary; the child rarely shows any skill in self-regulation. 1

Normalcy: Degree to which a child's physical appearance and/or behavior are socially agreeable to others in normal (mainstreamed) situations.

- Appearance and behavior are judged to be normal and offer no problems for integrating in everyday situations. 5
- Appearance and behavior are usually judged to be socially acceptable. 4
- Appearance and behavior are sometimes judged to be acceptable, but many people would object to integration into normal (mainstreamed) settings. 3
- Objections are raised so frequently concerning the child's appearance or behavior that involvement in normal settings is unlikely. 2
- Appearance or behavior is so abnormal that it prevents integration into normal settings. 1

nato, 1984; Bagnato, J.T. Neisworth, & Eaves, 1978). Results revealed the PODS to be sensitive enough to detect child status and progress when used by parents, teachers, and interdisciplinary team members and when completed independently to determine congruence. Inter-rater reliability was found to be .96 when the ratings of preschool teachers and psychologists were compared and .77 when the ratings of four team members were compared on 54 multihandicapped preschoolers. These data confirmed the hypothesis that standardized clinical judgments can provide valuable data for monitoring child status and progress. On the basis of these preliminary results, the authors concluded that the PODS held promise as a reliable method of standardizing and profiling clinical impressions of significant adults who work with preschool children. Concurrent validity data were also collected, comparing the PODS completed by the occupational therapist, the Bayley Scales of Infant Development/Gesell Developmental Schedules completed by the psychologist, and the Developmental Profile completed by the mother. Intercorrelations were as follows: PODS versus BSID/GDS: .89; PODS versus DP: .66.

Recent research has begun on the revised edition of the PODS (Bagnato et al., 1987; Bagnato & J.T. Neisworth, 1987). The authors studied the program and developmental/behavioral characteristics of both normal and handicapped preschoolers enrolled in 13 HCEEP-funded, integrated day care programs across the United States ($N = 45$). The Perceptions of Developmental Status (PODS) and the Developmental Profile (Alpern, Boll, & Shearer, 1984) were used in this descriptive and concurrent validity research. Both scales were completed independently by teachers, case managers, and other team members. Interscale agreement was .83 for the handicapped and .75 for the nonhandicapped groups. Both scales revealed congruent results in estimating both the functional levels and diagnostic categories for the groups. No significant differences in total or cluster scores were evident for either group of day care children. The results supported the reliability and validity of the clinical perceptions of diverse day care staff, the screening instruments themselves, and the functional utility of clinical judgment sources of data in monitoring child status and progress.

PODS is also functionally appropriate for a child in the kindergarten-transition age range, the area examined in the next section of close-ups.

KINDERGARTEN TRANSITION

Multidimensional psychoeducational assessment batteries have become prominent in recent years. The objective is to compare cognitive and learning or achievement abilities of children in the same norm group. The *Woodcock-Johnson Psychoeducational Battery* (WJPEB) (Woodcock & Johnson, 1977) is the best and most widely used example of this recent trend in instrument development. The preschool cluster of the WJPEB effectively fulfills the needs of assessment of preschool-to-school transition skills in various cognitive and learning subareas.

Woodcock-Johnson Psychoeducational Battery (WJPEB)—Preschool Cluster

Author(s): R.W. Woodcock, M.B. Johnson
Year: 1977
Publisher: DLM/Teaching Resources
Address: PO Box 4000, One DLM Park, Allen, TX 75002
Phone: 1 (800) 527-4747
Cost: $175 +

Assessment type: Norm-based; multidimensional assessment of cognitive, conceptual, and preacademic learning abilities.

Age range: 3-8 + years (usually administered for age 3 through Grade 1).

Domains/Contexts: 6 subtests: picture vocabulary, spatial relations, memory for sentences, visual-auditory learning, blending, and quantitative concepts.

Handicap options: Flip-card, easel format; motivating tasks; varied response modes (e.g., pointing) and item presentations (e.g., verbal rehearsal) are instructionally relevant and adaptable to mild disabilities.

Curricular links: Hierarchical task order and processes sampled are important for K-transition programming, particularly such prerequisites as memory, letter-word recognition, dictation, calculation.

Scoring/Sample: Basal-ceiling criteria and pass-fail scoring percentiles; grade and age equivalents; standard scores; instructional ranges, cluster and individual subtest scores available.

Technical support: Norm group $N = 4,732$ individuals (ages 3-8); reliability and predictive and concurrent validity are adequate; independence of subscales is not supported.

Training needed: Supervised training and experience regarding administration, scoring, and interpretation.

Critique:
- Excellent cognitive and preacademic measurement of learning abilities.
- Preschool cluster is clinically valuable but has not been the focus in research studies; 1989 revision.
- Provides diagnostic and achievement/instructional data on same norm group.
- Valuable for K-transition and high-risk LD assessments.

Citation:
McGrew, K. (1986). *Clinical interpretation of the WJ Tests of Cognitive Ability.* Orlando, FL: Grune & Stratton.

The WJPEB departs from a strict developmental approach to assessment, yet combines hierarchical arrangement of tasks with a wide sampling of basic concepts. The preschool cluster of the WJPEB appraises six cognitive areas: picture vocabulary, spatial relations, memory for sentences, visual-auditory learning, blending, and quantitative concepts. Also, six subareas from the achievement sections are sampled, including letter-word identification, applied problems, dictation, science, social studies, and humanities. The effective age range of these assessments is 3 to 6 years (Grade 1).

One of the most creative and clinically useful dimensions of the preschool cluster is the appraisal of prereading skills. Memory for sentences, visual-auditory learning, and letter-word identification provide a basic assessment of both process and product abilities. For example, through the letter-word subtest one can observe

Exhibit 4–15   Sample from the Visual-Auditory Learning Subtest of the WJPEB

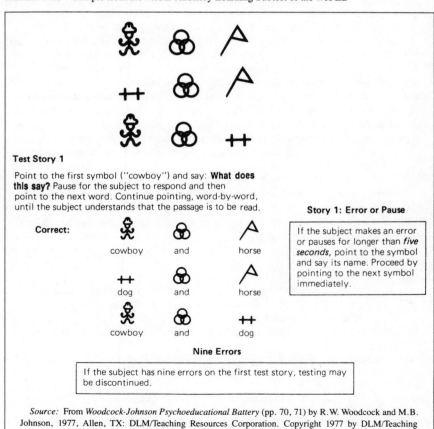

Test Story 1

Point to the first symbol ("cowboy") and say: **What does this say?** Pause for the subject to respond and then point to the next word. Continue pointing, word-by-word, until the subject understands that the passage is to be read.

Story 1: Error or Pause

If the subject makes an error or pauses for longer than *five seconds*, point to the symbol and say its name. Proceed by pointing to the next symbol immediately.

Correct:

cowboy   and   horse

dog   and   horse

cowboy   and   dog

Nine Errors

If the subject has nine errors on the first test story, testing may be discontinued.

Source: From *Woodcock-Johnson Psychoeducational Battery* (pp. 70, 71) by R.W. Woodcock and M.B. Johnson, 1977, Allen, TX: DLM/Teaching Resources Corporation. Copyright 1977 by DLM/Teaching Resources Corporation. Reprinted by permission.

the child's recognition of basic forms. The visual-auditory task uses a rebus format to analyze whether the child can recognize and remember words when paired with graphic symbols and then recall them by reading passages composed of the symbols (see Exhibit 4-15). This sample offers a possible predictor of the preschool-kindergarten child's reading needs and potential for progress. For the assessment of preschoolers at risk for learning disabilities, this represents an important dimension.

Within the field of early childhood special education, the WJPEB appears to be seriously underused. In fact, in the two most recent surveys of instrument use in preschool psychology and special education (Johnson & Beauchamp, 1987; NASP/APA Special Interest Preschool Group, 1987), the WJPEB was not even reported or rated by respondents! Yet the WJPEB is a notably invaluable instrument for use with young exceptional children who need to be evaluated for placement in traditional kindergarten, diagnostic kindergarten, and developmental kindergarten settings. It is especially important in identifying precursors of learning disabilities and in offering general targets for program planning when coupled with various basic concept and kindergarten instructional materials. The 1988 revision of the WJPEB is an important advance.

Criterion-referenced instruments can be particularly valuable in the comprehensive evaluation of 4- to 5-year-old children who are educationally at-risk. The *Cognitive Skills Assessment Battery* (CSAB) (Boehm & Slater, 1974) is one of the oldest and best of these diagnostic/prescriptive transition scales. The CSAB was designed to appraise and profile systematically the competencies of prekindergarten- and kindergarten-age children. The competencies included in the battery represent those that were reviewed by curriculum specialists and teachers in the field as most predictive of success in kindergarten and first grade.

The CSAB broadly samples skills in six major domains: (1) orientation toward the environment, (2) coordination, (3) discrimination, (4) memory, (5) comprehension, and (6) concept formation (see Table 4-6). Flexible and instructionally useful methods of scoring responses at various levels of knowledge acquisition are available. For example, on a language task, the assessor can score whether the child can identify (1) or label (2) pictured concepts (e.g., round, red, swimming) or has neither capability (N). The scale is very motivating in its easel, flip-card format and colored pictures.

Field-test data are available on $N = 898$ children for fall prekindergarten and kindergarten evaluations. Percentages of children responding correctly and incorrectly to each item (for low and middle SES at the prekindergarten and kindergarten levels) serve as a rough determination of the standing of individual children on the content.

The CSAB was designed after a content review of curricular materials during the preschool-to-kindergarten/first grade transition period. For this reason, it is particularly valuable as a diagnostic/prescriptive, criterion-referenced instrument for this age range. When a question arises regarding "achievement" abilities in preschool children, the CSAB, when used as part of a larger battery, enables diagnos-

Table 4-6 Competency Areas Included in the CSAB

Orientation Toward Environment	Coordination	Discrimination	Memory	Comprehension and Concept Formation
Basic information	Large muscle coordination	Color identification	Auditory memory-meaningful words	Number knowledge
Body parts	Visual-motor coordination	Shape identification	Auditory memory-sentence recall	Letter naming
Response during assessment		Symbol and letter discrimination	Visual memory	Vocabulary
		Visual-auditory discrimination	Picture and story comprehension	Information from pictures
		Auditory discrimination	Letter naming	Picture comprehension
			Number knowledge	Story comprehension
			Multiple directions	Multiple directions

Cognitive Skills Assessment Battery (CSAB)

Author(s): A.M. Boehm, B.S. Slater
Year: 1974
Publisher: Teachers College Press
Address: Teachers College, Columbia University, New York, NY
Cost: $20+

Assessment type: Criterion-referenced, curriculum-based assessment of pre-requisite preschool and kindergarten learning abilities.
Age range: 4-5 years.
Domains/Contexts: 20 subdomains within 5 domains: orientation toward environment, coordination, discrimination, memory, comprehension, and concept formation.
Handicap options: Nonspecific; offers continuum scoring option for functional level of response; can be modified to accommodate yes-no pointing or multiple-choice modes.
Curricular links: Learning processes are typical of the content emphasized in K programs.
Scoring/Sample: 3 levels: 2 = gives answer verbally/labels, 1 = identifies answer, N = shows neither skill; provides percentages of children responding at each level.
Technical support: N = 898 prekindergarten and kindergarten children (low and middle SES) in urban, suburban, and rural settings; representative content validity.
Training needed: Minimal; familiarity with materials and format/primarily for teacher/aide use.

Critique:
- Motivating and informal measure of prerequisite learning abilities.
- Details strengths and weaknesses to target curriculum objectives.
- General normative comparisons complement its criterion referencing.

ticians to determine ability-achievement discrepancies clinically and to offer programming targets.

The *Bracken Basic Concept Scale* (BBCS) (Bracken, 1984) is both a diagnostic tool and a comprehensive instructional program for the 2½- to 8-year-old child. It is unique in that it targets 258 concepts that are important content prerequisites for developing thinking skills in transition-age children. Moreover, it combines both norm-referenced and criterion-referenced elements to link assessment and instruction effectively for the young child with mild disabilities, particularly those that may be precursors of later learning disabilities. Developmental school psychologists and preschool-to-school transition teams are well advised to include the BBCS as a crucial addition to their prescriptive assessment batteries.

Bracken Basic Concept Scale (BBCS)

Author(s):   B.A. Bracken
Year: 1984
Publisher: The Psychological Corporation
Address: 555 Academic Court, San Antonio, TX 78204
Phone: 1 (800) 228-0752
Cost: $98+

Assessment type: Norm-based; hybrid norm- and criterion-referenced measure to diagnose concept deficiencies and to plan instructional programs, using the Bracken Concept Development program.
Age range: 2½-8 years.
Domains/Contexts: 258 concepts in 11 subtest categories: color, letter identification, numbers/counting, comparisons, shapes, direction/position, social/emotional, size, texture/material, quantity, time/sequence.
Handicap options: Multiple-choice format and pointing response is appropriate for preschoolers with communication problems; development research with matched deaf and hearing children ($N = 34$).
Curricular links: Items hierarchically arranged within concept categories so that instructional objectives can be identified and linked with the Bracken Concept Development program.
Scoring/Sample: Percentile ranks and standard scores for subtests, composite scores, and concept age equivalents; 20-30 minute administration time.
Technical support: $N = 1,109$ children; concurrent and diagnostic validity studies are highly supportive of the scale.
Training needed: Appropriate for use by school psychologists, teachers, speech/language clinicians, and educational diagnosticians; thorough reading of manual and practice with standardized procedures.

Critique:
- Represents the most detailed concept scale available.
- Combines technical adequacy and high instructional relevance.
- Links to matched "concept curriculum."
- Hierarchically arranged concepts offer a developmental base.
- Can be considered a preschool-kindergarten "achievement test."

Citation:
Bracken, B.A. (1987). Limitations of preschool instruments and standards for minimal levels of technical adequacy. *Journal of Psychoeducational Assessment, 4,* 313–326.

Exhibit 4–16 Sample Concept Items in the BBCS

IV. COMPARISONS   Subtotal _____

You may record the child's response by circling the frame number of the incorrect response

Item	Score		Response			
1. which fruit are **different**	① ⓪	1	2	3	4
2. which person is reading something **other than a book**	① ⓪	1	2	3	4
3. which boats are **alike**	① ⓪	1	2	3	4
4. which balloons are the **same**	① ⓪	1	2	3	4
5. which boxes are **not the same**	① ⓪	1	2	3	4
6. which cans are of **equal** size	① ⓪	1	2	3	4
7. which hats are **identical**	① ⓪	1	2	3	4

VII. SOCIAL/EMOTIONAL   Subtotal _____

You may record the child's response by circling the frame number of the incorrect response

Item	Score		Response			
1. the **man**	① ⓪	1	2	3	4
2. the **boy**	① ⓪	1	2	3	4
3. the **girl**	① ⓪	1	2	3	4
4. which child is **sick**	① ⓪	1	2	3	4
5. who is **angry**	① ⓪	1	2	3	4
6. which child is **happy**	① ⓪	1	2	3	4
7. who is **sad**	① ⓪	1	2	3	4
8. the **brothers**	① ⓪	1	2	3	4
9. which child is **afraid**	① ⓪	1	2	3	4

Source: Reproduced by permission from the *Bracken Basic Concept Scale*. Copyright © 1984, 1986 by The Psychological Corporation. All rights reserved.

Because the BBCS focuses on skills, concepts, and objectives that detail "transition" targets, it can be used to guide a team in determining whether individual children are in need of a broad range of special services that will promote mainstreaming opportunities (see Exhibit 4-16). In addition, in content and structure, it allows teams to detect basic concept deficiencies, provide tailored instruction, and evaluate child progress and program effectiveness. Through the use of percentile ranks, standard subtest and composite scores, and "concept ages," the BBCS characterizes concept knowledge in comparative terms and then prescribes objectives for instruction based upon this appraisal.

While not an adaptive instrument, the BBCS uses an easel multiple-choice format that only requires the child to point to the correct response. This format allows various response modes to be accommodated; thus, the scale incorporates features that allow modifications. This is particularly valuable for the child with communication disorders.

McCarthy Scales of Children's Abilities (MSCA)

Author(s):   D. McCarthy
Year: 1972
Publisher: The Psychological Corporation
Address: 555 Academic Court, San Antonio, TX 78204
Phone: 1 (800) 228-0752
Cost: $300 +

Assessment type: Norm-based; diagnoses degree of cognitive and neuro-developmental deficits.

Age range: 2½-8½ years.

Domains/Contexts: 18 subdomains within 6 global scales: verbal, perceptual-performance, quantitative, general cognitive, memory, and motor.

Handicap options: Minimal; not appropriate for children with significant language disorders or the severely handicapped, due to GCI limit of 50.

Curricular links: Samples many prerequisite memory, information-processing, perceptual-motor, and conceptual skills that are commonly emphasized in preschool and K programs.

Scoring/Sample: Developmental age scores for each subtest and standard scores.

Technical support: N = 1,032 children; excellent reliability and validity data.

Training needed: Extensive supervised training and experience; requires use and interpretation by a psychologist.

Critique:
- Primarily measures neuropsychological and learning processes.
- Excellent bridge between preschool and school emphases.
- To be used cautiously with language-disordered children as an "IQ" measure.
- Needs restandardization based on recent census.

Citations:

Naglieri, J.A. (1980). Comparison of McCarthy General Cognitive Index and WISC-R IQ for educable mentally retarded, learning disabled, and normal children. *Psychological Reports, 47,* 591–596.

Naglieri, J.A. (1985). Normal children's performance on the McCarthy Scales, Kaufman Assessment Battery, and Peabody Individual Achievement Test. *Journal of Psychoeducational Assessment, 3:* 123–129.

The BBCS is highly motivating, simple to use, economical, and brief (20-30 minutes). It offers crucial diagnostic-prescriptive data that are both clinically and educationally purposeful. The author is to be commended for developing a technically strong, narrow-focus measure that blends assessment and program dimensions so well.

The *McCarthy Scales of Children's Abilities* (MSCA) (McCarthy, 1972) is conceptualized as a measure of cognitive functioning in preschool children. However, ongoing research and clinical work with the instrument suggest that it may be better viewed as an effective measure of neurodevelopmental and learning readiness that taps various prerequisite functions, such as attention, memory, information processing, language, and neuromotor function (see Exhibit 4-17). Results with handicapped children on the MSCA often are much lower than those on the SBIS and WISC-R intellectual scales (Sattler, 1982).

The MSCA covers the 2½- to 8½-year age range, sampling strengths and weaknesses across 18 subtests and six global scales: verbal, perceptual-performance, quantitative, memory, motor, and general cognitive. Each subtest is scored with a mean of 50 and standard deviation of 10; its general cognitive index (GCI) (composite) has a mean of 100 and standard deviation of 16. The scale was normed on 1,032 children and stratified on multiple variables. Reliability and validity data are excellent for individual diagnosis. Analysis of neurodevelopmental strengths and weaknesses is aided by the derivation of developmental age scores for each subtest and the GCI.

The MSCA should be used cautiously with language-disordered preschoolers and those who are observed to be at high risk for learning disabilities due to attention, neuromotor, communication, and information processing problems. The caution stems from the fact that the GCI on the scale underestimates the overall abilities of learning-disabled children and classifies them as mildly retarded. For diagnostic purposes, diagnosticians are admonished to convert each major subscale to IQ equivalents so that, clinically, a profile results and characterizes discrepancies in functioning. In this manner, the MSCA becomes a practical measure of neurodevelopmental functioning in such subtle areas as memory for both meaningful and nonmeaningful information (i.e., Verbal Memory I and II; numerical memory).

As an important measure of transition skills, the MSCA enables team members to evaluate many practical precursors for learning disabilities and higher-level language learning disorders (e.g., word retrieval). A content analysis of the subskills sampled offers clinicians diagnostic information that can be readily translated into programming objectives that target school readiness concerns. The *Beginning Milestones* curriculum provides a good complementary match with the MSCA.

The *Pictorial Test of Intelligence* (PTI) (French, 1964) is designed as a measure of general intellectual functioning for both normal and physically handicapped children, even though it was not standardized on physically impaired children. The

Exhibit 4–17   Subtests and Scoring Form for the MSCA

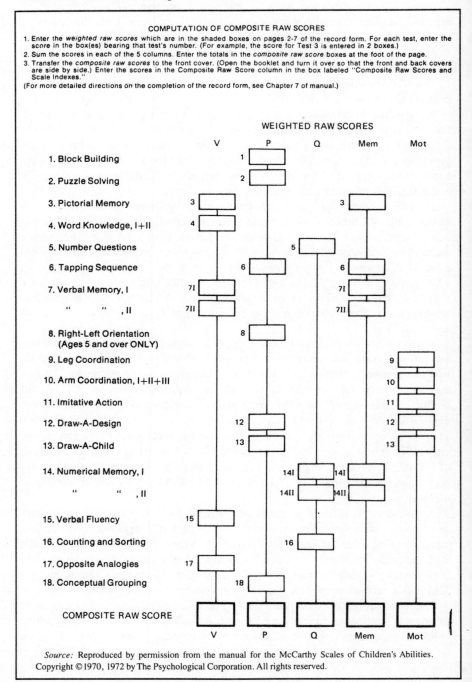

Pictorial Test of Intelligence (PTI)

Author(s):   J.L. French
Year: 1964
Publisher: Riverside Publishing Company
Address: 8420 Bryn Mawr Avenue, Chicago, IL 60631
Cost: $90+

Assessment type: Norm-based; surveys general cognitive abilities through comprehension of pictured concepts by a nonverbal gestural response.

Age range: 3-9 years.

Domains/Contexts: 3 product subtests: picture vocabulary, information and comprehension, size and number; 3 process subtests: form discrimination, similarities, and immediate recall.

Handicap options: Requires no verbal response from child and allows many responses to accommodate physically handicapped children (e.g., eye localization, head or light pointer, yes-no, multiple-choice, gesture); oversized picture cards and tilted easel format help children with neuromotor and visual problems.

Curricular links: Samples the categories of preacademic concepts stressed in kindergarten curricula.

Scoring/Sample: Mental ages for each subtest, percentiles, short form scores, and deviation IQ.

Technical support: N = 1,830 children representative of United States in 1960 census; field testing but no norms for physically handicapped, none included in norm group; excellent reliability and validity.

Training needed: Should be given by a psychologist or with supervision.

Critique:
- Superb nonverbal adaptive measure of cognitive skills.
- The best designed adaptive measure to date.
- Limitations due to dated norms and black line, repetitive pictures.
- Items increase in difficulty but are not developmental.
- Is an indispensible measure that must be restandardized.

Citation:
Sawyer, R.N. (1974). A factor analytic study of the PTI. *Journal of Educational and Psychological Measurement, 39,* 613–623.

Exhibit 4–18 Sample "Product" Subtest from the PTI

Information and Comprehension

Item	Label	T	L	B	R		Item	Label	T	L	B	R	
I-1a	Cuts	T	L	B	R	R	I-11	W/Broom	T	L	B	R	L
I-1b	Presses Clothes	T	L	B	R	T	I-12	Run fastest	T	L	B	R	L
I-2	Pour	T	L	B	R	L	I-13	Milk people	T	L	B	R	R
I-3	Temperature	T	L	B	R	L	I-14	Heaviest	T	L	B	R	B
I-4a	Keeps dry	T	L	B	R	T	I-15	Carry most	T	L	B	R	L
I-4b	Used to fight	T	L	B	R	L	I-16	Seal eats	T	L	B	R	L
I-5a	See	T	L	B	R	B	I-17	Real smallest	T	L	B	R	L
I-5b	Smell	T	L	B	R	B	I-18	Real biggest	T	L	B	R	T
I-6a	Grow ground	T	L	B	R	T							
I-6b	Eat most	T	L	B	R	T	I-19	Man always	T	L	B	R	B
I-7a	Man rides	T	L	B	R	L	I-20	Quarter past 8	T	L	B	R	T
I-7b	I carry	T	L	B	R	B	I-21	Paper made	T	L	B	R	R
I-8	G Y R B 3/4	+	+		−	+	I-22	Not eyelid	T	L	B	R	R
I-9	Butterfly	T	L	B	R	B	I-23	House must	T	L	B	R	R
I-10	W/Needle	T	L	B	R	L	I-24	Closest	T	L	B	R	L

I C TOTAL . . . .

Source: This exhibit is reproduced from the *Pictorial Test of Intelligence* by J.L. French, copyright © 1964 by The Riverside Publishing Company. Reprinted with permission of the Publisher. All rights reserved.

device's most adaptive feature is that alternative response modes can be incorporated into its structure, that is, formats for eye localization, head pointing, multiple-choice, and yes-no. The use of large picture cards allows the child to select one of four widely spaced pictured stimuli requested by the examiner and thus reveals the child's comprehension of specific areas of information.

The PTI covers the 3- to 8-year age range. It surveys six subdomain functions: (1) picture vocabulary, (2) form discrimination, (3) information and comprehension, (4) similarities, (5) size and number, and (6) immediate recall. Three subtests assess developing cognitive "processes," like form discrimination, and three subtests measure "product" information derived through general learning experiences in the environment, for example, information and comprehension (see Exhibit 4-18). Raw scores on the total test and on each of the subtests can be converted to mental ages, deviation IQs ($\bar{X} = 100, S = 16$), and percentiles by using the norm tables. Thus, a diagnostic profile of cognitive skills is provided.

The PTI is arguably the best standardized adaptive measure available, although the norms are now quite dated. The sample consisted of 1,830 children, ages 3 to 8, selected as representative of the United States population. The norm group was based on the 1960 census and stratified according to geographic region, community size, occupation level, and sex. Reliability and validity studies on the instrument attest to its adequacy for making instructional decisions.

The PTI should be considered one of the most useful and technically adequate specialized measures. Its excellent alternative response format makes it particularly valuable when assessing young cerebral palsied children, even though its structure is not strictly developmental in nature. The major drawback of the PTI concerns how quickly very young children can become bored and distracted by a format consisting of multiple black and white drawings and what is essentially a repetitive response (pointing) mode; periodic breaks are essential to temper these limitations. Finally, although the PTI results should be interpreted by a trained school psychologist, the scale can be effectively administered by teachers with supervision and used as a general guide to programming. It is an invaluable component of any adaptive diagnostic battery.

HOME

Perhaps the most widely used measure of the content, quality, and responsiveness of young children's home environments is the *Home Observation for Measurement of the Environment* (HOME) (Caldwell & Bradley, 1978). The reliability and validity of the HOME inventory for normal infants and preschoolers has been well-established, but research on its application in populations of developmentally disabled children is only now emerging. The HOME inventory is appropriate for

Home Observation for Measurement of the Environment (HOME)

Author(s):   B. Caldwell, R.A. Bradley
Year: 1978
Publisher: Author
Address: Human Development, University of Arkansas, Little Rock, AR
Cost: NA

Assessment type: Ecological; judgment-based analysis of the social and physical home environment.

Age range: 0-72 months (2 sections: 0-36 months, 36-72 months).

Domains/Contexts: 0-36 months: 45 items in 6 categories—emotional responsivity of mother, avoidance of restriction, environmental organization, play materials, maternal involvement, stimulation opportunities; 36-72 months: 80 items in 7 categories—stimulation, mature behavior, language environment, avoidance of restriction, pride/affection/thoughtfulness, masculine stimulation, independence.

Handicap options: Needs revision to be sensitive to the interactive needs and issues of handicapped children and parents.

Curricular links: Serves as a criterion-referenced tool to detect factors that require modification to optimize the home environment.

Scoring/Sample: Yes/no scoring; multiple raters are useful.

Technical support: One of the most widely researched early childhood devices; norm-based data for comparative purposes; adequate reliability and validity for screening purposes.

Training needed: Professional and paraprofessional use; good observational skills and sensitivity to family needs and family integrity and dignity, especially in harsh circumstances.

Critique:
• Premier ecological assessment scale.
• Essential in family service operations.
• Needs revision for cultural differences and handicap-appropriateness.

children from birth to 72 months. The first section (0- to 36-month age range) appraises such clusters of home ecological attributes as emotional and verbal responsivity of the mother, avoidance of restriction and punishment, organization of the physical and temporal environment, provision of adequate play materials, and opportunities for variety in daily stimulation. Similar dimensions are tapped in Section 2 for the 37- to 72-month-old child: provision of stimulation through equippunishment; pride, affection, and thoughtfulness; masculine stimulation; and independence from parent control) (see Exhibit 4-19).

Exhibit 4-19 Sample Items from the HOME Inventory

Ages 0-36 Months

Yes   No

I. Emotional and verbal responsivity of mother

1. Mother spontaneously vocalizes to child at least twice during visit (excluding scolding).

2. Mother responds to child's vocalizations with a verbal response.

3. Mother tells child the name of some object during visit or says name of person or object in a "teaching" style.

4. Mother's speech is distinct, clear, and audible.

5. Mother initiates verbal interchanges with observer—asks questions and makes spontaneous comments.

6. Mother expresses ideas freely and easily and uses statements of appropriate length for conversation (e.g., gives more than brief answers).

7. Mother permits child occasionally to engage in "messy" type of play.

8. Mother spontaneously praises child's qualities of behavior twice during visit.

9. When speaking of or to child, mother's voice conveys positive feeling.

10. Mother caresses or kisses child at least once during visit.

11. Mother shows some positive emotional responses to praise of child offered by visitor.

Ages 36-72 Months

Yes   No

II. Stimulation of mature behavior

22-29 Child is encouraged to learn the following:

22. Colors.

23. Shapes.

24. Patterned speech (nursery rhymes, prayers, songs, TV commercials, etc.).

25. The alphabet.

26. To tell time.

27. Spatial relationships (up, down, under, big, little, etc.).

28. Numbers.

29. To read a few words.

30. Tries to get child to pick up and put away toys after play session—without help.

31. Child is taught rules of social behavior which involve recognition of rights of others.

32. Parent teaches child some simple manners—to say, "Please," "Thank you," "I'm sorry."

33. Some delay of food gratification is demanded of the child, e.g., not to whine or demand food unless within ½ hour of mealtime.

Source: From *Home Observation for Measurement of the Environment* (pp. 130, 134) by B. Caldwell and R. A. Bradley, 1978, Little Rock, AR: University of Arkansas at Little Rock. Copyright 1978 by University of Arkansas at Little Rock. Reprinted by permission.

Parenting Stress Index (PSI)

Author(s):	R.R. Abidin
Year:	1983
Publisher:	CPPC
Address:	4 Conant Square, Brandon, VT 05733
Phone:	(802) 247-6871
Cost:	$30 +

Assessment type: Interactive/norm-based; diagnostic profile of perceived child and parent stress.

Age range: 1-60 + months.

Domains/Contexts: 13 subdomains within 4 major domains: total stress, child domain, parent domain, life stress.

Handicap options: Based on parent perceptions and report, thus providing social validity to the assessment and broadening the information base for treatment; 5-point rating scale of agreement-disagreement with item content.

Curricular links: Individual items bear directly on degree of life stress and disruption in the parent-child interaction. Items regarding mood, anxiety, and child misbehavior offer goals for the IFSP and therapy or counseling.

Scoring/Sample: Raw scores convert to percentile ranks for each domain and subdomain, yielding descriptive and diagnostic data and cut-offs of "pathology"; broad interview, self-report data.

Technical support: Norms/$N = 534$; adequate reliability and validity for diagnosis and prescription; separate norms for four diagnostic groups.

Training needed: Thorough familiarity with manual and procedure; good interviewing skills; should be administered to and monitored with parent by social worker or psychologist.

Critique:
- Effectively phrases items in "self-statements" to capitalize on parent emotions.
- Sensitively samples broad moods and behaviors.
- Should include parent-infant items to extend its use.
- Needs wider field testing with severely handicapped preschoolers and their parents.

Exhibit 4–20 Examples of Domains, Subdomains, and Items from the PSI

Domains	Sample Items
Child Domain Score Adaptability Acceptability Demandingness Mood Distract/Hyper Reinforces Parent	1. When my child wants something, my child usually keeps trying to get it. 2. My child is so active that it exhausts me. 3. My child appears disorganized and is easily distracted. 4. Compared to most, my child has more difficulty concentrating and paying attention. 5. My child will often stay occupied with a toy for more than 10 minutes. 6. My child wanders away much more than I expected.
Parent Domain Score Depression Attachment Restriction of Role Sense of Competence Social Isolation Relation to Spouse Parent Health	7. My child is much more active than I expected. 69. I find myself giving up more of my life to meet my children's needs than I ever expected. 70. I feel trapped by my responsibilities as a parent. 71. I often feel that my children's needs control my life. 62. It takes a long time for parents to develop close, warm feelings for their children. 63. I expected to have closer and warmer feelings for my child than I do and this bothers me.
Life Stress (Optional Scale)	

Source: From *Parenting Stress Index,* ed 2, by R.R. Abidin, 1986, Charlottesville, VA: Pediatric Psychology Press. Copyright 1986 by R.R. Abidin. Reprinted by permission.

The HOME is an effective tool for analyzing the stimulating quality of the home environment and for providing tangible guidelines about ways to intervene when necessary. Its adaptation for handicapped infants, preschoolers, and families is overdue.

Much interest is apparent in the design and development of instruments to assess the social and physical aspects of the child's environment. These are termed ecological assessment procedures; they include appraisals of family dynamics, parent-child interaction and stress, characteristics of the preschool classroom setting, and aspects of the home environment. With the federal mandate to devise family service plans, such family or ecological measures will be increasingly needed.

One of the most important and elusive ecological dimensions is analysis of family interactive stress. The *Parenting Stress Index* (PSI) (Abidin, 1983) is currently the best example of an economical, sensitive, and practical strategy for assessing

Family Needs Survey (FNS)

Author(s): D.B. Bailey, R.J. Simeonsson
Year: 1985
Publisher: Don Bailey, PhD
Address: Frank Porter Graham, Child Development Center,
University of North Carolina, Chapel Hill, NC 27514
Phone: (919) 962-5579
Cost: NA

Assessment type: Judgment-based; parent self-report of personal, social, child, economic, health, and family needs.
Age range: Infant-preschool.
Domains/Contexts: 6 clusters: needs for information, needs for support, explaining to others, community services, financial needs, family functioning; includes an open-ended "essay" question.
Handicap options: Parent reports of self and child needs.
Curricular links: Clearly identifies parent perceptions of the greatest areas of need and highlights goals for counseling, support, problem solving, and social service and medical interventions.
Scoring/Sample: 7-point Likert rating scale (1 = definitely do not need help, 2 = not sure, 3 = definitely need help).
Technical support: Preliminary field testing and technical studies on $N = 34$ two-parent families; moderate mother-father agreement and stability over 6-month period.
Training needed: Thorough knowledge of manual and parent interview skills, despite self-report format.

Critique:
- One of the best of the recently developed parent-family measures.
- Addresses areas of chronic need that affect family coping.
- Simple and readable.
- Answers immediately suggest intervention goals/options.
- Needs field testing with various "family" types (e.g., single parent, grandparent), child disabilities, and cultural groups.

Citation:
Bailey, D.B., & Simeonsson, R.J. (1988). Assessing needs of families with handicapped infants. *Journal of Special Education, 22*(1), 117–127.

this factor. The PSI allows the parents to rate their level of agreement with a series of "self-statements" reflecting the feelings, emotional turmoil, and images they experience in dealing with their child within the family context (see Exhibit 4-20). The self-statements are worded personally so that they tap the specific moods, anxieties, and expectations that most parents typically report (e.g., "My child is so active that it exhausts me," "I feel trapped by my responsibilities as a parent"). The PSI samples such stressful feelings related to the child as hyperactivity, demandingness, and the tendency to reinforce the parent. Similarly, it taps various parent perspectives, such as sense of competence, health, and relationship with the spouse. The PSI characterizes both the child's contribution to the problem as well as various parent factors that interact, resulting in a stressful life experience.

The PSI is a technically adequate instrument that can be used with confidence. Its use of parent perceptions allows it to have immediate and practical programming implications to plan family goals and reduce stress in various relationships. The system can be used to diagnose degree of interaction pathology or stress, to plan goals focused on reducing anxiety and promoting behavioral control and perhaps economical and social support, and finally to evaluate the impact of treatment. The PSI serves to link diagnosis and programming and progress evaluation, with the parent-child and family dynamics as the targets of treatment.

Caution should be observed, however, in the use of the scale with handicapped preschoolers. The PSI wording suggests that the scale is most effectively used with parents of learning-disabled and behaviorally and affectively disordered preschoolers. Use of the scale with more severely disabled children (e.g., autistic, cerebral palsied, and mentally retarded children) is judged to be least effective, since the items do not sample many of the unique attachment problems that stress the parents' relationships with their children. This caution operates despite the fact that the PSI was normed partially on 40 cerebral palsied children and their parents.

The author is to be commended for developing a practical tool that is both norm-referenced and loosely criterion-referenced in its content. The separate profiles on children and families with various problems—including hyperactivity, cerebral palsy, child abuse, developmental delay, as well as normal patterns—offer a precious comparative resource. The item content poignantly samples real-life parent perceptions and distress and thus holds tangible implications for therapy and counseling.

In response to the mandates of PL 99-457, researchers are beginning to design and field-test instruments that integrate parents and families into the early-intervention process. An important point to remember, however, is that such instruments must enable parents to "self-report" about their various needs in social, economic, health, personal, and child areas while also helping program personnel and the parents identify the best tailored program to meet both the infant's and the parents' needs. Such instruments are experimental at this time, few in number, and generally of undetermined technical adequacy; yet they represent an important development for the future in the early-intervention field.

Exhibit 4-21   Selected Self-Report Statements from the FNS

	No Help	Not Sure	Need Help
Needs for information			
1. I need more information about my child's condition or disability.	1	2	3
2. I need more information about how to handle my child's behavior.	1	2	3
Needs for support			
1. I need to have someone in my family that I can talk to about problems.	1	2	3
2. I need to have more friends that I can talk to.	1	2	3
Explaining to others			
1. I need more help in explaining my child's condition to either my parents or my spouse's parents.	1	2	3
2. My spouse needs help in understanding and accepting our child's condition.	1	2	3
Community services			
1. I need help in locating a doctor who understands me and my child's needs.	1	2	3
2. I need help locating a dentist who will see my child.	1	2	3
Financial needs			
1. I need more help in paying for expenses such as food, housing, medical care, clothing, or transportation.	1	2	3
2. I need more help in getting special equipment for my child's needs.	1	2	3
Family functioning			
1. Our family needs help in discussing problems and reaching solutions.	1	2	3
2. Our family needs help in learning how to support each other during difficult times.	1	2	3

Source: From *Family Needs Survey* by D. Bailey and R.J. Simeonsson, 1985, Chapel Hill, NC: University of North Carolina. Copyright 1985 by University of North Carolina. Reprinted by permission.

The *Family Needs Survey* (FNS) (Bailey & Simeonsson, 1985) is an important example of this type of instrument. As Exhibit 4-21 illustrates, its self-statements are organized into six clusters that tap the feelings and concerns of parents about themselves, their infant, and their family (e.g., "I need help locating a doctor who understands me and my child's needs," "I need to have more friends that I can talk to"). In a sense, these clusters focus the concerns of the parent and identify specific areas of pressing need. They are criterion-referenced—or more accurately, intervention-focused—so that they immediately suggest program goals and strategies ("I need more information about my child's condition or disability"). The

Early Childhood Environment Rating Scale (ECERS)

Author(s): T. Harms, R. Clifford
Year: 1980
Publisher: Teachers College Press
Address: Columbia University, Teachers College Press, New York, NY
Phone: 1 (800) 391-4000
Cost: $30 +

Assessment type: Ecological; judgment-based observation, rating, and analysis of the features of the preschool classroom that influence child adjustment and learning.

Age range: Preschool to kindergarten.

Domains/Contexts: 37 features in 7 domains: personal care routines, furnishings and displays, language-reasoning experiences, fine/gross motor activities, creative activities, social development, adult needs.

Handicap options: Recent revisions include items sensitive to the needs of young handicapped children in both integrated and specialized settings.

Curricular links: Scale serves as a type of criterion-referenced tool to detect factors that require modification in order to optimize the early childhood classroom setting.

Scoring/Sample: 7-point rating scale (1 = inadequate, 7 = excellent) with operational definitions.

Technical support: Field use in regular, integrated, and specialized early childhood settings.

Training needed: Knowledge of child development and educational implications; thorough reading and practice with the scale.

Critique:
- Simple, economical, yet effective.
- Valuable for evaluating the match between setting and individual child needs.
- Excellent administrative tool to enable programs to "self-evaluate."
- Handicapped revision must be better field-tested and standardized.

Citation:
Bailey, D.B., Clifford, R.M., & Harms, T. (1982). Comparison of preschool environments for handicapped and nonhandicapped children. *Topics in Early Childhood Special Education, 2*(1), 9–20.

Exhibit 4–22 Scale Items in the ECERS

GREETING / DEPARTURE

ITEM		PERSONAL CARE ROUTINES
Inadequate	1	No plans made. Greeting children is often neglected; departure not prepared for.
	2	●
Minimal	3	Informally understood that someone will greet and acknowledge departure.
	4	●
Good	5	Plans made to insure warm greeting and organized departure. Staff member(s) assigned responsibility for greeting and departure of children. (Ex. Conversation on arrival; art work and clothes ready for departure).
	6	●
Excellent	7	Everything in 5 (*Good*) plus parents greeted as well as children. Staff use greeting and departure as information sharing time to relate warmly to parents.

Source: Reprinted and adapted by permission of the publisher from Harms, Thelma & Clifford, Richard, *Early Childhood Environment Rating Scale*. (New York: Teachers College Press, © 1980 by Thelma Harms & Richard Clifford. All rights reserved.), p. 11.

Teaching Skills Inventory (TSI)

Author(s):   C. Robinson, S. Rosenberg
Year: 1985
Publisher: Steven A. Rosenberg, PhD
Address: Department of Psychology, University of Nebraska,
             444 South 44th Street, Omaha, NE 68131
Cost: NA

Assessment type: Judgment-based; observation and rating of parent-child interaction patterns in teaching-oriented play.

Age range: Birth to 36 months.

Domains/Contexts: 10 items/behavioral patterns assessed through observation and videotaping, including parent sensitivity to child cues, child-initiated activities, use of appropriate communication level, and positive feedback to child; uses operational definitions.

Handicap options: Field-test use with various disabilities: Down syndrome, spina bifida, cerebral palsy, deaf-blind, and multihandicapped; focus on parent's adjustment to child's developmental level and behavioral style.

Curricular links: Provides goal/guidelines for parent training; compatible behaviors with newly developed interactive curricula like TIP and PBP.

Scoring/Sample: Ratings on a 1-7 Likert scale (1 = almost always shows behavior, 7 = almost never shows behavior).

Technical support: $N = 57$ infant-mother pairs of various disabilities; content from recent interactive developmental research; good internal consistency, but only moderate inter-rater agreement ($R = .76$).

Training needed: Knowledge of the item operational definitions and training to establish inter-rater reliability.

Critique:
- Offers important appraisal of parent "teaching" skills.
- Item definitions need greater clarity to increase reliability.
- Based on solid developmental interactive research.
- Needs a matched component curriculum.

Citation:
Rosenberg, S., Robinson, C., & Beckman, P. (1984). Teaching Skills Inventory: A measure of parent performance. *Journal of the Division for Early Childhood, 8*(2), 107–113.

developers have completed initial field testing with the FNS on parents of infants with various disabilities. Preliminary technical adequacy data in terms of stability and mother-father agreement are encouraging (Bailey & Simeonsson, 1988).

The FNS represents a very important advance in the field. It is an instrument that blends simplicity, technical soundness, and intervention utility.

PROGRAM

The influence of the preschool environment on child behavior and developmental progress is an area of strong interest and concern. The *Early Childhood*

Exhibit 4-23   Selected Subscale Items from the TSI

1. *The frequency of child initiated activities is:*

   7. Almost all of the activities were initiated by the child.
   6. Most of the activities were initiated by the child.
   5. More than half of the activities were initiated by the child.
   4. An equal number of activities were initiated by the adult and the child.
   3. Less than half of the activities were initiated by the child.
   2. Most of the activities were initiated by the adult.
   1. Almost all activities were initiated by the adult.

2. *This parent is appropriately sensitive and responsive to the child's cues and moods, both positive and negative:*

   7. The adult is appropriately sensitive almost all of the time.
   6. The adult is appropriately sensitive most of the time.
   5. The adult is appropriately sensitive more than half of the time.
   4. The adult is appropriately sensitive half of the time.
   3. The adult is appropriately sensitive less than half of the time.
   2. The adult is inappropriate in response most of the time.
   1. The adult is inappropriate in response to the child's interests and moods in almost all interactions.

Source: From *Development & Use of the Teaching Skills Inventory* by S. Rosenberg and S. Robinson, 1985. Developed for the North Dakota Department of Public Instruction. Reprinted by permission.

Environment Rating Scale (ECERS) (Harms & Clifford, 1980) is one of the few instruments that operationalizes features to distinguish adequate and inadequate settings and that offers suggestions for rearrangement and improvement of those settings. In essence, the ECERS is a "curriculum" for administrators that addresses effective preschool program design. The ECERS is composed of 37 items organized into seven sections: (1) personal care routines, (2) furnishings and display for children, (3) language-reasoning experiences, (4) fine and gross motor activities, (5) creative activities, (6) social development, (7) and adult needs (see Exhibit 4-22). Through direct observation, one can rate these program dimensions, resulting in a profile of preschool program characteristics. Ratings are based on a 7-point scale. The ECERS focuses upon both the physical aspects of the preschool environment and the interactions between teacher and child and child-child groupings.

While typically used in regular early childhood settings, the ECERS has been used increasingly in special preschool environments. Recent research with the scale to evaluate preschools for handicapped children indicates that on 32 percent of the items, special preschoolers were rated much lower than those in normal settings (Bailey, Harms, & Clifford, 1982). A revision of the ECERS includes additional items for programs that integrate handicapped preschoolers, and a complementary measure addresses the best characteristics for home day care programs.

The ECERS fulfills a pressing need in a relatively uncharted early-intervention area. Whereas most environmental observation systems are cumbersome and time-consuming for data collection, the ECERS uses a simple procedure to focus on important factors that influence the child's adjustment and learning. With the integration into more normalized settings, early interventionists must address these program design issues that influence the success of treatment of young exceptional children.

The *Teaching Skills Inventory* (TSI) (Robinson & Rosenberg, 1985) is designed to provide early interventionists with specific ecological information about the parent/caregiver's ability to interact with a young at-risk child, especially on instructional or play tasks. It is an interactive measure that enables the team to identify strengths and limitations in the parent's style of interacting in play with the child by surveying various dimensions, such as use of praise, choice of tasks appropriate for the child's developmental stage, developmentally appropriate use of language for directions and comments, and sensitivity to the child's moods (see Exhibit 4-23). Through naturalistic observation, this behavioral survey presents the team with starting points for parent education in the use of effective instructional/ therapeutic techniques to promote child growth.

The TSI is still being field tested and shows only moderate inter-rater agreement. However, the scale was field tested with 57 infant-caregiver pairs for children with various disabilities. While the item definitions appear to need greater clarity to increase reliability, the authors have created a clinically effective format to assess parent interactive skills; they have constructed a method of simplifying a very complex analysis without trivializing it. Early-intervention programs will find this a very valuable addition to their curriculum-based assessment methods, particularly for developing one aspect of the IFSP.

5

Developmental Curricula:
Design and Content

Teachers are always faced with the question of what to teach; this is especially true at the preschool level. Later schooling usually becomes tilted toward academic achievement; here reading, writing, arithmetic, social studies, vocational preparation, and so forth dominate the program content. At the preschool level, however, there is considerable understandable controversy over what is appropriate and teachable content. The curriculum becomes the center of this controversy, since it is the "what-to-teach" part of the preschool program, that is, a basic set or pattern of educational objectives. The curriculum provides the potential objectives for children at various ages and stages of development.

What is the "right" curriculum depends not only on the developmental needs of the children but also on the professional and personal characteristics of the teacher. A curriculum that is well-suited for a given child will probably not be taught effectively if the teacher disagrees with the objectives or associated teaching methods. An optimal program is one in which there exists a good match or relationship among teacher characteristics, curriculum materials, and children (Safford, 1978). Parents, and, hopefully, also the child, should concur with the educational (i.e., curricular) content of the preschool program. Most curriculum developers agree on program goals when they are stated in general and abstract terms. Thus, few experts would object to such program goals as achieving self-respect, acquiring an appreciation of one's culture, caring about others, problem solving, gaining independence, and so on. But when these general goals are broken down into smaller parts and when specific behaviors are stated, the trouble really begins.

It should not be surprising, in view of this controversy, that a variety of preschool curricula has been developed and promoted by various factions in early childhood education (see Bagnato, J.T. Neisworth, & Capone, 1987). Indeed, hundreds of published curricula are available. Many are essentially similar or are only variations of others. On the other hand, many curricula are quite distinct, reflecting differing philosophies concerning child development and the role of the preschool experience (see Appendix B for summaries of prominent curricula).

Given the scope and sequence of potential developmental objectives, development assessment can provide guidelines for where to begin and where to go among the curricular objectives. Obviously, it is not possible to link assessment to program objectives when there is no organized set of objectives. A curriculum is the *sine qua non* for prescriptive developmental assessment, since the prescriptions are written in terms of recommended entry and intended curricular objectives.

MODELS FOR CURRICULAR CONTENT

The actual goals and objectives of a curriculum are to a large extent determined by the theoretical approach guiding its construction. While there are various ways to discuss content, in this chapter we are concerned with those models or approaches that provide the content of the major curricula available in early childhood special education: developmental milestones, cognitive-developmental, functional/adaptive, and interactive/transactional models.

Developmental Milestones Model

Empirical research in child development has accumulated much information on the landmark skills or "developmental tasks" evidenced by children at various ages

(Bayley, 1969; Gesell, 1923; Havinghurst, 1956; Knobloch, Stevens, & Malone, 1980). This information base tells us the usual direction, sequence, and onset of major capabilities. Most norm-based assessment instruments rely on testing or observing for such developmental milestones. Curricula that incorporate these developmental milestones usually also include objectives that are precursive to each milestone. Through the technique of task analysis, which breaks milestones down into simpler components, a given developmental milestone might have dozens of subskills or "readiness" skills. The skill of eating with a spoon, for example, is preceded by many other skills normally developed earlier, such as chewing and swallowing, eye-hand coordination, and grasping. If a child is unable to spoon-feed, instruction can begin on tasks earlier in the hierarchy. When the preschooler still cannot perform the earlier skill, the teacher can keep moving back in the hierarchy until an objective is found that the child has mastered. Instruction can proceed forward from that point.

Thus, hierarchies of objectives are provided, from earliest or easiest to later or more difficult. The hierarchies are developed through observation, empirical trials, task analysis, or sometimes sheer logic. Sometimes "professional consensus" (Bailey & Wolery, 1984) is employed to provide a sequence of skills subordinate to a milestone.

The developmental task or milestone approach offers a strong program format and content. Children's development can be assessed; treatment, instruction, or other intervention can be delivered; child progress can be tracked; and program impact can be evaluated—all with reference to developmental milestones. Thus, developmental hierarchies provide not only instructional objectives but also diagnostic profiles of a child's current capabilities. Finding where a child is within a hierarchy is a relatively rapid way to evaluate developmental status.

As might be suspected, the developmental milestones included in most curricula and assessment instruments come from research with nonhandicapped populations. More recently, however, information has been published regarding developmental patterns typical of a specific handicapped population. Often the age at which development is evidenced is later when compared with the nonhandicapped norm (see Table 5-1). Generally, however, the sequence and pattern of development are the same, although alternate paths to the same capability are sometimes developed. This has implications for when to attempt to teach a skill and how to task-analyze it.

The developmental task approach is used by many programs that include handicapped youngsters. Many early educators advocate using a developmental milestone curriculum because it is highly structured and sequenced and permits informal developmental assessment. Additionally, a comprehensive, developmentally sequenced curriculum almost invites "mainstreaming." Children of varying developmental levels can be readily accommodated. Frequently, these curricula are built to include children with developmental ages 0 to 5 and are particularly appropriate for mildly to moderately handicapped as well as nonhandicapped youngsters. However, a developmental milestone approach is often not appropri-

Table 5–1 Developmental Norms for Two Handicap Groups

Process	Normal (months)	Blind (months)	Cerebral palsy (months)
Reach and grasp	3 to 5	10	14
Tactile-auditory patterns	4 to 6	9 to 12	15 to 20
Repeats purposeful acts	4 to 8	14	18
Extends arms to mom	3 to 5	8 to 12	18
Spontaneous smile	1 to 2	12	4
Object constancy	6 to 8	15 to 20	18
Separation anxiety	8 to 12	24 to 36	24
Word/object/person match	12 to 14	20	18
Self-references (I, me)	30	36 to 54	42
Actual object representation	24 to 30	60	Incomplete
Reciprocal games (Peek-A-Boo)	6 to 8	14	12 to 14

ate for children with severe sensory or neurophysical handicaps who must use alternative sensory or response modes to act on the environment (Bailey & Wolery, 1984; Haley, 1989). Because use of normal milestones may not make sense with these children, functional and adaptive curricular models (to be discussed) are being developed to meet their needs.

Cognitive-Developmental Model

Jean Piaget's speculations and research have produced major contributions to early childhood assessment and curricula. His 1952 publication *The Origins of Intelligence in Children* provided the theoretical basis for practical applications in assessment and education. Other specialists (Brazelton, 1973; Bricker, in press; Dunst, 1981; Uzgiris and Hunt, 1975a) have used Piaget's observations to devise developmental goals and objectives. Piaget (1952) identified six critical concepts that are assumed to be the foundations for later learning: (1) object permanence, (2) means-end relations, (3) operational causality, (4) imitation, (5) spatial awareness, and (6) object function. Each of these concepts progresses through (almost) unvarying stages. Thus, a cognitive-developmental curriculum contains the steps in the progression of each concept through stages of the sensorimotor period. These developmental hierarchies provide a blueprint for appraising conceptual skills and for guiding instruction during the developmental period.

Curricula based on theories of development (such as Piaget's) contain objectives that are logically related and consistent. Thus, specific predictable sequences can be used to guide instruction. Recall that the developmental milestone approach is not theory-based but is rather an empirically based compilation of skills observed in typical children of various age groups. Such skills may meet psychometric criteria, that is, they may distinguish between age groups for norming purposes;

this, however, does not necessarily mean that the skills are crucial teaching objectives or that they are sequenced in a teachable manner.

Another feature of a cognitive-theory-based curriculum is the use of developmental stage, rather than age attainment (although stages are related to age). With such a curriculum, the teacher attempts to help the child to progress through each step in the predicted stage. Once accomplished, the next stage (dependent on the previous one) becomes the goal.

In addition to conceptual development, Piaget's theory suggests guidelines for the related areas of language and social development; however, other major curricular concerns—for example, fine and gross motor development, self-care, and affective development—are not adequately addressed to permit the construction of comprehensive curricula.

Functional and Adaptive Model

A functional curriculum has two major characteristics: First, it emphasizes the learning of skills that have immediate utility and motivation for the child; major life skills and adaptive behaviors are analyzed to identify components and sequences that can be taught and have rather immediate consequence. Second, "functionality" can refer to emphasis on the function of a behavior, rather than on the form and shape of the behavior per se. For example, some emerging curricula for neurologically impaired youngsters (Haley, 1989) delineate desirable functions or effects (e.g., opens doors) rather than developmental skills (e.g., pincer grasp, eye-hand coordination). Thus, the functional model offers great promise for handicapped children who may have deficient but alternative sensory or response capabilities.

Some programs have been designed to accommodate specific handicapping conditions. Curricula can be purchased for the visually limited, for autistic, motorically impaired, and language-delayed children, and for children with Down's syndrome. These "dedicated" curricula have clear advantages, since they follow a model of developmental milestones adaptive or sensitive to the alternative sensory or response modalities that are likely to be needed. In addition to such dedicated curricula, several good infant and comprehensive curricula provide suggestions for adapting or altering materials and activities for specific handicaps. Sometimes these curricula can be used in a mainstream setting, using the adaptations to accommodate enrolled handicapped youngsters.

Interactive/Transactional Model

There is increasing interest in examining and facilitating constructive caregiver-child interaction as a primary method for promoting child development. Especially during the newborn-infant period, the quality of interaction may indeed set the stage for subsequent cognitive and social development. Enhancement of the stimulus and response opportunities offered by the social and physical context of the child, rather than specific child behaviors, becomes the focus of concern. Most important is the match between caregiver or environmental events and the child's current capabilities, interests, and behavioral style (pace, mood, manner of reacting); teaching efforts that do not meet these three matching criteria are not seen as being productive. Thus, it is not just the content of an objective that is important; how it relates to the child's interests and behavioral state is also a major concern (Mahoney & Powell, 1986).

The transactional model is built on child development research (Bell, 1979; Bell & Harper, 1977; Sameroff & Chandler, 1975) that recognizes the impact of child characteristics and behavior on the caregiver (and vice versa) and the need for mothers to feel comfortable with their children (Bromwich, 1981). With new effort to develop and implement IFSPs, various transactional curricula may be available to optimize family-child reciprocity and mutually satisfying adult-child exchanges. Unlike the other curricular approaches, the transactional model emphasizes the dynamics of interaction (how to match and relate to the child) in order to promote child progress. Table 5-2 compares the four curriculum models.

CATEGORIES OF CURRICULA

As a result of some 15 years of research and development, many developmental curricula are now commercially available. These curricula may be grouped or typed according to intended child population, setting, or other characteristics. In this section, we identify three major developmental age groups as a basis for curriculum selection: newborn-infant, infant-preschool, and kindergarten-transition.

Newborn-Infant

A growing number of curricula are becoming available for use with children ages 0 to 2. Piagetian theory particularly has greatly influenced the design and content of infant curricula. These curricula focus on detecting and facilitating critical dimensions of cognitive development but may be supplemented with objectives based on developmental milestones within social, emotional, and motor domains.

Infant-Preschool

Infant-preschool curricula are designed to accommodate infant-to-preschool children ages 0 to 5. There are obvious advantages to using the same system to cover the birth to preschool range, and most programs include separately packaged infant and preschool components.

Table 5–2 Comparison of Four Curriculum Models

Model	Premise for Objectives	Advantages/Disadvantages
Developmental milestones	Skills evidenced by nonhandicapped children at various age levels. Based on empirical research and observation of normal development. Main objective: differentiate age groups, although subskills may be derived through task analysis or professional judgment.	**Advantages:** Normative comparisons. Ease of linkage with traditional developmental milestone assessment devices. **Disadvantages:** Objectives are based on assessment items that psychometrically differentiate among age groups. Such objectives may not be developmentally important or systematically related to each other.
Cognitive-developmental (Piagetian)	Skills evidenced by nonhandicapped children at various (theory-based) stage levels. Stages and sequence of steps within stages somewhat invariant, although timing varies with handicap.	**Advantage:** Sequence of steps in teaching stage level are specified, providing clear instructional goals for what must be taught first. **Disadvantage:** Piagetian theory somewhat restricted to cognitive and language development; other objectives must be provided.
Functional and adaptive	Objectives are those of immediate utility to child and for future success in predictable environments. Readiness or precursive skills are identified through task analysis rather than developmental prerequisites.	**Advantage:** Particularly suited for severely handicapped children to provide immediate success, motivation, and mastery in current situation—especially since normal milestone may not be feasible or even appropriate. **Disadvantage:** Child may not be prepared to succeed in subsequent environments since broad developmental milestones and prerequisites are not emphasized.
Interactive/transitional	Derived from child development research and theory. Objectives are actually for caregivers, designed to promote constructive and progressive adult-child transactions; these social dynamics then should produce optimal child attainment of developmental milestones.	**Advantages:** Parent-child dynamics crucial for early learning. Approach well-suited to a family-systems approach and to improving parent as well as child capabilities. **Disadvantage:** Promoting desirable interaction does not guarantee selection of child objectives; many parents may not be ready, willing, or able to transact.

Kindergarten Transition

More and more educators are recognizing the problems involved in transitioning a child from preschool to kindergarten and then to the primary grades. A few curricula that accommodate this transitional period are now commercially available.

Because of the increasing need for such curricula, it is likely that more will be developed to accommodate mainstreaming of handicapped youngsters.

ORGANIZATION OF CURRICULUM CONTENT

Objectives within the different domains of a curriculum should be organized in hierarchies or clear sequences that are based on child development research. Curricula should provide behavior expansion opportunities (Bagnato, J.T. Neisworth, & Capone, 1987) for the child, caregiver, or both. By adding new skills to the child's repertoire, the gaps in development often seen with special needs children can be filled. By developing behavioral variability across materials, settings, and response modes, skills can be generalized to situations outside the teaching environment (Mori & J.T. Neisworth, 1983).

As stated earlier, a curriculum is a collection of educational objectives, the content of which will vary according to the underlying approach. Depending on the nature of the content, curricula usually involve several areas or domains. Typically, each domain is made up of an array of related objectives; there may be dozens or hundreds of objectives grouped under each domain.

There are three common types of organization for the objectives within a curriculum (Wood & Hurley, 1977). Lists of developmental objectives are usually arranged in hierarchies. When each domain contains separate and unrelated hierarchical lists, the curriculum is using *parallel organization*. With this system, the teacher can proceed with instruction in a given domain even though the child may be having trouble in another domain. With parallel organization, progress in one domain is not directly tied to progress in another. Many skills include components of other skills, and in such cases assignment to a particular domain is rather arbitrary.

As noted previously, progress within a given domain is often at least indirectly related to accomplishments in other domains. *Crossover organization or cross-referencing* recognizes and emphasizes this interrelatedness of developmental objectives. Many tasks faced by children involve competence across several areas. Thus, cross-referencing is a sensible approach that alerts a teacher to the interrelatedness (and artificial separation) of domains. This organizational design helps to prevent "lopsided" programming.

Teachers of school-age children often favor *spiral organization*. Similar to the crossover organization, a spiral organization consists of sequences of interrelated modules for several domains. Objectives from different domains are taught and "revisited" later in more detail (Bloom, 1956). Skills can be introduced in a simple fashion. As other parts of the spiral are mastered, the skill can be learned more thoroughly and with greater elaboration. For example, children may initially learn to tell time by the hour and half hour. Later, as time concepts, visual discrimination, and other skills are developed, minutes and then seconds can be introduced. Thus, the spiral organization teaches prerequisite skills and stresses the interrelatedness of developmental progress. Exhibit 5-1 presents a visual comparison of the three organizational styles.

CONSIDERATIONS IN CURRICULUM EVALUATION

Depending on the purpose, some curricula are better than others. Like developmental assessment devices, developmental curricula are usually designed for certain age ranges, specific handicaps, and particular settings. The following considerations should be helpful in selecting curricula that best meet particular child/parent needs.

Target Population

When considering a particular curriculum, it is important to look at the developmental age and handicap of the children for whom it was designed. Curricula are usually targeted for infants, preschoolers, or both. For example, the *Hawaii Early Learning Profile Activity Guide* (Furono et al., 1979) was developed for infants birth to 3 years. The *Developmental Communications Curriculum* (Hanna, Lippert, & Harris, 1982) targets developmental ages 1 to 5 years. It is specifically prepared for children who exhibit communication delays. The developmental ages

Exhibit 5-1 Curriculum Organization

Parallel Organization			
Social	*Motor*	*Language*	*Cognition*
Task 1	Task 4	Task 7	Task 10
Task 2	Task 5	Task 8	Task 11
Task 3	Task 6	Task 9	Task 12
Crossover or Cross-Referenced Organization			
Social	*Motor*	*Language*	*Cognition*
Task 1	Task 4	Task 5	Task 8
Task 2	Task 2	Task 6	Task 1
Task 3	Task 5	Task 7	Task 5
Spiral Organization			
	Language		
Task 1	Task 1 +	Task 1 + +	Task 1 + + +

of the children in a program are the major concern; if children fall within the developmental age range but are chronologically older, care needs to be taken to adapt activities with a focus on age appropriateness.

In addition to developmental age, the curriculum may be sensitive to, or even designed for, a particular handicapped population. The *Carolina Curriculum for Handicapped Infants* (Johnson-Martin, Jen, & Attermier, 1986) presents alternative behaviors for children with particular handicaps, such as visual or physical impairments. Curricula that are dedicated to specific handicaps or that employ functional objectives can be especially helpful for children with more serious sensory and/or response limitations (see Exhibit 5-2).

Exhibit 5–2 Behavior Areas of the Carolina Curriculum for Handicapped Infants and Infants at Risk

AREA:　6. Functional Use of Objects and Symbolic Play
BEHAVIOR:　6i. Plays spontaneously with variety of objects, demonstrating their functions

Position of Child:　Any position that facilitates use of arms and hands
Materials:　Hairbrush, ball, squeaky toy, cup, spoon, doll, and so forth

Teaching procedures	Steps for learning/evaluation
Give the child a box of objects and observe what he or she does with each one while playing with it.	*Record* + if the child:
If the child does not use the object functionally, say, "Show me what you do with the _____."	1. Plays spontaneously with an object, demonstrating its functions.
If the child does not spontaneously use items functionally, go back to modeling the correct use of objects and encouraging the child to imitate.	*Criterion:* Child plays spontaneously with a variety of objects (4 or more), demonstrating their functions; 4 of 5 trials for 3 days.
For the *visually impaired* child, be sure to select objects that are familiar to the child and easily distinguishable by touch.	
For the *physically handicapped* child, try to find objects whose functions can be demonstrated within the constraints of the child's motor deficits. If little motor behavior is possible, try telling the child, "The _____ is for _____," as you demonstrate usage. Then, once in a while use the object incorrectly and ask the child, "Is this what we do with the _____?" or simply look for signs of amusement or other indications of understanding.	

Source: Johnson-Martin, Nancy, Jens, Kenneth G., and Attermeier, Susan M. (1986). *The Carolina Curriculum for Handicapped Infants and Infants At Risk.* Baltimore: Paul H. Brookes Publishing Co. Copyright ©1986 by Nancy Johnson-Martin, Kenneth G. Jens, and Susan M. Attermeier. Reprinted by permission.

Intended Setting

The setting for a program involves such considerations as whether it will be used on an individual or small-group basis and in the home, center, or hospital. For a home-based program, clearly written individual lessons (see Exhibit 5-3) and interesting tracking suggestions are needed if parents are to serve as the primary instructors. If a "parent-as-teacher" approach does not seem appropriate, transactional or interactive curricula may better fit a collaborative, family-focused approach (Dunst, 1985; 1986; Dunst & Trivette, in press; Dunst, Trivette, McWilliams, & Galant, in press).

Center- and hospital-based programs may employ both individual and small-group instructional arrangements. Programs may be implemented by paraprofessionals, parents, and/or volunteers in conjunction with professionals. Curricula designed for home use are often simpler and easier to use than those developed for centers, where greater staff effort and time can be expended. Thus, *Small Wonder* (Karnes, 1981) is attractive and helpful to many parents, even though it does not offer the scope and precision often necessary for handicapped children. Another example of a dedicated curriculum, *Education for Multihandicapped Infants* (Wallens, Elder, & Hastings, 1979), was developed for use by nurses in neonatal intensive care units. It furnishes important developmental stimulation activities that nurses and others can employ to offset the possible delays associated with early infant isolation and treatment.

Comprehensiveness and Balance

A curriculum should include all areas of development. A variety of objectives within all major domains provides for a balanced program. If a curriculum emphasized only self-help and motor skills, it would lack appeal for normally developing children; at the same time, it would limit the opportunities for handicapped children to develop skills in other areas. The *HICOMP Preschool Curriculum* (Willoughby-Herb, & J.T. Neisworth, 1980), for example, has specific listings in a hierarchy of 800 developmental behaviors or objectives for children from birth through 5 years in four domains: communication, own-care, motor, and problem solving. Some curricula for handicapped children are tilted toward one area (e.g., self-help). This type of approach inhibits parallel progress across other developmental areas (Mori & J.T. Neisworth, 1989). As educators develop integrated and mainstreamed preschool programs, the need for a comprehensive and balanced curriculum becomes even more important. A good comprehensive or "broad-spectrum" curriculum (Sparling, in press) can offer sufficient developmental objectives across the major domains for most children. Adaptations for specific handicaps further expand the utility of these curricula. It must be remembered, however, that the severity of the handicap may dictate a more specialized or "narrow-spectrum" curriculum. Therapists (occupational, physical, speech, and

Exhibit 5–3 Sample Teaching Activities for Parents of an Infant with Down Syndrome

Consequences:
(+) 1.   Praise the child for removing objects and allow her to play with the objects.
(−) 2.   If the child does not reach and remove, prompt this activity as indicated in the steps.

5.4: Places Ring on Peg
Goal: Child will place a ring on a peg.
Position: Supported sitting
Materials Needed: Plastic or wooden peg or dowel
                                  Plastic rings or rubber rings from canning lids
Teaching Activities:
1.   Prerequisite: Activity for "Puts Objects into Containers" (4.2).
2.   Either purchase or make a peg—a wooden base with a pole inserted. Rings can be rubber rings from canning lids, plastic or metal bracelets, or plastic rings from a toy store.
3.   Show your child how to put the rings on, then take them off and say, "You put the ring on."
4.   Physically prompt your child through the activity by gradually removing the amount of assistance you provide. For example, you might want to prompt your child completely by placing your hand over the child's hand. Later you might want to remove your guidance to just prompting the child at the wrist, then at the forearm, and finally at the child's elbow to get the child started placing the ring.
5.   Make this activity more difficult over time by using rings of graduated or smaller sizes.
6.   Steps:
     (1) Child places 1 ring on peg.
     (2) Child places 2-3 rings on peg.
     (3) Child places 4-5 rings on peg.
Consequences:
(+) 1.   Praise the child for putting each ring on the peg.
(−) 2.   If the child has difficulty placing the ring on the peg, increase your prompting and then remove it.

5.5: Dangles and Shakes Objects
Goal: Child will hold the end of an object, such as the string to which an object is fastened, and dangle it in the air; child will shake objects.
Position: Supported sitting
Materials Needed: Toys on strings, toys that rattle
Teaching Activities:
1.   Tie a large ring or bracelet on a string and hand the end of the string to your child.
2.   Dangling is usually easier if the child is seated on someone's lap so that there is adequate room to move the object.
3.   Show the child how to dangle the object, bouncing it up and down; then let her try it.

Source: From *Teaching the Infant with Down Syndrome: A Guide for Parents and Professionals* (p. 170) by M. Hanson, 1986, Austin, TX: PRO-ED. Copyright 1986 by PRO-ED. Reprinted by permission.

others) often use a specialized curriculum in conjunction with a comprehensive program in order to provide the precision needed in a specific trouble area.

Normalization and Integration

Helping exceptional children fit into the mainstream of life is an important goal for educators. A curriculum should involve objectives and methods that progressively move the child to more normal functioning. Instructional techniques should also move from specialized, contrived strategies toward more normal or typical ones (J.T. Neisworth & Madle, 1975). A curriculum that is comprehensive and broad in its scope can be used with children of varying degrees of development. In this way, the children can be more easily integrated into mainstream classrooms and programs. By varying the difficulty of a fine motor task, for example, children with different abilities could enjoy an activity together in spite of developmental differences. One child might be finger painting with one color on a table from a wheelchair; a second may be painting with several colors using conventional paper at the same table; a third might be combining paint and another substance to design a textured painting to illustrate a story dictated by the teacher. All should have the opportunity to participate in conversation, sharing, and enjoyment of a group activity; to the casual observer, all three of the above children would be finger painting. With adaptations, curricula designed for nonhandicapped or mixed groups are often excellent ones for mainstream settings. Comprehensive curricula are usually the best choices for these circumstances.

Family and Parent Involvement

Educators who work with exceptional children soon learn the importance of family involvement and support. Indeed, family involvement is seen as necessary for the developmental progress of young children. Both logic and expanding research indicate that family involvement promotes the child's development, benefits siblings, and enhances generalization and maintenance.

Under PL 99-457, family involvement becomes essential for a complete curriculum for infant and preschool programs. The need can be met in several ways by various curricula. The *Developmental Programming for Infants and Young Children* (Brown & Donovan, 1985) has parents as the focus of the program. Others, such as *Beginning Milestones* (Sheridan, Murphy, Black, Puckett, & Allie, 1986), provide parents with letters (available in English and Spanish) to coordinate home and school instruction. Transactional curricula may be especially helpful for use in home-family settings when social processes, rather than merely child behavior, are the focus.

Required Training and Utility

A curriculum can be effective only when it is implemented correctly. Some curricula are theoretically sound, have excellent content, and would constitute a powerful program if they were thoroughly implemented. Unfortunately, the time and effort required by some curricula weigh heavily against their use, and many copies of curricula gather dust in storage closets. To be useful, a curriculum must be used.

Some curricula include a thorough instructional manual; others require a training workshop. When working with handicapped children, additional training or consultation with specialists is often needed. This additional support is usually quite practical and assists in the better implementation of the curriculum.

The clarity and organization of the individual lessons are also of concern. Daily plans should be consistent with the conceptual basis of the curriculum. Necessary materials, objectives, criteria, and adaptations should be clearly understood and presented for ease of use. The users should be able to put the plans into effect with effort focused on the child rather than on extraneous preparation (see Exhibit 5-4).

The curriculum needs to fit the capabilities and desires of the program staff as well as the program's budget and physical facilities. Thus, a full understanding of the program's overall philosophy and resources is needed to make a good curriculum selection.

Exhibit 5–4 Lesson from the Hawaii Early Learning Profile

3.11 KICKS RECIPROCALLY (1½-2½ mo.)

The child, when excited, will kick her legs up and down in an alternating fashion, while lying in supine.

1. Move the child's legs up and down alternately in a slow, easy rhythmical manner while singing a song. One leg bends at the hip and knee, while the other leg is straightened at the hip and knee.
2. Place brightly colored straps around the child's ankles. Have the child's head slightly elevated so she can see the movement and talk about her feet and legs.
3. Place bells on the ankles to jingle during movement.
4. For a child with hypertonic muscles, do this exercise on a beach ball. First relax his trunk, arms and legs by gentle rotational movements on the ball. After the child is relaxed, try any of the above mentioned activities.
5. Reinforce any voluntary kicking movements with smiles, praise and/or touching.
6. For a child with some kicking skills, hang things in her crib to kick, e.g., the large rabbit "Thumper" which can be strung across the crib.

Source: From *Hawaii Early Learning Profile* (p. 75) by S. Furono et al., 1985, Palo Alto, CA: VORT Corporation. Copyright 1985 by VORT Corporation. Reprinted by permission.

Progress Monitoring

A well-organized curriculum should permit easy recording of child progress. Formative evaluation can be accomplished by using a simple checklist or chart that is marked and dated. Summative evaluation can be done in a similar manner. Some curricula include criteria for mastery of an objective; with others, an individual teacher may set the standards. In either case, behavioral objectives with clear criteria enhance the evaluation process.

Monitoring child progress is important for two major purposes. First, teachers and therapists need feedback on the effect of intervention; continual (formative) evaluation supplies such information. Second, parents, agencies, and other professionals need periodic reports on the child's developmental status. Curriculum-based assessment detects what the child can and cannot do (entry points), tracks progress (formative), profiles accumulated (summative) achievement, and produces corrective feedback to adjust instruction (J.T. Neisworth & Bagnato, 1986, 1988).

Services provided under PL 99-457 involve parents, cooperating agencies, and public and private schools. A curriculum that offers a clear record of child progress can aid in communication among all those involved and thus can result in a more effective program for the child (see Exhibits 5-5 and 5-6).

Data or Information Base

Most curricula are developed through armchair speculation, logic, and the cutting and pasting of existing curricula. Once developed, many such curricula lack data on their effectiveness. Educators must demand to "see the data" before adopting something as crucial as a curriculum. Ideally there should be evidence concerning the effectiveness and efficiency of the curriculum with the kind of children for whom it is intended. Field testing on at least several hundred children would provide an adequate data base. The data obtained through actual use by teachers in the "real world" can provide important evidence to consider.

The potential user should look for the following information within the data set:

- the number and kinds of children with whom the curriculum has been used
- the number of times it has been used, the sites where it has been in effect, and the length of time it has been in use
- child-progress information, especially criterion-referenced evidence of progress within the curriculum and/or of developmental growth detected on standardized, norm-referenced tests
- teacher ratings of the utility of the curriculum (a curriculum may be well-designed and effective in the laboratory but still fail to meet realistic demands)

Exhibit 5–5 Child Progress Record from the Early Learning Accomplishment Profile

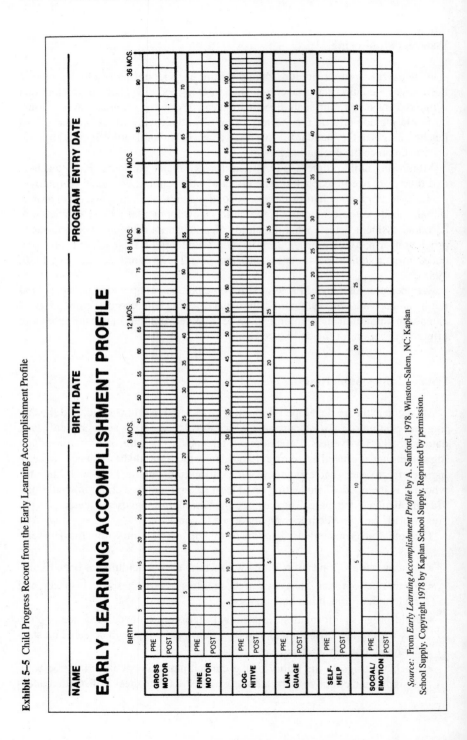

Source: From *Early Learning Accomplishment Profile* by A. Sanford, 1978. Winston-Salem, NC: Kaplan School Supply. Copyright 1978 by Kaplan School Supply. Reprinted by permission.

Exhibit 5–6 Record of Progress on a Specific Objective from Teaching the Infant with Down Syndrome

TARGET SKILL: *Reaching*

Date: 4/1 4/2 4/3 4/4 4/5 4/6 4/7

+10	+10	+10	+10	(+10)	10	10
+9	+9	+9	+9	+9	9	9
+8	+8	(+8)	(+8)	+8	8	8
-7	(+7)	+7	+7	+7	7	7
(-6)	-6	+6	+6	+6	6	6
+5	+5	-5	+5	+5	5	5
-4	+4	+4	+4	+4	4	4
-3	+3	+3	-3	+3	3	3
+2	-2	+2	-2	+2	2	2
+1	-1	-1	+1	+1	1	1
0	0	0	0	0	0	0

Source: From *Teaching the Infant with Down Syndrome: A Guide for Parents and Professionals* (p. 63) by M. Hanson, 1986, Austin, TX: PRO-ED. Copyright 1986 by PRO-ED. Reprinted by permission.

Durability

Curriculum materials come in a variety of formats and packages. Some are presented in kit form, while others are contained in a manual with reproducible forms or lessons. Material that is well-organized and sturdy and can be used by more than one professional or parent at the same time can be an economical benefit in a program. When making a selection, the type of program (home-, center-, or hospital-based) and the number of people who will be using the materials should also be considered. Materials and lesson plans should be adaptable for special handicapping conditions and have generalization potential. If the materials or manuals are to be shared or used by different instructors, one should consider how many will be needed to implement fully the curriculum. Also to be considered are the consumables and extra materials needed for the program on a regular basis. Finally, the cost must fit the program's budget; curriculum prices can range from $48 to $300.

MAKING THE CHOICE

Before deciding on a curriculum for a particular program, those making the selection need to have a clear understanding of the program—its philosophy, goals, and staff; the children and families to be served; and the available resources (both physical and financial). The relevant information can be gathered through surveys, interviews, and/or observations. After the program's mission and characteristics are identified, the needs of the program can be matched to a curriculum that best serves those needs. By learning about the curriculum before enrolling their child, parents will have a better understanding of what to expect of the program and what is expected of them. They will be better able to determine if the program will meet the particular needs of their child and family. For some parents, an intense home-based program may be the most helpful and valuable; for others, due to a variety of reasons, a center-based program or a home-based program of less intensity may better suit their needs.

In summary, a good developmental curriculum will provide

- scope and sequence of objectives
- focus for program planning, staff training, and parent involvement
- systematic and low-effort approach to writing IEPs
- entry objectives for placement in the program
- basis for curriculum-based assessment
- ready linkage with most developmental assessment devices
- progress tracking along curricular objectives that can be shared with parents
- differential progress checks across domains
- formative and summative curriculum-based program evaluation

The curriculum evaluation format in Exhibit 5-7 takes into account the various concerns in selecting a curriculum. Such a format can be very helpful in organizing information, comparing curricula, and providing a common basis for professional discussion, thereby aiding the selection process.

Exhibit 5–7 Curriculum Evaluation Format

CURRICULUM _____	PUBLISHER _____
TARGET POPULATION	PROGRAM TYPE
AREAS COVERED	
ARE THESE AREAS BALANCED? _____ SEQUENCED? _____	
TYPE OF ORGANIZATION	
INTEGRATION POSSIBILITIES	LINKAGE POSSIBILITIES
FAMILY INVOLVEMENT POTENTIAL	
TRAINING NEEDED	
LESSON PLANS	
ADAPTABLE TO HANDICAPPED CHILDREN	
MONITORING: DAILY/LONG RANGE	
WAS THE CURRICULUM TESTED? WITH WHAT TYPE OF CHILDREN? HOW MANY?	
IS THE MATERIAL DURABLE? WELL ORGANIZED?	
COST: BASIC PROGRAM? CONSUMABLES? EXTRA MANUALS?	

6

Close-ups of Exemplary Developmental Curricula

Important Considerations in Matching Curricula with Programs
    Developmental Age of Enrolled Children
    Kind and Severity of Handicaps
    Intended Setting
    Time/Effort/Cost Considerations

Newborn-Infant Curricula
    Learning Accomplishment Profile (LAP) and Early Learning Accomplishment Profile
        (E-LAP)
    Carolina Curriculum for Handicapped Infants and Infants at Risk (CCHI)
    Evaluation and Programming System for Infants and Young Children (EPS)
    Small Wonder/You and Your Small Wonder (SW)
    Working with Parents and Infants/Parent Behavior Progression (PBP)
    Seattle Inventory of Early Learning Software (SIEL)

Infant-Preschool
    Learning Accomplishment Profile (LAP)
    HICOMP Preschool Curriculum (HICOMP)
    Hawaii Early Learning Profile and Help for Special Preschoolers (HELP)
    Developmental Programming for Infants and Young Children (DPIYC)
    Oregon Project Curriculum for Visually Impaired and Blind Preschool Children (OPC)
    Individualized Assessment and Treatment for Autistic and Developmentally Disabled
        Children (IATA)
    Developmental Communication Curriculum (DCC)
    Transactional Intervention Program (TRIP)

Kindergarten-Transition
    Beginning Milestones (BM)
    BRIGANCE Prescriptive Readiness: Strategies and Practice (BPR)

Selecting the curricula to feature in this chapter was a difficult but interesting task. When considered as a group, there is much more to choose from than just a few years ago. Many curricula have distinct advantages that make them ideal—for particular purposes and circumstances (see Table 6-1). As in the case of developmental assessment instruments, there is no Holy Grail that will provide all the answers. On the other hand, selecting the right curriculum for the job need not be a confusing or trial-and-error effort. Indeed, when the choice has been narrowed down to just a few curricula, less critical features (binding, format, packaging) may be used to make a final decision.

IMPORTANT CONSIDERATIONS IN MATCHING CURRICULA WITH PROGRAMS

In general, four main factors should be considered when selecting a curriculum congruent with a program: (1) the developmental age of the enrolled children, (2) the kind and severity of the children's handicaps, (3) the intended setting, and (4) time/effort/cost considerations.

Developmental Age of Enrolled Children

In considering developmental ages, the childhood chronological age ranges usually addressed are infancy (0-2 years), preschool (3-5 years), and transition/readiness (5-6 years). Some early childhood materials may be appropriately employed with older but developmentally less mature children (e.g., severely retarded school-age youngsters). Getting the right developmental age match between curriculum and enrolled children is essential, but will not usually be a problem. When a child's developmental age falls between groups (infant-preschool), the use of two curricula may be necessary within the same year. Also, it is often the case that a child may be functioning at an infant level in one domain of development but be at preschool levels in others. Comprehensive developmental curricula offer a strong advantage in this regard; they provide a "nonstop program" from 0 to 5 years, and a few even extend into kindergarten.

Kind and Severity of Handicaps

Generally speaking, more severe handicaps require dedicated curricula, in which objectives and methods are tailored to the sensory and/or response capabilities of the child. As an illustration, the Developmental Communications Curriculum is devoted to language development in ages 1 to 5 for children with language delays, children who do not respond to traditional language therapy, and low- and nonverbal children. Note that this curriculum addresses only the communication and related cognition domains. As is usually the case, dedicated curricula sacrifice breadth for depth. Accordingly, a dedicated curriculum is frequently used along with a comprehensive one.

Table 6–1   An Overview of Exemplary Curricula

Curriculum	Focus	Author	Publisher
Newborn-Infant			
Carolina Curriculum for Handicapped Infants and Infants at Risk (CCHI)	Handicap-sensitive	Johnson-Martin, Jens, & Attermeier	Paul Brookes Publishing Company
Evaluation and Programming for Infants and Young Children (EPSI)	Handicap-sensitive	Bricker, Bailey, Gunnerlock, Buhl, & Slentz	American Guidance Service
Early Learning Accomplishment Profile (E-LAP)	Developmental milestones	Glover, Preminger, & Sanford	Kaplan School Supply
Infant Learning	Handicap-sensitive	Dunst	DLM/Teaching Resources Corporation
Small Wonder (SW)	Developmental milestones	Karnes	American Guidance Service
Teaching the Infant with Down Syndrome (TIDS)	Handicap-sensitive	Hanson	PRO-ED
Education for Multihandicapped Infants (EMI)	Handicap-sensitive	Wallens, Elder, & Hastings	Children's Medical Center U of Va
Learning Through Play (LTP)	Cognitive development	Fewell & Vadsy	DLM/Teaching Resources Corporation
Infants and Toddlers with Neuromotor Delays (ITND)	Handicap-sensitive	Connors, Williamson, & Siep	Teachers College Press
Parent Behavior Progression (PBP)	Interactive	Bromwich	PRO-ED
Seattle Inventory of Early Learning (SIEL)	Handicap-sensitive	Schlater, Fewell, & Sandal	Specialty Software Etc.
Infant-Preschool			
HICOMP	Developmental milestones	Willoughby-Herb & Neisworth	Psychological Corporation
Hawaii Early Learning Profile (HELP)	Handicap-sensitive	Furono, O'Reilly, Hoska, Insatauka, Allman, & Zeisloft	VORT Corporation
Learning Accomplishment Profile (LAP)	Developmental milestones	Sanford	Kaplan School Supply

Curriculum	Focus	Author	Publisher
Portage Guide to Early Education (PGEE)	Developmental milestones	Bluma, Shearer, Frohman, & Hillard	CESA 5
Adaptive Play for Special Needs Children	Handicap-sensitive	Musselwhite	College Hill Press
Developmental Programming for Infants and Young Children (DPIYC)	Developmental milestones	Brown & Donovan	University of Michigan Press
Clark Early Language Program (CELP)	Handicap-sensitive	Clark & Moore	DLM/Teaching Resources Corporation
Peabody Developmental Motor Scales and Activity Cards (PDMS)	Handicap-sensitive	Folio & Fewell	DLM/Teaching Resources Corporation
Individualized Assessment and Treatment for Autistic and Developmentally Delayed Children (IATA)	Handicap-sensitive	Schopler & Reichler	PRO-ED
Oregon Project Curriculum for Visually Impaired and Blind Preschoolers (OPC)	Handicap-sensitive	Brown, Simmons, & Methvin	Jackson County Education Service District
Developmental Communication Curriculum (DCC)	Handicap-sensitive	Hanna, Lippert, & Harris	Charles E. Merrill Publishing Company
Transactional Intervention Program (TRIP)	Interactive	Mahoney & Powell	Pediatric Research and Training Center University of Conn.
Arizona Basic Assessment and Curriculum Utilization System (ABACUS)	Developmental milestones	McCarthy, Lund, Bos, Vaughn, & Glatke	Love Publishing Company

Table 6–1   continued

Table 6–1   continued

Curriculum	Focus	Author	Publisher
	Kindergarten-Transition		
Beginning Milestones (BM)	Handicap-sensitive	Sheridan, Murphy, Black, Puckett, & Allie	DLM/Teaching Resources Corporation
BRIGANCE Prescriptive Readiness: Strategies and Practices (PRSP)	Developmental milestones	Brigance	Curriculum Associates

Since there are several excellent handicap-sensitive curricula, these should be given consideration when child characteristics dictate. Certainly, curricula dedicated to visually limited, hearing-impaired, or neuromotor-handicapped children can provide objectives and instructional activities more appropriately and precisely than curricula designed for all children.

Intended Setting

Some curricula are useful across settings, especially when some training is provided. Preschool, day care, home, and hospital settings are the usual contexts for special-needs children. It may be advantageous to select a curriculum to fit a particular setting and staff. For example, the *Education for Multihandicapped Infants* (EMI) was developed for use by nurses in a neonatal intensive care unit. Since hospitalized infants are at a critical time of development, a curriculum to guide caregivers at such a time may be critical in preempting developmental risks and delays.

Home-based instruction makes special demands on the itinerant teacher and parents; it also complicates the choice of a curriculum. Frequently, parents need a simple, low-effort program to interact with and teach their child. In such cases, curricula designed with parents in mind are the best choices—even though they may not be the best ones for the center-based professional. *Small Wonder*, for example, is particularly useful for parents and day care staff in that it uses a simple "recipe box" format to provide key developmental activities. The *Parent Behavior Progression* curriculum is specifically designed to help the parent build parent-child interactive skills. Thus, "who is the teacher?" and "where will instruction take place?" may be the major questions to answer in determining curriculum choice.

Time/Effort/Cost Considerations

Unfortunately, the "hassle factor" and the cost of a curriculum may in many cases cause it to be rejected. Some excellent curricula are difficult to implement, and some require considerable effort to track child progress. Again, there seems to be a trade-off between precision and effort. There are several programs, however, that provide adequate child data with reduced effort. The *Learning Accomplishment Profile* (LAP) curriculum and the *Hawaii Early Learning Profile* (HELP) monitor progress without undue demands on the busy teacher.

The budgets of the institutions where the curriculum is to be used should also be considered. When it is impossible to fund the purchase of a new curriculum, there are often methods to circumvent the problem. One might borrow a sample copy from another school district or educational materials center, or the curriculum might be used with a selected number of students for a prescribed period of time to determine if it is suitable. In trying to convince parents and supervisors of the merits of a particular curriculum to fit both teacher and student needs, relevant data collected from a trial group of youngsters may provide the evidence needed to ensure its purchase. Publishing companies and authors are often willing to provide free copies of a curriculum if, in return, feedback on the progress of the enrolled students is provided. Often the cost of a curriculum is greatly increased because it includes a kit of instructional activities/materials (dolls, cups, blocks, beads, puppets); often these materials can be gathered separately by the teacher or parent volunteers, thereby saving money.

In some situations, aides, parents, volunteers, or student teachers are available to assist the teacher. In these cases, a good curriculum that may require more effort should be considered. Paraprofessionals with adequate training and experience can be involved in the implementation of most curricula with teacher supervision. The overall benefit derived from proper training will outweigh the training time.

Before purchasing a new curriculum, it is sensible to have a trial period in which to study or use it. As noted earlier, publishing companies often will offer a trial period to enable the user to examine a curriculum to see if it is suitable for use with particular students. Educational materials centers, common in larger school systems, often receive complimentary copies of curricula; calling such centers for information should be a first step when considering curricula to preview. Local colleges and universities will also have sample copies of curricula. Colleges of education, psychology, and human development are major centers for developing such materials, and individual professors in such institutions can suggest other sources of help.

Considering the wide range of type and quality among available curricula and the demands of early-intervention settings, we have selected 16 curricula as warranting particular examination and review in the remainder of the chapter. These curricula are organized in three categories: (1) newborn-infant, (2) infant-preschool, and (3) kindergarten-transition. In each of these categories, normal developmental and handicap-sensitive examples are provided.

NEWBORN-INFANT CURRICULA

Early Learning Accomplishment Profile (E-LAP)

Author(s):   E.M. Glover, J. Preminger, A. Sanford
Date: 1979
Publisher: Kaplan School Supply
Address: P.O. Box 609, Lewisville, NC 27023-0610
Phone: 1 (800) 334-2014, NC (800) 642-0610

Focus: Developmental milestones.
Target population: Birth to 3 years.
Program type: Can be used in home- or center-based programs for individuals and some small groups.
Content area: Fine and gross motor, language, self-help, social and cognitive skills.
Data system: Profile for summative recording.
Materials/Cost: Kit profile: English $6, Spanish $7; early learning activity cards: $35.
Training needed: Knowledge of the target population; two-day workshop is suggested.
Quality of materials: Profile is soft-bound booklet; activity cards are organized in plastic file box.
Family involvement: Activities can be used with parent in home-based program.

Comment:
- Requires minimal training.
- Use of profile aids in IEP or IFSP development.
- Variety of skills at each level.
- No formative data system.
- Widely used program.
- Adaptations needed for handicaps.

Learning Accomplishment Profile (LAP) and Early Learning Accomplishment Profile (E-LAP)

Organization

The LAP curriculum content is arranged in a parallel mode, employing a task-analysis model. Both the manual and the profile contain careful documentation of the original sources for individual items.

The program comprises three main parts:

1. The *Learning Accomplishment Profile* (LAP) serves as a means of ongoing assessment of progress by the teacher/parent who is most familiar with the child (birth to 6 years).

2. The *Early Learning Accomplishment Profile* (E-LAP) provides a wide selection of skills within each age range for ongoing assessment (birth to 3 years).
3. The *Learning Accomplishment Profile Diagnostic Assessment* (LAP-D) (birth to 6 years) is designed to serve three primary purposes:

- evaluation of the child's entry skills prior to the start of intervention
- evaluation of the child's exit skills after participation in a given program
- validation of the intervention program itself

The LAP-D is not meant to serve as an ongoing assessment tool, as a clinical assessment, as a means to label children, or as a tool to identify children for special class placement.

Additional products extend the use of the program and provide variety in activities. They include *A Planning Guide: The Preschool Curriculum,* learning activity cards (for both the LAP and the E-LAP), a *Planning Guide for Gifted Preschoolers,* and supplemental books and audiovisual aids for staff and parents. These products assist in developing mainstreamed or integrated programs.

The LAP curriculum can be used in center- or home-based programs with individuals or small groups. There are no special adaptations noted for specific handicapping conditions. In developing alternative activities, consultation with specialists would be advisable.

Linkage

The program provides for linkage through the LAP-D and the profile. Both are designed to individualize recordkeeping. For the program to function effectively, each child should have a personal profile in which daily attempts or achievements of objectives can be recorded. The writing of IEPs and IFSPs is enhanced by the use of the profile's listing of short- and long-range goals (see Exhibit 6-1).

Training

The LAP curriculum was designed to require minimal training of the personnel responsible for implementation of the specific objectives and suggested activities. Familiarity with the Bayley Scales of Infant Development, the Denver Developmental Screening Test, or other norm-referenced tests helps to generalize knowledge to the curriculum objectives. Interventionists using the curriculum need skill in observation and recording of behavior.

A two-day training workshop is recommended to ensure consistency of behaviors among staff and/or parents as they use the LAP core products. In order to maintain uniformity throughout the period of implementation, refresher sessions are recommended during the first 1½ years.

Additional assistance in developing specific behaviorally defined strategies to achieve teaching objectives and in accommodating various handicaps is required. Consultation with specialists would optimize use of the LAP curriculum for children with specific handicapping conditions.

Exhibit 6-1 Sample Sheet for Recording Skill-Sequence Development, LAP, Part 2

Bibliog. Source	Behavior	Age (Dev.)	Assessment Date*	Date of Achievement	Comments (Criteria, Materials, Problems, Etc.)
3	Manipulates egg beater	27 months	+ 9/12/73		Whipped soap suds. Teacher held handle.
9	Enjoys finger painting	30 – 35 months	+ 9/20/73		Finger painted on formica table – 10 min.
9	Makes mud and sand pies	30 – 35 months	+ 9/24/73		made sand pies using tea set.
13	Paints strokes, dots and circular shapes on easel	30 – 35 months	+ 9/27/73		Imitated teacher w/ ½" brush
6	Cuts with scissors	35 months	+ 10/2/73		cut ½" partially cut strips (2 whacks)
13	Picks up pins, thread, etc., with each eye separately covered	36 – 48 months	− 10/3/73		These will
7	Drives nails and pegs	36 – 48 months	/ 10/4/73		
13	Builds tower of nine cubes	36 – 48 months	− 10/5/73		become
7	Holds crayon with fingers	36 – 48 months	+ 10/8/73		objectives
3	Strings 4 beads	36 – 48 months	− 10/8/73		for this child
13	Can close fist and wiggle thumb in imitation, R&L	36 – 48 months			
11	Puts 6 round pegs in round holes on pegboard	36 – 48 months			

*Mark + for positive demonstration of skills
Mark – for negative demonstration of skills

Note: ← - - - -
The child has demonstrated a dev. age of 35 mos. in Fine Motor Skills.

Failure on 4 of 5 items represents ceiling.

Source: From *Learning Accomplishment Profile* by A. Sanford, 1978, Lewisville, NC: Kaplan School Supply. Copyright 1978 by Kaplan School Supply. Reprinted by permission.

Family Involvement

The program can be adapted for use in a home-based program. The activity cards could be used by a home visitor with several families. Two of the supplemental products—*Working with Parents* and *Programs for Parents of Preschoolers*—give additional information on using the program with families.

Research Support

The LAP has been field tested with both handicapped and nonhandicapped children. The curriculum has been used in a variety of programs. The rate of development for participants in Learning Experiences, an Alternative Program for Preschoolers and Parents (LEAP) was measured in part by using the LAP (Hoyson, Jamieson, & Strain, 1984).

User Friendly

The LAP curriculum materials can be used with a minimal amount of training. Recordkeeping for monitoring progress is adequate. With the use of supplemental materials, activities can be expanded. Materials for the LAP-D are available in a well-organized kit. The kit is convenient, but its cost may limit its accessibility for some programs with limited funds. Parent-involvement opportunities are possible. Finally, as noted, there is a need for assistance in making adaptations for specific handicapping conditions.

Carolina Curriculum for Handicapped Infants and Infants at Risk (CCHI)

Organization

The CCHI is based on a normal developmental sequence but does not assume even development in all areas. Item order is determined by a logical teaching sequence rather than by mean age levels. The curriculum assumes that some children, particularly those with severe handicaps, will never be "normal," even with extensive intervention. Adaptive skills are taught to replace normal skills when necessary.

Basic content of the curriculum was determined through a review of developmental skills found on norm-referenced tests, skills defined by the *Uzgiris and Hunt Ordinal Scales of Psychological Development*, skills in the tactile integration area as compiled by Callier and Azusa in the *Callier-Azusa Scale*, and skills judged to be alternatives to "normal" skills for specific handicapping conditions. The authors also included some skills they felt were important for social development and motivation. The skills were reviewed by specialists in the various areas before the final selections were made.

In the CCHI, the traditional areas of development (cognition, communication/language, social skills/adaptations, self-help, fine motor, and gross motor) are ex-

The Carolina Curriculum for Handicapped Infants
and Infants at Risk (CCHI)

Author(s):   N. Johnson-Martin, K.G. Jens, S. Attermeier
Date: 1986
Publisher: Paul H. Brookes Publishing Company
Address: P.O. Box 10624, Baltimore, MD 21285-0624
Phone: (301) 337-9580

Focus: Handicap-sensitive.
Target population: Handicapped infants; developmental age range: birth to 24 months.
Program type: Small-group or individual instruction; center- or home-based.
Content area: Fine motor, gross motor, cognition/language, self-help, social skills/adaptation.
Data system: Individual assessment logs and developmental progress charts.
Materials/Cost: Manual $29.50 (includes one chart); charts 10 @ $16.95.
Training needed: User should be familiar with basic principles of learning and assessment appropriate for working with handicapped population; can be used by professionals, paraprofessionals and parents (with staff support); consultation with professionals encouraged.
Quality of materials: Manual in well-organized spiral notebook.
Family involvement: Importance of family involvement emphasized; activities can be incorporated in daily routines.

Comment:
- Family involvement.
- Alternative behavior for infants with particular handicap.
- Plans clear and easy to implement.
- Good data system.

panded to 24 areas (see Table 6-2). This expansion allows for logical sequencing. The following principles of teaching are fundamental to the CCHI:

- Consequences count.
- Make the consequences effective.
- Break a task into small steps.
- Provide sameness and change.
- "Set Up" success.
- Build learning experiences into daily routines.
- Allow for quiet time.

Table 6-2   Areas of development in *The Carolina Curriculum for Handicapped Infants and Infants at Risk*

Traditional areas	CCHI areas
Cognition	Tactile Integration and Manipulation Auditory Localization and Object Permanence Visual Pursuit and Object Permanence Object Permanence (Visual-Motor) Spatial Concepts Functional Use of Objects and Symbolic Play Control over Physical Environment "Readiness" Concepts
Communication/Language	Responses to Communication from Others Gestural Imitation Gestural Communication Vocal Imitation Vocal Communication
Social Skills/Adaptation	Social Skills Self-Direction
Self-Help	Feeding Grooming Dresssing
Fine Motor	Reaching and Grasping Object Manipulation Bilateral Hand Activity
Gross Motor	Gross Motor Activities: Stomach Gross Motor Activities: Back Gross Motor Activities: Upright

Source: Johnson-Martin, Nancy, Jens, Kenneth G., and Attermeier, Susan M. (1986). *The Carolina Curriculum for Handicapped Infants and Infants at Risk.* Baltimore: Paul H. Brookes Publishing Co. Copyright © 1986 by Nancy Johnson-Martin, Kenneth G. Jens, and Susan M. Attermeier. Reprinted by permission.

Linkage

Children can fit into the CCHI program through the use of the assessment log and information obtained from other sources, such as parents and previous evaluations. Curricular items can then be selected to develop an appropriate program. The authors stress the importance of encouraging development in areas of strength as well as weakness. IEP and IFSP development is easier with the data system.

The importance of data collection is emphasized. The progress chart (Exhibit 6-2) provides for summative recordings, while the activity sheets (Exhibit 6-3) provide formative data.

Training

The CCHI is designed for use by professionals and paraprofessionals. Parents can use the program with support and guidance from professionals. Throughout the program, consultation with specialists is encouraged.

Exhibit 6-2 Carolina Curriculum Developmental Progress Chart

Developmental Progress Chart

Name: _____

Date: _____

⬚ No norms available.   ■ Items beyond this point are necessary only for certain populations (see Assessment Log).

	Sequence	0 - 3 mo.	3 - 6 mo.	6 - 9 mo.	9 - 12 mo.	12 - 15 mo.	15 - 18 mo.	18 - 21 mo.	21 - 24 mo.
Cognition	1 Tactile Integration and Manipulation	a	b c	d e f	g h	i	j	k	
	2 Auditory Localization and Object Permanence	a b c	d e	f g	h	i	j	k	
	3 Visual Pursuit and Object Permanence	a b c d e	f	g	h	i	j	k	
	4 Object Permanence (Visual-Motor)	a	b c	d e f g	h				i
	5 Spatial Concepts	a	c d	e	g	h		l	n
	6 Functional Use of Objects and Symbolic Play	a	b	d e	g	h	i	k	l
	7 Control over Physical Environment	a	b c	d	e	f	g	h	i
	8 'Readiness' Concepts						a b	c d	e f g
Communication/Language	9 Responses to Communication from Others	a	b	c d e f g	h i	j k	l m n o p	q r s	t u v w
	10 Gestural Imitation	a				g			
	11 Gestural Communication	a	b	c d e f	g h i	j k	l m n	o	
	12 Vocal Imitation	a	b c d	e f g h	i		i j	k	
	13 Vocal Communication	a b c d	e f g h	i	j k	l m n	o p	q r s	t u v
	14 Social Skills	a b c	d e f	g	h i j k l	m	n o	p q	r s
S.S.A.*	15 Self-Direction	a	b						
	16 Feeding	a	b c	d e	f g h	i j k	l m n o	p q r	
Self-Help	17 Grooming					a	b	c	d
	18 Dressing					b	c d e	d e f	d e f g
Fine Motor	19 Reaching and Grasping	a	b	c d e f	g h i j k l	m	n o	p q	r s
	20 Object Manipulation	a	b	e f	g h i j k l	m	n o	p q	r s
	21 Bilateral Hand Activity	a	b	c d e	f	g	h i	j k	l m n
Fine Motor	22 Gross Motor Activities Stomach	a	b	c d e f g	m n o	p	a b	c d	c d
	23 Gross Motor Activities Back	a b c d	e f g				a	a b	b c d
Gross Motor	24 Gross Motor Activities Upright	a	b	c	d e f g h i	j	i v a b	c d	e

*S.S.A. - Social Skills Adaptation.

Source: Johnson-Martin, Nancy, Jens, Kenneth G., and Attermeier, Susan M. (1986). *The Carolina Curriculum for Handicapped Infants and Infants at Risk.* Baltimore: Paul H. Brookes Publishing Co. Copyright ©1986 by Nancy Johnson-Martin, Kenneth G. Jens, and Susan M. Attermeier. Reprinted by permission.

Exhibit 6–3 Carolina Curriculum: Example of an Individual Activity Sheet

Individual Activity Sheet

Student _____ Date begun _____

Teacher _____ Curriculum number _____

Target behavior (goal)

Training method (description of positioning, materials, and toys needed, etc.)

Steps

Step 1 _____

Step 2 _____

Step 3 _____

Criterion

State of the child																						

Trials	5 5 5 5 5 4 4 4 4 4 3 3 3 3 3 2 2 2 2 2 1 1 1 1 1		5 5 5 5 5 4 4 4 4 4 3 3 3 3 3 2 2 2 2 2 1 1 1 1 1		5 5 5 5 5 4 4 4 4 4 3 3 3 3 3 2 2 2 2 2 1 1 1 1 1		5 5 5 5 5 4 4 4 4 4 3 3 3 3 3 2 2 2 2 2 1 1 1 1 1

Step																							
Date																							

State of the child																						

Trials	5 5 5 5 5 4 4 4 4 4 3 3 3 3 3 2 2 2 2 2 1 1 1 1 1		5 5 5 5 5 4 4 4 4 4 3 3 3 3 3 2 2 2 2 2 1 1 1 1 1		5 5 5 5 5 4 4 4 4 4 3 3 3 3 3 2 2 2 2 2 1 1 1 1 1		5 5 5 5 5 4 4 4 4 4 3 3 3 3 3 2 2 2 2 2 1 1 1 1 1

Step																							
Date																							

Comments:

Source: Johnson-Martin, Nancy, Jens, Kenneth G., and Attermeier, Susan M. (1986). *The Carolina Curriculum for Handicapped Infants and Infants at Risk.* Baltimore: Paul H. Brookes Publishing Co. Copyright ©1986 by Nancy Johnson-Martin, Kenneth G. Jens, and Susan M. Attermeier. Reprinted by permission.

Family Involvement

The importance of the family is recognized by the authors of the CCHI. The curriculum encourages the building of learning experiences into daily routines. The plans are clearly written and, with support, can be used by parents (see Exhibit 6-4).

Research Support

The first version of the CCHI (birth to 12 months) was field tested with useful data collected on 96 children with three degrees of handicapping conditions (mild, moderate, and severe/profound). The current version (birth to 24 months) is an extension of the original, with changes based on suggestions from the field testing. Characteristics of the population and child progress results are shown in Exhibits 6-5 and 6-6.

Exhibit 6–4   Carolina Curriculum: Gestural Imitation Area

AREA: **10. Gestural Imitation**
BEHAVIOR: 10a. Looks at person talking and gesturing

Position of Child: Sitting or lying down
Materials: No materials needed other than a vibrant person with an engaging smile!

Teaching procedures	Steps for learning/evaluation
Place the child in a position that allows full eye contact between the child and teacher/caregiver. Get child's attention while talking and gesturing to child for communicative purposes. Use clear gestures (e.g., raising hands when you say, "Do you want to get up?" or making the sign for "Daddy" when you say "Daddy"). Remember: Pace your talking and gesturing to the "style and pace" of the child. Be aware of what he or she is doing. If child does not look at you, try to get his or her attention with an object, then put the object down and see if child looks at you.	***Record*** + if the child: 1. Looks at person communicating with him or her momentarily; and 2. Looks at person communicating with him or her for 30 seconds or more. ***Criterion:*** Child looks at the person communicating with him or her for 30 seconds or more; 4 of 5 trials on 3 separate days.

Note: This series of items is an attempt to bring meaning to the child's gestural repertoire. It is not a replacement for oral language. but, instead, an important building block that will facilitate a general communication link between the child and another person. Once a communicative link is established and meaning is attached to gestures, a more efficient means of communication can be established.

Source: Johnson-Martin, Nancy, Jens, Kenneth G., and Attermeier, Susan M. (1986). *The Carolina Curriculum for Handicapped Infants and Infants at Risk.* Baltimore: Paul H. Brookes Publishing Co. Copyright ©1986 by Nancy Johnson-Martin, Kenneth G. Jens, and Susan M. Attermeier. Reprinted by permission.

Exhibit 6–5 Carolina Curriculum: Field Test Results

Table 4. Child progress data: Differences in numbers of items passed between assessments in sequences worked on and not worked on during first and second field-test periods

Degree of handicapping conditions	W_1	NW_1	W_2	NW_2
Mild	$N = 15$ $M = 10.07$ $SD = 6.23$	$N = 15$ $M = 5.37$ $SD = 4.63$	$N = 11$ $M = 10.95$ $SD = 4.95$	$N = 11$ $M = 6.14$ $SD = 3.81$
		$t = 3.16$*		$t = 2.84$*
Moderate	$N = 19$ $M = 9.26$ $SD = 6.72$	$N = 19$ $M = 5.42$ $SD = 4.79$	$N = 15$ $M = 10.00$ $SD = 8.45$	$N = 15$ $M = 6.13$ $SD = 4.34$
		$t = 2.77$*		$t = 0.84$*
Severe/profound	$N = 58$ $M = 3.84$ $SD = 4.51$	$N = 58$ $M = 2.58$ $SD = 4.88$	$N = 39$ $M = 2.42$ $SD = 4.38$	$N = 39$ $M = 1.99$ $SD = 4.13$
		$t = 2.77$*		$t = 0.84$*

Note: W refers to the sequences worked on; NW to sequences not worked on; numerical subscripts denote whether the data come from the first or the second field-test period.

*Differences between means are significant at the .01 level (one-tailed *t*-test).

Source: Johnson-Martin, Nancy, Jens, Kenneth G., and Attermeier, Susan M. (1986). *The Carolina Curriculum for Handicapped Infants and Infants at Risk.* Baltimore: Paul H. Brookes Publishing Co. Copyright ©1986 by Nancy Johnson-Martin, Kenneth G. Jens, and Susan M. Attermeier. Reprinted by permission.

Exhibit 6–6 The Carolina Curriculum: Child Progress Data in Motor Sequences

Table 5. Child progress data in motor sequences

Level of handicap	GM_1	GM_2	FM_1	FM_2
Mild	$N = 17$ $M = 4.18$ $SD = 3.59$	$N = 10$ $M = 4.10$ $SD = 2.14$	$N = 14$ $M = 3.61$ $SD = 3.53$	$N = 10$ $M = 4.90$ $SD = 1.88$
Moderate	$N = 19$ $M = 2.26$ $SD = 2.67$	$N = 17$ $M = 2.50$ $SD = 3.19$	$N = 19$ $M = 3.55$ $SD = 4.24$	$N = 17$ $M = 3.74$ $SD = 4.30$
Severe/profound	$N = 57$ $M = 0.63$ $SD = 1.10$	$N = 39$ $M = 0.51$ $SD = 1.00$	$N = 57$ $M = 0.94$ $SD = 1.59$	$N = 39$ $M = 0.62$ $SD = 1.41$

Note: GM, gross motor; FM, fine motor; numerical subscripts denote whether the data come from the first or second field-test period.

Source: Johnson-Martin, Nancy, Jens, Kenneth G., and Attermeier, Susan M. (1986). *The Carolina Curriculum for Handicapped Infants and Infants at Risk.* Baltimore: Paul H. Brookes Publishing Co. Copyright ©1986 by Nancy Johnson-Martin, Kenneth G. Jens, and Susan M. Attermeier. Reprinted by permission.

The overall results indicated that the curriculum could be used without extensive training and was useful for assessment and program planning. There were reservations noted with regard to its effect with severe and profoundly handicapped children. Additional reservations were noted in its use with children over 4 years. This is above the age ceiling for the curriculum, though the results do not indicate a clear upper limit for use. The authors note that more data are needed.

User Friendly

The CCHI plans for a variety of activities are clearly written for ease of use. Additional information on special adaptations for handicapping conditions are noted. IEP or IFSP development is enhanced by the well-organized data system. The training needed is within the range of most programs. The curriculum can be used for home- and center-based programs.

Evaluation and Programming System for Infants and Young Children (EPS)

Organization

The curriculum of the Evaluation and Programming System for Infants and Young Children employs an activity-based instructional format. Skills are taught by embedding the training into everyday functional activities that hold the interest of the child. Because of the relevant antecedents and consequences, problems of motivation and attention are decreased.

Activities are selected that can meet varied individual goals for a diverse group of children in an interesting and challenging manner. Additional selection considerations are that the activities (1) allow for the grouping of similar objectives of different children into one activity; (2) allow for the grouping of different goals for the same child into one activity; (3) are adaptable for varying ages and skill levels; (4) minimize the need for adult direction and assistance; and (5) are child-initiated, when possible, to enhance motivation.

The curriculum material details schedules, staffing needs, organization of materials, and environment and classroom behavior management procedures. Guidelines are provided for compliance, transition among activities, group management, free play, and the handling of aggressive and destructive behavior. As can be seen, goals, criteria, materials, program steps, and teaching procedures are detailed for ease of use.

Data collection for the system is well-planned and organized. The information needed for each child is clearly stated. Correct/incorrect responses can be marked over the Numbers 1 to 5 for each child for each behavior. The information can then be transferred to individual multiband graphs. "Post-it" note slips can be used for individual objective selections within the data grids. The data are double-marked when a transfer is made; however, the ease of using only one sheet during group activities would seem to compensate for the inconvenience involved.

Evaluation and Programming System for Infants and Young Children (EPS)
Author(s): D. Bricker, E. Bailey, S. Gunnerlock, M. Buhl, K. Slentz Date: 1986 Publisher: Author Address: University of Oregon, Human Development

Focus: Handicap-sensitive.

Target population: Children at risk or handicapped with a developmental age of 1 month to 3 years.

Program type: Small-group, center-based; could also be used in home-based program.

Content area: Fine and gross motor, self-care, cognitive, social-communication, social.

Data system: Data-collection grids allow for monitoring of more than one child; summary graphs.

Materials/Cost: Material not yet commercially available.

Training needed: Knowledge of early development; careful examination and study of curriculum materials; can be used in direct service and by specialists.

Quality of materials: Sample materials in sturdy book form; normal classroom materials needed.

Family involvement: EPS-PI (parent form for assessment) provides an opportunity for parent input; this could be used as a means to teach parents developmental sequences.

Comment:
- Activity-based instruction.
- Behavior management techniques.
- Computer program to provide individual skills profile, IEPs, and program evaluation data.

Linkage

Bricker's curriculum is one of the few materials with built-in linkage procedures. This functional curriculum emphasizes child competencies that have immediate utility and relevance to the child. Both the assessment and curricular items focus on critical competencies. The system calls for direct observation under varying conditions (e.g., verbal or manual prompting) over several trials; thus, there is no gap between assessment and instruction. For example, Exhibit 6-7 stresses the competency of initiating and maintaining social interactions. The mastery criterion requires two or more social exchanges, such as "pat-a-cake" or clapping hands together. If a child does not meet the criterion, this item then becomes an instructional objective.

Exhibit 6–7 EPS-1 Strand A: Interaction with Adults

Functional Objective:	Initiates and maintains social interactions
Adaptive Criterion:	Interacts for 2> exchanges "Pat-a-cake"; Claps hands
Procedure:	Natural observation Verbal and manual prompt
Scoring:	+/1/− 3 trials

Source: From *Evaluation and Programming System: For Infants and Young Children: Assessment Level 1: Developmentally 1 Month to 3 Years* by D. Bricker, D. Gentry, E.J. Bailey, 1985, Eugene, OR: University of Oregon Center on Human Development.

Exhibit 6-8 illustrates yet another instance of a relevant target (i.e., use of a simple mechanical toy).

Training

The system's curriculum can be implemented by a staff knowledgeable of the target population. Prior to using the curriculum, inservice training is suggested. In order to maintain the efficiency of the program, a regular schedule of meetings is recommended; the full staff should meet twice a month. At these meetings, additional inservice topics, program changes, and other general information can be discussed. Weekly meetings for the interventionists and coordinators present an opportunity to inform one another of intervention progress and to share information. A third type of meeting would include all staff directly involved with a particular group of children and families; at these meetings, more detailed attention can be given to individual programs and needs.

The training aspect of the program requires a commitment of time for the planning and sharing of information among staff members. Through the sharing of information about a child's progress, successful techniques, new ideas, and the families involved, the program can be made more effective. In short, there needs

Exhibit 6–8 EPS-1 Strand C: Causality

Functional Objective:	Acts on mechanical/simple toy
Adaptive Criterion:	Acts on toy in any manner to make it move or sound
Procedure:	Natural observation Manual prompt and guidance
Scoring:	+/1/− 3 trials

Source: From *Evaluation and Programming System: For Infants and Young Children: Assessment Level 1: Developmentally 1 Month to 3 Years* by D. Bricker, D. Gentry, E.J. Bailey, 1985, Eugene, OR: University of Oregon Center on Human Development.

to be both an awareness of the need (which is usually understood) and a commitment of time to deal with the need (which is often the more difficult aspect).

Family Involvement

The family is directly involved in the home-based programs suggested by the system's curriculum. The basic concept of activity-based instruction brings the family into the program in a natural way. Thus, there is a need for close communication between staff and home in order to make progress with the child.

User Friendly

The activity-based instruction used in the curriculum embeds training in functional daily activities. The activities are of interest to the children, are functional, provide relevant antecedents and consequences, and aid in generalization and maintenance. The curriculum addresses everyday concerns of teachers and parents with adequate guidance and suggestions for the implementation of programs. In addition to the focus on curriculum issues within the program itself, the problems involved in the transition of children to another program or public school are addressed. This is an important aspect of the full educational picture that is often neglected by other curricula.

Small Wonder/You and Your Small Wonder (SW)

Organization

The *Small Wonder* program was originally developed as part of a research project on low-income families with young children. Its activities are developmentally sequenced. Targeted for normal development, the program provides information to parents and caregivers to enable them to provide an environment that encourages the child to explore and learn. The activity cards and user's guide include information on child development, as well as suggestions for activities to further that development. The emphasis is on the use of daily routines and activities as learning experiences. Included in the material are ideas and tips for play, health, and nutrition and on providing a stimulating and safe environment.

Materials needed for the program's activities are readily available and can be individualized. The user's guide notes modifications that can be made for handicapped children up to age 3. The guide suggests general teaching procedures, such as, "Once children learn a skill, encourage them to practice it. Add variety to practice by having them perform a skill in different situations" (Karnes, p. 41). Information on exactly how to help the baby would vary with each child, and assistance from a specialist would be needed. In spite of this limitation for handicapped children, the program does offer some good ideas and activities for parents and caregivers in providing opportunities for handicapped children to experience the fun and pleasure of learning and play.

Small Wonder (SW):
Level I (Birth to 18 Months), Level II (18 to 36 Months)

Author(s):　M.B. Karnes
Date:　　　1981
Publisher:　American Guidance Service
Address:　　Publishers' Building, Circle Pines, MN 55014-1796
Phone:　　　1 (800) 328-2560

Focus: Developmental milestones.

Target population: Level I: Birth to 18 months, remedially to age 3; Level II: 18 months to 36 months, remedially to age 5.

Program type: Parent/child home-based program; can also be used in a center-based program for individual and small-group settings.

Content area: Balance and motion skills, body awareness, cognitive skills, finger and hand skills, language development, listening skills, self-help skills, socialization and visual skills.

Data system: Level I diary, Level II progress chart.

Materials/Cost: Activity book: $9.95 ($8.95, 2-4; $7.95, 5 +); Level I and Level II kits: $198.

Training needed: Careful review of the manual; knowledge of child development.

Quality of materials: Sturdy box; durable, colorful pictures; activity cards are numbered and color-coded; activity books are well-organized, easy to read.

Family involvement: Activities are designed for home use, including ideas for sibling involvement.

Comment:
- Colorful, well-organized material.
- Family involvement.
- Material designed for normally developing children; adaptations needed for handicapped.
- Can be coordinated with IEP or IFSP.
- Minimal amount of training needed.

Linkage

Activities in the program are coded according to developmental level, enabling the user to match the results of an assessment. A summary of normal development is included in the user's guide, with a caution that development is an individual process. The diary and progress chart permit the monitoring of progress in a summative manner. For formative evaluation, the user would need to develop simple charts or graphs.

Training

The *Small Wonder* program is designed for parents, caregivers, and professionals. Information on child development is provided throughout the program. Users can learn as they progress through the program. The activity cards, picture cards, and user's guide offer tips on teaching and provide clear directions for activities. Each activity card lists the materials needed, what the child is learning, the nature of the activity, and other ideas to develop further the activity concept (see Exhibit 6-9). Because of the clarity of the cards, a minimal amount of training is needed to implement the program.

Family Involvement

The Small Wonder kits can be used in home-based programs and by parents in the home. The program *You and Your Small Wonder* complements the material in the Small Wonder kits. Together, the two components provide opportunities for parent/child interaction. The program activities can be incorporated into daily routines, and thus make learning a part of the family routine (see Exhibit 6-10).

Research Support

The original *Small Wonder* program was field-tested with 25 children at the Infant Day Care Center at the University of Illinois. Additional field testing was conducted with nonhandicapped and handicapped children from low- and middle-income families in centers. The final field testing involved 200 parents at 12 sites and included use in both homes and centers. Information from more than 2,000 evaluations was the basis for revision.

Parents' response to the program was positive. The program was viewed as offering support, an increase in knowledge of child development, and ideas to enhance the parent-child interactive relationship. It was found to be especially effective with first-time parents and caregivers and with teachers in centers, parenting classes, and high school child development classes. The actual data from the field testing are not presented with the material.

Articles in *Day Care and Early Education* (Fall 1979) and *Dimensions* (April 1980) comment on the Small Wonder curriculum and its usefulness.

User Friendly

Because of its organization and clarity of instruction, the Small Wonder program can be used comfortably and successfully by those involved with infants and toddlers. The emphasis is on enjoying and enhancing the interaction between parent and child or caregiver and child. The variety of the activities and the encouragement to individualize contribute to this goal. However, assistance is needed to modify the program for use with special-needs children. With those modifications, the program can provide a more "normal" environment for families. Additional modifications would be needed in the data-collection system in order to provide

Exhibit 6–9 Small Wonder Activity Card

Removing Lids

Preview
The baby removes a plastic lid from its container

Materials
- A plastic container with its lid a margarine tub or cottage cheese container
- Two or three things small enough to fit in the container but too large to swallow: jar lids, spools, nontoxic blocks

12-15 months

Baby is
- Coordinating eye movements and hand movements
- Learning that objects continue to exist when out of sight
- Learning to solve problems

Activity
Sit down on the floor across from your baby. Hold up the container in one hand and the objects in the other. Say, **Look at these things: I have some of your toys.** Place the objects inside the container and snap on the lid. Then give it to him.

Your baby may shake the container as he would a rattle. As he examines it, try to interest him in the objects inside. Tap the container and say, **What's inside the container?**

Place one hand over his to help him remove the plastic lid. Use your other hand to steady the container. **Ooooh What's inside? A (block) and a (spool).** **See!** Let him play with the objects for a moment or two, and then put them back in the container and close the lid.

Now you do it. Open the lid. Give the baby a minute or two to remove the lid. If he needs help, show him how to do it.

Have other family members help the baby practice this activity. You may want to carry a small container with you when you and the baby will have to wait in stores or offices.

Check your cabinets and shelves for containers with removable lids. When your baby can remove lids, he may open containers you want to keep covered. Place such containers out of his reach until he knows that he should not play with them.

Source: From *Small Wonder Kit A* (p. 107) by M.B. Karnes, 1981, Circle Pines, MN: American Guidance Service. Copyright 1981 by American Guidance Service. Reprinted by permission.

Exhibit 6–10 You and Your Small Wonder: Example of a Program Activity

4. LOOKING UP

Age Range
3-6 months

Materials
- Laundry to be folded

By this time your baby should be able to hold her head up at a 90° angle when you place her on her tummy. She'll enjoy looking around while she's in this position, at least for short periods of time. When you are sorting and folding laundry, you can play a looking game with your baby as she lies on her stomach.

Put a pile of clean laundry on the floor and place the baby nearby on her tummy so that she's facing you. As you remove each piece of clothing from the pile and fold it, talk to her: **"Look at this pretty shirt. It's your mommy's favorite one."**

Whenever you select a brightly colored item from the pile, use it to play a brief looking game. Stand over the baby's head out of her sight. Then lower the laundry item until it's in front of her face. Jiggle the item so that she watches it intently. Then slowly raise the piece of laundry and talk to the baby so that she looks up to see it: **"Look up. The shirt is over your head now."** If she sees your grinning face above her head, she may wiggle her body in excitement and do some "swimming" with her arms and legs.

Then drop the piece of laundry in front of your baby so that she can reach for it and examine it while you sort and fold other articles from the laundry pile.

5. TURNING TOWARD THE SOURCE OF A SOUND

Age Range
3-6 months

Materials
- Noisemaker

Your baby is quickly becoming more mobile. Although he is not yet crawling, he can twist his body in order to see all around him. By six months he can probably turn over from front to back *and* from back to front. You can take advantage of his increasing mobility to play a listening game while you dust and clean a room.

Lay your baby faceup on the floor in the middle of a room that you plan to dust. Carry a bell or other noisemaker with you while you clean the room. As you work, ring the bell and talk to your baby: **"(Baby's name), listen to the bell. It's over here."** He should then turn in the direction of the sound. If he doesn't, move within his view while you make the sound.* When he does look toward you, praise him and give a big smile: **"You found me. I have the bell!"** Move around the room and ring the noisemaker as you clean. From time to time, walk over to your baby and give him a kiss and a hug. Then ring the bell over his head and let him reach for it.

Turn your baby over and try this activity while he is lying on his tummy. He may even manage to pivot his body around in order to see you.

Source: From *You and Your Small Wonder* (p. 103) by M.B. Karnes, 1981, Circle Pines, MN: American Guidance Service. Copyright 1981 by American Guidance Service. Reprinted by permission.

adequate information for monitoring progress; though the system as offered gives general summative information, additional formative records would be needed for this purpose. Program activities could then be correlated with IFSP and IEP goals.

The materials for the *Small Wonder* program are durable, attractive, and varied. One kit can be used for a number of children and will last for a considerable period of time. Parts of the kit can be replaced without purchasing a complete new kit, thus further lengthening its use.

Working with Parents and Infants/Parent Behavior Progression (PBP)

Organization

Generally speaking, developmental curricula tend to be either infant curricula, which focus on the infant and needed skills (e.g., E-LAP), or curricula that seek to educate the parent to meet the needs of the child (e.g., Teaching your Infant with Down syndrome). In contrast, the approach taken by Bromwich was to develop an interaction model, in which the emphasis is on the importance and uniqueness of the interaction between parent and child and its relationship to development.

In this program, no single "best" way is suggested. Rather the focus is on a problem-solving process. Experts offer support, information, and encouragement to the parents to find the solution that best suits themselves and their child. Research supports the importance of this type of parent-child relationship.

Working with Parents and Infants
Parent Behavior Progression (PBP)

Author(s):   R. Bromwich
Date: 1978
Publisher: PRO-ED
Address: 5341 Industrial Blvd., Austin, TX 78735
Phone: (512) 892-3142

Focus: Interactive.
Target population: Parents and infants (birth to 3 years).
Program type: Home-based.
Content area: Interaction model: social-affective, cognitive motivational/language, motor, parenting-caregiving.
Data system: Parent behavior progression helps staff to organize observations and parent reports.
Materials/Cost: Book: $21.
Training needed: Knowledge of the target population; careful study of text.
Quality of materials: Soft-bound book.
Family involvement: Parents are the focus of the program, with consideration for the needs of siblings.

Comment:
- Individualized approach dependent on needs.
- Focus on mother-infant dyad.
- Program requires close coordination and communication between all involved.
- Program staff need low caseload for adequate implementation.
- Staff needs careful training and support.

The Bromwich approach uses reciprocal reading and responses between parent and child as the core of the model. Mutually pleasurable interaction between the parent and child is the short-term objective that enhances the long-term goal of infant development. An example of how the staff works toward that goal is shown in Exhibit 6-11.

Exhibit 6–11 Working with Parents and Infants: Example of Staff/Parent Interaction To Help the Parent To Enhance the Infant's Development

Table 1. Helping the parent to enhance the infant's development

The staff tries...	to help the parent...	...so that the infant will...
Social-Affective Area		
	to read accurately the infant's behavioral cues and to be responsive to them, e.g., to respond to the infant's smiles, signs of discomfort or distress, expression of feelings...	give clear cues and, in turn, be responsive to the parent.
	to initiate positive social interactions and social games, and to respond to the infant's playful behavior...	seek (initiate and respond to) social interaction in a manner pleasurable to both infant and parent.
	to show clearly positive affect in social interaction with the infant...	respond to and express affect with pleasurable interaction.
	to give clear cues to the infant that are consistent across gestural, verbal, and other affective channels of communication...	read the parent's cues accurately.
Cognitive-Motivational Area		
	to develop observational skills with respect to the infant's play interests, preferences, and skill level... (This will lead her to stimulate the infant's interest in his environment with appropriate materials and activities.)	play with materials that are satisfying and will focus on an activity and remain involved with it for a significant time interval.
	to find ways of "tuning in" to the infant's play and to interact with him in a manner that enhances his play, i.e., that is not intrusive and does not interfere with his goals and spontaneous activity...	be goal-oriented in some of his play; will experiment with materials and use them in a variety of ways; and will seek challenging and increasingly complex activities.
	to identify those activities from which the infant gets satisfaction on his own and those for which he needs the adult's participation in order for his play to be satisfying...	enjoy his play and his problem-solving and will play constructively by himself or seek the involvement of the adult with some toys.
Language Area		
	to acknowledge and to respond to the infant's cooing, babbling, and vocalizing...	continue to experiment with sounds and vocalizations.
	to understand the importance of reciprocal communication between infant and adult, so as to motivate her to initiate as well as respond to language...	initiate language communication as well as reciprocate with language.
	to become aware of the infant's interest in the human face and voice, so that she will then talk to the infant in a focused manner when he is looking at her face...	attend to the human voice and become increasingly interested in language.
	to realize the infant's ability to understand a great deal before he is able to say words... (This will encourage her to talk to the infant long before he is able to say words and to give him satisfying feedback as he makes attempts at language.)	increase his understanding of language (receptive language), and will be motivated to experiment with the use of words.

Source: From *Working with Parents and Infants* (p. 18) by R. Bromwich, 1978, Austin, TX: PRO-ED. Copyright 1978 by PRO-ED. Reprinted by permission.

Ten basic guidelines express the philosophy of the program:

1. enabling parents to remain in control
2. avoiding the "authority-layman" gap
3. dealing with parents' priorities and concerns
4. building on parents' strengths
5. respecting parents' goals for the infant
6. involving parents in planning
7. respecting individual styles of parent-infant interaction
8. using reinforcement is not enough
9. giving parents an "out"
10. sharing how it feels to get no response

These guidelines aid in ensuring consistency between implementation and the basic philosophy of the program.

Linkage

The assessment process used for the pilot program included observations and formal assessment tools. The observations were extensive, including home visits as well as observations at the center or clinic. Three instruments were used: (1) the Knobloch, Pasamanick, Shepherd Developmental Screening Inventory, (2) the Parent Behavior Progression (which was used to plan intervention and monitor progress), and (3) the Play Interaction Measure. Information was also available from the medical-nursing team that worked with the family as part of the overall program. An initial intervention plan, such as the one presented in Exhibit 6-12, was developed for each family.

The purpose of the Parent Behavior Progression (PBP) instrument is to sensitize the staff to the feelings, attitudes, and behaviors of the parents and thereby increase the effectiveness of interventionist efforts with the family. The PBP serves as a conceptual framework for observations and parent reports. Six levels of interaction are identified:

- *Level I:* The parent enjoys the infant.
- *Level II:* The parent is a sensitive observer of the infant, reads the infant's behavioral cues accurately, and is responsive to them.
- *Level III:* The parent engages in a type of interaction with the infant that is mutually satisfying and that provides opportunity for the development of the attachment.
- *Level IV:* The parent demonstrates an awareness of materials, activities, and experiences in the infant's current stage of development.
- *Level V:* The parent initiates new play activities, based on principles that the parent has internalized from personal experiences involving previous activities suggested to or modeled for the parent.

Exhibit 6-12 Working with Parents and Infants: Sample Goals from an Initial Intervention Plan

Goals	Rationale and considerations	Program plan	Evaluation plan
To increase social behavior of infant with parents; to increase parents' valuing of infant's social behavior and consequently their responses to it.	Infant's vocalizations are pleasurable to him; minimal eye contact observed between infant and mother; no social games observed or reported with infant. Mother enjoys talking to us.	Respond to and reward infant's vocalizations. Point out that infant is like mother—likes to "talk" too. Discuss with mother the importance of eye contact. In response to mother's questions, provide list of, and bring, suitable records and books. Model social games, nursery rhyme games.	Look for increase in infant's social and affective behavior with parent by second summary time, 4 months hence.
To help parents see importance of infant's language development at this stage, and increase their awareness of the effect of more language interaction on his overall development.	Infant's language subscores have gone down steadily (from 4-month Gesell to 9-month Gesell to 11-month KPS Inventory[a]). Quantity and variety of vocalizations have not increased between visits, nor has receptive language.	Model imitating and responding to infant's sounds. Model verbal games, physical closeness when talking with him, giving him time to respond. Try singing to him. Evoke mother's reaction to infant's responses. Ask mother to "keep track" of his vocalizations and other responses, and to share information with us.	Check infant's vocalizations and receptive language. Look for increase in language reciprocity with mother. Expect mother's spontaneous reports on infant's vocalizations and on what he understands.
To develop third caregiver's skills in play interaction with infant.	Third caregiver is teenager who spends several hours a day caring for infant.	Model presenting toys to infant and interacting with him to increase his interest and attention span.	Look for infant's increased pleasure in play and a longer attention span.

[a]Refers to Developmental Screening Inventory by Knobloch, Pasamanick, and Sherard, an infant development checklist used informally by the staff in the home.

Source: From *Working with Parents and Infants* (p. 43) by R. Bromwich, 1978, Austin, TX: PRO-ED. Copyright 1978 by PRO-ED. Reprinted by permission.

- *Level VI:* The parent independently generates a wide range of developmentally appropriate activities and experiences that are interesting to the infant, in both familiar and new situations and levels of the infant's development.

Parents need not progress through the levels one at a time; a parent may not be yet able to enjoy the infant but may still be able to engage in play activities with the infant. The PBP includes a behavioral checklist for use by the staff. Not all behaviors are appropriate for all parents, nor are all possible behaviors listed. The focus is on positive behaviors, with the realization that the parent may have negative feelings concerning the infant. A caution is noted in regard to individual differences: Staff need to be sensitive to the cultural characteristics of a given population, as well as being aware of the special needs of the parents of the handicapped children and of individual family crises. Overall, a sensitive, well-informed decision-making process is required.

Training

The staff involved with the pilot study were trained in child development and early childhood education, and all were experienced in working with parents and children. Additional experience with high-risk infants and parents and opportunities for observation of testing of infants by experts were also provided.

The staff met regularly to discuss the intervention procedure. Group problem-solving sessions were helpful in solving individual problems. Individual staff members were able to consult on a regular basis with the director concerning particular situations. Two interventionists were assigned to each family.

The support, training, and communication offered through the pilot program may, of course, not be available in other settings. Yet it is important that the factors involved in the pilot program be taken into account. For this type of program to be effective, communication and support among the members of the team are essential. Also, a careful and consistent orientation and study of the approach are necessary for successful implementation; the entire team must appreciate and support the program's basic philosophy.

Family Involvement

As noted earlier, the focus of the program is on parent-child interaction. The basic approach is extremely sensitive to the importance of the family in the development of the child. Intervention strategies allow for individual differences and respect for the rights and desires of the parents. In addition, efforts are made to involve family members other than the primary caregiver.

Research Support

The pilot intervention program involved 30 families, each of whom had a preterm infant (born at 37 weeks' gestation age or earlier and weighing 2,500 g or less). The families were diversified regarding socioeconomic status, ethnic origin, working and nonworking mothers, family makeup, and problems of the infants.

Further information on the results of the pilot study can be found in Sigman and Pamelee (1979). Longitudinal evaluation of the preterm infant appears in Field, Sostek, Goldberg, and Shuman (1979).

User Friendly

The program book is designed to be a tool and guide for those who work with at-risk infants and their parents. To develop a program, the user must carefully assess, plan, and then intervene in a manner that is quite different from the usual approach. Careful training, support, and communication are needed among those involved. A different attitude toward parents is also essential. From a quick overview, this approach may not appear to be user friendly in the sense that an interventionist can quickly reach into the program and pull out a solution for a family. However, the approach is in fact extremely user friendly in terms of its potential for achieving long-term results in parent-child interaction and optimum child development. A basic decision to commit oneself to the philosophy of the approach and then to provide the necessary resources to support that commitment is, however, an essential first step.

Seattle Inventory of Early Learning Software (SIEL)

Organization

The Seattle Inventory of Early Learning (SIEL) software is a menu-driven educational computer system designed to

- manage children's demographic, mailing, and test information
- compute developmental age scores for the five domains of the SIEL assessment
- generate personalized home activity packages from a data base of 650 activities (see example in Exhibit 6-13)
- generate SIEL test reports for tracking children's progress (see Exhibit 6-14)
- generate demographic and mailing reports
- print mailing labels
- add activities to the existing activity data base
- generate data files for statistical analysis

Linkage

The SIEL software is linked with the Seattle Inventory of Early Learning Test developed by Fewell and Sandal (1987). The inventory's developmental checklist

---

Seattle Inventory of Early Learning Software (SIEL)

Author(s):   A.L. Schlater
Date: 1987
Publisher: Specialty Software Etc.
Address: 7535 57th Place N.E., Seattle, WA 98115
Phone: (206) 525-5090 or 543-4011

Focus: Handicap-sensitive.
Target population: Young children (birth to 3 years) and their families.
Program type: Individually home-based.
Content area: Cognition, language, gross motor, perceptual/fine motor and self-help organized within daily routines.
Data system: Program offers means to monitor progress, maintain records, and track test results; based on EIDP sales.
Materials/Cost: $4,000.
Training needed: Knowledge of and experience with the target population; minimal knowledge of computer use.
Quality of materials: IBM-compatible computer with more than 256k RAM needed.
Family involvement: Program revolves around family routine; activities are adapted to fit individual family life- styles.

Comment:
- Ease in individualizing and recordkeeping.
- Activities adjusted to fit family needs and schedule.
- Purpose of the activities is clearly explained.
- Linkage with Seattle Inventory of Early Learning Test (e.g., EIDP).
- Program can be easily changed or updated without excessive use of staff time.

(0-3) (incorporating EIDP scales), which can be administered by parents and educators, assesses performance in five domains: (1) gross motor, (2) language, (3) fine/perceptual motor, (4) self-help, and (5) cognition. Results of the test are the basis for the home activity packages, which contain activities organized around nine daily routines: (1) mealtime, (2) mealtime games, (3) naptime, (4) bathtime, (5) playing with others, (6) playing independently, (7) communication, (8) diapering/dressing, and (9) exercise.

Training

The SIEL program, designed by parents and early childhood educators, permits adaptations for some special needs. Consultation on an individual basis serves to enhance program effectiveness.

Exhibit 6–13 Seattle Inventory of Early Learning Software: Example of a Home Activity Package

---

HOME ACTIVITIES FOR Laura One

MEALTIME

1. Laura can begin to eat solid foods by biting (or gumming) crackers such as graham crackers, arrowroot cookies, rice crackers, etc. You may want to avoid wheat and sugar items. Begin with foods that soften easily in your child's mouth and are firm enough to break off in small bites. First break off a piece of cracker for your child to hold. Allow Laura to bring the cracker to her mouth, assisting only if needed. You may need to provide support just under the child's elbow for her to bring crackers to the mouth and bite/gum independently. When Laura is beginning to eat solid foods you should be sure to watch her in case she chokes. Also observe your child for any allergic responses to new foods.

2. This activity will help Laura learn to hold her bottle. As you are giving Laura a bottle, hold it back from her mouth at midline where her eyes focus on the nipple. When her eyes are on the nipple, prompt her arms to reach toward the bottle. Assist as you place her hands on the bottle, then cover with your hands. Do this several times at each feeding and observe whether the reaching toward the bottle becomes more routine. Praise these efforts and encourage longer periods of independent holding.

3. In this activity Laura learns to hold her bottle. One of the first tasks a child learns to do for him- or herself is to learn to take a bottle. To help Laura learn this task, place her hands around the bottle with your hands over her hands. Gradually remove your hands when you feel her hands are securely in place. Do this when she first begins to feed, as she is likely to tire and will not be as successful in managing the bottle later. Gradually reduce your support as Laura appears to be catching on to the process and your expectations. Be sure to add a few smiles and words of praise when Laura begins to gain this independence.

4. Allow Laura to practice picking up small pieces of food and help her get these to her mouth. Laura will be better able to finger feed independently when she has mastered a "controlled release" of objects (putting objects in a container or stacking blocks). For finger feeding, try cheerios, teething cookies, and slightly cooked vegetables.

MEALTIME GAMES

1. Help Laura practice sitting in a baby-size chair. You might use a high chair, or baby seat that attaches to the table. At first you will need to add blankets or foam inserts to give Laura additional support through the trunk and hips. As Laura gains strength, you can gradually reduce this support. Remember that you want Laura to sit with a fairly straight back and to be able to use her hands.

NAPTIME

1. This is a beginning memory game. Does Laura have a favorite stuffed animal in her crib? If so, play a little game with it when getting Laura up from a nap or ready for a bath. Attract her attention to the toy. Shake it in front of her face. Then drop a blanket or diaper over part of the toy. Encourage Laura to pull on the blanket to see the whole toy. Then, when she gets the toy, let her play with it.

BATHTIME

1. Practice "scooping" in the bathtub. Show Laura how to scoop water, bubbles, soap, or small toys using the same scooping action she would use to scoop food from her tray. Show her how to scoop objects, and then splash them, or let them fall. Scoop the water fast and try to make bubbles, then scoop up the bubbles.

Exhibit 6–13 continued

PLAYING WITH OTHERS
1. Gather toys that have a front/back or right/wrong side (mirror, cup, cat, doll). Present these toys to the child, one at a time, upside down or backwards. If Laura turns the toy the correct way, smile and let her play with the toy. If Laura doesn't turn the toy, help her find the correct side. Then try the activity again.
2. This is an activity to encourage babbling. Sit Laura on the floor and place a large rubber ball in her lap or between her legs. Sit across from her and bang the ball with your hands and say "bang bang" or "wam wam." Take Laura's hands and do the same thing. Repeat any sound she says and make it into two bisyllables: if she says "oo," you say "boo boo." What you will try to do here, is try to use a repetitive hand/arm movement paired with sounds (boo-boo). Laura may begin to produce two syllable sounds following your model.
3. Sit in a comfortable spot with Laura. Call her name through a hollow cardboard tube, then say "aaah." Give her the tube and encourage her to make a sound. Take turns making sounds through the hollow tube. Eventually begin to make consonant-vowel combinations (e.g., baba, dada, maba) and encourage Laura to imitate. Vary your pitch and intonation pattern. Encourage Laura to do the same.
4. A pegboard will give Laura opportunities to practice many skills. To get the peg, she must lift the peg up and out. Then she must use her index finger, in isolation, to poke the holes. Later she must accurately place the peg to get it back in the pegboard. Make a pegboard by cutting holes into the lid of a shoe box. Use large crayons or clothespins for pegs. Cut the holes just large enough for the pegs to fit. Secure the lid on the shoe box with tape, string, or a rubberband. Present the pegboard with all the pegs in their places. Help Laura to take them out. Later, you can encourage Laura to give them to you, or to place them in another container. Give them back to Laura and help her to put them back into their holes.

PLAYING INDEPENDENTLY
1. Let Laura play on the floor to practice her mobility skills. Place Laura on her tummy. Place a few interesting toys in front of Laura and to either side. The toys should be just out of Laura's reach. Laura will have to move to get a toy.

DIAPERING/DRESSING
1. As you diaper or dress Laura, spend some time in face-to-face conversations. Talk briefly to Laura, in an animated way, then pause and listen for her sounds. Eventually, she may begin to respond with cooing and vowel sounds. Imitate any sounds she makes. You can encourage more consonant sounds by gently brushing her lips with a clean diaper, sock, or wash cloth when it is her turn to talk. Early consonant sounds she may make are d, n, and b. Later, she will begin to make sounds beginning with t, p, and m.
2. Sounds or vocalizations that Laura makes will change from being mostly vowels early in life to becoming combinations of vowels and consonants in subsequent months. Laura will often begin to make vowel sounds when she is alone, after feeding, or after just waking up from a nap. Early vocal sounds are called "cooing" sounds. Laura will often make these cooing sounds in your presence, and this is a good time to begin having "talk times" with her. Babies, in the early months, often talk more when parents are talking. Later, they begin to take turns making sounds. After Laura has been making sounds for some time, try imitating her sounds and waiting for a response. Laura will probably not imitate your sounds exactly, and may even stop in surprise. By imitating her sounds, you encourage her to continue vocalizing, and she will begin to respond more to your imitations.
3. After Laura begins to repeat consonants in a "babbling" pattern such as dadada, bababa, papapa, you should hear more variation in vowels and consonants. For example, dadida,

Exhibit 6–13 continued

biba, etc. may be some patterns Laura will use. Also at this time, Laura should begin to imitate sounds more readily when you initially copy the sounds she makes. Laura's increasing imitation skills make it possible to encourage greater sound variety, since many children may only repeat their favorite sounds at this time such as dada. Note the sounds you hear Laura make when playing with others and when alone. Some early consonants include the lip sounds b, m, p; the tongue-tip sounds d, t, n; and the back sounds k, g. Expand Laura's sound repertoire at play with a hand mirror and imitate any sound she produces. After a few "turns" on both sides, slightly change from her sounds to a different sound. An example would be to change from d to n or b to m so that the sound is still a lip, tongue-tip, or back sound.

EXERCISES

1. This exercise lets Laura practice rolling from back to tummy. Place Laura on her back. Bend her right knee. Attract her attention to the left so that her head and eyes turn left, and move her right knee and hip forwards and across to the left. Laura should roll onto her tummy, and her left arm will be under her body. Wait briefly to see if she can bring her left arm out independently. If not, push lightly over her right hip to help Laura lift her left shoulder to free her arm. Repeat exercise to the other side.

2. This activity will help Laura sit independently. Sit on the floor with Laura placed between your legs. Your abdomen and legs will help support her in a sitting position. Give Laura a toy to play with or sit in front of a mirror. Let her play with the toy or watch the reflection in the mirror. As Laura demonstrates more control in sitting, begin to decrease the support you are providing with your body.

Home Activity Package for Laura One

Child Number:	0001	Test Date:	5/25/86
Test Number:	001	Corrected/Birth Date:	7/05/85
Sex:	F	Chronological Age:	10
Location:	02 CENTER PROGRAM	Enrollment Date:	5/25/86
Condition:	03 OTHER	Time in Intervention:	0

	Test Item	Age Range (Months)
MEALTIME		
1. Introduce cracker—1st time—graham (be aware of allergies)	510	3-5
2. Reaches and holds bottle	512	3-5
3. Learns to hold bottle	512	3-5
4. Picks up bits of food and puts in mouth	416	6-8
MEALTIME GAMES		
1. Child sits in high chair, baby seat	315	6-8
NAPTIME		
1. Pulls blanket off, sees partially hidden stuffed animal	113	6-8

Exhibit 6–13 continued

BATHTIME

1. During bath encourage child to scoop water, toys, etc.	416	6-8

PLAYING WITH OTHERS

1. Turns objects to correct side	117	6-8
2. Produces bisyllables while banging ball	216	6-8
3. Makes sounds through hollow tube	219	9-11
4. Pegboards facilitate many skills (make pegboard)	419	9-11

PLAYING INDEPENDENTLY

1. Child on tummy, reaches, turns for toys	314	6-8

DIAPERING/DRESSING

1. Imitate child's vocalizations—encourage consonant sounds	216	6-8
2. Beginning stage of sound imitation (6-8)	216	6-8
3. Imitate a variety of consonant sounds	219	9-11

EXERCISES

1. Child rolls from back to tummy	314	6-8
2. Practices sitting between parent's legs	315	6-8

Source: From *Seattle Inventory of Early Learning Software* by A.L. Schlater, 1987, Seattle, WA: Specialty Software Etc. Copyright 1987 by Specialty Software Etc. Reprinted by permission.

Family Involvement

The program revolves around daily routines in the home. Parents are the primary interventionists. Activities can be designed to include other family members.

Research Support

Review of the SIEL material does not indicate research support for the effectiveness of the program.

User Friendly

The SIEL software enables the user to combine technology and personal expertise. The software tasks provide the means to organize a program, monitor progress, individualize programming, and maintain records. A demonstration disk is available to preview the program. On-line help information makes the menu-driven program easy to use; individual programs can be altered with relatively little effort once the system is learned, thereby encouraging more accurate and up-to-date programming. If a central data base is maintained, administrators, supervisors, and others involved in a program can review and add to the records at will and the records can be better organized, more clearly written, and maintained with

Exhibit 6–14 Seattle Inventory of Early Learning Software: Example of Test Report on a Child's Progress

```
                           TEST ENTRY SCREEN                              (I-1)
   TEST ENTRY
   01   Child Number   0001                    Laura One
        ( \ Child Number or Child Name)

   02   Test Number       001             Chronological Age          10 (months)
   03   Test Date          05-25-1986     Time in Intervention         0 (months)

   04   COGNITION   06  LANGUAGE  08   MOTOR     10  P/FM     12   SELF/HELP
        01> 113         01> 217         01> 310      01> 418       01>511
        02> 114         02> 219         02> 313      02> 420       02> 512


   TOTAL PASSES
   05      15       07      17       09     13      11     18    13      11
   DA SCORE (months)
           6.00             7.00            5.00           8.00          4.00

   CHANGE ?
```

Source: From *Seattle Inventory of Early Learning Software* by A.L. Schlater, 1987, Seattle, WA: Specialty Software Etc. Copyright 1987 by Specialty Software Etc. Reprinted by permission.

less effort and time on the part of the teaching and clerical staff. The initial cost of a computer and printer may present a problem for some programs; however, the long-term savings in time and efficiency in programming could offset the cost.

INFANT-PRESCHOOL

HICOMP Preschool Curriculum (HICOMP)

Organization

HICOMP is an acronym for "higher competencies" in the four domains of communication, own-care, motor, and problem solving. In theoretical organization, the HICOMP curriculum takes a developmental task approach. It is suitable for use with normal, developmentally delayed, and multihandicapped children. It has been adopted by infant development centers, Head Start centers, child care centers, and private and public preschools and kindergartens.

The content of the HICOMP curriculum is arranged primarily in a spiral mode. The four domains contain lists of separate hierarchical objectives. There are 800 objectives, thus making the four lists quite comprehensive of behavior exhibited by children from birth through 5 years of age. Room is provided at the end of each domain for consumers to add their own special objectives.

Crossover is found throughout the curriculum. The HICOMP guide provides a reference list of the objectives that are identical in several domains. These items are also starred in the curriculum (see Exhibit 6-15).

Learning Accomplishment Profile (LAP)

Author(s):	E.M. Glover, J. Preminger, A. Sanford
Date:	1977
Publisher:	Kaplan School Supply
Address:	P.O. Box 609, Lewisville, NC 27023-0609
Phone:	1 (800) 334-2014 NC 1 (800) 642-0610

Focus: Developmental milestones.

Target population: Birth to 5 years.

Program type: Small group or individual in center- or home-based program.

Content area: Fine and gross motor, language, self-help, social and cognitive skills.

Data system: Profile provides for summative recording.

Materials/Cost: LAP kit consists of LAP Profile: English $6, Spanish $7; Learning Activities for Young Children, $35.

Training needed: Knowledge of the target population; two-day workshop is suggested.

Quality of materials: Profile is contained in soft-bound booklet; manual is hardback three-ring binder; activity cards are in plastic file box.

Family involvement: Activities can be used with parents in home-based program.

Comments:
- Requires minimal training.
- Profile provides summative record; need to develop formative.
- No adaptations for handicaps.
- Kit is expensive.
- Activities correlate with assessment; caution against teaching to the assessment.

Note: See full description on pp. 158-161.

Behavioral strategies for implementing the developmental objectives and evaluation techniques to detect child progress are provided. The page of the HICOMP guide shown in Exhibit 6-16 is a portion of the section describing the strategy of "shaping." The guide also covers such topics as

- planning accelerating consequences, using six methods
- planning decelerating consequences, using five methods
- placing (linking) a child into the curriculum sequence, using results from an assessment scale
- planning lessons and programs that include sample lesson-plan formats and sample IEPs
- examples of reinforcers, including recipes for nutritious snacks

HICOMP Preschool Curriculum (HICOMP)

Author(s): S.J. Willoughby-Herb, J.T. Neisworth
Date: 1980
Publisher: Psychological Corporation
Address: 55 Academia Court, San Antonio, TX 78204
Phone: 1 (800) 228-0752

Focus: Developmental milestones.
Target population: Handicapped and nonhandicapped, birth to 5 years.
Program type: Small group or individual center-based; behavioral emphasis.
Content area: Communication, own care, motor and problem solving.
Data system: Easily scored formative system.
Materials/Cost: Complete kit $85, scales 12 for $11.
Training needed: Thorough study of curriculum guide; workshop suggested (half day for professionals, full day for paraprofessionals).
Quality of materials: Sturdy ringed binder.
Family involvement: Activities could be used in home-based program.

Comment:
- Source for mainstreamed or integrated program.
- Good data-collection system.
- 800 objectives and lesson plans.
- IEP and IFSP correlation.

Linkage

The HICOMP guide provides a means of placing the child in the program based on assessment results. It also provides for linkage with IEP or IFSP planning. The evaluation system permits ongoing monitoring of child progress.

One of the attractive features of the HICOMP curriculum is its easy method of recordkeeping, as shown in Exhibit 6-17. Unlike the LAP, which has three places to record a child's progress, the HICOMP has only one. The teacher or parent, of course, may use additional records, such as individual charts or graphs, to record additional data on a child's progress on particular objectives in the curriculum. Because HICOMP's recordkeeping method is designed so efficiently, it leaves more time for the parent or teacher to work with the individual child or groups of children. Time is a precious element when planning for young children.

Training

It is possible to implement the HICOMP curriculum with a thorough study of the guide. Clearly stated procedures for assessing and placing a child in the curriculum are provided. Explanations of how to teach the specific objectives are included, along with suggested lesson plans and strategies. Criteria to determine whether or not a specific objective has been attained are also presented.

Exhibit 6–15   A Sample Page from the HICOMP Curriculum

Domain and year level are listed at the top of each page of the curriculum. The code number in column 1 indicates the domain, the year, the subdomain which is simply a "broad skill area" within each domain, and the general objective. The general objective is printed in column 2. It serves as a starting point for you to identify the specific goal(s) for your lesson plan. The child's entry level skills should be marked in column 3. In columns 4 and 5, you can record the date when instruction began and ended on a specific objective. Specific teaching strategies (column 6) are recommended for each objective. It is not essential that you use the recommended strategy, but this notation in column 6 indicates which of the strategies described in Chapter 5 have been field tested and found appropriate. Similarly, the evaluation techniques, described in Chapter 4, listed in column 7 are optional. You may supplement or substitute another means of determining whether a child has achieved a given objective. The remaining columns are self-explanatory.

COMMUNICATION – Year 1 – Page 1

Col. 1	Col. 2	Col. 3	Col. 4	Col. 5	Col. 6	Col. 7			
Objective Number	General Objective	Pretest	Date Begun	Date Ended	Strategy	Evaluation Technique	Comments: Activities:	Materials:	
C-1-1.1	Vocalizes a pleasant sound				1,3	3			
C-1-1	Language Related Play								
C-1-1.1	Vocalizes a pleasant sound				1,3	3			
C-1-1.2	Vocalizes frequently				1,3	3			
C-1-1.3	Vocalizes varied sounds				1,3	11			
C-1-1.4	Repeats particular sounds (e.g., ah-goo)				1,3	3			
C-1-1.5	Varies loudness, pitch, and speed of sounds playfully				1,3	11			
C-1-1.6	Laughs when played with (e.g., in familiar game)				1,3	11			
C-1-1.7*	Vocalizes amusing sounds (e.g., coughs, animal sounds)				1,3	11			
C-1-1.8	Repeats syllables over and over (e.g., di-di-di, da-da-da-da)				1,3	11			
C-1-1.9	Repeats performance laughed at				1	11			
C-1-1.10	Babbles or hums along with the rhythm of a game or with music				1,3	11			
C-1-1.11	Uses jargon with toys or persons				1,3	11			
C-1-1.12	Cooperates in game (e.g., during "pat-a-cake")				1	11			

Source: From *HICOMP* (p. 29) by S.J. Willoughby-Herb and J.T. Neisworth, 1980, San Antonio, TX: Psychological Corporation. Copyright 1980 by Psychological Corporation. Reprinted by permission.

Exhibit 6–16 Portion of the HICOMP Guide Describing Strategy of Shaping

Strategies for Promoting Accomplishment of the HICOMP Developmental Activities

There are many time-honored as well as new methods that preschool educators and child development experts find useful. Many of these techniques are based on principles of learning and development. We have identified *ten basic strategies* based on modern learning theory. These instructional strategies are employed in teaching the objectives in the *Developmental Activities Handbook* and can be useful in teaching almost any new behavior that you select. Mastery of these ten strategies will provide you with a valuable set of effective professional skills for teaching and therapy with young children.

The ten strategies are:

1. Shaping	6. Questioning
2. Modeling	7. Activity pairing
3. Verbal prompting	8. Chaining
4. Visual prompting	9. Behavior rehearsal
5. Manual guidance	10. Discrimination learning

Each of these strategies is described in the following pages along with general guidelines for using the strategy, examples of its use in the four domains of development, and work forms which can be copied to assist you in planning for the use of the strategy.

Strategy 1: SHAPING

Often we are faced with teaching new, difficult behaviors to children. We cannot simply ask a two-year-old to throw a ball across the room and expect that he or she will then do it. The child will, at first, experience difficulty in aiming the ball in the correct direction and/or in throwing the ball such a great distance. Nor can we simply *wait* for the child to accomplish such a difficult task, so that we can reinforce its complete performance. We must reinforce small approaches toward the intended objective. For example, we would at first reward the child for simply throwing the ball. After the child becomes proficient at the first approximation of the task, reinforcement is withheld until the child more closely approximates the desired behavior. Thus, we might tell the child, "Good, but now throw it to *me*." Then we would only reinforce throws that came *toward* the teacher.

In shaping, *the teacher cannot always predetermine the steps in the shaping process but must watch the child closely and reinforce even slight progress toward the developmental objective.* Some typical shaping sequences are given below:

1. In the Communication curriculum we find the following objective: Child repeats proper sentence when teacher says, "Mary, say this: 'Give me the pencil.' "

   The child's typical responses during shaping could proceed from

   a) "Pencil," to

   b) "Give pencil," to

   c) "Give me pencil," to

   d) "Give me the pencil."

2. In the Own-care curriculum we find the following objective: Upon entering, the child will leave parent and happily join activities. The child's typical responses during shaping might proceed through the sequence

   a) child leaves parent, but is in tears;

   b) child leaves parent, but looks sad;

   c) child leaves parent and watches others play;

   d) child leaves parent and walks over to the play group;

   e) child leaves parent and joins an activity;

   f) child leaves parent and happily joins an activity.

Exhibit 6–16 continued

3. In Motor curriculum one objective is that the child will walk across the balance beam without falling. The child's typical responses during shaping might be
   a) child puts one foot on balance beam;
   b) child walks along balance beam with one foot on floor,
   c) child stands on balance beam upon both feet,
   d) child takes two steps and is allowed down.
   The required number of steps would then be gradually increased until the child walks all the way across the beam.

4. In the Problem-solving curriculum an objective is that the child will recall four objects that he has been shown. The child's typical responses during shaping would likely be
   a) child recalls 1 or 2 items;
   b) child recalls 3 items;
   c) child recalls all 4 items.

Remember that shaping works *if* you

Use a reinforcer that really *is* a reinforcer. Be certain the child will work for the thing or event that you are using as a reinforcer.

Don't demand too much too soon. Be patient and generous!

WORK FORM
Planning for the use of a Shaping Strategy

Select an objective from the listing of developmental objectives and state possible steps toward approximation of the objective for a child who has been having difficulty in learning.

1. _____

2. _____

3. _____

4. _____

5. _____

6. _____

7. _____

Source: From *HICOMP* (pp. 5-6) by S.J. Willoughby-Herb and J.T. Neisworth, 1980, San Antonio, TX: Psychological Corporation. Copyright 1980 by Psychological Corporation. Reprinted by permission.

A HICOMP workshop for child care workers and teachers explains how to "link" a child's results on a norm-referenced test, like the Gesell Developmental Schedule (Gesell, 1949), or on a criterion-referenced test, like the LAP-D, to the HICOMP curriculum. This workshop can be covered in one day with lay personnel and in a half day with professional personnel.

Exhibit 6–17 Portion of HICOMP Guide Showing Method of Recordkeeping

---

Keeping Track of Child Progress

The term "evaluation" refers to data collection methods that you can use to detect and record when a child has learned an objective. The eleven forms of evaluation described here do not exhaust all possibilities. They may suggest to you additional options. The *HICOMP Track Record* is a convenient way to record accomplishment of the Developmental Activities. The eleven types of evaluation described below provide additional ways to assess skills as they are developed.

Evaluation 1:

CHECKLISTS WITH CRITERIA

Typically a checklist outlines the behavior of interest to the teacher, and often a simple "yes" or "no" is all that is required for evaluation. Can a child remove his coat or not? The *HICOMP Track Record* is really a large checklist that can be used to "keep track" of a child's progress through the curriculum. The *Track Record* is particularly useful with parents to display their child's progress and current developmental status.

The form of this evaluation may be one of simply marking the behavior with a check. However, a plus, minus, or question mark can also provide an easy answer to whether a child can or cannot perform a specific behavior.

Example:

Scissor cutting checklist

Behavior criteria	*Yes*	*No*	*Sometimes*
1. Places finger and thumb in correct scissor holes.	[ ]	[ ]	[ ]
2. Opens and shuts scissors repeatedly.	[ ]	[ ]	[ ]
3. Places scissors perpendicular to paper.	[ ]	[ ]	[ ]
4. Holds paper firmly in place when cutting (i.e., for 3 openings and shuttings of the scissors).	[ ]	[ ]	[ ]
5. Moves scissors ahead after cutting for 3 openings and shuttings.	[ ]	[ ]	[ ]
6. Cuts a line 2″ long	[ ]	[ ]	[ ]
7. Cuts a line 4″ long	[ ]	[ ]	[ ]

Source: From *HICOMP* (p. 20) by S.J. Willoughby-Herb and J.T. Neisworth, 1980, San Antonio, TX: Psychological Corporation. Copyright 1980 by Psychological Corporation. Reprinted by permission.

User Friendly

HICOMP curriculum materials have undergone several revisions. The manuals are in paperback but have plastic bindings that enable the user to fold back pages easily to record data. The printing is of high quality and large enough to be read while in the process of working with the child. A variety of activities, a complete data-collection system, and a well-organized presentation of materials combine to make the curriculum practical, interesting, and adaptable for use with preschool children.

Research Support

The HICOMP curriculum was developed through an HCEEP grant. Employing a model-integrated setting, the objectives, activities, and data-collection system were refined with 12 handicapped and 12 nonhandicapped 3- to 5-year-olds. After 3 years of development, the curriculum was field tested with over 1,200 preschoolers across three Department of Defense preschool centers and numerous private and Head Start centers. After 3 years of field testing, HICOMP became commercially available. Content validity and concurrent validities with developmental assessment instruments are reported in Bagnato (1981), Bagnato and J.T. Neisworth (1980), Bagnato and J.T. Neisworth (1983), and MacTurk and J.T. Neisworth (1978). HICOMP materials include a listing of HICOMP objectives linked to parallel items found in several widely used assessment instruments, permitting informal estimates of concurrence and age norms.

Family Involvement

The HICOMP manual contains numerous suggestions for home-based activities for parent-child interaction. The curriculum is not, however, focused on parent involvement and does not supply separate home-related materials.

Hawaii Early Learning Profile
and Help for Special Preschoolers (HELP)

Organization

The Hawaii Early Learning Profile (HELP) curriculum consists of assessment devices and activity guides for both infants (birth to 3 years) and preschoolers (3 to 6 years). The activities were developed for use with handicapped children. Due to the sequential developmental arrangement of skills and activities, the program is appropriate for normally developing children as well.

Content areas include self-help, motor skill, communication, social skills, and cognitive development. The motor skills area presents wheelchair and swimming skills in addition to the usual motor skills. Included within social skills are adaptive behaviors, responsible behaviors, interpersonal relations, personal welfare/safety, and social manners. Cognitive development covers attention span/task completion, basic reading skills, math skills, writing skills, reasoning skills, and music/rhythm skills. Communication includes auditory perception/listening skills, language comprehension skills, language skills, sign language skills and speech reading skills. Activities in all areas make use of everyday routines and situations. There seems to have been a conscious effort to provide activities that will enhance normalization. This type of a focus can aid in lessening the tendency to teach to a specific or unnatural situation.

Another special feature of HELP is the inclusion of activities, like attention and task completion, for older developmentally delayed children (see Exhibit 6-18).

Hawaii Early Learning Profile (HELP)
and Help for Special Preschoolers

Author(s): S. Furono, K. O'Reilly, C.M. Hoska, T. Instauka,
            T.L. Allman, B. Zeisloft
Date: 1985
Publisher: VORT Corporation
Address: PO Box 60880, Palo Alto, CA 94306
Phone: (412) 322-8282

Focus: Handicap-sensitive.
Target population: Handicapped infants birth to 3 years; preschoolers 3 to 6 years.
Program type: Individual home- or center-based.
Content area: Gross and fine motor, cognition, expressive language, social and emotional development, and self-help.
Data system: HELP charts are used to identify current mastery of skills, needs, and objectives and for recording and visually tracking progress.
Materials/Cost: Activity guide (birth to 3 years): $17.95; activities binder (3 to 6 years): $34.95; HELP charts: $2.95, $2.45 for 10 + ; HELP When a Parent is Handicapped: $21.95; Help for Parents: $3.95; Help at Home: $59.95.
Training needed: Knowledge of and experience with handicapped infants; consultation with other professionals encouraged.
Quality of materials: Sturdy spiral notebook.
Family involvement: Guides for parents: When a Parent is Handicapped (techniques for involving blind, deaf, physically disabled and mentally retarded parents), and HELP for Parents of Children with Special Needs (additional parent information and a means of recordkeeping).

Comment:
- Precautions and suggestions for intervention with particular handicapping conditions.
- Family involvement.
- Microcomputer planning and recordkeeping system available.
- Plans clearly written with a variety of activities.

Skills need to be taught in an age-appropriate manner, and these activities focus attention on that need.

HELP can be used in a variety of settings. The infant curriculum lends itself to both home- and center-based programs. Preschool activities are mainly small-group oriented; with a little adaptation, they can also be used successfully in a home setting. Permission is given to duplicate the activities for direct use only. In this way, an interventionist could leave copies of activities in the home, thus correlating activities between the two settings.

Exhibit 6–18 HELP Curriculum Activities for Preschoolers at-Risk for Learning Disabilities

---

23. ATTENTION SPAN/TASK COMPLETION

23.01 Completes 10% of task with some attention and reinforcing.

ACTIVITIES:

1. Prepare a simple puzzle of ten or fewer pieces by taping all but two of the pieces in place.
2. Start with all but the easiest pieces taped in place on the puzzle board.
3. Have the child sit at a table and give her the one or two pieces not already in place.
4. Instruct her to place the puzzle piece in the exposed/correct area.
5. Guide her hand to help her place the pieces.
6. As she succeeds with one piece, remove tape to increase the difficulty.

SUGGESTIONS/NOTES:

_____

_____

_____

_____

23.02 Starts a task only when reminded.

ACTIVITIES:

1. Demonstrate a variety of fun activities from drawing to puzzle boards.
2. Tell the child he can select one of the activities.
3. Provide him with the necessary materials, and tell him to start the task within the next minute.
4. Set a timer for one minute.
5. Tell the child to start, and start the timer.
6. Praise the child for getting a quick start, and help him if necessary.
7. Vary by introducing less desirable tasks such as cleaning up.

SUGGESTIONS/NOTES:

_____

_____

_____

_____

Source: From *Help for Special Preschoolers: Activities Binder* (p. 113) by Santa Cruz County Office of Education, 1987, Santa Cruz, CA: Santa Cruz County Office of Education. Copyright 1987 by Santa Cruz County Office of Education. Reprinted by permission of VORT Corporation.

Linkage

Assessment is a part of the HELP program. The teacher can link the results of the HELP checklist (Exhibit 6-19) to the activities. The checklist and chart provide a record of progress. Computer planning and recordkeeping software is available for use with the Apple II family or IBM-PC and compatibles. Use of the software can assist in planning, monitoring, and ensuring efficient use of staff time and resources.

Training

The user should have knowledge of and experience with the target population. Careful examination and study of the manuals are important to permit constructive use of the curriculum. Consultation with specialists is stressed throughout the activities. Cautions concerning particular handicapping conditions are noted.

Additional skills are needed to ensure proper implementation of the program. In some instances, the teacher is called on to observe a child and determine the presence or absence of a given behavior. Thus, training in observation is needed. Teachers also need to be able to develop behavioral objectives. A limited description of a behavioral objective is given, but further training or experience would be helpful. Skill in the use of modeling, prompting, and reinforcement procedures would also enhance the effectiveness of the program. These skills may be a part of the repertoire of a teacher trained in special education but are not often found in a curriculum for early childhood teachers.

Family Involvement

The HELP curriculum can be used in home-based programs. The activities from the computer program or copies of activities in the regular curriculum can be given to parents to use at home. The plans are clear and easily interpreted.

Activities used in the program capitalize on normal routines. Users are encouraged to plan activities that take into consideration family resources, strengths, interests, and time availability. The focus is on using play as a means of family involvement.

User Friendly

The overall HELP curriculum and assessment instruments are clearly written and well organized. Progress can be monitored and can be made even easier with the available computer software. Activities are interesting, and the required materials are reasonable in cost. The program respects the individual needs of the child and the family by providing precautions and suggestions for intervention in cases that involve stress in infants, ideas for older delayed children, consideration of family differences, and a variety of individual activities.

Exhibit 6–19 HELP Assessment Checklist

Age (mo.)	Item No.	Skill	Assessment Dates		Comments
		3.0 GROSS MOTOR (continued)			
16-17	3.89	Stands on one foot with help			
17-19	3.90	Walks upstairs with one hand held			
17-18½	3.91	Carries large toy while walking			
17-18½	3.92	Pushes and pulls large toys or boxes around the floor			
17½-19½	3.93	Walks independently on eight inch board			
17½-18½	3.94	Tries to stand on two inch balance beam			
17½-19	3.95	Backs into small chair or slides sideways			
18-24½	3.96	Kicks ball forward			
18-20	3.97	Throws ball into a box			
18-24	3.98	Moves on "ride on" toys without pedals			
18-24	3.99	Runs fairly well			
18-21	3.100	Climbs forward on adult chair, turns around and sits			
19-21	3.101	Walks downstairs with one hand held			
19-24	3.102	Picks up toy from floor without falling			
20-21	3.103	Squats in play			
20-22	3.104	Stands from supine by rolling to side			
20½-21½	3.105	Walks a few steps with one foot on two inch balance beam			
22-24	3.106	Walks upstairs holding rail – both feet on step			
22-30	3.107	Jumps in place both feet			
23-26	3.108	Goes up and down slide			
23-25½	3.109	Stands on tiptoes			
23-25	3.110	Walks with legs closer together			
24-26	3.111	Catches large ball			
24-30	3.112	Rides tricycle			
24-36	3.113	Imitates simple bilateral movements of limbs, head and trunk			
24-25½	3.114	Walks upstairs alone – both feet on step			
24-26	3.115	Walks downstairs holding rail – both feet on step			
24-30	3.116	Jumps a distance of eight inches to fourteen inches			
24-26½	3.117	Jumps from bottom step			
24-30	3.118	Runs – stops without holding and avoids obstacles			
24-26	3.119	Walks on line in general direction			
24-30	3.120	Walks between parallel lines eight inches apart			
24½-26	3.121	Stands on two inch balance beam with both feet			
24-30	3.122	Imitates one foot standing			
25½-27	3.123	Walks downstairs alone – both feet on step			
25½-30	3.124	Walks on tip-toes a few steps			
27-29	3.125	Jumps backwards			
27½-28½	3.126	Attempts step on two inch balance beam			
28-29½	3.127	Walks backward ten feet			
29-32	3.128	Jumps sidewards			
29-31	3.129	Jumps on trampoline with adult holding hands			
30-32	3.130	Alternates steps part way on two inch balance beam			
30-34	3.131	Walks upstairs alternating feet			
30-36	3.132	Jumps over string two to eight inches high			
30-36	3.133	Hops on one foot			

Source: Copyright 1984 by VORT Corporation. Reprinted by permission.

Developmental Programming for Infants and Young Children (DPIYC)

Organization

Developmental Programming for Infants and Children is organized in five volumes. Volumes 1, 2, and 3 contain an assessment, a profile, and intervention activities for infants from birth to 3 years. The assessment, profile and application

---

Developmental Programming for Infants and Young Children (DPIYC)

Author(s): Sara Brown, Carol M. Donovan
Date: 1985
Publisher: University of Michigan Press
Address: P O Box 1104, Ann Arbor, MI 48106
Phone: (313) 764-4392

Focus: Developmental milestones.
Target population: Children with a developmental age of birth to 36 months.
Program type: Individual home-based program that can be adapted to center and clinical settings.
Content area: Perceptual/fine motor, cognition, language, social/emotional development, self-care, and gross motor.
Data system: Part of the complete program and linked to assessment devices; there is no specific data sheet for the activities; EIDP or PDP developmental scales.
Materials/Cost: Books 1, 2, 3 (birth to 36 months): $16; Books 4, 5 (preschool): $12.50; test booklet: $1.50.
Training needed: Professionals train parents; consultation with other professionals is recommended.
Quality of materials: Sturdy spiral notebook.
Family involvement: Parents are the focus of the program; professionals offer training and support and monitor progress.

Comment:
- Parents are the focus of the program.
- Adaptations for handicap noted.
- Cautions alert user to inappropriate activities for certain handicaps.
- Need to develop own behavioral objectives and formative evaluation collection method beyond EIDP and PDP scales.
- Designed especially for use by interdisciplinary teams.

---

activities for preschoolers are found in Volumes 4 and 5. The curriculum content is arranged in a parallel mode with a crossover of specific objectives. The activities are designed for professionals who are training parents and are meant to supplement specific therapies from specialists. Ongoing consultation with other members of a multidisciplinary or transdisciplinary team is essential to the formalization and implementation of an appropriate program for each child.

Activities include adaptation suggestions for particular handicapping conditions. Exhibit 6-20 illustrates the symbols used throughout the plans and notes basic adaptations for handicaps. A section of the manual presents a general discussion of ways to alter activities for specific handicaps.

Exhibit 6–20 Developmental Programming for Infants and Young Children: Plan Symbols and Adaptations for Handicaps

---

KEY

The following symbols are used consistently throughout the book. They describe an adaptation of the activities due to a child's handicap and the appropriate teaching method for a given short-term goal.

O. *Omit only if the child cannot be expected to achieve the goal because of handicapping condition. Use alternative activity if given (see page 13).*

NC. *No changes in activities are necessary (see page 11).*

MA. *Only minor adaptations are necessary to make the activities appropriate, for example:*

Hearing Impaired: *Give oral and gestural cues consistent with the alternative communication system being used. Continue to talk to the child and to label objects so that any residual hearing may be tapped. Continue amplification if used. Substitute signs or symbols for words when appropriate.*

Motorically Involved: *Position the hypertonic child in a relaxed position where s/he can achieve maximal use of the motor patterns s/he exhibits being careful not to encourage inappropriate compensation patterns. Encourage eye pointing if the child is unable to use his/her hands and arms or unable to speak.*

Visually Impaired. *Use bright colors and large objects to effectively tap any residual sight. Encourage the child to consistently wear corrective glasses if prescribed. Compensate for lack of vision by substituting objects with sounds, textures, and smells.*

Numbered Activities. *These activities are sequenced in order of difficulty. The first activity should be achieved with a degree of success (50 percent) before the next activity is used unless a given handicap does not allow successful completion.*

Source: From *Developmental Programming for Infants and Young Children* by S. Brown and C.M. Donovan, 1985, Ann Arbor, MI: The University of Michigan Press. Copyright 1985 by The University of Michigan Press. Reprinted by permission.

Linkage

Volumes 1 and 4 provide assessment instruments: *Early Intervention Developmental Profile* (EIDP) and *Preschool Developmental Profile* (PDP). These are to be used in conjunction with information from other evaluations to determine a child's strengths and weaknesses. The program's profiles (Exhibit 6-21) are used to record the results of the assessment, assist in program planning, and provide a means for summative evaluation. Some type of recording sheet would need to be developed for daily or weekly data collection.

The program guides the user in the formation of behavioral objectives, resulting in a list of sample six-month objectives, as seen in Exhibit 6-22. The objectives are then translated into activities, such as those shown in Exhibit 6-23.

Activities for preschoolers are designed to provide the added socialization benefits of a center-based setting. Group activities are more common for this age level

Exhibit 6–21 Developmental Programming for Infants and Young Children: Assessment Profile

NAME _____ **Perceptual/Fine Motor**

ITEM NUMBER	DEVELOPMENTAL LEVELS AND ITEMS	DATE	DATE	DATE	DATE
	0–2 months				
*1	Responds to different light intensities				
2	Focuses momentarily on face or soft light				
3	Follows moving object horizontally and vertically				
4	Follows moving object through most of a circular path				
	3–5 months				
*5	Integration of grasp reflex				
6	Reaches for dangling object				
7	Moves head to track moving object				
8	Fingers own hands in play at midline				
9	Uses ulnar palmar prehension				
10	Reaches for cube and touches it				
11	Uses radial palmar prehension (uses thumb and two fingers)				
12	Transfers toy from hand to hand				
	6–8 months				
13	Pulls one peg out of pegboard				
14	Rakes or scoops up raisin and attains it				
15	Has complete thumb opposition on cube				
16	Uses inferior pincer grasp with raisin				
	9–11 months				
17	Pokes with isolated index finger				
18	Drops a block with voluntary release				
19	Uses neat pincer grasp with raisin				
20	Attempts to imitate scribble (holds crayon to paper)				
21	Holds crayon adaptively				

* = reflex, righting reaction, protective response, or equilibrium reaction   *Developmental Programming for Infants and Young Children Volume 2 Early Intervention Developmental Profile*

Source: From *Developmental Programming for Infants and Young Children* by S. Brown and C.M. Donovan, 1985, Ann Arbor, MI: The University of Michigan Press. Copyright 1985 by The University of Michigan Press. Reprinted by permission.

Exhibit 6–22 Developmental Programming for Infants and Young Children: Sample Behavioral Objectives

---

Sample 6-Month Objectives from 12/4/78 Evaluation of K.S., Birthdate 12/26/73

Perceptual/Fine Motor
1. K.S. will imitate movements of the arms which require stabilization of the shoulder and elbow while isolated movements are made at the fingers or wrist.
2. K.S. will copy shapes which combine intersections of horizontal and vertical planes, using clay, Lincoln Logs, Tinker Toys, etc.

Cognition
1. K.S. will count to 10 using one-to-one correspondence.
2. K.S. will classify geometric shapes according to curves and angles.

Language
1. K.S. will describe objects according to their functions.
2. K.S. will describe to the teacher's aide what she did during free play.

Social
1. K.S. will work on a task or project with another child until the task or project is completed.
2. K.S. will knock and wait for a reply before entering the classroom's lavatory.

Self Care
1. K.S. will unbutton and button large buttons on a button board.
2. K.S. will wash and dry her face before and after snack time without assistance.

Gross Motor
1. K.S. will imitate bilateral movements made with the entire arm or leg.
2. K.S. will maintain her balance while moving on a narrow base of support.

Note: These objectives relate to June 1979 assessment.

Source: From *Developmental Programming for Infants and Young Children* (p. 60) by S. Brown and C.M. Donovan, 1985, Ann Arbor, MI: The University of Michigan Press. Copyright 1985 by The University of Michigan Press. Reprinted by permission.

---

and provide opportunities to learn or practice skills in a natural setting. Infant activities are mainly individual activities that could be implemented in either a home- or center-based program.

Training

The program is designed for professionals and paraprofessionals, who then train parents in home-based programs or who teach directly in center-home settings. A good background in child development and a knowledge of the target population are assumed. Skill in working with parents and other professionals involved with the child is important. Throughout the program, the emphasis is on the need for ongoing consultation with specialists. Some information about writing behavioral objectives is included; however, additional training may be needed. The plans do

Exhibit 6–23 Developmental Programming for Infants and Young Children: Objective Activities

---

Profile item 109:
  Defines concrete labels.

Behavioral objective:
  Susan will describe and give the use for three objects not present during a guessing game *(What does it look like? What do we use it for?)*

Underlying concepts of the objective are:
  1. receptive language (understands the question *What?* as asking for a description)
  2. expressive language (is able to use modifiers to describe an object)
  3. part-whole relations (is able to break an object into its component properties: size, shape, use)
  4. mental image (is able to hold an image of the object in memory)
  5. cognitive constructs (has basic constructs of size, shape, and use relationships; can make comparisons—*it is round like an orange, but bigger*—beach bɛ.'l). Suggested objects are ball, shoe, cup, spoon, hat.

Alternative activities:
  a. Using a stereognosis bag where the child's only cues to describe can be gained by feeling an object, ask the child *What does it look like? What do we use it for?*
  b. Play a guessing game, asking, *What things are round?* or *teeny?* or *blue?* allowing the children to walk around the room looking for objects which fit a descriptive term.
  c. Play a riddle game (such as *What is round, soft, and has a hole in the middle?*) where the children have to supply the label.

Source: From *Developmental Programming for Infants and Young Children* (p. 61) by S. Brown and C.M. Donovan, 1985, Ann Arbor, MI: The University of Michigan Press. Copyright 1985 by The University of Michigan Press. Reprinted by permission.

---

not address the need for particular prompts or suggest reinforcement ideas; additional training in this area would clearly complement implementation of the program.

Family Involvement

The home is the focus of the program. The activities for the infant seek to increase the parents' confidence in their ability as parents and to improve parent-child interaction. Such activities are often a part of a home-based program with close parent participation. For preschoolers, the opportunity for socialization with their peers is best served in center-based programs. If the interventionists are familiar with the child's daily schedule at home, they can help the family incorporate activities into daily routines by pointing out times when logical opportunities are available. A schedule like that shown in Exhibit 6-24 can help the parent fit activities into the family schedule. Since it is important that the activities be consistent at the home and center, a simple chart to ensure this can be developed, and the parent can assist in collecting data and graphing progress.

Exhibit 6–24 Developmental Programming for Infants and Young Children: Activity Schedule

In order to aid the family to incorporate many activities in the routine, the programmer must be familiar with their daily schedules that involve the child. Examples of how general developmental activities can be worked into the daily schedule are as follows:

7:00	Arising (dressing, toileting, and hygiene activities)
7:30	Breakfast (eating, tooth-brushing activities)
8:00	Educational TV (language, cognition, positioning, and sitting)
9:00	Housework (self-care, social, dramatic play, sweeping floors, making beds, washing dishes)
10:00	Snack (feeding; social and self-care activities such as putting on an apron, using a napkin, washing hands, spreading peanut butter)
10:30	Playtime (inside—cognitive and fine motor: clay molding, coloring, drawing, puzzles)
12:00	Lunch (feeding, setting table, using dishes)
1:00	Quiet time (language and cognition: records, puzzles, finger plays)
1:30	Nap (dressing activities)
3:00	Snack (social: tea party or "picnic" with siblings or neighbors)
3:30	Playtime (outside—gross motor activities: walking, climbing, swinging, ball play, tricycling)
5:30	Supper preparation (self-care and social activities such as cooking)
6:00	Supper (language: time to be a part of the whole family conversations)
6:30	Playtime (roughhousing with father, playing with siblings)
7:30	Bath (hygiene, dressing, toileting)
8:00	Bedtime (language: story time)

Source: From *Developmental Programming for Infants and Young Children* (p. 62) by S. Brown and C.M. Donovan, 1985, Ann Arbor, MI: The University of Michigan Press. Copyright 1985 by The University of Michigan Press. Reprinted by permission.

Research Support

Concurrent validity of the *Early Intervention Developmental Profile* was examined during 1973-1976 project activities. Table 6-3 shows the correlation coefficients for developmental levels attained on the profile and on standardized instruments.

As a result of field testing with handicapped and nonhandicapped children, the final form of the *Preschool Developmental Profile* was developed. Information on the testing sites and disabilities of the children in the studies is included in the manual. Actual results are not given (see also Bagnato, 1984; Bagnato & Neisworth, 1985; Bagnato & Mayes, 1986; Bagnato & Murphy, 1989).

User Friendly

The program offers a complete package for linkage of assessment to curriculum. All the basic elements are provided. Some special adaptations and cautions for spe-

Table 6–3 Developmental Programming for Infants and Young Children: Correlation
Coefficients for Developmental Levels

TABLE 1. Correlation Coefficients Between Developmental Levels Attained on the Profile and on
Standardized Instruments

Profile Scale	Bayley Mental Scale (N = 13)	Bayley Motor Scale (N = 7)	Vineland Social Maturity Scale (N = 12)	REEL (N = 11)	Clinical Motor Evaluation (N = 14)
Cognition	.96***	.82***	.90***	.55	.68
Perceptual/Fine Motor	.91***	.84***	.93***	.44	.82*
Gross Motor	.87***	.95*	.84***	.33	.84*
Language	.90***	.62*	.85***	.75**	.36
Social/Emotional	.96***a	.88***	.91***b	.51	.83*
Self-care	.80**	.66**	.77**	.55	.81*c

***p ≤ .001   a. N = 12
**p ≤ .01   b. N = 11
*p ≤ .05   c. N = 13

TABLE 2. Correlation Coefficients Among the Six Profile Scales

	Self-care (N = 14)	Social/ Emotional (N = 13)	Language (N = 14)	Gross Motor (N = 14)	Perceptual/ Fine Motor (N = 14)
Cognition	.73**	.95***	.89***	.81***	.90***
Perceptual/Fine Motor	.87***	.93***	.72**	.87***	
Gross Motor	.74**	.91***	.59*		
Language	.59*	.83***			
Social/Emotional	.85***a				

***p ≤ .001   a. N = 13
**p ≤ .01
*p ≤ .05

Source: From *Developmental Programming for Infants and Young Children* (p. 3) by S. Brown and C.M.
Donovan, 1985, Ann Arbor, MI: The University of Michigan Press. Copyright 1985 by The University of
Michigan Press. Reprinted by permission.

cific handicaps are given. The curriculum can be used for both handicapped and
nonhandicapped, thus permitting use in mainstreamed and integrated settings.
Training requirements and cost fall within the range of most programs.

There are several ways the basic elements could be expanded. A means of
monitoring progress on a daily or weekly basis would enable the user to comply
with the data-collection needs of IEP and IFSP development and would facilitate
effective programming. Additional background and training in the development of
behavioral objectives and in specific teaching methods (such as prompting and
reinforcement) and a larger array of activities or alternative activities would further
enhance the program.

Oregon Project Curriculum for Visually Impaired
and Blind Preschool Children (OPC)

Author(s):   D. Brown, V. Simmons, J. Mehtvin
Date: 1979
Publisher: Jackson County Education Service District
Address: 101 N. Grape Street, Medford, OR 97501
Phone: (503) 776-8580

Focus: Handicap-sensitive.
Target population: Visually impaired/blind children (birth to 6 years).
Program type: Home-based; can be used in center or institution with individuals or small groups.
Content area: Cognitive, language, self-help, socialization, fine and gross motor.
Data system: Weekly recording sheet suggested; permission given to duplicate; skills inventory for summative evaluation.
Materials/Cost: Teacher's manual: $60 (includes five skills inventory booklets).
Training needed: Knowledge of development of visually impaired preschool children; skill in use of prescriptive teaching methods.
Quality of materials: Well-organized, sturdy binder; plans clearly written.
Family involvement: Need for cooperation between teacher and parent emphasized; activities designed for home use.

Comment:
- Family involvement.
- Clear summative data system.
- Reasonable cost.
- Precursors to independent skills at 6 years of age.

Oregon Project Curriculum for Visually Impaired and Blind Preschool Children (OPC)

Organization

The format for the Oregon Project Curriculum for Visually Impaired and Blind Preschool Children is a sequence matching that of normal development. The authors believe that children with visual impairment develop in a normal pattern, with some skills taking longer or appearing later in the cycle. Within the sequence, six areas of development are emphasized: cognitive, language, self-help, socialization, fine motor, and gross motor. A coding system is used to note skills that are appropriate for a child with a particular visual problem or that the child may develop at a slower rate or later than other children (see Exhibit 6-25). Compensatory skills are included in the curriculum.

Exhibit 6–25 Oregon Project Curriculum Coding System

---

* May not be appropriate for totally blind child.
(Example: "Socialization 10* – Reaches for and pats at mirror image")

b May be appropriate only for child who will be a braille reader.
(Example: "Fine Motor 78[b] – Inserts paper into brailler")

° May be appropriate only for child who will need orientation and mobility training.
(Example: "Gross Motor 60° – Runs trailing a wall or rope")

+May be acquired at later age by totally blind child.
(Example: "Gross Motor 33 + – Walks independently")

These codes are a guide rather than absolute indicators. The decision regarding whether or not to teach coded skills should be based upon degree of vision and other individual circumstances. The visual stimulation skills in the early part of Fine Motor 1*, 2*, 3*, 5* should be attempted if the child has eyes and there is the least suspicion of some vision.

Source: From *Oregon Project Curriculum for Visually Impaired and Blind Preschool Children* by D. Brown, V. Simmons, and J. Mehtvin, 1979, Medford, OR: Jackson County Education Service District. Copyright 1979 by Jackson County Education Service District. Reprinted by permission.

Linkage

Assessment of the child in the home is viewed as the best approach for this program, since early intervention will likely take place in that setting. Prior to use of the skills inventory (part of the curriculum), teachers are encouraged to assess the child using a simple normative test. Suggested tests include the Maxfield-Buchholz adaptation of the Vineland Social Maturity Scale for Blind Preschool Children (Maxfield & Buchholz, 1957) and the Alpern-Boll Developmental Profile (Alpern, Boll, & Shearer, 1984). These or similar instruments provide a means for additional summative evaluation.

The skills inventory permits one to link the assessment with the curriculum (see Exhibit 6-26). Long-range goals and short-range objectives for IEP or IFSP development can be formulated from the results of the inventory. Progress can be monitored through the use of the weekly recording sheets and the profile.

Training

The curriculum is designed to be used with prescriptive teaching procedures. A description of the teaching method is found in the manual. The activity sheet (Exhibit 6-27) indicates the behavioral objectives and the teaching and recording procedures to be used. Additional information on task analysis and reinforcement is included. Also noted are sources the user may use to obtain additional ideas and information on various aspects of the prescriptive teaching method. Use of the curriculum is facilitated by a knowledge of the target population, a careful study of the manual, and close consultation with others involved with the child's care and education.

Exhibit 6–26 Oregon Project Curriculum Skills Inventory: Cognitive Area

C O G N I T I V E AGE LEVEL 0-1	Dates:	ASSESSMENTS	OBJECTIVES HAS		
			Date Init	Date Ach	SKILL ✔
1 Alerts to daily tactual stimulation (body massaged with lotion)					
2 Familiar person holds, rocks, cuddles and talks to child 3 or more times each day					
3 Adult provides simultaneous sight, sound, smell, taste, and/or feel of simple event or object (bath, food cooking)					
4 + Removes cloth from face					
5 Touches new objects randomly (feels furry blanket)					
6 + Searches visually or tactually for object that has been removed from vision or touch					
7 + Picks up brightly colored or sound producing toy which child has dropped within arm's reach					
8 + Finds hidden object under container placed within reach (musical toy under box)					
9 + Puts down one object deliberately to reach for another					
10 Adult provides simultaneous sight, sound, smell, taste and/or feel of complex events and objects (shopping, picnicking)					
AGE LEVEL 1-2					
11 Examines variety of liquid and semi-solid substances (foods) with hands					
12 Plays with simple toys appropriately					
13 + Opens container to find sound-maker (ticking clock in box)					
14 + Discovers objects under cover in variety of locations (pans in cupboard, cake in cakepan)					
15 Stacks 3 blocks					
16 Selects, from group of 3, object identical to given object (simple matching)					
17 Names 4 common items when they are presented					
+ May be acquired at later age by totally blind child					

Source: From Oregon Project Curriculum for Visually Impaired and Blind Preschool Children *by D. Brown, V. Simmons, and J. Mehtvin. 1979, Medford, OR: Jackson County Education Service District. Copyright 1979 by Jackson County Education Service District. Reprinted by permission.*

Exhibit 6–27 Oregon Project Curriculum: Activity Sheet, Cognitive Area

Child's Name __KIM__

Teacher's Name __KAREN__

Date __MAY 26, 1979__

SKILL AREA AND NO. ___ COGNITIVE 72

SKILL: __NAMES SHAPES: CIRCLE, SQUARE AND TRIANGLE__

BEHAVIORAL OBJECTIVE:
Kim will name circle, square and triangle 2 out of 3 times each for 3 consecutive days when presented with shapes.

RECORDING PROCEDURE:
Each time Kim correctly names the shape presented, record X in the appropriate space. Record 0 if she does not name shape correctly.

TEACHING PROCEDURE:

Have shapes and formboard ready with Kim seated at small table. As you sit across from her, tell her you are going to play a game with shapes.

Give her one of the shapes and say "What is this shape?" Help her explore the object if necessary. If Kim correctly names the shape, praise her and let her put the shape in the formboard. Record X on the chart.

If Kim does not correctly name the shape, say "This is a _____.", as you guide her hand around the shape. Point out features of the shape ("The circle is round and smooth; the square has four sharp points, the triangle has three sharp points, etc.") Record 0 on the chart.

Present each shape 3 times each day. Be sure to vary the time of day the task is presented (one day morning, next day before bed) and the order in which the shapes are presented.

Weekly Recording Sheet

Items/Trials	Pre Test M	T	W	Th	F	Sat	Sun	Post Test M
circle 1	0	0	X	0	X	X	X	X
2	0	X	X	X	X	X	X	X
3	X	X	X	X	X	X	X	X (23)
square 1	0	0	0	X	X	X	X	X
2	X	X	X	X	X	X	X	X
3	0	X	X	0	0	X	X	X
triangle 1	0	0	0	0	X	X	X	0
2	0	0	0	0	0	0	0	X
3	0	X	X	X	X	X	X	X

Days of Week

Source: From *Oregon Project Curriculum for Visually Impaired and Blind Preschool Children* by D. Brown, V. Simmons, and J. Mehtvin, 1979, Medford, OR: Jackson County Education Service District. Copyright 1979 by Jackson County Education Service District. Reprinted by permission.

Family Involvement

The program is targeted as a home-based model. Activities are encouraged in normal situations and at usual times. The lessons are clearly written and make use of household items and natural settings. Parents and teachers are viewed as partners. Home visits of 1½ hours per week are recommended.

If the program were to be adapted for center use, the use of daily routines and activities would enhance the carryover to the home and family. Activities could be shared with parents through conferences, workshops, or teacher-designed home communication sheets. Thus the partnership between parent and teacher would remain an integral part of the program.

Research Support

The Oregon project curriculum was field tested in nine sites (75 visually impaired children) in Oregon and Arizona. Data were collected on 53 children (26 girls and 27 boys) ranging in age from a few months to 8 years. Further details on the results of the field testing can be found in Green and Straugh (1979).

User Friendly

The overall design of the curriculum facilitates its use by professionals and paraprofessionals. The linkage with the assessment and the emphasis on parent involvement are compatible with PL 94-142 and PL 99-457 requirements. Clearly written plans and an adequate data system combine to make a practical and functional curriculum.

Initial use of the curriculum will require extra time and resources for designing, securing, and adapting materials for the individual activities. There is no fixed list of materials; the required books, pictures, and other materials need to be assembled by the user. However, the materials are not extensive or particularly expensive. In most teaching situations, after using the curriculum and assembling an initial set of materials, one would need to change or adapt the materials only to fit a particular child's needs and interests.

Individualized Assessment and Treatment for Autistic and Developmentally Disabled Children (IATA)

Organization

Individualized Assessment and Treatment for Autistic and Developmentally Disabled Children is organized in three volumes. Volume 1, the *Psychoeducational Profile* (PEP), is used to assess the abilities of the child. Seven areas of learning functions are examined: (1) imitation, (2) perception, (3) gross motor, (4) fine motor, (5) eye-hand integration, (6) cognitive performance, and (7) cognitive verbal.

Individualized Assessment and Treatment for Autistic
and Developmentally Disabled Children (IATA)

Author(s):   E. Schopler, R. Reichler
Date: 1979
Publisher: PRO-ED
Address: 5341 Industrial Oaks Blvd., Austin, TX 78735
Phone: (512) 892-3142

Focus: Handicap-sensitive.
Target population: Children functioning at preschool level within the chrono-
logical age range of 1 to 12 years; autistic preschoolers.
Program type: Individual, center- or home-based.
Content area: Imitation, perception, fine and gross motor, eye-hand integra-
tion, cognitive performance, cognitive verbal skills.
Data system: PEP profile sheets.
Materials/Cost: Psychoeducational Profile: $29; profile sheets: $12; Teaching
Strategies for Parents and Professionals: $21; Teaching Activities for Autistic
Children: $59.
Training needed: Knowledge of and training with the target population.
Quality of materials: Ringed notebooks.
Family involvement: Strategies for parents included.

Comment:
- Linkage suggestions for IEP/IFSP and program development.
- 250 teaching activities and goals.
- Strategies for parents.

Volume 2 contains teaching strategies for parents and teachers. Volume 3 provides teaching activities. There is no attempt to provide a general curriculum for
the target population; due to the truly individual characteristics of this population,
such a curriculum is not conceivable. Progress toward individual goals can be
tracked through forms such as that shown in Exhibit 6-28. Exhibit 6-29 presents an
example of a plan to teach a specific objective at different levels of difficulty.

Linkage

The PEP enables the user to determine an entry point for the curriculum. Coordination with IEP and IFSP goals and objectives can then be made.

Training

A knowledge of the target population and experience working with children and
their families are essential. A careful study of the materials and ongoing consulta-
tions with other professionals will aid in planning and implementation.

Exhibit 6–28 Individualized Assessment and Treatment for Autistic and Developmentally Disabled
Children: Form for Tracking Progress

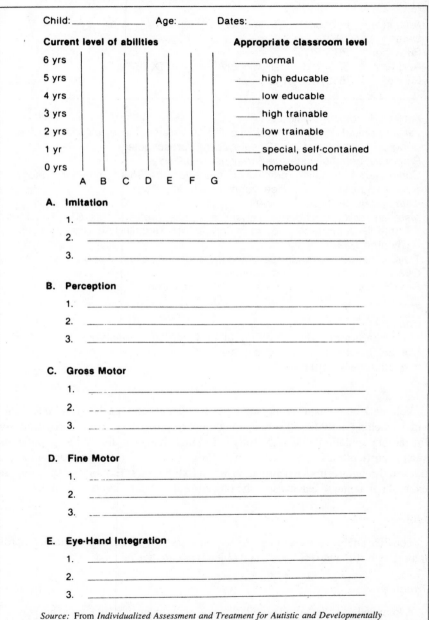

Exhibit 6–29 Individualized Assessment and Treatment for Autistic and Developmentally Disabled Children: Teaching Plan

---

Visual Perceptions

GOAL 1: TO SCAN AN AREA TO LOCATE A GIVEN OBJECT

Objective A: To scan the table to locate a correct puzzle piece.

Materials: Four-piece inset puzzle

Procedure: Place a simple puzzle on a cleared table, putting each piece at a different location around the table. Point to each piece in turn, directing the child to put *that* piece in. Once he understands that he is to place the pieces as you direct, then name each one, e.g., "put banana," or point to the hole that needs filling. Now the child will have to scan the area to find the correct piece.

Objective B: To scan the room to locate a given object.

Materials: Apple, ball, shoe, cup

Procedure: Place the objects around the room so that they are clearly visible to the child. Then sit next to him and ask him to "get apple." (If he has no receptive language, hold another apple up, showing him what to get.) The child now has to look at a distance, find what he wants, and move across the space without becoming distracted.

GOAL 2: TO INCREASE VISUAL TRACKING

Objective C: To observe a moving object.

Materials: Bubbles, ball, balloon, flashlight.

Procedure: Ask child to "look" at each object, and then take action.

Bubbles—Blow them into the air; child pops them with his fingers.

Ball—Sit on floor facing the child. Roll the ball to him, asking him to "catch" it. Gradually roll it slightly to the right or left side so he must reach over to catch it.

Balloon—Pat it into the air and teach child to pat it up again.

Flashlight—Seat child in one place, hand him the flashlight, ask him to make the light "hit" the place you name, i.e., a picture on the wall, a toy across the room, a person.

Source: From *Individualized Assessment and Treatment for Autistic and Developmentally Disabled Children* (p. 17) by E. Schopler and R. Reichler, 1979, Austin, TX: PRO-ED. Copyright 1979 by PRO-ED. Reprinted by permission.

Family Involvement

The importance of cooperation between teachers and parents is emphasized throughout the curriculum. Regular personal contact between teacher and parent is essential to implementation. Parents are encouraged to observe in the classroom and to share ideas they may have used successfully with their children. Home visits by the teachers are also considered to be important.

Communication and recording procedures are guided by both the parents' and the professional's need for information. Exhibit 6-30 shows a weekly home log, and Exhibit 6-31 presents a parent-teacher notebook; to facilitate communication, this notebook usually travels with the child and should be examined as soon as the child arrives at home or at school.

The following principles govern the professional's communications with parents:

- support to parents
- acceptance of individual differences
- appropriate and practical advice (e.g., "Never ask someone to do something you haven't done yourself.")
- parent's need for information

Research Support

Data concerning the effectiveness of the program can be found in Mittler (1981).

User Friendly

The curriculum and assessment offer a well-planned and reasonable program for children with handicaps that continue to puzzle educators. A variety of activities are provided, and strategies are carefully explained. Cooperation between home and school further enhances the potential for progress.

Developmental Communication Curriculum (DCC)

Organization

The Developmental Communication Curriculum (DCC), which was developed under a grant from the Buhl Foundation of Pittsburgh, uses play as its context. Play is defined as "the spontaneous activity of children which begins in infancy with the exploration and manipulation of the environment, through stages of make-believe and pretend to participation in games with rules" (Hanna, Lippert, & Harris, 1982, p. 2). The DCC covers four chronologically ordered stages: (1) prelinguistic (birth to 12 months, (2) symbolic (9 to 21 months), (3) symbolic relationships (18 to 36 months), and (4) complex symbolic relations (over 30 months). Within each stage, the concept of communication is viewed from three domains: function, form, and content. This organization serves as a means of analyzing communication in behavioral terms.

Placement in the curriculum is based partly on the results of the DCC inventory. Results are reported in the placement profile (see Exhibit 6-32). With this information, behavioral objectives are formulated, based on three selection criteria:

Exhibit 6–30 Individualized Assessment and Treatment for Autistic and Developmentally Disabled
Children: Weekly Home Log

PAGE 1: HOME TEACHING

How much time did you spend on the Home Teaching Program each day this week?
 Monday — 45 minutes
 Wednesday — 1 hour
 Sunday — 1 hour

What were your goals?
 Goals: To get Robin to spell simple words using sounds of letters. To help Robin understand the concept "more" and "one more."

What progress?
 Progress: He understands the first and last sound, but I have to emphasize the sounds
 much of the time. I'm not sure about "more." Sometimes he does OK and not so good
 another time.

Any problems? (What have you tried? What worked? Describe child's response.)
 Problems: He still gets silly, laughs a lot when a task is hard for him. He usually calms
 down if I give more help, but not if I scold him.

Do you want some new activities to teach?
 New activities: None yet. I'm not sure how fussy to be about his writing.

PAGE 2: SELF-HELP SKILLS (Eating, dressing, toileting, etc.)

What are you working on?
 Goals: Asking for more, not grabbing food. Learning to wipe and flush toilet.

What progress?
 Progress: So-so. He can ask for more but forgets. Toileting depends on his mood, and
 how soon I get to him. A little progress, I think.

Any problems? (What have you tried? What worked? Describe child's response.)
 Problems: I'm trying moving the serving dishes out of reach so I don't have to prompt
 him to ask or scold grabbing behavior. Don't know if this will help but it makes meals a
 bit pleasanter.

Are your goals too difficult? Is he ready for new goals?
 New goals: No, two at a time is plenty.

Source: From *Individualized Assessment and Treatment for Autistic and Developmentally Disabled Children* (p. 154) by E. Schopler and R. Reichler, 1979, Austin, TX: PRO-ED. Copyright 1979 by PRO-ED.
Reprinted by permission.

---

1. The objectives must teach skills a child needs to develop practical, effective
   communication with another person.
2. The objectives must allow for or teach prerequisite skills for communication
   in a variety of expressive modalities.
3. The objectives must be developmentally sound and appropriate to the repertoire of a preschool child.

The DCC activity handbook contains over 300 activities designed to encourage
and stimulate language growth. Flexibility and adaptation of activities are pro-

Exhibit 6–31 Individualized Assessment and Treatment for Autistic and Developmentally Disabled
Children: Parent-Teacher Notebook

TEACHER REPORT — 9/20
   General.   This has been a good week. Jamie is much calmer and has
had only four temper outbursts. We think he is settling down into the
classroom routines again after the summer vacation. He is beginning to
seek our attention and tell us what he wants; he's used "ball," "tickle,"
and "bathroom" signs spontaneously this week. On 3 days he let Tony
play next to him at the sand table without pushing or hitting. He is taking
one small taste of every food at lunch now, and, believe it or not, he tried a
piece of lettuce without any prompt.
   Lessons.   The color sorting is really solid now and we are moving on
to a new task — matching a row of alternating colored pegs. Jamie is
working on sorting pictures of food versus clothing. I am using the chart I
showed you of pictures illustrating classroom events. Jamie goes and
points to the picture of what he wants to do next (bathroom, water foun-
tain, sand table, etc.). This is making sense to him. Can you come in next
week one afternoon? I would like to show you this chart and how he uses
it. I think it might be useful for you at home. I also have two new signs to
show you: "outside" and "open."
   Home suggestions.   I agree with your idea for controlling his behavior when you have company (i.e., giving him a special activity to *do* while
you are talking). Why not put some of these in shoe boxes so they will be
ready when you need them. Activities we have used at school that he likes
are: cutting strips of paper, threading beads, coloring within a stencil, and
using Lego blocks. You might also try play-do and a plastic knife. It will
probably work better if the shoe box games are only used for these
special "company" times. He is more interested in materials that are a bit
new, not always available.

Source: From *Individualized Assessment and Treatment for Autistic and Developmentally Disabled Children* (p. 156) by E. Schopler and R. Reichler, 1979, Austin, TX: PRO-ED. Copyright 1979 by PRO-ED.
Reprinted by permission.

moted. A wide range of activities is included for both individuals and groups. The
suggested curricular and teaching strategies encompass functional language use
(e.g., teach language in the contexts in which it is used), good teaching methods
(e.g., isolate significant features, highlight sequences), and effective management
techniques (e.g., aim for social reinforcers).

Recognizing the need for organized evaluation of child progress, the authors
present 46 probes, with a general scheduling guideline dependent on student contact time. The probes are linked with objectives in the curriculum. Although the
activities are similar to those found in the handbook, the materials and procedures

Developmental Communication Curriculum

Author(s):	R.P. Hanna, E.A. Lippert, A.B. Harris
Date:	1982
Publisher:	Charles E. Merrill Publishing Company
Address:	1300 Alum Creek Drive, Columbus, OH 48106
Phone:	1 (800) 233-5682, Ohio: call collect (614) 258-8441

Focus: Handicap-sensitive.

Target population: Developmental ages 1 to 5 years; language and hearing-impaired.

Program type: Individual, center- or home-based.

Content area: Communication skills taught in the context of play.

Data system: The curriculum guide contains probes that provide a means to monitor and organize records of progress objectively.

Materials/Cost: Complete program includes Curriculum Guide, Activities Handbook, 12 copies each of Development Communication Inventory (DCI), and the Parent News: $85; additional DCI: 12 for $20; additional Parent News: 12 for $20.

Training needed: Training in working with the target population in speech and language development.

Quality of materials: Material presented in spiral notebook.

Family involvement: Parent News offers descriptions of communication developments.

Comment:
- Organized by categories rather than objectives.
- Makes use of augmentative communication.
- Parent communication through *Parent News*.
- Means to verify teacher and parent observation of child's ability to communicate.

vary, thereby encouraging spontaneity of expression and generalization of concepts. For optimum use of the probes, it is suggested that a trained observer record the data. Important considerations in achieving accurate data collection are noted. Exhibit 6-33 shows the record form used for the probes.

Additional issues included in the DCC curriculum guide concern: (1) parent programs, (2) choosing an augmentative expressive system, (3) working with the physically handicapped, (4) staff development and training, and (5) administration concerns. These issues address some of the needs of a program beyond the actual curriculum itself. Under PL 99-457, many new programs will be developed and many existing programs will expand with special considerations to the infant/preschool level. This section of the DCC takes a look at some of these considerations in a way that should prove helpful to teachers and administrators.

Exhibit 6–32 Developmental Communication Curriculum: Placement Profile

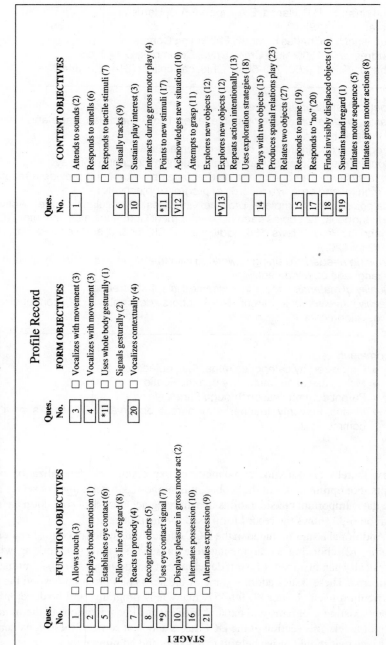

Profile Record

FUNCTION OBJECTIVES

Ques. No.	
1	☐ Allows touch (3)
2	☐ Displays broad emotion (1)
5	☐ Establishes eye contact (6)
	☐ Follows line of regard (8)
7	☐ Reacts to prosody (4)
8	☐ Recognizes others (5)
*9	☐ Uses eye contact signal (7)
10	☐ Displays pleasure in gross motor act (2)
16	☐ Alternates possession (10)
21	☐ Alternates expression (9)

STAGE I

FORM OBJECTIVES

Ques. No.	
3	☐ Vocalizes with movement (3)
4	☐ Vocalizes with movement (3)
*11	☐ Uses whole body gesturally (1)
	☐ Signals gesturally (2)
20	☐ Vocalizes contextually (4)

CONTENT OBJECTIVES

Ques. No.	
1	☐ Attends to sounds (2)
	☐ Responds to smells (6)
	☐ Responds to tactile stimuli (7)
6	☐ Visually tracks (9)
10	☐ Sustains play interest (3)
	☐ Interacts during gross motor play (4)
*11	☐ Points to new stimuli (17)
V12	☐ Acknowledges new situation (10)
	☐ Attempts to grasp (11)
	☐ Explores new objects (12)
*V13	☐ Explores new objects (12)
	☐ Repeats action intentionally (13)
	☐ Uses exploration strategies (18)
14	☐ Plays with two objects (15)
	☐ Produces spatial relations play (23)
	☐ Relates two objects (27)
15	☐ Responds to name (19)
17	☐ Responds to "no" (20)
18	☐ Finds invisibly displaced objects (16)
*19	☐ Sustains hand regard (1)
	☐ Imitates motor sequence (5)
	☐ Imitates gross motor actions (8)

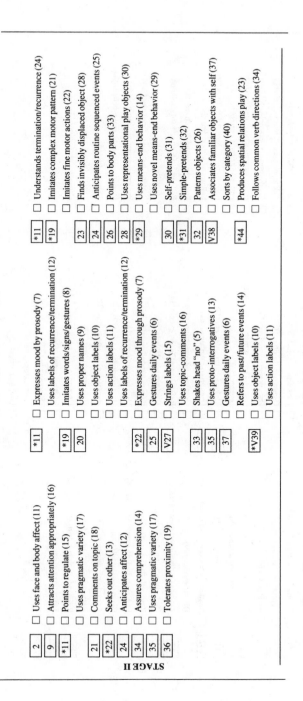

STAGE II

2	☐ Uses face and body affect (11)
9	☐ Attracts attention appropriately (16)
*11	☐ Points to regulate (15)
	☐ Uses pragmatic variety (17)
21	☐ Comments on topic (18)
*22	☐ Seeks out other (13)
24	☐ Anticipates affect (12)
34	☐ Assures comprehension (14)
35	☐ Uses pragmatic variety (17)
36	☐ Tolerates proximity (19)

*11	☐ Expresses mood by prosody (7)
	☐ Uses labels of recurrence/termination (12)
*19	☐ Imitates words/signs/gestures (8)
20	☐ Uses proper names (9)
	☐ Uses object labels (10)
	☐ Uses action labels (11)
	☐ Uses labels of recurrence/termination (12)
*22	☐ Expresses mood through prosody (7)
25	☐ Gestures daily events (6)
V27	☐ Strings labels (15)
33	☐ Uses topic-comments (16)
	☐ Shakes head "no" (5)
35	☐ Uses proto-interrogatives (13)
37	☐ Gestures daily events (6)
*V39	☐ Refers to past/future events (14)
	☐ Uses object labels (10)
	☐ Uses action labels (11)

*11	☐ Understands termination/recurrence (24)
*19	☐ Imitates complex motor pattern (21)
	☐ Imitates fine motor actions (22)
23	☐ Finds invisibly displaced object (28)
24	☐ Anticipates routine sequenced events (25)
26	☐ Points to body parts (33)
28	☐ Uses representational play objects (30)
*29	☐ Uses means-end behavior (14)
	☐ Uses novel means-end behavior (29)
30	☐ Self-pretends (31)
*31	☐ Simple-pretends (32)
32	☐ Patterns objects (26)
V38	☐ Associates familiar objects with self (37)
	☐ Sorts by category (40)
*44	☐ Produces spatial relations play (23)
	☐ Follows common verb directions (34)

Exhibit 6-32 continued

2	☐ Expresses mood variety (20)	**V27**	☐ Uses possessive-object (31)	**V27**	☐ Follows 3-4 semantic relation directions
	☐ Labels moods (20)		☐ Uses agent-action (32)	***V44**	☐ Selects labeled object (35)
*11	☐ Appropriately stops others (22)		☐ Uses action-object (33)		☐ Selects labeled picture (36)
*19	☐ Repeats another's message (37)		☐ Uses attribute-object (34)		☐ Acknowledges accuracy of label (38)
21	☐ Adds new information (36)		☐ Uses preposition-object (35)		☐ Chooses several examples of label (39)
34	☐ Revises message (25)		☐ Uses 3-4 term semantically-related events (36)		☐ Follows agent-action directives (48)
	☐ Alters rate and volume (28)				☐ Follows attributive directives (49)
35	☐ Asks simple questions (31)	**33**	☐ Makes yes/no judgments (20)		☐ Follows prepositional directives (50)
V42	☐ Includes necessary information (26)	**35**	☐ Uses proto-interrogatives (13)		☐ Follows adverbial directives (51)
	☐ Directs another (29)		☐ Uses true interrogatives (23)		☐ Follows pronoun directives (52)
43	☐ Attends for duration of message (33)	**37**	☐ Refers to past/future events (14)		☐ Follows 3-4 term semantic relations directives (53)
*V44	☐ Understands you/me; I/you (27)		☐ Uses temporal labels (30)		
45	☐ Responds to direction (32)	***V39**	☐ Uses expanded nouns (17)	**48**	☐ Pantomimes use without object (41)
46	☐ Expresses lack of comprehension (24)		☐ Uses sensory verbs (18)	**49**	☐ Pantomimes personal/animal (43)
	☐ Gives news of self (30)		☐ Uses expanded verbs (19)		☐ Produces domestic make-believe (44)
	☐ Asks simple question (31)		☐ Uses possessive pronouns (21)		☐ Takes on role (45)
	☐ Responds to question (34)		☐ Uses prepositions (22)	**50**	☐ Labels abstract object (42)
47	☐ Responds to changed affect (23)		☐ Uses uncombined attributes (24)	**51**	☐ Organizes play scene (47)
60	☐ Takes turns in game (35)		☐ Uses personal pronouns (26)		
			☐ Uses adverbs (27)		
			☐ Uses texture labels (28)		
			☐ Uses quantifiers (29)		
		40	☐ Present progressive marker (37)		
			☐ Plurals (38)		
		41	☐ Uses color labels (25)		
		45	☐ Uses true interrogatives (23)		

STAGE III

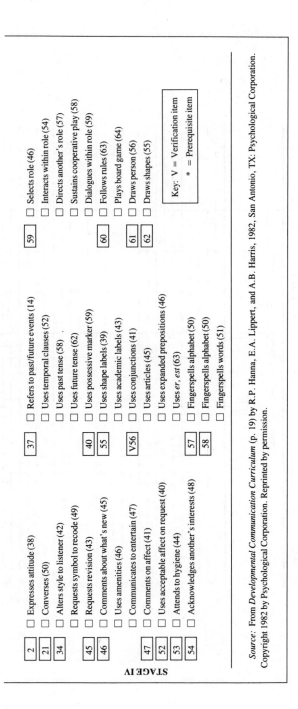

STAGE IV

2	☐ Expresses attitude (38)	37 ☐ Refers to past/future events (14)
21	☐ Converses (50)	☐ Uses temporal clauses (52)
34	☐ Alters style to listener (42)	☐ Uses past tense (58)
	☐ Requests symbol to recode (49)	☐ Uses future tense (62)
45	☐ Requests revision (43)	40 ☐ Uses possessive marker (59)
46	☐ Comments about what's new (45)	55 ☐ Uses shape labels (39)
	☐ Uses amenities (46)	☐ Uses academic labels (43)
	☐ Communicates to entertain (47)	V56 ☐ Uses conjunctions (41)
47	☐ Comments on affect (41)	☐ Uses articles (45)
52	☐ Uses acceptable affect on request (40)	☐ Uses expanded prepositions (46)
53	☐ Attends to hygiene (44)	☐ Uses *er*, *est* (63)
54	☐ Acknowledges another's interests (48)	57 ☐ Fingerspells alphabet (50)
		58 ☐ Fingerspells alphabet (50)
		☐ Fingerspells words (51)

59	☐ Selects role (46)
	☐ Interacts within role (54)
	☐ Directs another's role (57)
	☐ Sustains cooperative play (58)
	☐ Dialogues within role (59)
60	☐ Follows rules (63)
	☐ Plays board game (64)
61	☐ Draws person (56)
62	☐ Draws shapes (55)

Key: V = Verification item
       * = Prerequisite item

Source: From *Developmental Communication Curriculum* (p. 19) by R.P. Hanna, E.A. Lippert, and A.B. Harris, 1982, San Antonio, TX: Psychological Corporation. Copyright 1982 by Psychological Corporation. Reprinted by permission.

Exhibit 6–33 Developmental Communication Curriculum: Probe Record Form

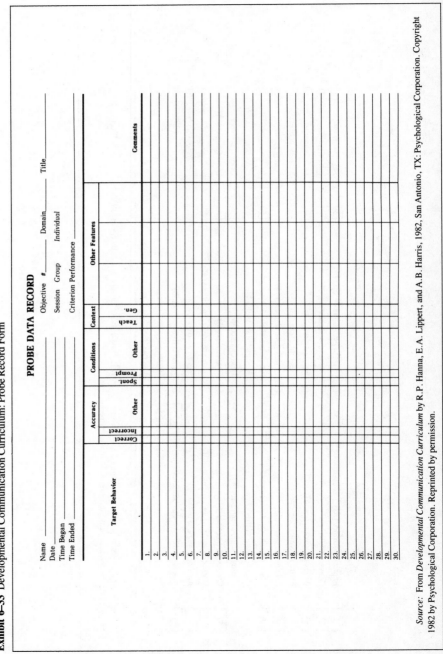

Source: From *Developmental Communication Curriculum* by R.P. Hanna, E.A. Lippert, and A.B. Harris, 1982, San Antonio, TX: Psychological Corporation. Copyright 1982 by Psychological Corporation. Reprinted by permission.

Linkage

The DCC inventory, which is linked with the curricular model, is meant to be used as a part of a complete evaluation of communication function. Comprising two parts (Part 1, direct instruction with the child; Part 2, questions posed to the caregiver), the inventory enables the user to place a child in the curriculum. Physical limitations and the quality of the child's response are considered in administration.

Training

The DCC curriculum is designed for use by special education teachers, speech/language pathologists, hearing therapists, preschool and primary teachers, and child developmental specialists.

Family Involvement

The authors recognize the need for dependence on the parents as informants, observers, teachers, models, counselors, and advocates for their children. At the conclusion of the initial evaluation, it is suggested that the parents receive a copy of the *Parent News,* which is a part of the DCC. This publication is viewed as a stimulus for a regular exchange of information between parents and teachers.

Research Support

No information on research support was provided in the material reviewed.

User Friendly

The DCC presents a well-organized language program with a means for linkage and data collection. Activities, probes, and material on paracurricular issues are clearly written for ease of understanding and use. Within the curriculum, flexibility allows for adaptation for special needs, spontaneity of communication, creativity in teaching style, and functional use of language in a situation that is natural to all children—play.

Transactional Intervention Program (TRIP)

Organization

The Transactional Intervention Program (TRIP) is a child-centered approach to developmental intervention with young handicapped children. The quality of the interaction between the children and their caregivers and teachers is the focus of the program. By enhancing this interaction, the program seeks to increase the frequency of the children's active engagement.

The theory that children's learning and development are a result of their own intrinsically motivated activity is the basis for the approach. Adults are encouraged

Transactional Intervention Program (TRIP)

Author(s): G. Mahoney, A. Powell
Date: 1986
Publisher: Pediatric Research and Training Center/University of Connecticut School of Medicine
Address: Farmington, CT 06032
Phone: (203) 674-1485

Focus: Interactive.
Target population: Young handicapped children (birth to 5 years).
Program type: Individual (child/caregiver/teacher), home- or center-based.
Content area: Turntaking, interactional match, and adult-child interactive skills.
Data system: Developmental profile.
Materials/Cost: NA.
Training needed: Teacher or therapist familiar with the needs of young handicapped children and their families, skilled in observation and transactional intervention, and with good interpersonal skills.
Quality of materials: Soft-bound binder.
Family involvement: Parents/caregivers are essential to the implementation of the program.

Comment:
- Child-centered approach, spontaneous.
- Focuses on interaction between parent/caregiver and child rather than direct instruction.
- Careful training and selection of staff.

to interact in ways that will cause the children to be motivated to learn and develop new skills. Children, parents, and teachers have specific roles, which, when understood and performed, can lead to fulfilling interaction and development. The emphasis is on a match between the child's developmental level, behavioral style, and interest. The program provides information on the roles of children, parents, and teachers; turn taking, which is an essential skill for interaction; interactional matching; and how to develop adult-child interactive skills.

Linkage

The TRIP developmental profile focuses on six domains: (1) cognitive, (2) language, (3) social functioning, (4) fine motor, (5) gross motor, and (6) self-help. According to the authors, the profile can be used for three purposes: (1) observation of behavior, (2) setting expectations, and (3) monitoring the match between children's behavior and aspects of their environment.

To aid in observation, the TRIP worksheet (Exhibit 6-34) includes a description of what the observer is to look for, general observations, estimates of developmen-

Exhibit 6–34 TRIP Developmental Profile Worksheet: Cognition Area

---

COGNITION

Child's Name _____

Observe the child in a variety of situations involving play with toys. Some things to think about as you observe are:

- What kinds of toys or objects does the child typically choose and enjoy playing with?
- How does the child use or play with materials? (for example, does the child look, bang, mouth, wave, throw or use them functionally?)
- Does the child demonstrate a variety of behavior with toys? Are there particular activities of behaviors that are dominant or repetitive in the child's play?
- What is the child's behavioral style typically like in play with toys? (for example, is the child's style deliberate or impulsive, slow or fast-paced?)

General Observations:

_____

_____

_____

_____

Estimated Developmental Age: _____

Based on your observations, rate each of the following characteristics of the child's play with toys. Use a scale from 1 to 7, where 1 = lowest and 7 = highest.

	Rating	*Comments*
Enjoyment	_____	_____
Practice	_____	_____
Exploration	_____	_____
Curiosity	_____	_____
Persistence	_____	_____
Problem Solving	_____	_____
Overall Engagement	_____	_____

Source: From *Transactional Intervention Program* (p. 13) by G. Mahoney and A. Powell, 1986, Farmington, CT: University of Connecticut. Copyright 1986 by University of Connecticut. Reprinted by permission.

---

tal age, and ratings of the characteristics of the child's play. Information on the use of the profile for other purposes is provided in the teacher's guide.

Training

The TRIP pilot program was implemented by certified teachers and therapists. In reviewing the program, it is evident that more than just "academic" knowledge of the target population is necessary for successful implementation. The ability to observe and interpret children's behavior accurately, skill in working with families, and a clear understanding of the basic approach are essential. Good planning and organizational skills, coupled with flexibility and good listening skills, would further enhance a quality replication of the program.

Family Involvement

The participation of the parent/caregiver is essential for the program to operate effectively. The authors and others contend that little progress can be made in early intervention programs without parental involvement.

Research Support

The research support found in the teacher's guide is derived from the T.O.T.E. program conducted in Woodhaven, Michigan. This program served children who were 2 to 30 months of age and eligible for special education services. Two hours of weekly home instruction were provided by teachers and therapists. Data on the children's progress are shown in Table 6-4.

According to Mahoney and Powell (1986), these data support two conclusions: (1) interactional behavior can be modified by instructional procedures in the TRIP, and (2) the amount of gain seen with children is directly related to the degree to which parents can modify their behavior in accordance with the general goals of the program.

Table 6–4   Comparison of Children's Performance in TRIP Intervention

Variable	Low Directive (N = 11)	Groups Medium Directive (N = 10)	High Directive (N = 13)	Significance*
Developmental age, pre	12.00	10.60	9.92	NS
Developmental age, post	19.92	16.30	14.00	.0096
Language age, pre	12.42	11.05	8.58	NS
Language age, post	24.27	18.00	14.24	.0413
Motor age, pre	9.17	7.75	9.18	NS
Motor age, post	14.50	12.50	12.90	NS
Chronological age, pre	18.42	18.50	17.00	NS
Months of intervention	11.08	9.60	9.76	NS

* Significance for pretest comparisons are ANOVA's; significance for posttest comparisons are analyses of covariance that are partialed on pretest performance.

Source: From *Transactional Intervention Program* (p. 51) by G. Mahoney and A. Powell, 1986, Farmington, CT: University of Connecticut. Copyright 1986 by University of Connecticut. Reprinted by permission.

User Friendly

The TRIP focuses on an essential element: the interaction between the parents and their children. The program thus requires a shift in approach by many interventionists (parents and teachers). Interventionists who feel "safe" in curricula structures with specific guidelines, tasks, objectives, and data-collection methods may feel threatened by this approach.

From a theoretical viewpoint, the transactional approach is sound, productive, and beneficial to the child and family. From a practical implementation viewpoint, the program requires careful training, a commitment to and an understanding of the approach, excellent interpersonal skills, and support from administrators. Availability of the requisite resources should be carefully considered when evaluating this program for a particular use.

KINDERGARTEN-TRANSITION

The following two kindergarten-transition curricula are reviewed in this section:

1. Beginning Milestones
2. Brigance Prescriptive Readiness: Strategies and Practices

Beginning Milestones (BM)

Organization

Language is the cornerstone of the Beginning Milestones curriculum. The curriculum was developed for use with young children (about 4 years of age) for whom English is a second language or who, due to socioeconomic background, lack adequate knowledge for the correct use of English. Activities in the areas of communication, motor and socioemotional development, and fine arts are designed to enhance overall development with special emphasis on language development.

The Peek-at-a-Week plan book offers a plan for 36 weeks of instruction. Developmental milestones are identified, and activities and procedures to achieve those milestones are suggested in the resource guide. The guide contains suggestions for making the activities easier or more difficult, depending upon the abilities of the children. There are no specific suggestions for children with particular handicaps. The ideas are of a general nature, such as limiting or increasing the number of items or concepts presented.

The program offers information on teaching strategies (modeling, fading, etc.), discipline, positive reinforcement, classroom management, child development, and enrichment activities. A section on multicultural considerations discusses some important things a teacher needs to be aware of when working with children

Beginning Milestones (BM)

Author(s):   S. Sheridan, D. Murphy, J. Black, M. Puckett, E. Allie
Date: 1986
Publisher: DLM/Teaching Resources Corporation
Address: One DLM Park, Allen, TX 75002
Phone: 1 (800) 527-4747, Texas 1 (800) 442-4711

Focus: Handicap-sensitive.
Target population: 18 months to 5 years.
Program type: Small-group or individual instruction; center- or home-based.
Content area: Communication development, cognitive development, motor development, fine arts, social/emotional development.
Data system: Informal checklists for observation of skills and student performance.
Materials/Cost: Complete curriculum: $150; milestones, materials, and manipulatives: $300.
Training needed: Knowledge of the target population and a careful study of manual.
Quality of materials: Manual in spiral notebook form; colorful, durable picture cards; carrying case provided.
Family involvement: Parent letters provide suggestions for activity to enrich classroom instruction.

Comment:
- Good system for beginning teacher.
- Multicultural considerations.
- Parent letters in English and Spanish.
- All-purpose library of 300 full-color pictures.

from other cultures. Both English and Spanish are used in the manual and parent information material. The All-Purpose Photo Library I is an optional component that contains 272 full-color photo cards.

Linkage

The program encourages both formal (three times a year) and informal (on a regular basis) assessment. The teacher's checklist (Exhibit 6-35), provided in the manual, can be reproduced for each child. The checklist covers such areas as health, language, self-concept, motor skills, general knowledge, and creativity/imagination/rhythms. Student performance checklists (again reproducible) are provided for each unit (see Exhibit 6-36). Teachers can note whether skills are emerging (concepts applied 40 percent to 70 percent of the time) or mastered (concepts applied at least 80 percent of the time). An additional section allows for comments. Both checklists are valuable sources of information for parent conferences, individual progress, and IEP or IFSP development.

Exhibit 6–35 Beginning Milestones: Teacher's Checklist

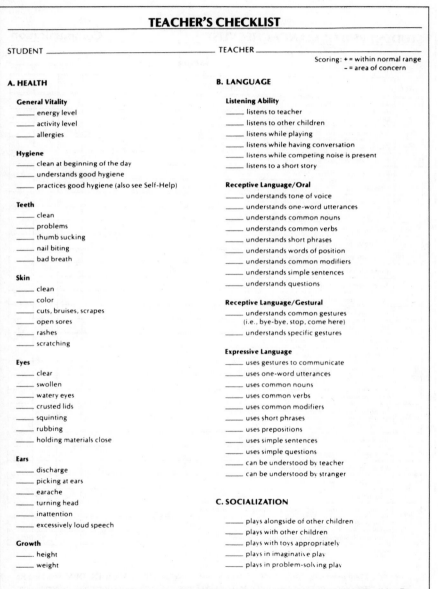

TEACHER'S CHECKLIST

STUDENT _____ TEACHER _____

Scoring: + = within normal range
– = area of concern

A. HEALTH

General Vitality
_____ energy level
_____ activity level
_____ allergies

Hygiene
_____ clean at beginning of the day
_____ understands good hygiene
_____ practices good hygiene (also see Self-Help)

Teeth
_____ clean
_____ problems
_____ thumb sucking
_____ nail biting
_____ bad breath

Skin
_____ clean
_____ color
_____ cuts, bruises, scrapes
_____ open sores
_____ rashes
_____ scratching

Eyes
_____ clear
_____ swollen
_____ watery eyes
_____ crusted lids
_____ squinting
_____ rubbing
_____ holding materials close

Ears
_____ discharge
_____ picking at ears
_____ earache
_____ turning head
_____ inattention
_____ excessively loud speech

Growth
_____ height
_____ weight

B. LANGUAGE

Listening Ability
_____ listens to teacher
_____ listens to other children
_____ listens while playing
_____ listens while having conversation
_____ listens while competing noise is present
_____ listens to a short story

Receptive Language/Oral
_____ understands tone of voice
_____ understands one-word utterances
_____ understands common nouns
_____ understands common verbs
_____ understands short phrases
_____ understands words of position
_____ understands common modifiers
_____ understands simple sentences
_____ understands questions

Receptive Language/Gestural
_____ understands common gestures
          (i.e., bye-bye, stop, come here)
_____ understands specific gestures

Expressive Language
_____ uses gestures to communicate
_____ uses one-word utterances
_____ uses common nouns
_____ uses common verbs
_____ uses common modifiers
_____ uses short phrases
_____ uses prepositions
_____ uses simple sentences
_____ uses simple questions
_____ can be understood by teacher
_____ can be understood by stranger

C. SOCIALIZATION

_____ plays alongside of other children
_____ plays with other children
_____ plays with toys appropriately
_____ plays in imaginative play
_____ plays in problem-solving play

Source: From *Beginning Milestones* (p. 16) by S. Sheridan et al., 1986, Allen, TX: DLM/Teaching Resources Corporation. Copyright 1986 by DLM/Teaching Resources Corporation. Reprinted by permission.

Exhibit 6–36 Beginning Milestones: Student Performance Checklist for Communication Area

STUDENT PERFORMANCE CHECKLIST   Communication

STUDENT _____ TEACHER _____

UNIT	OBJECTIVE	I	E	M
1	Attends without interruption			
	Listens to stories			
2	Focuses attention without interruption			
	Demonstrates enjoyment of stories			
3	Participates in finger plays, rhymes, chants			
4	Responds appropriately to gestures			
	Uses gestures			
5	Responds appropriately to facial expressions			
	Uses facial expressions appropriately			
6	Describes feelings			
7	Demonstrates understanding of familiar signs			
	Responds appropriately to familiar signs			
8	Pantomimes familiar actions			
	Names familiar actions			
9	Demonstrates understanding that sounds are heard			
10	Identifies familiar sounds			
11	Imitates familiar sounds			
12	Responds to different tones of voice			
13	Identifies specific body parts			
	Names specific body parts			
14	Identifies common nouns			
	Uses common nouns			
15	Identifies common nouns			
	Uses common nouns			
16	Identifies familiar animals			
	Names familiar animals			
17	Responds to words, phrases, sentences			
18	Uses intelligible word units			
	Uses phrases			
19	Communicates in words, phrases, sentences			
	Uses intelligible speech			
20	Expresses feelings and ideas with a variety of words			

Source: From *Beginning Milestones* (p. 20) by S. Sheridan et al., 1986, Allen, TX: DLM/Teaching Resources Corporation. Copyright 1986 by DLM/Teaching Resources Corporation. Reprinted by permission.

The assessment procedures are general in nature. Additional experience and assessments (some suggested in the manual) are needed to focus on special problems or needs other than those on which the curriculum is focused.

Training

Training with and knowledge of the target population and normal child development are needed to implement the program. The material is clearly presented and can be successfully used after a study of the manual. The user is encouraged to use the suggestions offered and to develop ideas and procedures that fit the needs and abilities of the teacher and the students. Further consultation with and support from other professionals would be needed for children with additional handicaps.

Family Involvement

The importance of parent involvement and communication is stressed. Ideas for conferences, home visits, and parent letters are presented. Sample parent letters in both English and Spanish are provided and can be reproduced (see Exhibit 6-37). The letters can be used as guides for a beginning teacher and can be adapted by the user to achieve a more personalized effect.

Exhibit 6–37 Beginning Milestones: Sample Parent Letter in Spanish

---

CARTA PARA PADRES 27—Engrudo: "Plastilina" Casera

Muy estimados padres,

Esta semana hicimos adornos de "plastilina" casera. Preparamos la "masa," cortamos los adornos, y los pintamos.

Aqui tiene la receta

1 taza de harina
1 taza de sal
1 cucharada de aceite
colorante para pasteles
Mezclar la harina y la sal. Agregar el aceite.
Agregar el agua lentamente hasta que se
convierta en masa; agregar unas gotitas
de colorante para pasteles.
Formar los adornos o con molde para galletas
o con las manos.

Haga que su hijo le ayude a Mamá a preparar las tortillas para toda la familia.
Que pasen buen fin de semana.

Atentamente,
La maestra de su hijo

Source: From *Beginning Milestones* by S. Sheridan et al., 1986, Allen, TX: DLM/Teaching Resources Corporation. Copyright 1986 by DLM/Teaching Resources Corporation. Reprinted by permission.

Research Support

No research support is indicated in the program material.

User Friendly

The material and organization of the Beginning Milestones curriculum makes it especially attractive to a beginning teacher. In designing the program, the authors considered the needs of the new teacher—where to start, how to set up a classroom, how to track progress, how to talk with parents, how to discipline, and where to seek additional information. For the more experienced teacher, the curriculum offers ideas and suggestions that can be expanded and personalized.

The material is presented in sturdy ringed notebooks that can be carried in a plastic carrying case. The checklists and parent letters can be reproduced, thereby reducing costs. The plans are clear and easily understood.

BRIGANCE Prescriptive Readiness: Strategies and Practice (BPR)

Organization

The BRIGANCE Prescriptive Readiness Strategies and Practice curriculum is designed as a resource for use with children who are developmentally from 4 to 6 years of age. Each section in the manual covers the following subjects: objective, rationale, sequence, recommendations for effective teaching, indications of and possible reasons for learning difficulties, teaching activities, enrichment activities, related learning opportunities, read-to-me books (which can be found in most public libraries), commercial materials, correlation with BRIGANCE assessment materials, and references.

Objectives focus on all areas of development (language, motor, social, self-help, cognition, and writing and reading readiness skills). The curriculum offers the user a variety of strategies, materials, and suggestions for activities that can be adapted according to teaching style, situation, and students' needs. The readiness strategies can be used by themselves or in conjunction with other BRIGANCE assessment materials or basal programs.

Linkage

Each section of the curriculum is cross-referenced with BRIGANCE assessment materials, specifically the *Comprehensive Inventory of Basic Skills* (CIBS), the *Inventory of Basic Skills* (IBS), the *Inventory of Early Development* (IED), the *K & 1 Screen* (K & 1), and the *Assessment of Basic Skills* (ABS) (Spanish edition) (see Table 6-5). Teachers are encouraged to use observation skills to monitor progress. The section on indications of and possible reasons for learning difficulties can be reviewed to aid in the observation. The linkage with well-known and widely used assessment tools can be helpful in enhancing communication among

BRIGANCE Prescriptive Readiness: Strategies and Practice (BPR)

Author(s): A. Brigance
Date: 1985
Publisher: Curriculum Associates, Inc.
Address: 5 Esquire Road, North Billerica, MA 01862-9987
Phone: 1 (800) 225-0248, MA (800) 354-2665

Focus: Developmental milestones.
Target population: Prekindergarten to first grade.
Program type: Center/school based; group and individual; could be adapted for home use.
Content area: Gross and fine motor, language, self-help, visual motor and pre-academic.
Data system: Correlates with BRIGANCE assessments; each lesson notes correlation point.
Materials/Cost: $99.50; sampler available; request order number TH400.
Training needed: Early childhood educational training.
Quality of materials: Large sturdy binder; clear and well-organized lesson plans.
Family involvement: Parent letters inform parents of material covered and offer suggestions for home activities.

Comment:
- Well-organized presentation facilitates use.
- Behaviors that could indicate learning problems are noted.
- Variety of activities.
- Family involvement.

professionals and transition to elementary schools where the assessments may be in use.

Training

Experience with and knowledge of the target population, coupled with a careful study of the manual, will enable one to use the curriculum successfully. Consultation with specialists is needed to adapt activities for specific handicapping conditions.

Family Involvement

Ideas for parent involvement can be found in the recommendations for effective teaching presented throughout the manual. In addition, parent letters describing specific classroom activities are provided for reproduction (see Exhibit 6-38). The original letters are lengthy; however, individual teachers could adapt them for use with different parent groups. Certain parents may respond better to a simpler for-

Table 6–5 BRIGANCE Prescriptive Readiness Strategies and Practice: Correlations with BRIGANCE Assessment Materials

	Assessment	*Record Book*
CIBS (Green)	3	2
IBS (Blue)	10	2
IED (Yellow)	149-151	16
K&1 (White)	13	K
ABS (Orange)	3	2

Source: From *BRIGANCE® Prescriptive Readiness Strategies and Practice* by A. Brigance, 1985, North Billerica, MA: Curriculum Associates, Inc. Copyright 1985 by Curriculum Associates, Inc. Reprinted by permission. BRIGANCE is a registered trademark of Curriculum Associates, Inc.

Exhibit 6–38 BRIGANCE Prescriptive Readiness: Strategies and Practice—Sample Parent Letter

Dear Parents:

Your child is working on walking skills (walking a straight line, walking a circular line, walking on tiptoe, walking forward heel-to-toe, walking backward toe-to-heel, walking in scissor steps).

You can help your child develop these walking skills by demonstrating and allowing your child time to imitate. Give your child lots of encouragement!

Here are some activities you might try:

1. Before asking your child to perform specific walking skills, have your child experiment with different ways of walking. Ask your child to walk on his or her heels. Then, have your child walk using the sides of the feet. Next, have your child walk with the toes pointed in or out. Finally, have your child walk with the toes pointed straight ahead. Ask your child which way of walking feels the most comfortable. Demonstrate and discuss the correct way to walk.

2. Use masking tape on the floor to make a straight line. Say, "Walk on tiptoe on the line." Demonstrate. Practice other walking skills on the line of masking tape.

3. Play Mother (Father), May I? with your child. Establish a starting point. Tell your child to walk a straight line. Before your child moves, he or she must ask permission by saying, "Mother, may I?" You should respond with, "Yes, you may walk a straight line." This is a good way to reinforce verbal directions. Your child must go back to the starting point if he or she forgets to say, "Mother, may I?"

4. Here are a few books that deal with the subject of movement and walking:
   Burton and Dudley by Marjorie Weinman Sharmat.
   One Step, Two... by Charlotte Zolotow.
   Try It Again, Sam: Safety When You Walk by Judith Viorst.

Source: From *BRIGANCE® Prescriptive Readiness Strategies and Practice* by A. Brigance, 1985, North Billerica, MA: Curriculum Associates, Inc. Copyright 1985 by Curriculum Associates, Inc. Reprinted by permission. BRIGANCE is a registered trademark of Curriculum Associates, Inc.

mat with illustrations, perhaps as a part of a class newsletter; the children could participate in the development of such a newsletter.

Research Support

The curriculum has been field tested in at least 28 sites throughout the country. The material was adapted based on suggestions and field-testing results. The author does not list any specific results of the testing.

User Friendly

The well-organized material is presented in a large ring binder. Each section is designed for ease of use and contains a variety of ideas, activities, and resources. Depending upon the experience of the teacher and the resources available, activities can be altered or expanded to serve the needs of a wide range of children. The curriculum offers the security of a structured program for a beginning teacher and the challenge of different approaches for the more experienced educator. The material can be reproduced, thus making it more cost-efficient. Linkage to assessment enhances progress tracking and transition to other programs.

Adaptations and consultation with specialists are needed in order to use the curriculum effectively for children with specific handicaps. The range of activity suggestions and teaching ideas can provide a good base for use with the handicapped. With consultation, the curriculum has the potential for mainstreaming individual children or for designing an integrated program of interest to both delayed and normally developing children.

7

Forging the LINK: A Developmental Assessment/Curriculum Linkage System

Curriculum-based developmental assessment prescribes tailored interventions for young handicapped children and families. Many scales and curricula are available to link a program's assessment and intervention, as illustrated in Chapters 4 and 6; Table 7-1 suggests the best matches between those scales and curricula. Yet few programs have a system in place to integrate the information gained from these prescriptive instruments in order to maximize service delivery to children and families. Most early-intervention programs conduct their assessment and individualized programming efforts as if they were separate and distinct operations. Assessment must be prescriptive, or the effort will be time-consuming and unproductive. Moreover, in the absence of a framework that sequences assessment, intervention, and evaluation operations, programs will fail to be accountable for their services. They simply cannot document the benefits of their hard work with children and families and, therefore, cannot justify the difficult and expensive efforts of their teams. In short, early-intervention programs do not need more tests or more curricula; they do need a systematic framework that synchronizes assessment, intervention, and progress/program evaluation in economical, reasonable, and practical ways.

LINK: A Developmental Assessment/Curriculum Linkage System (Bagnato & Neisworth, 1989) was designed to systematize interdisciplinary team operations by establishing curriculum-based procedures as the foundation and structural "bridge" that link each phase in the assessment, intervention, and evaluation process (see LINK form ordering information in Appendix F). Chapters 2 and 3 presented a skeletal description of each of the phases in the LINK model. To review, the four phases and purposes are (1) screening/identification, (2) prescriptive developmental assessment/curriculum linkage, (3) programming/intervention, and (4) progress evaluation/monitoring. Each of these phases involves two levels of appraisal: administrative and clinical.

This chapter illustrates the step-by-step operation of the LINK system, including the selection of a prescriptive developmental assessment battery, the linkage between assessment tasks and curriculum objectives, and the evaluation of child progress and program impact, using developmental data derived from the scales and curricula. The practical application of the system is illustrated by a child case vignette on Vanessa. First, the case study presents, as background information, Vanessa's early developmental history, disabilities, and programming needs. Then, each phase in the LINK system is explained and illustrated procedurally to document Vanessa's entry into and progress in the intervention program.

APPLICATION OF THE LINK SYSTEM: A CASE STUDY— CEREBRAL PALSY

The following case vignette on Vanessa, a child with cerebral palsy, provides the relevant background information.

Table 7–1 Recommended Links between Developmental Scales and Developmental Curricula

Scale	Curriculum
Newborn-Infant	
Kent Infant Developmental Scale (KIDS)	Early Learning Accomplishment Profile (E-LAP)
Infant Psychological Development Scale (IPDS)	Infant Learning (IL) Carolina Curriculum for Handicapped Infants (CCHI)
Early Coping Inventory (ECI)	Parent Behavior Progression (PBP) Transactional Intervention Program (TRIP)
Teaching Skills Inventory (TSI)	Parent Behavior Progression (PBP)
Infant-Preschool	
BRIGANCE Diagnostic Inventory of Early Development (BDIED)	Learning Accomplishment Profile (LAP) HICOMP Hawaii Early Learning Profile (HELP) BRIGANCE Prescriptive Readiness: Strategies and Practice (BPR)
Learning Accomplishment Profile: Diagnostic Edition (LAP-D)	Learning Accomplishment Profile (LAP) HICOMP
Battelle Developmental Inventory (BDI)	
Griffiths Mental Development Scales (GMDS)	Hawaii Early Learning Profile (HELP) Developmental Programming for Infants and Young Children (DPIYC) Beginning Milestones (BM) HICOMP Learning Accomplishment Profile (LAP)
Scales of Early Communication Skills: Hearing Impaired (SECS)	Clark Early Language Program (CELP) Developmental Communication (DC)
Reynell-Zinkin Developmental Scales: Visually Impaired (RZS)	Oregon Project Curriculum: Blind and Visually Impaired (OPC)
Uniform Performance Assessment System (UPAS)	Evaluation and Programming System for Infants and Young Children (EPS-I) Hawaii Early Learning Profile (HELP) HICOMP Early Learning Accomplishment Profile (E-LAP)
Autism Screening Instrument for Educational Planning (ASIEP)	Individualized Assessment and Treatment: Autism (IATA)
Kindergarten-Transition	
Woodcock-Johnson: Preschool Cluster (WJPEB)	Beginning Milestones (BM) Hawaii Early Learning Profile (HELP)
McCarthy Scales of Children's Abilities (MSCA)	Beginning Milestones (BM) Hawaii Early Learning Profile (HELP)
Cognitive Skills Assessment Battery (CSAB)	Beginning Milestones (BM) BRIGANCE Prescriptive Readiness: Strategies and Practice (BPR) HICOMP

Forty-one marked a turning point for Mrs. Burns. She had always wanted a child, but the years had passed so quickly that the possibility had seemed remote. Now, she was pregnant. The uneasy mixture of excitement and apprehension grew. Her prenatal exams for Vanessa were fine, but her one previous miscarriage made her worry anyhow.

In her 7th month, complications arose. Because of a double footling breech presentation, Vanessa was delivered by C-section at 26 weeks' gestation weighing 2 pounds, 1 ounce. Apgars were 4 and 7 at 1 and 5 minutes, respectively. In addition, her condition was complicated by mild chronic lung disease, intraventricular hemorrhage, and patent ductus arteriosis. However, she progressed relatively well in the NICU of the regional university children's hospital and was discharged to home after 3 months in the hospital.

Despite her problems, Vanessa was an easy baby to care for, since she cried little and slept often. Yet, she had some difficulties adjusting to feeding from a bottle, since she could not suck very well. As she grew, Mrs. Burns and her husband became worried about Vanessa's unusual posturing of her legs and back. Her pediatricians were sensitive to these concerns but cautioned them to wait until Vanessa was about a year old to see if things changed. This did not soften their concerns, and the parents sought another evaluation. This time the pediatric diagnostic team at the local children's rehabilitation center confirmed the parents' worries. Because of her birth difficulties, Vanessa had experienced a brain insult that now showed itself as spastic quadriplegic cerebral palsy. Mr. and Mrs. Burns were devastated, yet relieved that their suspicions had been confirmed finally.

At 8 months of age, Vanessa was enrolled in a home-based infant intervention program. Since the family lived in a rural area, center-based, coordinated services had been hard to obtain. A cooperative effort between the local Easter Seals program and a nursery school at the local college had provided Vanessa specialized services as well as interactions with nonhandicapped friends once a week. Everyone believed that Vanessa understood nearly everything said to her; but her speech/language difficulties, poor head control, and inability to use her hands functionally complicated their ability to assess her accurately. When Vanessa began to use a consistent yes-no response, things began to change dramatically. The team began to concentrate on concept development and language understanding and use in their program for Vanessa.

It was becoming clearer that Vanessa was a severely physically handicapped child with near average intellectual abilities but significant language and motor problems. She could now be enrolled in the local early-intervention program operated by the school district; an initial evaluation was necessary to make this transition occur successfully for Vanessa and her parents. The Burnses have been stressed greatly by Vanessa's physical needs and their continuing search to find coordinated services for her. Their worries about her speech difficulties were strong, but her recent progress has made them hopeful. The opportunity to enroll her in the school district's program was viewed by them as a turning point in their lives.

Administrative Appraisal

Definition

Early-intervention programs are advised to use appraisal procedures that globally survey child and family status, needs, and progress. This global screening enables the team to conceptualize problems and objectives. Judgment-based assessment measures are valuable for this purpose. They enable team members to recognize and reconcile disparate perceptions and to reach consensus about service delivery goals and options. We consider this global depiction to be an administrative appraisal; it serves the organizing function of focusing the interdisciplinary team's decision making about child/family needs and programming. As a summative evaluation method, it provides the team with an economical way of monitoring progress and program impact via structured clinical impressions.

Phase 1: Screen/Identify

Programs must select and use a format by which team members can identify and highlight the most prominent needs of each special preschooler. This screening or "needs analysis" is the first phase in the LINK sequence. The process enables the team (whether composed of three or eight members) to make decisions about the perceived severity and nature of the child's functional capabilities and about the particular areas on which a comprehensive assessment should focus. The screening helps the team to select the type of prescriptive developmental assessment battery that will best promote intervention planning and to determine the probable services the child will need. We recommend use of the *System to Plan Early Childhood Services* (SPECS) (Bagnato & J.T. Neisworth, 1989b) as the administrative appraisal component of LINK. SPECS is a separate product that includes two clinical judgment instruments that rate child characteristics and service delivery/program needs: (1) Perceptions of Developmental Status (PODS) and (2) the Child Services Indicator.

The child study team of the local preschool program gathered a variety of data about Vanessa's developmental needs and completed the Personal Data Form from the LINK packet (see Exhibit 7-1). These data included records from her infant intervention program, parent interviews, observations of parent-child interaction at home, results from a brief receptive language screening measure, and reports from the pediatrician. Using the PODS to profile Vanessa's needs, each team member independently rated her capabilities on the 19 5-point subscales. Screening with the PODS allowed the team to identify areas requiring more focused and comprehensive assessment and thereby enhanced interdisciplinary communication and program planning.

Table 7-2 displays the independent team member ratings that led to the team's consensus of Vanessa's status. As can be observed, the team showed a high level of agreement that Vanessa appeared to demonstrate individually well-developed conceptual, problem-solving, and social skills but moderate-to-severe deficits in the

Exhibit 7–1 Vanessa's Personal Data Form from the LINK System Packet

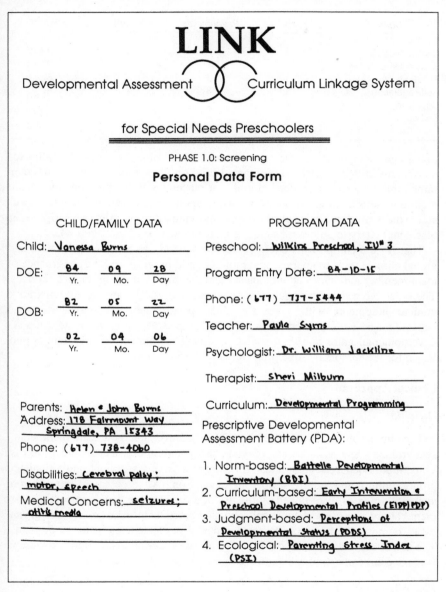

LINK

Developmental Assessment ⚭ Curriculum Linkage System

for Special Needs Preschoolers

PHASE 1.0: Screening

Personal Data Form

CHILD/FAMILY DATA

Child: **Vanessa Burns**

DOE: **84** Yr. **09** Mo. **28** Day

DOB: **82** Yr. **05** Mo. **22** Day

02 Yr. **04** Mo. **06** Day

Parents: **Helen & John Burns**
Address: **118 Fairmount Way**
Springdale, PA 15343
Phone: (**677**) **738-4060**

Disabilities: **Cerebral palsy; motor, speech**
Medical Concerns: **seizures; otitis media**

PROGRAM DATA

Preschool: **Wilkins Preschool, IU# 3**

Program Entry Date: **84-10-15**

Phone: (**677**) **737-5444**

Teacher: **Pavla Syms**

Psychologist: **Dr. William Jackline**

Therapist: **Sheri Milburn**

Curriculum: **Developmental Programming**

Prescriptive Developmental
Assessment Battery (PDA):

1. Norm-based: **Battelle Developmental Inventory (BDI)**
2. Curriculum-based: **Early Intervention & Preschool Developmental Profiles (EIPP/PDP)**
3. Judgment-based: **Perceptions of Developmental Status (PODS)**
4. Ecological: **Parenting Stress Index (PSI)**

fine motor, gross motor, self-care, and expressive language domains. Exhibit 7-2 graphs the team's consensus on the PODS Profile Sheet. These consensus ratings were transferred to the Child Services Indicator (see Exhibit 7-3) to help the team members translate their functional ratings into preliminary decisions about educa-

Table 7-2 Team Member PODS Cluster Comparisons for Vanessa

Domain	Teacher	Psychologist	Parent	Speech
Communication	2	2	3	2
Sensorimotor	1	1	1	2
Physical	3	4	3	3
Self-regulation	3	3	4	4
Cognitive	4	3	5	4
Self-social	4	4	5	3

tional and therapeutic services and to start to determine Vanessa's eligibility for enrollment in their preschool program. Based on these findings, the team determined that Vanessa was indeed eligible for placement in the program and would require various auxiliary services. Focusing upon the screened problem or "need" areas, the team could then select the most individually appropriate prescriptive assessment battery to guide curriculum goal planning (see Phase 2 below).

The SPECS components could serve subsequently as both administrative and global clinical tools to appraise and monitor child progress and the congruence of team member judgments about Vanessa and the impact of the program's services. The objective was to "triangulate" or evaluate congruence among administrative clinical judgments with Vanessa's actual performance on norm-based and curriculum-based instruments. Thus, SPECS helped the team to evaluate Vanessa's developmental gains and their social validity. The entire SPECS system is published for the authors by American Guidance Service, Inc.

Clinical Appraisal

Definition

The clinical appraisal aspect of the LINK system enabled the team members to synchronize their assessments of Vanessa's capabilities, needs, and progress. Thus, it provided a common thread for comprehensive assessment, individualized programming, and progress/program evaluation. All assessment-intervention-evaluation phases were linked by the use of a prescriptive developmental assessment battery. The clinical appraisal generated practical information regarding Vanessa's demonstrated functional developmental competencies in many domains. The assessments were conducted at program entry, during instruction and therapy (i.e., session/daily/weekly/monthly/quarterly) and at year's end.

Phase 2: Assess/Link

A sequence of five steps enabled psychologists and other team diagnosticians to identify curriculum entry points, thereby "linking" the results of norm-based and judgment-based scales with the curriculum used in the early intervention program (see Exhibit 7-4).

Exhibit 7–2 Team Consensus Ratings for Vanessa on the PODS Profile Sheet

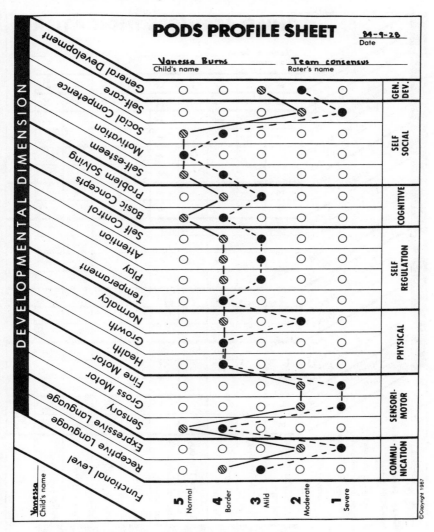

Step 1: Select prescriptive battery. A prescriptive developmental assessment battery (PDA) was chosen based upon Vanessa's functional disabilities and the content of the curriculum to be employed by the program. The PDA consists of at least four types of scales: norm-based, curriculum-based, judgment-based, and ecological.

Table 7-3 depicts the PDA especially selected for Vanessa. This PDA was sensitive to Vanessa's disabilities as a young spastic quadriplegic cerebral palsied child experiencing severe fine motor, gross motor, and expressive language/speech impairments. However, the PDA provided adaptations to reduce the impact of her

Exhibit 7–3 Team Consensus Judgments of Vanessa's Therapy Needs on the Child Services Indicator

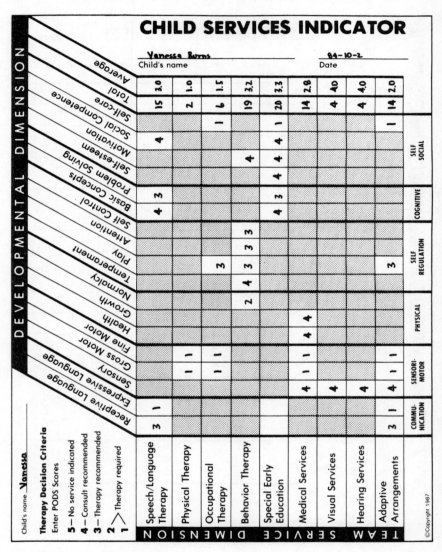

deficits and to determine her underlying, near-average cognitive, conceptual, and receptive language competencies. (Note that the focal measure of the PDA is an adaptive curriculum, in this case, *Developmental Programming for Infants and Young Children,* Moersch & Schafer, 1981).

Step 2: Determine functional levels. Once the most handicap-appropriate battery is chosen, the developmental school psychologist, together with other team

Exhibit 7–4 Five Steps in Linking Norm-Based and Curriculum-Based Instruments in Phase 2 of the LINK System

---

Step 1: Select prescriptive developmental assessment battery

Step 2: Determine functional levels in each developmental domain

Step 3: Conduct developmental task analysis of items in the norm-based scale

Step 4: Link assessment and curricular tasks using emerging or transitional competencies (1, PF, ±)

Step 5: Construct developmentally based reports of assessment results

---

members, administers the PDA over one or two sessions, ideally in both home and preschool settings in order to document the child's current levels and ranges of developmental skills within and across the major developmental and behavioral domains. The norm-based measure in the PDA serves to diagnose degree of developmental deficit and to establish general levels of functioning.

The *Battelle Developmental Inventory* (Newborg et al., 1984) served this diagnostic function for Vanessa, with results from the *Perceptions of Developmental Status* (Bagnato & J.T. Neisworth, 1989a) as complementary evidence regarding functional capabilities apparent in various settings, and as a basis for documenting the social validity or generalization of her behaviors.

Exhibit 7-5 profiles Vanessa's performance on the *Early Intervention Progress Profile*, the graph form that accompanies the LINK system. Vanessa's general levels of developmental functioning are graphed in the Program Entry column for each developmental/curricular domain: cognitive (C), language (L), perceptual/fine motor (PFM), socioemotional (SE), gross motor (GM), and self-care (SC). Developmental ages (DAs) and developmental quotients (DQs) describe her comparative functioning in normative terms (*note:* developmental quotient and rate are used interchangeably). The graphed scores are standard scores, ratio indexes, or age equivalents—depending upon the type of scale used. During the fourth phase of the LINK procedure, additional assessments are graphed to document rates of developmental progress during intervention.

Table 7–3 Prescriptive Developmental Assessment Battery for Vanessa

Type	Measure
Norm-based	Battelle Developmental Inventory (BDI)
Curriculum-based	Early Intervention Developmental Profile (EIDP)
	Preschool Developmental Profile (PDP) (in Developmental Programming for Infants and Young Children)
Judgment-based	Perceptions of Developmental Status (PODS)
Ecological	Parenting Stress Index (PSI)

Exhibit 7–5 Vanessa's Developmental Levels Graphed on the Early Intervention Progress Profile

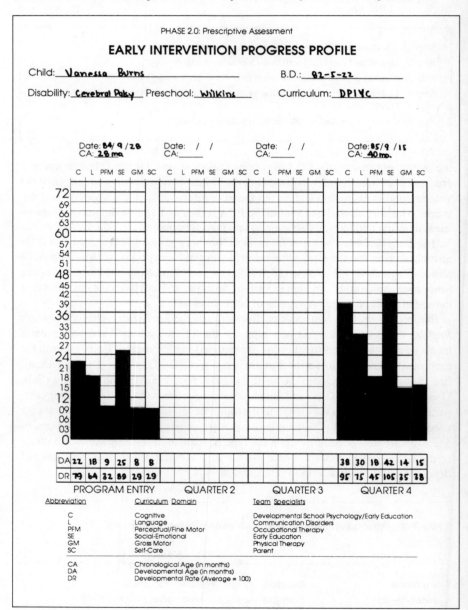

The developmental levels indicated in the prescriptive assessment of Vanessa on the BDI and EIDP scales, as shown in Exhibit 7-5, corroborated the team's clinical judgments on the PODS regarding her functional capabilities. In general, Vanessa demonstrated borderline cognitive capabilities; mild receptive and severe expressive language/speech deficits; and severe limitations in fine motor, gross motor, and self-care skills. With adaptations from the BDI, it was clear that Vanessa had acquired important conceptual abilities, despite her problems in exploring toys and objects with her hands and in moving about. She showed good selective attention skills in finding hidden objects, identifying concrete and some pictured objects, identifying missing or hidden toys in a two-choice discrimination task, and matching colors and shapes. Her individually strong competencies in initiating and maintaining interactions with adults and other children were further indications of her well-developed cognitive capabilities. Vanessa smiled at her successful completion of difficult tasks, gestured and made sounds to communicate with others, persisted in attempting to complete tasks, and played cooperative games with appropriate help. On the BDI, she showed cognitive capabilities that were most comparable to those expected at 22 months of age, progressing at approximately 79 percent of the rate expected for her age. This indicated borderline-to-mild cognitive deficits at entry into the program. However, her strong socioemotional skills were more like those of a 25-month-old child, progressing at nearly 90 percent of the rate expected. This suggested that Vanessa had acquired low-average abilities in the social interactive area. Her receptive language skills matched her current cognitive abilities, but her expressive and speech communication skills were limited by her oral-motor impairments and thus were severely affected.

Step 3: Conduct developmental task analysis. Curriculum linkage is accomplished primarily by matching the results of the norm-based assessment with the program's developmental curriculum. In practice, an analysis is made of items in the norm-based scale to determine the child's range of capabilities in reference to the developmental task analysis. Test tasks are matched with similar curriculum tasks to create a series of "curriculum entry" points that indicate the most appropriate goals to start instructional and therapeutic planning.

In general, the diagnostic specialist analyzes items within the norm-based scale to determine ranges of developmental skills and deficits. First, the child's basal skills, that is, all those tasks that the child can complete successfully for the child's developmental level, are identified. These *basal skills* indicate fully acquired competencies, usually represented by a +, a P, or a 2 score. Next, in the task analysis of increasingly difficult items, those tasks that the child has some difficulty completing but still show components of the required skill are identified. These are inconsistent behaviors, usually defined by the fact that the child can perform the skills perhaps 50 percent of the time or show some of the essential behaviors. These inconsistent skills are considered *emerging capabilities* and thus are represented by a ±, a 1, or a PF score. Finally, the child's *ceiling competencies* are determined. These are the skills that are most difficult for the child and are rarely displayed.

Exhibit 7–6 Analysis of Vanessa's Performance on Selected Tasks from the BDI

Subdomain: Memory

CG 11	0–5	Follows auditory stimulus	2
CG 12		Follows visual stimulus	2
CG 13	6–11	Uncovers hidden toy **(adapted)**	2
CG 14		Searches for removed object	2
CG 15	24–35	Repeats two-digit sequences	0
CG 16		Selects hand hiding toy ✦	1
CG 17	36–47	Recalls familiar objects ✦	1
CG 18	72–83	Repeats four-digit sequences	0
CG 19		Recalls facts from story presented orally	0
CG 20	84–95	Repeats six-digit sequences	0

Subdomain Score | **10**

Subdomain: Reasoning and Academic Skills

CG 21	6–11	Pulls string to obtain toy or ring **(adapted)**	2
CG 22	12–23	Reaches around barrier to obtain toy	2
CG 23	36–47	Responds to *one* and *one more* ✦	1
CG 24	48–59	Identifies sources of common actions	0
CG 25		Gives three objects on request	0
CG 26		Answers simple logic questions	0
CG 27		Completes opposite analogies	0
CG 28		Identifies larger of two numbers	0
CG 29	60–71	Selects single words from visual presentation	0
CG 30		Identifies missing parts of objects	0
CG 31		Recognizes picture absurdities	0

Source: From *Battelle Developmental Inventory,* 1984, 1988, Allen, TX: DLM/Teaching Resources. Copyright 1984, 1988 by LINC Associates. Reprinted by permission.

These behaviors are considered absent competencies in the task analysis, although the child may display them at a very low level of frequency or only with prompts. They are represented by − , 0, or F scores. Once this process is completed, a loose developmental task analysis results. Exhibit 7-6 shows this item task analysis for

Vanessa in two cognitive subdomains, memory and reasoning/academic skills, using Battelle Developmental Inventory results.

Step 4: LINK assessment/curricular tasks. Developmental assessment/curriculum linkages are based upon the *emerging skills* within the child's *"transitional range"* as identified during the task analysis. Each ±, 1, or PF item is extracted from the norm-based scale and sequenced in developmental order (least mature to most mature). Exhibits 7-7 and 7-8 illustrate how Vanessa's emerging competencies on the Battelle Developmental Inventory were matched with competencies (e.g., tasks) on the program's curriculum, *Developmental Programming for Infants and Young Children.*

It is worth emphasizing at this point that the item analysis and resulting curriculum entry points apply only to tasks within the child's developmental age range (i.e., transitional range), not those within the child's chronological age range. For this reason, for functional assessment purposes, it is reasonable to administer a measure that is appropriate for the developmental level, not the chronological age level, of the child. For example, one could reasonably administer the Bayley Scales of Infant Development to a 4-year-old with severe developmental retardation.

Emerging skills from the norm-based scale are matched with congruent tasks within the curriculum by following simple criteria. The tasks must be within a roughly similar developmental range (e.g., 12 to 18 months), the tasks must be similar in content and wording (e.g., recalls objects vs. names missing objects), and the tasks must have similar response requirements (e.g., discriminating among three shapes to identify the triangle form).

Exhibit 7-9 illustrates the completion of the Prescriptive Linkages Form from the LINK package of materials for Vanessa, using the norm- and curriculum-based results. Developmental transitions are the emerging (i.e., ±, 1, or PF) behaviors from the Battelle norm-based measures to be linked with curriculum tasks. Observe that four curriculum-entry targets or prescriptive linkages can be selected for each of the six developmental/curriculum domains: C, L, PFM, SE, GM, and SC. The center column allows one to establish a shorthand link index to identify specific matching tasks within the curriculum that are the most appropriate starting points for intervention and treatment. The LINK codes in Exhibit 7-9 are combined numbers and letters that identify the placement, and often also the domain, for each curriculum task (e.g., CG 16/M 4).

Step 5: Construct developmentally based reports. Psychologists and other diagnosticians who assess young children for program placement, prescription, and progress evaluation purposes must communicate their results effectively to program staff and parents. Research on the effectiveness of different styles of writing psychoeducational reports indicates that reports that are organized by functional or developmental domain and also contain information that is "eye catching" and easily accessible are more useful for individualized program planning than are traditional test-based psychological reports (Bagnato, 1980, 1981b; F. Prus & L. Prus, 1988).

Exhibit 7–7 Illustration of Vanessa's Current Skills on the BDI, Transferred to Congruent EIDP Curriculum Tasks

6–8 months					
56	Attains partially hidden object	+			
57	Looks to the floor when something falls	+			
58	Uncovers face	+			
59	Bangs object	+			
60	Rotates a bottle inverted less than 180° to drink	±			
61	Imitates hand movements already in his/her repertoire	+			
9–11 months					
62	Attains completely hidden object	+			
63	Pulls string to secure ring and succeeds	+			
64	Shows knowledge of toy hidden behind a screen	±			
65	Imitates facial movements inexactly	±			
66	Imperfectly imitates movements never performed before	−			
67	Rotates a bottle inverted 180° to drink	—			
68	Reacts to novel features of an object	±			

Developmental Programming for Infants and Young Children
Volume 2: Early Intervention Developmental Profile

ITEM NUMBER	*DEVELOPMENTAL LEVELS AND ITEMS*	DATE	DATE	DATE	DATE
12–15 months					
69	Imitates body action on a doll	±			
70	Repeatedly finds toy when hidden under one of several covers	+			
71	Lifts a ½-inch cube off a 1-inch cube	O			
72	Balances nine 1-inch cubes in a coffee cup	O			
16–19 months					
73	Repeatedly finds toy when hidden under multiple covers	±			
74	Uses a stick to try to attain an object out of reach (**Adp**)	±			
75	Retrieves raisin by inverting small vial	±			
76	Corrects imitations of new movements	—			
77	Deduces location of hidden object, single displacement	±			
78	Pulls cloth to reach object	—			

Source: From *Early Intervention Developmental Profile* (pp. 6, 7) by D.S. Schafer and M.S. Moersch, 1981, Ann Arbor, MI: The University of Michigan Press. Copyright 1981 by The University of Michigan Press. Reprinted by permission.

Exhibit 7-8 Illustration of the Match among Vanessa's Performances on the BDI Tasks and Similar DPIYC Curriculum Objectives

NORM Battelle Developmental Inventory (BDI)				CURRICULUM Developmental Programming for Infants and Young Children: Early Intervention Developmental Profile (EIDP)		
Age	Task	Score →	LINK Codes ←	Age	Task	Score
6-11 mo.	Searches removed object	2	CG 14/56	6- mo.	Attains hidden object	+
6-11 mo.	Pulls string for toy	2	CG 21/63	9-11 mo.	Pulls string for ring	+
12-23 mo.	Reaches around barrier	2	CG 22/64	9-11 mo.	Knows toy screened	+
24-35 mo.	Selects hand hiding toy	1	CG 16/77	16-19 mo.	Deduces toy location	±
24-35 mo.	Matches forms	1	CG 7/92	32-35 mo.	Matches 4 shapes	±
36-47 mo.	Recalls objects	1	CG 17/94	32-35 mo.	Names missing object	±
36-47 mo.	Identifies big, small	0	CG 23/163	28-31 mo.	Points to big, small	–

Exhibit 7–9 Vanessa's Prescriptive Curriculum Linkages

PHASE 2.1: Curriculum Linkage

Child: __Vanessa Burns__	Date: __84-10-15__	CA: __28 months__
Developmental Scale: __Battelle (BDI)__	Curriculum: __DPIYC : EIDP/PDP__	

PRESCRIPTIVE LINKAGES

DEVELOPMENTAL TRANSITIONS (±)	LINK CODES	CURRICULUM TARGETS
DA = 22 (18-30)	Cognitive	
Selects hand hiding toy	CG16/77C	Deduces toy location
Matches forms	CG7/92C	Matches 4 shapes
Recalls objects	CG17/94C	Names missing object
Responds to one & one more	CG23/89C	Understands "1" concept
DA = 18 (8-26)	Language	
Associates spoken words & objects	CM 5/L110	Looks at named objects & people
Follows 3+ verbal commands	CM6/L118	Follows familiar directions
Gives objects on request	CG25/L123	Selects 2 of 3 objects
Associates spoken words & pictures	CM19/L124	Points to 4 pictures
DA = 25 (21-32)	Social-Emotional	
Initiates social contacts	PS45/SE156	Initiates social games
Separates easily from parent	PS15/SE158	Plays apart from familiar person
Plays independently	PS47/SE159	Varies play with toy
Plays & shares with prompts	PS50/SE173	Shares with others in play
DA = 9 (9-12)	Perceptual/Fine Motor	
Release toy from grasp	M50/PFM 18	Drops block with release
Pulls open drawers	M49/PFM 23	Removes box cover
Reproduces lines	N68/PFM 31	Imitates crayon stroke
Places rings on post	N66/PFM 29	Places pegs
DA = 8 (6-10)	Gross Motor	
Operates switch toy	M69/PFM 52	Activates simple toy
Sits without support – 5 secs.	M4/GM 241	Sits trunk erect
Moves lying to sitting	M10/GM 236	Prone rolls to supine to sit
Lifts head on stomach	M2/GM 231	Prone – head –chest 90°
DA = 8 (8-10)	Self-Care	
Feeds with spoon	A20/SC183	Pickup spoon
Drinks from cup – assisted	A15/SC182	Drinks from cup with help
Feeds self, bite-sized pieces	A16/SC185	Finger feeds
	/SC191	Swallows with closed mouth

In terms of prescriptive curriculum linkages, Exhibit 7-10 presents the LINK form Early Childhood Program Prescriptions, which provides a fast, descriptive, easily accessible, and economical method for reporting assessment, curricular, and programming information to preschool teachers. The form, attached to the previous prescriptive linkage sheet, allows the psychologist to convey developmental

Exhibit 7–10 Preliminary Program/Intervention Guidelines for Vanessa and Her Parents

PHASE 3.0: Intervention
EARLY CHILDHOOD PROGRAM PRESCRIPTIONS

Child: <u>Vanessa Byrns</u>　　　　CA: <u>28 months</u>　　　　Date: <u>84-10-15</u>

DEVELOPMENTAL ASSESSMENT SUMMARY: Vanessa has acquired important conceptual and problem-solving skills despite her severe motor and speech impairments. Her ability to initiate and sustain interactions with others underscores her well-developed social and gestural communication skills. Programming must use technology to support her progress in various cognitive areas. The parents must be integral partners in the classroom as possible.

DEVELOPMENTAL PROGRAM GUIDELINES:

FEATURES	OPTIONS	COMMENTS
Instructional Setting	☐ Home-based ☒ Center-based ☐ Combo ☐ Hospital-based	Involve her in mainstream experiences regularly — maybe with daycare center
Instructional Methods	☒ Verbal prompts ☐ Physical prompts ☐ Shaping	She follows directions well — brief, active directions
Grouping Pattern	☐ 1:1 ☒ 1:1 & small group ☐ 1:1, small/large groups	Use peer-pairing toward groups of 6-8.
Adaptive Arrangements	☒ Special toys ☒ Communication system ☒ Wheelchair ☐ Room arrangement	Electromechanical toys for cause-effect play Computer & light pointer Adaptive chair & tray
Auxiliary Therapies	☒ Speech ☒ PT/OT ☒ Psychologist ☐ Pediatrician ☐ Sensory	Alternate communication system; consult re: appropriate switches;
Behavioral Strategies	☐ Primary reinforcement ☒ Token economy ☐ Behavioral contract ☒ Social praise ☐ Time out ☐ Planned ignoring	Maintain motivation with novel toys & tasks, social praise & stickers — tokens
Parent Participation	☐ Conference only ☒ Parent education/training ☒ Counseling/therapy	Counseling re: disability and stress reduction Behavior management

and behavioral performance to teachers, parents, and therapists in practical terms. In addition, it enables the psychologist to offer specific judgments about service delivery options and strategies that match with curricular goals; this involves consideration of seven program dimensions: (1) instructional setting, (2) instructional methods, (3) grouping pattern, (4) adaptive arrangements, (5) auxiliary therapies,

(6) behavioral strategies, and (7) parent participation. (See examples of complete developmentally based reports in Appendix C.)

Phase 3: Program/Intervene

The entire programming/intervention phase of the LINK system is beyond the scope of this book and is, in fact, a topic for a book by itself. However, Phase 3 encompasses certain linked assessment/intervention operations that are important for understanding how the whole LINK system operates.

Once prescriptive developmental linkages and curriculum entry targets have been tailored for a particular child, the teacher and therapists have the responsibility and flexibility to move the child within the curriculum's developmental task analysis for each domain. With the curriculum entry points from the developmental school psychologist as initial referents, program personnel can move the child's goals forward or backward in the task analysis of objectives, based upon several factors, including the mix of children with various disabilities in a classroom, the grouping patterns (small group, zone) within the setting, the desire to increase the child's motivation with easier tasks, and the desire to maintain a balanced emphasis on several domains simultaneously. Based on these initial goals, instructional and therapeutic plans and strategies can be designed by program personnel.

Exhibit 7-10 includes some preliminary recommendations on the design and strategies for instruction and therapy in Vanessa's individualized intervention plan. The developmental school psychologist and other diagnostic specialists, using LINK form Phase 3.0 Early Childhood Program Prescriptions, could present a shorthand summary of these suggestions that could be expanded upon during the child study team meeting. Preliminary suggestions for Vanessa recognized the great discrepancy between her cognitive capabilities and her speech and neuromotor impairments. Thus, regular mainstreaming experiences were important in order to continue to provide her with good social and language models and challenges. Small-group and peer pairing were indicated as an initial method of allowing her to practice her developing skills in a comfortable, manageable setting and then to integrate her gradually into larger group activities. Because of her physical disabilities, special attention had to be focused upon the appropriate selection and use of response-contingent and electromechanical toys to foster functional behaviors. An adaptive wheelchair was vital here to establish social interaction, head and trunk control during instruction, and spatial orientation to people and tasks. An alternative communication system had to be considered to support the expressive language skills that she might develop. Appropriate switches had to be examined to allow Vanessa to operate both toys and the computer systems. She was quite motivated for learning, but she gained an extra incentive through the use of social praise and tokens or stickers. Verbal prompts appeared to be all that was needed to maintain attention, task performance, and persistence. Finally, the program staff had to be sensitive and responsive in simultaneously addressing the parents' needs to reduce their stress, to educate them about Vanessa's capabilities and needs, to help them identify their goals for her and for the family, and to support them emotionally through individual parent counseling, and perhaps also through involvement, not only in the program but also in parent support groups.

Phase 4: Evaluate/Monitor

One of the most important but generally neglected phases of early-intervention operations is the evaluation and monitoring of both child progress and program effectiveness. Preschool program personnel frequently report that they are too understaffed to "retest" children or that program evaluation is too difficult and re-moved from everyday services to be important. The stark reality is that, without a progress/program evaluation system that enables them to document the benefits of their services and efforts, early-intervention programs may be engaging in unethi-cal and experimental practices with children. Assessment and intervention must be linked through program evaluation.

The child progress/program evaluation phase brings the LINK sequence full cycle. The full evaluation sequence enables programs to determine both effective and ineffective intervention practices and to modify those practices periodically for the benefit of children and families. As children make gains on the curriculum entry goals identified during Phase 2 and through the treatment plans and methods implemented during Phase 3, program evaluation focuses on these goals as criteria or "benchmarks" of progress. Thus, assessment, intervention, and evaluation maintain a consistent focus and underlying foundation—developmental cur-riculum goals.

Various methods are available for evaluating curricular progress (i.e., changes in development and behavior) during intervention. Each has its own technical ad-vantages and disadvantages; yet when several are combined, they can provide valu-able data regarding child gain and program impact. *Acquisition of curriculum competencies is the primary index of change.* Changes in norm-based, judgment-based, and ecological measures provide important corroborative evidence.

Two types of program evaluation methods are noteworthy: formative and sum-mative. *Formative evaluation* occurs on a regular basis throughout the period of early intervention. It involves the systematic observation of child behavior and adult-child/child-child interactions and the monitoring of attainment of curricular goals on a session, daily, weekly, monthly, and/or quarterly schedule, depending on the program's needs and resources. *Summative evaluation* involves compari-sons of baseline or preintervention functioning with follow-up or postintervention functioning. Generally, summative evaluation compares beginning-of-the-year with end-of-the-year functioning, using norm-based data. As a rule of thumb, sum-mative evaluation is usually based upon global data comparisons, such as develop-mental ages (DAs) and developmental quotients (DQs), whereas formative evalua-tion is usually based upon specific and discrete data comparisons, such as frequency and duration of behaviors and/or the number of curriculum goals at-tained within a specified time period, supplemented by other more global data. Nevertheless, developmental curricula, used for both summative and formative evaluation purposes, enable the early-intervention team to track and chart both general (e.g., DA, DQ, percentiles) and discrete (e.g., number of curricular goals attained, attention and on-task frequencies) units of change.

Exhibit 7-11 presents the Summative Child Progress/Program Evaluation Form 4.0 on Vanessa from the LINK package. This form is organized by the six developmental curricular domains cross-referenced with various evaluation indexes. Basically, first quarter (e.g., fall/winter) and fourth quarter (e.g., spring/summer) data are compared, using a variety of scores, including developmental ages and rates, gain scores, efficiency indexes, maturation-intervention comparisons, and curricular indexes. Each of these types of scores is reviewed in the following sections.

Developmental scores. With both norm-based and curriculum-based performances, the child's acquisition of skills can be converted into indexes of age functioning and developmental rate. These "standard scores" can be calculated either by using normative tables, if a standardized scale like the Battelle, Bayley, or McCarthy is used, or by the old ratio methods (DA/CA X 100).

Developmental ages (DAs) and developmental rates (DRs or DQs) indicate, respectively, the child's comparable age-equivalent functioning in each developmental domain and the child's rate or quotient of progress, with 100 considered an average from which deviations are calculated. For example, a DR of 75 indicates a functioning rate that is (in a simplistic manner) approximately 75 percent of that expected of a typical child. With a 40-month-old child like Vanessa, this rate converted to a DA equivalent of only 30 months in the language area, a mild deficit. In addition, with all young handicapped children, it is important to determine the child's developmental age *range* of functioning, from basal to ceiling levels, or the scattering of developmental capabilities. For example, at the fourth-quarter evaluation, although Vanessa was functioning at the 30-month level in language skills, her skills were widely scattered in this area—from a low of 22 months in expressive skills to a high of 34 months in identifying and recalling pictures, objects, and concepts from memory. This range might narrow or widen, based on later therapeutic gains; it might also have reflected purposeful as well as isolated splinter skills. Developmental Programming for Infants and Young Children (i.e., EIDP) and the Battelle Developmental Inventory were used to derive these progress indexes for Vanessa, as they were used previously to determine prescriptive curriculum entry linkages.

Developmental age gain is calculated over a specific period of intervention (e.g., 6 months or 12 months) by subtracting DA at program entry from DA at the end of that period. For Vanessa, the gain in the cognitive area was 16 months and in the perceptual fine motor area, 9 months, during the 12-month intervention period.

Intervention efficiency indexes. Controversy surrounds the use of efficiency indexes in early childhood special education (Bagnato & J.T. Neisworth, 1980; Jellnek, 1985; Simeonsson & Weigerink, 1975). However, when pragmatically coupled with other progress measures, such indexes can provide useful administrative evidence of child change and program impact.

Exhibit 7–11 Analysis of Vanessa's Developmental Progress and the Program's Therapeutic Impact

SUMMATIVE CHILD PROGRESS/PROGRAM EVALUATION SHEET

PHASE 4.0: Evaluation

Child: **Vanessa Burns**   C.A. **40 months**   Date: **85-9-18**

Developmental/ Curricular Domain	1ST Quarter			4th Quarter			DA Gain	IEI	CEI	M%	P%
	DA	DA Range	DQ	DA	DA Range	DQ					
COGNITIVE	22	18-30	79	38	36-45	95	16 mo.	1.3	1.5	59%	41%
LANGUAGE	18	8-26	64	30	22-34	75	12 mo.	1.0	.92	64%	36%
SOCIAL-EMOTIONAL	25	21-32	89	42	36-48	105	17 mo.	1.4	1.8	63%	37%
PERCEPTUAL/ FINE MOTOR	9	9-12	32	18	12-20	45	9 mo.	.75	.75	42%	58%
GROSS MOTOR	8	6-10	29	14	10-16	35	6 mo.	.50	.41	58%	42%
SELF-CARE	8	8-10	29	15	10-18	38	7 mo.	.58	.67	50%	50%
DEVELOPMENTAL AVERAGE	15		54	27		65	12 mo.	1.0	1.01	54%	46%

Bagnato and J.T. Neisworth (1980) proposed the *Intervention Efficiency Index* (IEI) to document simply how much developmental change (e.g., gain in age scores) was evident during the specific period of intervention. The index documents change during instruction and therapy. For example, for Vanessa in the cognitive area, a gain of 16 months during a 12-month period of structured intervention suggested a rate of growth that was 1.3 times that expected in normal child development (i.e., 1 month of development for each month of life).

Another efficiency measure, the *Curricular Efficiency Index* (CEI), was devised by Bagnato and J.T. Neisworth (1983), but it is generally unused in programs. This index compares the number of curriculum objectives achieved during a 1-month period by either a sample of nonhandicapped children or children in a specialized classroom with the number achieved by a handicapped preschooler. In essence, a "local program norm" or limited comparative sample is used to determine a child's relative standing for curriculum skill acquisition. For example, Vanessa achieved 12 cognitive objectives while the norm group achieved 8 objectives in the same 12-month period. This ratio (12:8) suggested a curricular efficiency rate that was 1.5 times the rate expected for her peers. Thus, IEI, CEI, and developmental ages and rates can be used to "triangulate" consistent evidence of child progress and program impact.

To calculate the IEI and CEI, the following formulas are used:

- The *Intervention Efficiency Index* (IEI) is a ratio of the child's developmental gain in months and the number of months the child has received program intervention. The IEI is calculated for each developmental domain:

$$\text{IEI} = \frac{\text{Number of months developmental gain (DA2} - \text{DA1)}}{\text{Number of months receiving program intervention}}$$

- The *Curriculum Efficiency Index* (CEI) is a ratio of the average number of curriculum objectives achieved by a child per month and the average number of curriculum objectives achieved by either a local normal sample of children or by the children in the child's own program. The CEI is calculated for each developmental domain:

$$\text{CEI} = \frac{\text{Number of curriculum objectives achieved by the child per month}}{\text{Number of curriculum objectives achieved by a group per month}}$$

Maturation/intervention percentages. Few programs use procedures that attempt to estimate the amount of relative gain that can be attributed to maturation effects versus intervention (i.e., treatment) effects (Bagnato & Mayes, 1986; Irwin & Wong, 1974). For young children with congenital disabilities (i.e., those with presumably constant or static disabilities and developmental rates), such as cerebral palsy, mental retardation, and autism), maturation/intervention comparisons are justifiable and practical.

Maturation percentages (M%) and *Intervention percentages* (I%) are calculated with reference to the child's own preintervention levels and rates of functioning. The use of such percentages assumes that children with "static" disabilities will maintain relatively constant rates of development and behavior in the absence of intervention or major environmental changes. Therefore, one uses preintervention rates as reference points and then projects the level at which the child will most probably be functioning at some later time, based on the historical reference point and presuming linearity of skill acquisition. This projection describes the child's maturation rate as a percentage. When the child is enrolled in a treatment program, the child's developmental rate is re-evaluated after a period of intervention. If the child's postintervention rate of progress exceeds the maturation rate, the amount of gain is attributed to treatment and is characterized as the intervention rate or percentage.

To compare the proportion of developmental gain that may be attributable to the effects of the child's maturation (M%) with that resulting from the effects of the program's intervention (I%), the following formulas are used:

$$M\% = \frac{\text{Expected maturational gain in months}}{\text{Actual developmental gain in months}}$$

$$I\% = \frac{\text{Actual developmental gain in months minus maturational gain expected}}{\text{Actual developmental gain in months}}$$

In the case of Vanessa, progress results (see Exhibit 7-11), M% and I% were calculated for each developmental/curricular domain. For example, in the cognitive area, the amount of maturational gain to be expected in a 12-month period of intervention was calculated, presuming she continued to progress at a preintervention DQ rate of .79. Multiplying 12 months by .79 resulted in an expected maturational gain of 9.5 months. This expected gain of 9.5 months was then divided by the actual developmental gain, which is 16 months, resulting in an M% of .59 or 59 percent. Thus, 59 percent of Vanessa's developmental gain of 16 months in the cognitive domain could be reasonably attributed to the effects of maturation; the remainder of the total percentage of gain could be reasonably attributable to the effects of intervention. Accordingly, the expected maturational gain was subtracted from the actual developmental gain (16.0 – 9.5 = 6.5 months) and this was then divided by the actual developmental gain (16 months) to determine the I% of 41 percent. Thus, 41 percent of Vanessa's progress in acquiring cognitive skills might have been attributable to the impact of the program's plan of instruction and therapy. Exhibit 7-11 indicates that Vanessa showed significant intervention effects in all developmental areas, despite her congenital neuromotor impairments. In theory, if a child continues to progress at the initial pretest developmental rate and no faster, the maturation effect would be 100 percent and the intervention percentage would be 0 percent. Therefore, any I% that exceeds 0 percent suggests an intervention effect.

Functional behavior ratings and program data. The final program evaluation strategy applies data for both clinical and administrative purposes. In the LINK system, judgment-based and ecological data sources are used to enhance assessments of child status, progress, and therapeutic impact. With Vanessa, data obtained from the observations of interdisciplinary team members and parents were recorded on the *Perceptions of Developmental Status* scale and the *Parenting Stress Index* (PSI).

As noted earlier, the PODS functionally rates behavior according to its maturity or problem-severity based upon observation and clinical judgment. A rating of 5 indicates normal functioning, 4 indicates borderline, 3 mild deficit, 2 moderate deficit, and 1 severe functional deficits. This rating provides a shorthand method of characterizing functional levels after intervention.

Exhibit 7-2 shows the observed progress of Vanessa on the PODS scale, using a team consensus. After 12 months of intervention, she had generally progressed from a severe-to-mild level of overall disability, which corroborated the curriculum results. Finally, the parent's scores on the PSI had decreased, indicating that they believed that they experienced less stress after 1 year of programming.

Permanent product data can also be a rich source of progress information. Such characteristics as type of grouping pattern, behavior management strategies, days per week in programming, adaptive aids, auxiliary therapies, and medical involvement are all program product information indicating specific service delivery options implemented by the program. At the end of the intervention period, the team can once again reconsider these areas and determine if the "intensity" of the service delivery needs has decreased—a clear, practical index of child change.

DEVELOPMENTALLY BASED ASSESSMENT REPORTS

Diagnostic reports are perhaps the primary vehicles through which psychologists and diagnostic specialists communicate their results to teachers and parents. Yet, teachers and parents complain regularly that the reports they receive help them very little in understanding the strengths, weaknesses, and needs of a child. Traditional reports are criticized as being authoritarian in tone, test-centered, ambiguous, and jargon-filled. The major disadvantage of traditional diagnostic reports is that they do not convey information in either content or form that is practical for individualized program planning. Perceptions about the value and effectiveness of school psychological services are influenced heavily by the manner in which one writes a report.

Apart from the innate limitations of the traditional style of writing reports, traditional reports are totally inappropriate with handicapped infants and preschoolers. The developmental base in early intervention and its intervention-focused purpose argue for a different style of reporting assessment results. Clearly, developmentally-based assessment reports are the most effective means for communicating diagnostic data as a basis for prescribing preschool programs (see Appendix C).

Developmental versus Traditional Assessment Reports

Field-based research demonstrates that developmental reports are more effective than traditional psychoeducational reports in enabling preschool teachers to construct individualized programs for young handicapped children (Bagnato, 1980, 1981b).

Bagnato and J.T. Neisworth (1979) developed a pragmatic procedure for translating assessment results from traditional norm-referenced measures so that they could be linked with tasks in frequently used preschool curricula. Bagnato (1980, 1981a, 1981b) coupled this "linkage" procedure with a translated form of report writing to determine whether different styles of writing diagnostic reports could influence the decision making and goal selection of teachers in programs for handicapped preschoolers.

Inservice workshops and simulated exercises were conducted with groups of early childhood teachers ($N = 48$) in order to analyze the characteristics of diagnostic reports that make them useful to teachers for individualized curriculum planning. The study was designed to explore general differences between two styles of writing diagnostic reports: traditional and translated. The study also sought to analyze the differential accuracy with which teachers could "match" diagnostic results to curriculum goals, using the two reporting styles. An expert panel of six school psychologists and early special educators evaluated the accuracy of teacher-constructed linkages in practice IEPs.

In the study, 48 teachers in early childhood programs for handicapped children enrolled in workshops to learn how to analyze developmental reports in order to identify diagnostic data that could be "linked" with curriculum objectives as a basis for forming individualized instructional goal plans. All of the teachers had 1 to 5 years' experience working with handicapped infants and preschoolers, as well as familiarity in the use of developmental curricula for child programming. The teachers represented a wide spectrum of training, ranging from experience as child care aides to master's level training in special education.

First, the teachers were assigned to either an experimental or a control group. Each experimental and control group received specific training on how to link assessment results to curriculum goals. However, the experimental group received a "translated" report and the control group received the usual traditional report, as a basis for designing instructional objectives. The assessment information contained in the two different types of reports provided the basis for constructing linkages.

A diagnostic report dealing with the developmental performance of a handicapped preschooler was selected from clinic pediatric files by an expert panel. The psychoeducational assessment data from the diagnostic report were first used in original form to represent the traditional type of report typically provided by school psychologists. This traditional report included both a quantitative and a qualitative breakdown of assessment results. It was organized by traditional subheadings of background information, behavioral observations, tests administered, results, analysis, and discussion. Global recommendations were suggested.

The diagnostic data from the traditional report were then reanalyzed and reorganized to create a translated developmental report. The translated format had three major divisions: (1) a diagnostic profile of variations in age-level functioning across several behavioral areas; (2) a narrative organized by functional and developmental domains that involved behavioral descriptions of the child's capabilities, deficits, learning style, and instructional needs; and (3) a description of developmental/learning targets to guide program planning as derived from the assessment results (see Appendix C).

Teachers in the experimental group used the translated report and those in the control group used the traditional report, as a basis for selecting instructional objectives from the developmental curriculum employed in their programs (HICOMP or Memphis) that best matched the developmental problems discussed in each type of report. The results showed that the experimental group teachers who used the translated report were more stable, accurate, and productive in constructing individualized linkages, compared with the control group teachers who used the traditional report. While inservice training was a moderately effective factor, the greatest impact in focusing teacher judgment for the purpose of matching diagnostic and programming data can be attributed to the greater efficacy of translated, compared with traditional, diagnostic reporting procedures (88 percent vs. 54 percent) (see Tables 7-4 and 7-5).

Table 7–4 Assessment Reports and Curriculum Planning

	HICOMP		Memphis	
Report Style	Links	%	Links	%
Traditional	145	53	128	55
Developmental	334	87	330	86

Note: N = 48.

Table 7–5 Assessment Reports and Curriculum Planning

	HICOMP		Memphis	
Curriculum Domain Links	Trad %	Dev %	Trad %	Dev %
Communication	48	87	41	89
Problem-solving	54	82	39	86
Motor	62	92	49	95
Self-care	57	86	56	89

Note: N = 48.

Distinguishing Features of Developmentally Based Reports

Four major dimensions distinguish developmental reports from traditional reports: (1) purpose, (2) organization, (3) content, and (4) application. Exhibit 7-12 summarizes these dimensions in shorthand form; Appendix C provides a sample translated or developmentally based assessment report.

Purpose

Traditional reports serve the primary purpose of norm-referenced assessment and categorical diagnosis. In contrast, developmental reports serve the objective of criterion-referenced or curriculum-based assessment, prescribing individualized programs within a functional or developmental framework. Developmental reports convey functional assessment information in a form that enables preschool teachers and therapists accurately to identify curriculum goals that match the child's disabilities and the developmental content of the curriculum employed by the program.

Organization

Traditional diagnostic reports are organized in terms of the tests administered and thus describe the child only in terms of the limited glimpse offered by struc-

---

Exhibit 7–12 Distinguishing Dimensions of Developmentally Based Reports

1. Purpose
   - Prescribes rather than diagnoses
   - Links to curriculum goals
2. Organization
   - Organized by developmental/behavioral domains
   - Uses advance and summary organizers
   - Lists goals and strategies
3. Content
   - Cites multisource, multidomain data
   - Stresses curricular focus
   - Explains impact of disabilities
   - Emphasizes serial progress data
   - Balances qualitative and quantitative data
   - Cites DA, $\pm$, range, DQ
   - Includes "process" variables
   - Uses behavioral descriptions
4. Application
   - Offers curricular links
   - Describes intervention options
   - Provides progress/program impact data

tured testing procedures. Developmental reports are, in contrast, organized by functional or developmental and behavioral domains. This allows a broader description of child functioning by incorporating evidence of the child's overall response to specific people and conditions that reflect the child's capabilities in each domain. More practically, developmental reports, because of their multidomain organization, are structurally compatible with most preschool curricula and thus easily facilitate goal planning and decision making.

Developmental reports concentrate on the use of concise, descriptive, easily accessible, and highlighted information. Effective presentation of information is the central focus, somewhat akin to the manner in which news is reported in the newspaper *USA Today*. Advance and summary organizers are used to alert the reader to the information that will be and has been communicated. This includes placing the summary section first and renaming it a general synopsis. This initial section provides a capsule summary of the child's disabilities, strengths and limitations and of general programming needs. Lists are used to highlight goals, reinforcement preferences, behavior problems, and strategies that worked to manage behavior and promote learning, based on the assessment.

Content

Traditional diagnostic reports stress quantitative data, which have limited use in program planning. Developmental reports, because of their organization and focus, offer a broader and richer range of information. Developmental reports use data derived from multiple sources (e.g., people, methods) across multiple functional areas; they discuss the impact of the child's sensory and neuromotor impairments on cognitive, language, and social functioning. Developmental reports use various methods to profile both quantitative and qualitative information over time in order to document status and progress. Thus, developmental indexes (e.g., DA, DQ, range) are synthesized with basal, ceiling, and transitional skills and with process data. Process variables include attention, behavioral style, motivation, reinforcement needs, need for containment, prompts, redirection, and disciplinary strategies. Behavioral descriptions are primary. All data are reported so that they can facilitate curriculum goal planning and the establishment of instructional/therapeutic techniques to match the child's skills and needs.

Application

Traditional diagnostic reports serve only an administrative function—documenting that some direct or indirect service was provided to the child, teacher, or parent. Developmental reports, in sharp contrast, are the beginning phase in program planning. They serve as the bridge to translate assessment data into treatment terms. In short, they decipher assessment data in practical terms to link assessment, intervention, and evaluation purposes and functions in early intervention.

8

LINK Case Vignettes of Young Handicapped Children

Early-intervention programs and their interdisciplinary teams are severely challenged by the complex needs of children with both congenital and acquired disabilities. Repeatedly, program personnel report that they need guidance on the most effective combination of methods for assessing and programming for children with specific disorders. The LINK system offers an easily understood and efficient framework for applying curriculum-based assessment to prescribe individualized goals and options for handicapped infants, preschoolers, and their families.

Case studies can begin to provide some direction, since they present realistic problems that require pragmatic solutions. This chapter presents a series of case vignettes that address assessment and programming issues for young children with specific disabilities: premature infant birth, Down syndrome, autism, visual impairment, hearing impairment, and traumatic brain injury. The case vignettes illustrate each phase in the LINK sequence, including the selection of a handicap-sensitive prescriptive developmental assessment battery, curriculum entry points for individualized programming, an initial plan for service delivery and intervention, and an overview of child progress and program impact. An applied case exercise on a child with language/learning disabilities at transition into kindergarten concludes the chapter, providing an example of how the LINK procedure can be applied to a typical child in most programs.

CASE VIGNETTE 1: PREMATURE INFANT BIRTH

Sheila Vaughan's pregnancy was progressing normally until she developed an infection with fever at 26 weeks' gestation and began to have labor contractions. In spite of medications to stop labor, she delivered a 1 lb, 13 oz (820 g) baby boy. Both Sheila and her husband, Tom, work in a health care profession and were acutely aware of the possible adverse outcomes their son could face. They strongly objected to and refused medical treatment for their infant. The neonatologists, after trying persuasion, had to obtain a court order to provide the needed treatment to sustain Timmy's life.

Timmy was hospitalized for the first 4 months of his life, during which time he was intubated and placed on a mechanical ventilator for 2 months; he developed pneumonia several times. His multiple problems due to prematurity included sepsis, hyaline membrane disease, IVH, and bronchopulmonary dysplasia. He suffered a cerebral hemorrhage and later experienced seizures and bouts of apnea. He also had mild retinopathy of prematurity, which seemed to resolve by the time of discharge; but doubts remained. When Timmy was discharged from the neonatal intensive care unit (NICU) at 4 months of age, his parents had to be trained in CPR and in the use of an apnea monitoring machine. These extra factors caused them additional stress and anxiety.

Tom and Sheila were very apprehensive and ambivalent about caring for Timmy at home and began to feel the stress of the past 4 months on their marriage. Services were provided to them by the infant follow-up program of the local children's hospital. Timmy immediately began to receive home-based physical therapy for his motor problems that had resulted from the hemorrhage and seizures. A developmental assessment took place when Timmy was 4½ months old (1½ months corrected for prematurity). The parents were concerned about possible disabilities, such as mental retardation and cerebral palsy and the emotional impact of the traumatic birth on his "baby feelings." Also, they wanted to feel more in control of his progress by being able to do things to help him develop at home. Overall, Timmy's parents were encouraged about his development but apprehensive about his future. They wanted to enroll him in a specialized program to help him "move faster."

Phase 1: Screen/Identify

A home visitor from the local Easter Seals' Baby Steps program, who had previously met the Vaughans while Timmy was in the hospital, arrived at the Vaughan home to interview the parents and to observe Timmy's behavior firsthand. The social worker for the NICU at the university hospital had had the foresight to contact the home visitor. This made the transition much easier for the parents, who were very anxious and fearful about taking Timmy home. The social worker cooperated with the hospital transition team to make sure the parents understood how to use Timmy's portable monitors and deal with his physical and behavioral needs. This also gave the home visitor an opportunity to assess Timmy's development over time and to appraise the quality of the parents' interactions with him. While Timmy had changed developmentally in positive ways, the parents still needed a great deal of help in coping with their mixed feelings, as well as with Timmy's multiple needs. The home worker, a social worker trained in infant development, decided to use observation and parent and professional judgment measures to screen Timmy's current neurobehavioral capabilities. She chose three scales: the Early Coping Inventory (ECI), the Parent Behavior Progression (PBP) scale, and the Infant Temperament Scale (ITS).

The home worker's initial observations, reported to the team, indicated that Timmy had strong emerging social interactive skills but little ability to use his hands to explore toys; he did not seem to understand that he was capable of influencing his world with his behavior. His style of behavior was still disorganized and still retained the qualities observed in a premature baby functioning at a late gestational age; he often coughed, sneezed, and became easily overstimulated if one tried to keep his attention focused too long on a toy or activity or made too many physical demands on him.

The parents' interaction with Timmy was highly variable. In general, Sheila Vaughan felt "afraid that he would break" and typically soothed him and held him carefully; in contrast, Tom Vaughan often avoided touching Timmy; when he did take Timmy at his wife's urging, his behavior was too active and abrupt and "out of sync," with Timmy's facial expressions indicating that it was too much. The team considered all these factors in designing a program for Timmy and his parents (see Exhibit 8-1).

Phase 2: Assess/LINK

With the social worker's observations as the focus, the team met to profile Timmy's and his parents' needs. Table 8-1 presents the prescriptive battery they selected in order to tailor Timmy's comprehensive intervention plan. Once the battery was selected, a two-person transdisciplinary team (the developmental psychologist and the physical therapist), with the parents observing, assessed Timmy's

---

Table 8–1 Timmy's Prescriptive Developmental Assessment Battery

Type	Scale
Norm-based	Infant Psychological Development Scale (IPDS)
Curriculum-based	Carolina Curriculum for At-Risk and Handicapped Infants (CCHI)
Judgment-based	Brazelton Neonatal Behavioral Assessment Scale (BNBAS) Early Coping Inventory (ECI) Infant Temperament Scale (ITS)
Ecological	Parent Behavior Progression (PBP)

Exhibit 8–1 Timmy's Personal Data Form

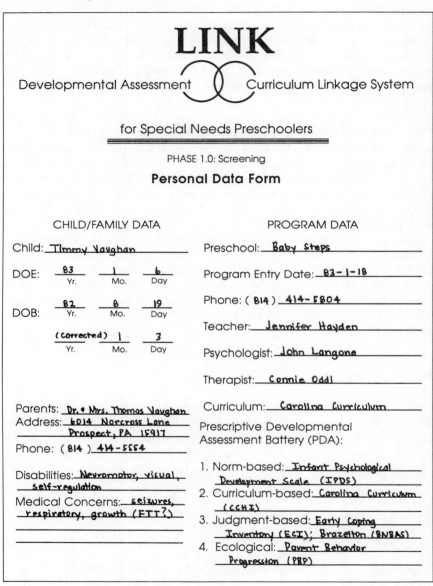

LINK

Developmental Assessment ⬤⬤ Curriculum Linkage System

for Special Needs Preschoolers

PHASE 1.0: Screening

Personal Data Form

CHILD/FAMILY DATA

Child: _Timmy Vaughan_

DOE: __83__ __1__ __6__
      Yr.   Mo.   Day

DOB: __82__ __8__ __19__
      Yr.   Mo.   Day

(Corrected) __1__ __3__
      Yr.   Mo.   Day

Parents: _Dr. + Mrs. Thomas Vaughan_
Address: _6014 Norcross Lane_
Prospect, PA 15917
Phone: (814) _414-5554_

Disabilities: _Neuromotor, visual,_
self-regulation
Medical Concerns: _seizures,_
respiratory, growth (FTT?)

PROGRAM DATA

Preschool: _Baby Steps_

Program Entry Date: _83-1-18_

Phone: (814) _414-5804_

Teacher: _Jennifer Hayden_

Psychologist: _John Langone_

Therapist: _Connie Oddi_

Curriculum: _Carolina Curriculum_

Prescriptive Developmental
Assessment Battery (PDA):

1. Norm-based: _Infant Psychological_
Development Scale (IPDS)
2. Curriculum-based: _Carolina Curriculum_
(CCHI)
3. Judgment-based: _Early Coping_
Inventory (ECI); Brazelton (BNBAS)
4. Ecological: _Parent Behavior_
Progression (PBP)

capabilities in three different situations: with the parents, in a feeder seat, and on a floor mat. Restricting the team to two persons ensured that Timmy would not be overstimulated and that his system would not be overtaxed by too many people and too many competing environmental demands.

Cognitive and Self-Regulatory Capabilities

Exhibit 8-2 profiles Timmy's neurobehavioral, social, interactive, and self-regulatory capabilities. Timmy showed a range of cognitive, neurodevelopmental, and adaptive skills that spanned the 2-week to 2-month age levels. Within this pattern of skills, he showed his strongest capabilities at a level that was comparable to

Exhibit 8–2 Prescriptive Assessment Profile for Timmy

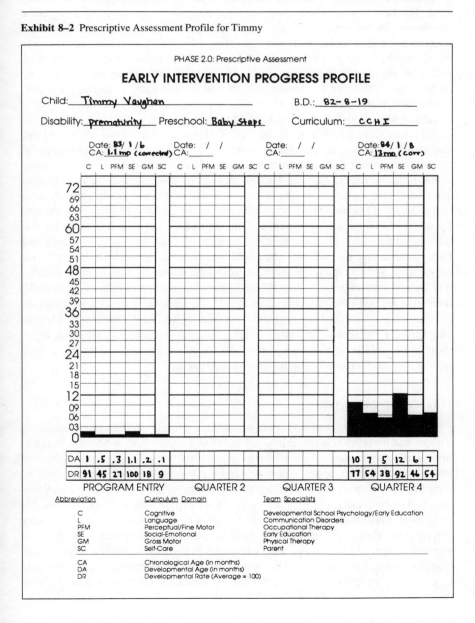

PHASE 2.0: Prescriptive Assessment

EARLY INTERVENTION PROGRESS PROFILE

Child: **Timmy Vaughan**   B.D.: **82-8-19**

Disability: **Prematurity**   Preschool: **Baby Steps**   Curriculum: **C C H I**

Date: **83/ 1 /6**   Date: / /   Date: / /   Date: **84/ 1 /8**
CA: **1·1 mo *(corrected)*** CA:_____   CA:_____   CA: **13 mo (Corr)**

	C	L	PFM	SE	GM	SC
DA	1	.5	.3	1.1	.2	.1
DR	91	45	27	100	18	9

Quarter 4:

	C	L	PFM	SE	GM	SC
DA	10	7	5	12	6	7
DR	77	54	38	92	46	54

PROGRAM ENTRY   QUARTER 2   QUARTER 3   QUARTER 4

Abbreviation	Curriculum Domain	Team Specialists
C	Cognitive	Developmental School Psychology/Early Education
L	Language	Communication Disorders
PFM	Perceptual/Fine Motor	Occupational Therapy
SE	Social-Emotional	Early Education
GM	Gross Motor	Physical Therapy
SC	Self-Care	Parent
CA	Chronological Age (in months)	
DA	Developmental Age (in months)	
DR	Developmental Rate (Average = 100)	

that expected of an average child of 1 month and 12 days of age. This cognitive developmental level indicated skills in adaptive motor behaviors, attention, and visual and auditory responses, as well as a style of behavioral organization, that appeared to be within the average range for Timmy's corrected age.

Specifically, Timmy showed strong visual attention for faces. He exhibited a great deal of eye brightening and widening to new stimuli presented in his visual field. His behaviors to show awareness and adaptation were eye blinking and a startle to bells, buzzer, and a rattle, as well as eye widening with some delay to a squeeze toy with a squeaker. Timmy also showed intermittent raising of his hands to his mouth, sucking movements of the lips, and lip smacking in anticipation of various events and in social responses to the faces of adults in beginning imitative patterns. He attempted to console himself with a hand suck, evidencing his continuing behavioral organization and ability to gain greater self-control.

Timmy was an alert and sociable child who attempted to maintain a variety of social interactions with adults. He molded well into an adult's body when held and responded actively to stimulation. He exhibited a reflex smile, but the quality of the smile appeared to change with a variety of circumstances. He showed good visual focusing during feeding. He also showed several instances of vocalization and coos during face-to-face interactions with adults. He was easily upset by position changes of his body when being held, but he appeared to recover well and was consoled most often by the presence of an adult's face and by soft talking. He discriminated the "feel" of his mother and father by the movements of his hands and feet—more active movements when held by his father, in contrast with reduced movements when in the more soothing, nurturing embrace of his mother. Finally, it is important to note that Timmy showed strong habituation to a variety of stimuli, indicating his ability to process and selectively "screen out" repetitive stimulation. He showed good vertical and horizontal coordination of his eyes, as well as beginning circular patterns in following objects. He showed some social smile in responding to adults and also responded with anticipation and interest to a cloth placed over his face in a beginning peek-a-boo game.

Parent-Infant Interaction

The PBP and direct observation provided a sample of the contributions of Timmy and his parents in social interactive behavior. Both Tom and Sheila Vaughan appeared quite stressed by their interactions with Timmy. Caring for his physical needs, observing the apnea monitor, watching for evidence of seizures, and attempting to cope with their mixed feelings had drained them of energy. Timmy was attached to them both, and they did make efforts to play with and care for him, but they were afraid that they were "doing things wrong." Sheila Vaughan was very effective in calming Timmy and in getting his best eye contact and "smiling," but she was very afraid that being more active with him would produce a seizure. Tom Vaughan wanted to play with Timmy and felt that he slept too much and would never learn if people "tiptoed around him." As noted, his interactions and play with

Timmy were active, quick, and often abrupt; Timmy often cried and was upset by this. Because of the difficulties involved in these play times, Tom Vaughan felt that his wife should be the only one to play with Timmy until he was older. This produced arguments and some resentment between them. The team had to be sensitive to each of their needs and, through counseling, demonstration, and manageable goals, intended to promote better interactions between the parents and Timmy.

Exhibit 8-3 presents the goals and prescriptive linkages that constituted Timmy's individualized program. Note that the emphasis in the goals of intervention was the parent-infant interaction. The program attempted to promote Timmy's most capable area—his social and affective competencies. Visual attention, smiling, reciprocal cooing, eye widening and brightening, and anticipatory responses were Timmy's contributions to the interaction. His parents had to support these skills by pacing their stimulation of him so that it did not overwhelm his self-regulatory capabilities.

Phase 3: Program/Intervene

The psychologist and other team members met to negotiate skeletal developmental program guidelines. As shown in Exhibit 8-4, these guidelines initially focused the treatment upon the parent-infant interaction in the home. Here it was important that one of the team members be a "transdisciplinary" professional who could integrate all of the team goals into activities that would generalize skills across several settings: feeding routines, sleep routines, bathing, and play time. Multisensory toys would be selected and used to prompt behaviors that had a lower arousal threshold. The parents would be partners in this therapy, learning developmental techniques; they would also be afforded the opportunity to participate in counseling designed to explore and resolve their ambivalence and fears about Timmy.

Phase 4: Evaluate/Monitor

Timmy participated in home-based intervention for 12 months. He made notable progress on gross motor, self-care, and social communication goals (see Exhibit 8-5). As he matured, however, his deficits became clearer. Upon his entrance into the program, he had been diagnosed as a child with spastic diplegic cerebral palsy.

Subsequently, Timmy continued to show relative difficulties in the neuromotor, language, and play areas. At the same time, his interaction with his mother and father changed considerably. Both parents were much more consistent in regulating and pacing their social exchanges with him; consequently, his behavior was less disorganized, and he became stressed and upset much less frequently. This made the interaction with his father much more positive and enjoyable, and Sheila Vaughan was now able to increase her activity with Timmy and increase his posi-

Exhibit 8–3 Timmy's Prescriptive Developmental Linkages

PHASE 2.1: Curriculum Linkage

Child: Timmy Vaughan   Date: 83-1-b   CA: 1 mo, 3 days (corrected)

Developmental Scale: IPDS; BNBAS; ECI; PBP Curriculum: CCHI

PRESCRIPTIVE LINKAGES

DEVELOPMENTAL TRANSITIONS (±)	LINK CODES	CURRICULUM TARGETS
DA = 1 (1wk–1.5)	Cognitive	
Tracks object – 180° arc	I 1d/ 3a	Visually tracks side to side
Increased activity with toy present	II E8/ 11a	Anticipates regular events
Vocalize–smile to adult talking	IV E34/ 12a /9b	Vocalizes to person talking
Alternates glance bet. objs.	X 1/ 5a	Shifts attention 1 object to another
DA = .5 (1wk–3wk)	Language	
Responds to voice	IIIA E20/ 9a	Quiets to voice
Vocalizes vs. crying	IIIA 1/ 13c	Vocalizes to get attention
Positive emotions to cooing by adult	IIIA 2a/ 9b	Smiles to talking & gesture
Increased motor activity to face	BNBAS/ 3e /11e	Reacts to caregivers face + disappear
DA = 1.1 (1–2)	Social-Emotional	
Consoles self sucking fist	BNBAS/ 6a/14a	Moves hand to mouth
Smiles–vocalizes to maintain inter.	PBP/ 9b	Smiles to person talking
Face–face visual attention	BNBAS/ 14f	Attract adult by smile–eye contact
Increased endurance in play–social	ECI/	Maintains longer eye contact
DA = .3 (1wk–3wk)	Perceptual/Fine Motor	
Searches for sound with eyes	X E38/ 2b	Visually searches for sound
Grasps finger /toy	XI E48/ 19c	Grasps object placed in hand
Retains rattle in hand 5–10 secs.	XI E49/ 21d	Both hands on toy – midline
Alternates looking bet. objs.	X 1/ 20f	Glance 1 object to other in hand
DA = .2 (1wk–3wk)	Gross Motor	
Prone – head up, turns both sides	BNBAS/ 22a	Lifts head, frees nose
Tone increases at shoulder	BNBAS/ 24a	Head steady when held
Head–shoulder tone ↑ in pull-to-sit	BNBAS/	
DA = .1 (1wk–3wk)	Self-Care	
Sucks on bottle nipple	BNBAS / 1ba	Sucks from nipple smoothly
Coordinates suck–swallow	BNBAS/ 1bd	Gags infrequently

tive play with her. She viewed him now less as a vulnerable baby "who might break" and more as a "fighter." It was decided that Timmy would be enrolled gradually in a combined center-based and home-based program the following year, as his endurance increased and as his parents felt more comfortable with the change.

Exhibit 8–4 Timmy's Developmental Program Guidelines

PHASE 3.0: Intervention
EARLY CHILDHOOD PROGRAM PRESCRIPTIONS

Child: <u>Timmy Vaughan</u> CA: <u>1.1 months</u> Date: <u>83-1-15</u>

DEVELOPMENTAL ASSESSMENT SUMMARY: Timmy has gained important neurobehavioral skills in view of his birth complications. Seizures, low endurance, easy overstimulation, and low self-regulation must be heavily considered in designing his program. Most important intervention goals should promote the parent-infant interaction. These include helping the parents to be consistent in pacing their play and care with Timmy. Combined social and sensorimotor goals are the focus.

DEVELOPMENTAL PROGRAM GUIDELINES:

FEATURES	OPTIONS	COMMENTS
Instructional Setting	☒ Home-based ☐ Center-based ☐ Combo ☐ Hospital-based	1 therapist to deliver integrated program
Instructional Methods	☒ Verbal prompts ☒ Physical prompts ☐ Shaping	Integrate goals into daily routines—use toys to prompt behavior
Grouping Pattern	☒ 1:1 ☐ 1:1 & small group ☐ 1:1, small/large groups	parent-therapist-infant pace
Adaptive Arrangements	☒ Special toys ☒ Communication system ☐ Wheelchair ☐ Room arrangement	Use multisensory toys. Use several positions: feeder seat, prone, supine, at shoulder
Auxiliary Therapies	☐ Speech ☒ PT/OT ☐ Psychologist ☒ Pediatrician ☐ Sensory	Consider PT service delivery (2) teacher input. Monitor seizures and suspected FTT
Behavioral Strategies	☐ Primary reinforcement ☐ Token economy ☐ Behavioral contract ☒ Social praise ☐ Time out ☐ Planned ignoring	Face-face interactions
Parent Participation	☐ Conference only ☒ Parent education/training ☒ Counseling/therapy	Parents as therapists. Couple therapy—psych.

Exhibit 8-5 Timmy's Developmental Progress Evaluation

PHASE 4.0: Evaluation

SUMMATIVE CHILD PROGRESS/PROGRAM EVALUATION SHEET

Child: Timmy Vaughan   C.A. 13 months (corrected)   Date: 84-1-8

Developmental/ Curricular Domain	1st Quarter			4th Quarter			DA Gain	IEI	CEI	M%	P%
	DA	DA Range	DQ	DA	DA Range	DQ					
COGNITIVE	1	(.1–1.5)	91	10	(8–12)	77	9	.75	.84	100%	0%
LANGUAGE	.5	(.1–.9)	45	7	(6–10)	54	6.5	.54	.50	83%	17%
SOCIAL-EMOTIONAL	1.1	(1–2)	100	12	(10–14)	92	10.9	.91	.99	100%	0%
PERCEPTUAL/ FINE MOTOR	.3	(.1–.9)	27	5	(4–8)	38	4.7	.39	.49	69%	31%
GROSS MOTOR	.2	(.1–.9)	18	6	(5–10)	46	5.8	.48	.40	37%	63%
SELF-CARE	.1	(.1–.9)	9	7	(6–10)	54	6.9	.58	.60	16%	84%
DEVELOPMENTAL AVERAGE	.53	—	46	7.8	—	60	7.3	.61	.70	79%	21%

CASE VIGNETTE 2: DOWN SYNDROME

Jeremy was a full-term infant born by cesarean section due to fetal distress. Ms. Bowers was 19 years old. Her labor lasted about 5 hours. Jeremy had developed jaundice but did not require any phototherapy and so was sent home after a 5-day hospital stay. Ms. Bowers was extremely tired from the delivery and stayed with her mother over the first month after discharge. During this time, Jeremy seemed to sleep longer than expected. Of most concern to Ms. Bowers, recently separated from her husband, was the fact that Jeremy seemed to be very floppy, compared with most other babies and seemed to have a "funny-looking" face. Over the next 5 months, this became more pronounced as he was unable to lift his head and roll. At 6 months of age, Jeremy was diagnosed as having Down syndrome due to translocation rather than trisomy.

Jeremy was enrolled in home-based programming through the local ARC program at 8 months of age. This consisted mostly of physical therapy once a week until he was 4 years old. Over this time, Jeremy's acquisition of developmental skills was far behind that of many other handicapped children. He did not walk until he was 4 years old. His developmental course was interrupted by various hospitalizations for eye surgery (for strabismus), tubes for ear infections, and bowel compaction and dehydration.

Ms. Bowers and her therapist were concerned because Jeremy was now losing many of the skills that he had previously achieved, particularly in self-feeding, social interaction, and language use. He previously had said "mama," would wave "bye," and could imitate animal sounds. Now, he no longer fed himself with a spoon and did not look at people when they were present. Yet, he still continued to gain in gross motor development. His mother felt that his loss of skills coincided with a severe strep infection of several months' duration, with one fever of 104 degrees. Jeremy now showed some head-banging and hand-flapping behavior when excited or when too many people were around. Ms. Bowers wanted Jeremy to be evaluated and placed in a center that could help him regain his lost skills.

Phase 1: Screen/Identify

Ms. Bowers and the physical therapist met with the team from the local ARC program (see Exhibit 8-6). The team had previously observed Jeremy in the home, and the purpose of the present meeting was to gather each member's perceptions of Jeremy's current functional capabilities. Exhibit 8-7 profiles these impressions.

It was clear that Ms. Bowers and the team were in close agreement about Jeremy's needs. He was viewed as having severe deficits across most developmental domains, with the exception of gross motor skills and some fine motor manipulative behaviors. Based on this screening, the team selected a battery of sensitive measures that could detect specific competencies to be shaped in Jeremy's program.

Exhibit 8–6 Jeremy's Personal Data Form

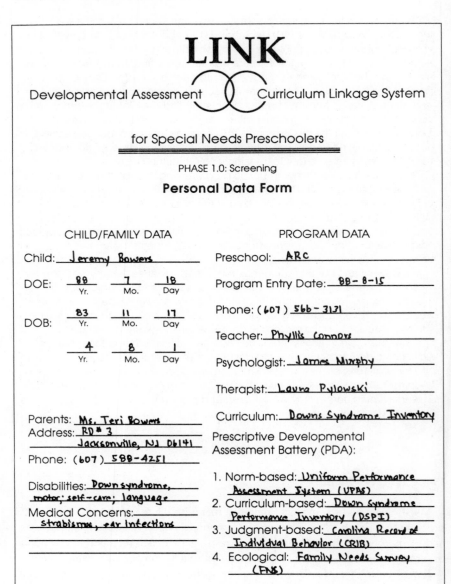

LINK

Developmental Assessment ⃝⃝ Curriculum Linkage System

for Special Needs Preschoolers

PHASE 1.0: Screening

Personal Data Form

CHILD/FAMILY DATA

Child: **Jeremy Bowers**

DOE: **88** Yr. **7** Mo. **18** Day

DOB: **83** Yr. **11** Mo. **17** Day

4 Yr. **8** Mo. **1** Day

Parents: **Ms. Teri Bowers**
Address: **RD # 3**
Jacksonville, NJ 06141
Phone: (**607**) **588-4251**

Disabilities: **Down syndrome,**
motor; self-care; language
Medical Concerns:
strabismus, ear infections

PROGRAM DATA

Preschool: **ARC**

Program Entry Date: **88- 8-15**

Phone: (**607**) **566 - 3131**

Teacher: **Phyllis Connors**

Psychologist: **James Murphy**

Therapist: **Laura Pylowski**

Curriculum: **Downs Syndrome Inventory**

Prescriptive Developmental
Assessment Battery (PDA):

1. Norm-based: **Uniform Performance**
   Assessment System (UPAS)
2. Curriculum-based: **Down Syndrome**
   Performance Inventory (DSPI)
3. Judgment-based: **Carolina Record of**
   Individual Behavior (CRIB)
4. Ecological: **Family Needs Survey**
   (FNS)

Exhibit 8–7 Team PODS Profile for Jeremy

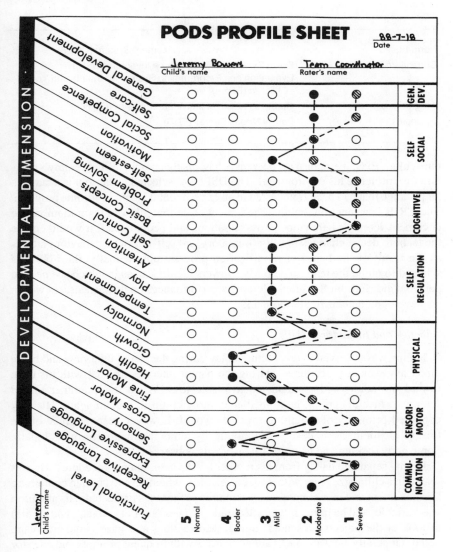

Phase 2: Assess/LINK

The team chose a battery of four instruments that would be sensitive to Jeremy's current developmental difficulties (see Table 8-2). The UPAS was chosen as the hybrid norm/criterion scale, since it contains more differentiated skills at lower functional levels to accommodate Jeremy's severe deficits. In addition, as in the

Table 8–2 Jeremy's Prescriptive Developmental Assessment Battery

Type	Scale
Norm-based	Uniform Performance Assessment System (UPAS)
Curriculum-based	Down Syndrome Performance Inventory (DSPI)
	Evaluation and Programming System for Infants and Young Children (EPS-I)
Judgment-based	Carolina Record of Individual Behavior (CRIB)
Ecological	Family Needs Survey (FNS)

curriculum EPS, it emphasizes operant behaviors that would reflect Jeremy's capability to influence his environment. The DSPI was selected because it is a curricular package that had been field tested in an experimental Down syndrome program. The CRIB is a functional clinical judgment scale that allowed team members to document Jeremy's behaviors across situations and people; also, it would enable the team to detect changes in self-stimulatory and self-injurious behavior patterns as the result of the behavior modification programming. Finally, the FNS was selected to guide the team to help Ms. Bowers identify areas in which she needed personal aid. Exhibit 8-8 graphs Jeremy's performances on these measures within six developmental/curricular domains.

Affective and Behavioral Skills

Jeremy was observed in unstructured play during the parent interview and in the direct assessment procedures. During the parent interview, he sat with his back toward the adults and manipulated available toys. When the examiner turned Jeremy to face the group, he immediately turned himself around again. His play consisted primarily of mouthing toys. He would, however, respond most of the time to his mother's request of "no mouth" by removing the toy from his mouth. Some body rocking and head rocking were also observed.

Jeremy separated easily from his mother for the assessment procedures. He was seated in a child-size chair with deep barrel arms, which assisted him in containing his movement and in maintaining his attention to the tasks presented. His attention was variable, and he frequently needed multiple cues (auditory, visual, and tactile) to look at the objects presented. Some head rocking and gaze avoidance were noted. Generally, he was able to attend to tasks with frequent prompts and cues for periods of approximately 10 minutes. Interspersing periods of gross motor activities with tasks demanding fine motor and cognitive skills appeared to assist his ability to attend to tasks. On one occasion, he demonstrated apparent frustration by scratching the examiner's arm when he was unable to reach around a transparent screen to obtain a toy. He did not, however, use scratching on a regular basis to avoid interaction. Jeremy was occasionally observed to respond by smiling to social rewards, such as hand clapping and praise. He also demonstrated a differential

Exhibit 8–8 Jeremy's Developmental Levels

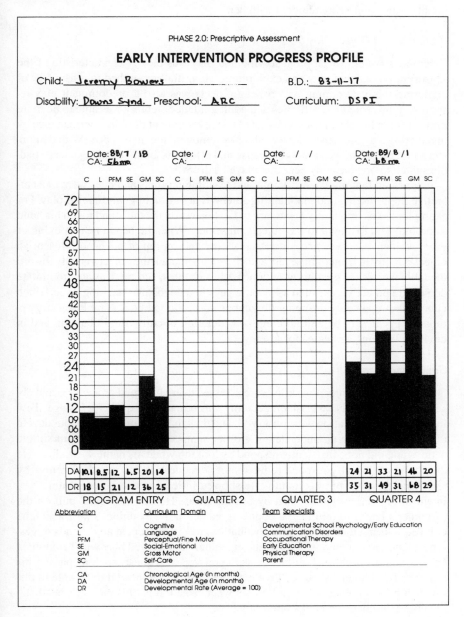

PHASE 2.0: Prescriptive Assessment

EARLY INTERVENTION PROGRESS PROFILE

Child: **Jeremy Bowers**   B.D.: **83-11-17**

Disability: **Downs Synd.** Preschool: **ARC**   Curriculum: **DSPI**

Date: **86/7 /18**   Date: / /   Date: / /   Date: **89/8 /1**
CA: **56mo**   CA:_____   CA:_____   CA: **66 mo.**

	C	L	PFM	SE	GM	SC	C	L	PFM	SE	GM	SC	C	L	PFM	SE	GM	SC	C	L	PFM	SE	GM	SC
DA	10.1	8.5	12	6.5	20	14													24	21	33	21	46	20
DR	18	15	21	12	36	25													35	31	49	31	68	29

PROGRAM ENTRY	QUARTER 2	QUARTER 3	QUARTER 4

Abbreviation	Curriculum Domain	Team Specialists
C	Cognitive	Developmental School Psychology/Early Education
L	Language	Communication Disorders
PFM	Perceptual/Fine Motor	Occupational Therapy
SE	Social-Emotional	Early Education
GM	Gross Motor	Physical Therapy
SC	Self-Care	Parent
CA	Chronological Age (in months)	
DA	Developmental Age (in months)	
DR	Developmental Rate (Average = 100)	

response to his mother after the assessment procedures by vocalizing and extending his arms upon being reunited with her.

Cognitive and Object Play Skills

Jeremy's pattern of problem solving and play was clearly characteristic of the sensorimotor stage of play and exploration. He initially mouthed toys as a way of exploring them. Dropping or throwing objects was also a predominant play response. With structured activities and adult guidance, Jeremy was able to be more purposeful in his play. He demonstrated the development of object permanence by uncovering a toy hidden under a cloth or by removing the lid of a box. With demonstration, he also showed emerging cause and effect reasoning by using a large paddle switch to operate a toy bear that played a drum.

It appeared that multisensory toys and teaching prompts and cues were most effective in promoting and maintaining Jeremy's attention in goal-directed play. For example, it was frequently necessary to tap objects on the table and touch his hand to prompt him to attend to the objects presented. When he began head rocking or gaze avoidance, it was necessary to place a hand on top of his head, present an object directly in front of his eyes, and allow him to track the object visually toward the table in order to gain his attention. With such cues, Jeremy was able to imitate demonstrated activities, such as placing pegs in a pegboard, stacking three 1-inch cubes, and repeatedly dropping tiny cubes into a slotted box. A multisensory approach appeared to be an important consideration in curriculum planning and in devising learning strategies for Jeremy.

Communication Skills

Jeremy's communication skills were assessed using informal procedures and observation. During the assessment, Jeremy was remarkably quiet for his age. Few instances of vocalization were observed, and they included only vowel sounds. He did not demonstrate an understanding of the names of familiar objects or simple actions and did not consistently respond by looking when his name was called. He did, however, usually respond to his mother's request of "no mouth, Jeremy" by removing the toy from his mouth. He showed little spontaneous communicative intent in his actions, other than by turning away. He did, however, pull on the examiner's hands to reinitiate a bouncing game on the examiner's lap, which he enjoyed. During the course of the evaluation, he did not repeat any sounds or gestures requested or demonstrated by the examiner. In observed play with his mother, he was able to perform familiar games upon verbal request, such as patting his mother's hand when asked to "give her five." He also appeared to be able to distinguish between his mother and others when asked to pat his mother's head and then the examiner's head in a familiar game.

Jeremy's severe lack of receptive and expressive language was of great concern. He did communicate on a very basic level; and it was decided that this basic, holistic, tactile communication should be encouraged and built upon. It was also agreed that nonverbal symbolic systems such as sign language should be explored as an alternative means of communication.

Prescriptive Linkages

It was vital that Jeremy's IEP (see Exhibit 8-9) place a premium on the following four goals initially: (1) to increase his social communication skills in both verbal and nonverbal areas; (2) to increase his purposeful goal-directed play skills at his current developmental level; (3) to reduce his self-stimulatory behaviors and increase eye contact and self-regulatory skills; and (4) to promote activities of daily living, such as the establishment of independent spoon feeding. To these ends, it was crucial that his educational team recognize his current developmental levels, which were most typical of a child at approximately 1 year of age. It was felt that introducing tasks that required higher level skills would likely result in reduced attention and increased frustration and withdrawal, as evidenced by Jeremy's scratching and hair pulling. It was agreed that frequent monitoring of Jeremy's levels and progress through both developmental and curriculum-based assessments would help target his current abilities and needs.

Phase 3: Program/Intervene

It was clear that the use of highly structured methods in a low-distraction setting would best promote Jeremy's learning (see Exhibit 8-10). It was agreed that reinforcement contingencies and environmental controls should be directed toward eye contact, attention to tasks, and imitation of gestures and actions. The goal was to increase the occurrence of the reinforced response (e.g., toy play or attention to task) with a decrease in inattention and self-stimulatory behaviors. Initial areas of social communication skills could include attention to visual and auditory events, vocal and motor exchanges with others, and the use of sound and gestures to interact with others. Teaching objects in the cognitive domain would be used to capitalize on Jeremy's beginning cause-and-effect reasoning skills, such as acting on a simple and/or mechanical toy to produce an action and reproducing part of an interactive game or action in order to continue the event. The latter skill was seen when Jeremy raised his arms and pulled on the examiner's hands to reinitiate a lap-bouncing game. It was felt that such responses should be rewarded in an attempt to generalize the communicative and cause-and-effect responses to other actions. The use of multisensory approaches and multiple cues (auditory, visual, and tactile) appeared to be most effective in establishing and maintaining Jeremy's attention and play skills.

Phase 4: Evaluate/Monitor

In his first year in the ARC program, though Jeremy's functional problems still indicated a high level of disability, the program had a major impact in shaping and

Exhibit 8–9 Jeremy's Prescriptive Developmental Linkages

PHASE 2.1: Curriculum Linkage

Child: __Jeremy Bowers__   Date: __88-8-1__   CA: __5b months__

Developmental Scale: __UPAS ; CRIB ; BSID__   Curriculum: __DSPI ; EPS__

PRESCRIPTIVE LINKAGES

DEVELOPMENTAL TRANSITIONS (±)	LINK CODES	CURRICULUM TARGETS
DA = 10 (6–12)	**Cognitive**	
Focus on face & toys – track 180°	PA 3 / EPS 1.2	Focuses & follows obj./person
Uncovers hidden object	BSID 8b / EPS 2.1	Locates disappearing object
Activates simple & mechanical toy	PA 11/ EPS 1.2	Acts on simple, mech. toy
Rings on stick	PA 11/ L₂ 24	Puts 3–5 rings on stick
DA = 8 (6–9)	**Language**	
Emits vowel-consonant combos	C 32 / EPS 2.1	Consistent consonant–vowels
Imitates nonspeech sounds	C 37/ EPS 2.2	Uses non-speific sounds
Respond to "come here"	C 6/ EPS 2.3	Carries out 1-step direction –cue
Responds to word & gesture	C 5/ EPS 1.1	Responds © vocal or gesture
DA = 6 (4–7)	**Social-Emotional**	
Responds to adult social behavior	EPS 2.2/ L₂ 2	Responds to greeting by adult
Initiates simple game © adult	EPS 2.1/ EPS 2.1	Initiates game © adult
Smiles to familiar adult	EPS 1.2/ L₁ 2,3	Smiles responsively & spont.
↓ self-stimulation & injury	UPAS 2b/ CRIB	↓ hand-flap, scratch, head-bang
DA = 12 (10–15)	**Perceptual/Fine Motor**	
Turns book pages	PA 13/ L₂, 2b	Turns book pages singly
Hammers pegs	PA 15/ L₂, 30, 1315	Pounds, hits pegs © hammer
Release object into target	EPS 5.1/ L₂ 27-28	Turns knobs & door handles
Rotates wrist –horizontal	EPS 1.1/ L₂ 27-28	Turns knobs & handles
DA = 20 (15–21)	**Gross Motor**	
Walk with object – 2 hands	GM 23/ L₂, 1b	Lifts & carries object
Push cart to spot	GM 24/ L₂/14,15	Pushes carriage or wagon
Kick ball	GM 61/ L₂, 20	Kicks ball
Jump down in place	GM 38/ L₂, 11	Jumps in place
DA = 14 (10–15)	**Self-Care**	
Eat solid food w/ spoon	SS b/ L₂, 14	Feeds self with spoon
Self-remove sock	SS 12/ L₂, 20, 21	Removes socks & shoes
Sit on toilet	SS 23/ L₂, 17	Sits on toilet
Wash-dry hands	SS 27/ L₃, 1b	Wash-dry hands © assistance

enhancing his adaptive skills (see Exhibit 8-11). The program was responsible for significant and generalizable increases in his social, communication, play, and object-manipulation skills. Behavior analysis revealed that Jeremy's episodes of hand flapping, scratching self and others, and head banging had been reduced to a few instances of a few minutes each day. During play and interaction, such

Exhibit 8–10 Jeremy's Program Guidelines

PHASE 3.0: Intervention
EARLY CHILDHOOD PROGRAM PRESCRIPTIONS

Child: __Jeremy Bowers__   CA: __56 months__   Date: __88-7-21__

DEVELOPMENTAL ASSESSMENT SUMMARY: Jeremy's performance indicates severe functional deficits in important social communication, behavior, self-regulatory, and adaptive domains. His self-stimulatory patterns are becoming more frequent and of greater duration, particularly with stress & frustration. A premium must be placed on enhancing social interaction, object play and adaptive, self-care skills while ↓ self-injury and self-stimulation.

DEVELOPMENTAL PROGRAM GUIDELINES:

FEATURES	OPTIONS	COMMENTS
Instructional Setting	☐ Home-based ☒ Center-based ☐ Combo ☐ Hospital-based	5 full days / week Reduce distractions
Instructional Methods	☒ Verbal prompts ☒ Physical prompts ☒ Shaping	Prompt and shape initiation of toy & social play
Grouping Pattern	☐ 1:1 ☒ 1:1 & small group ☐ 1:1, small/large groups	1-1 for instructional sessions; pair with 1 higher peer occasionally
Adaptive Arrangements	☒ Special toys ☒ Communication system ☐ Wheelchair ☐ Room arrangement	Response-contingent & multisensory toys Reinforce communication prerequisites/try signs
Auxiliary Therapies	☒ Speech ☒ PT/OT ☒ Psychologist ☐ Pediatrician ☐ Sensory	Consult re: integrate language in classroom Beh Plan: self-stim. ↓ ↑ play ↑ language Identify best PT setting
Behavioral Strategies	☒ Primary reinforcement ☐ Token economy ☐ Behavioral contract ☒ Social praise ☐ Time out ☐ Planned ignoring	Focus on social, but pair primary as needed Identify activity reinforcers
Parent Participation	☐ Conference only ☒ Parent education/training ☐ Counseling/therapy	Parent group (S) MH/MR Mother as teacher Respite care; support

stereotypies were rarely observed; during unoccupied times, they were somewhat more frequent, even though he was now capable of occupying himself with various toys. The reduction in atypical behaviors was accompanied by increases in social communication and object play. Nevertheless, his caregivers still needed to provide for most of Jeremy's daily living needs.

Exhibit 8–11 Developmental Progress and Program Impact Data for Jeremy

PHASE 4.0: Evaluation

SUMMATIVE CHILD PROGRESS/PROGRAM EVALUATION SHEET

Child: Jeremy Bowers   C.A. 68 months   Date: 89-8-1

Developmental/ Curricular Domain	1st Quarter			4th Quarter			DA Gain	IEI	CEI	M%	P%
	DA	DA Range	DQ	DA	DA Range	DQ					
COGNITIVE	10.1	(6–12)	18	24	(18–28)	35	13.9	1.16	1.10	16%	84%
LANGUAGE	8.5	(6–9)	15	21	(12–21)	31	12.5	1.04	.97	14%	86%
SOCIAL-EMOTIONAL	6.5	(4–7)	12	21	(14–24)	31	14.5	1.21	.95	17%	83%
PERCEPTUAL/ FINE MOTOR	12	(10–15)	21	33	(24–34)	49	21	1.75	1.20	12%	88%
GROSS MOTOR	20	(15–21)	36	46	(42–50)	68	26	2.17	1.58	17%	83%
SELF-CARE	14	(10–15)	25	20	(15–21)	29	6	.50	.42	50%	50%
DEVELOPMENTAL AVERAGE	11.9	(4–21)	20	21.5	(12–56)	40	15.6	1.30	1.12	15%	85%

CASE VIGNETTE 3: AUTISM

Derek was always a puzzle. When he was a newborn, he was very difficult to feed and did not seem to enjoy cuddling and playing simple games like "peek-a-boo." In fact, the parents reported that he seemed to "look through" them when he was on his back, on the floor, or in the crib. He walked early compared with their older child, and at one point seemed to be beginning to understand how to play with toys and with adults purposefully. Yet, by the time he was 2½ years old, it was clear that something was very wrong with Derek's behavior. He learned several words but rarely used them for their objects; more importantly, he did not seem to understand that words should be used to tell people what you want. Derek resisted eye contact with adults and refused being held; he spent much of his time alone and would wander about the room twirling in circles, watching his fingers, and echoing words and phrases that he had heard on T.V. In bed at night, he would often rock repetitively so hard that he would bang his head on the wall, but he never seemed to get hurt. Finally, Derek often appeared to be afraid of various sounds and would cup his ears, roam the room, and make rhythmic sounds when a loud car passed or a siren sounded.

Derek and his parents lived in a very rural area. It took them several years to believe friends and relatives when they said that Derek's behavior was abnormal for any age. They were particularly concerned about his lack of language and his inability to play with the toys they bought him. Despite their isolation, Derek's mother began to read about special children. She felt that she knew what was wrong, but her husband insisted that Derek was just stubborn and would outgrow "his little world." She did, however, convince her husband that specialists had to evaluate Derek so that they could understand him and help him. She approached the local school district for guidance, since Derek had never received services before.

Phase 1: Screen/Identify

At the mother's request, a social worker and an itinerant teacher from the school district's pupil appraisal center visited Derek at home. Through observation and interview, they gathered developmental information. At the close of their first session, they asked the parents if they would be willing to bring Derek to their center for a more detailed evaluation.

The next day they presented their initial impressions to the program supervisor who coordinated the team meeting. Their initial judgments are profiled on the PODS Profile Sheet in Exhibit 8-12. In their profile, they indicated that Derek had moderate-to-severe deficits in several areas, especially communication and social interaction skills. Given these deficits and Derek's atypical behaviors, they were concerned about autism. Also, they were concerned about a significant degree of mental retardation. The team members concluded their meeting with the decision to enroll Derek initially in their preschool-kindergarten diagnostic program, since he had recently turned 6 years old but had never been involved in a classroom ex-

Exhibit 8–12 Derek's PODS Profile

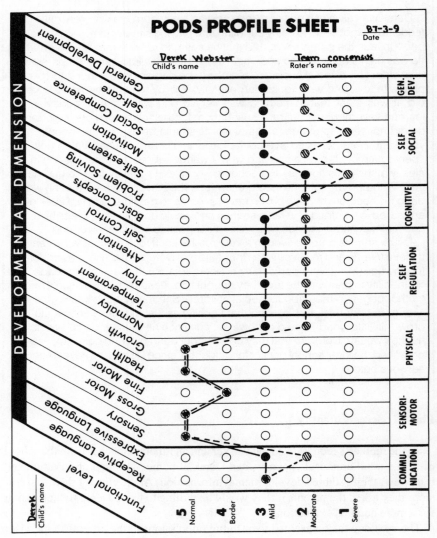

perience before, except for participation in Sunday school (see Exhibit 8-13). At this point, they wanted to analyze more fully his developmental competencies, using both structured and unstructured methods, since he was difficult to keep on task. They chose a flexible diagnostic battery that allowed them to assess Derek's adaptive behaviors and atypical behavior patterns.

Exhibit 8–13 Derek's Personal Data Form

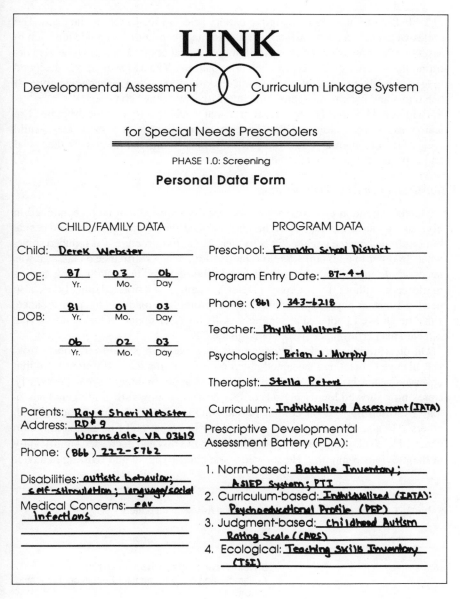

LINK

Developmental Assessment 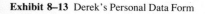 Curriculum Linkage System

for Special Needs Preschoolers

PHASE 1.0: Screening

Personal Data Form

CHILD/FAMILY DATA

Child: **Derek Webster**

DOE: **87** Yr. **03** Mo. **06** Day

DOB: **81** Yr. **01** Mo. **03** Day

06 Yr. **02** Mo. **03** Day

Parents: **Ray & Sheri Webster**
Address: **RD # 9**
Wornsdale, VA 03619
Phone: (**866**) **222-5762**

Disabilities: **autistic behavior;**
self-stimulation; language/social
Medical Concerns: **ear**
infections

PROGRAM DATA

Preschool: **Franklin School District**

Program Entry Date: **87-4-1**

Phone: (**861**) **343-6218**

Teacher: **Phyllis Walters**

Psychologist: **Brian J. Murphy**

Therapist: **Stella Peters**

Curriculum: **Individualized Assessment (IATA)**

Prescriptive Developmental
Assessment Battery (PDA):

1. Norm-based: **Battelle Inventory;**
   ASIEP System; PTI
2. Curriculum-based: **Individualized (IATA);**
   Psychoeducational Profile (PEP)
3. Judgment-based: **Childhood Autism**
   Rating Scale (CARS)
4. Ecological: **Teaching Skills Inventory**
   (TSI)

Phase 2: Assess/LINK

Table 8-3 outlines the prescriptive battery selected for Derek by the team. The scales were chosen for their flexible qualities and their ability to guide the team in assessing his cognitive, communication, and social competencies, while also defining the severity of his atypical behavior patterns. The assessment was designed to lead to goals for curriculum planning or skill building and for reducing atypical behaviors and increasing appropriate interactive and play behaviors.

Exhibit 8-14 graphs Derek's developmental levels at entry into the program. The team's assessment indicated that Derek was functioning at a moderate-to-mild level of developmental retardation, with the most significant deficits in the social and expressive communication domains.

Social and Behavioral Observations

Derek's attention difficulties and overactivity required that he be contained in his seat with an arm gently about his shoulders, as the psychologist kneeled beside him, until he became engaged in activities. Then, the structure was reduced somewhat. In order to maintain attention, motivation, and performance on tasks, it was necessary to intersperse the more focused, high-demand tasks with active toys as reinforcers; without this approach, Derek's attention deteriorated quickly. He also needed constant physical and verbal-visual prompts to maintain his performance, since he showed poor visual scanning skills on discrimination tasks; this deficit affected his performance particularly on the PTI.

On discrimination tasks, Derek's limit remained a three- to four- choice task; yet, his eye contact and sustained attention were dramatically different from that observed when home intervention had begun approximately 1 year previously. Derek now showed longer periods of face-to-face gazing with smiling and laughing. He often hugged on command and sought greater emotional contact with others. He also showed greater participation in verbal and fine motor imitation games. He displayed some echolalic behavior, but this had decreased significantly in the previous 3 months. He showed some hand-flapping and twirling behavior

---

Table 8–3   Derek's Prescriptive Developmental Assessment Battery

Type	Scale
Norm-based	Battelle Developmental Inventory (BDI)
	Autism Screening Instrument for Educational Planning (ASIEP)
	Pictorial Test of Intelligence (PTI)
Curriculum-based	Psychoeducational Profile (PEP): IATA
Judgment-based	Childhood Autism Rating Scale (CARS)
Ecological	Teaching Skills Inventory (TSI)

Exhibit 8–14 Prescriptive Assessment Profile for Derek

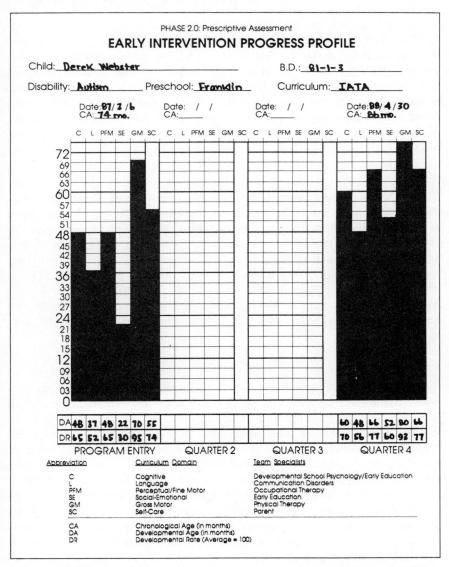

PHASE 2.0: Prescriptive Assessment

EARLY INTERVENTION PROGRESS PROFILE

Child: **Derek Webster**   B.D.: **81-1-3**

Disability: **Autism**   Preschool: **Franklin**   Curriculum: **IATA**

	PROGRAM ENTRY	QUARTER 2	QUARTER 3	QUARTER 4
Date	**87/3/6** CA: **74 mo.**	/ / CA:	/ / CA:	**88/4/30** CA: **88 mo.**

	C	L	PFM	SE	GM	SC																C	L	PFM	SE	GM	SC
DA	48	37	48	22	70	55																60	48	66	52	80	66
DR	65	52	65	30	95	74																70	56	77	60	93	77

Abbreviation	Curriculum Domain	Team Specialists
C	Cognitive	Developmental School Psychology/Early Education
L	Language	Communication Disorders
PFM	Perceptual/Fine Motor	Occupational Therapy
SE	Social-Emotional	Early Education
GM	Gross Motor	Physical Therapy
SC	Self-Care	Parent
CA	Chronological Age (in months)	
DA	Developmental Age (in months)	
DR	Developmental Rate (Average = 100)	

when excited; yet, when engaged in tasks, he exhibited fewer instances of these stereotypies.

Conceptual

Derek's least-developed cognitive skills were apparent in the conceptual area. He knew some colors, shapes, and positional and size concepts. However, he showed limitations in understanding opposites, number concepts, and spatial concepts and in doing memory tasks requiring attention. His strongest cognitive skills were evident in remembering and recalling pictures presented visually, in defining basic words (coat, towel, car), in grouping words into generic categories ("things to eat"), and in identifying missing details in pictures. In nonverbal problem solving on the PTI, Derek's performance was limited by poor visual scanning and attention, although he showed conceptual knowledge at the 5-year level. For example, he was able to match clothes to appropriate persons on a discrimination task. When his attention was focused, he was capable of showing good visual problem solving, as shown in his completion of a missing parts task (wagon—"the wheel broke off").

Attention

Derek's selective and sustained attention skills were much like those expected at the 18- to 24-month level. His impulsivity and distractibility were hindrances to his understanding and performance on tasks. He appeared to be capable of learning through visual cues, modeling, and guided performance with physical prompts; and he could repeat actions. In contrast, his attention to auditorily presented material was significantly limited. Thus, he had difficulty remembering numbers and unrelated words presented in a series and had great difficulty attending to a story and recalling details, even in short eight-word forms or descriptive sentences. He needed much work in careful visual scanning and comparing on tasks that had three to four choices.

Language

Derek's pattern of capabilities showed a large discrepancy between language understanding and use. He had great difficulty expressing definitions beyond objects and functions; even though he might have understood the concept, he could not express his thoughts in coherent sentences or phrases. He showed many of the word retrieval deficits displayed by children with neurologically based language disorders. For example, because he had difficulty recalling a particular word for a concept, he often gave associative responses, such as identifying a horn as "a tune" or a lock as "a key." Finally, he had difficulty remembering more than two or three words or elements presented in a direction. Typically, he quickly said the last word that was presented before it disintegrated in memory. With more meaningful forms (short sentences), he tried to repeat the details in telegraphic fashion before he forgot. He showed strong increases, however, in his ability to imitate fine motor actions and gestures.

Perceptual Fine Motor

One of Derek's weaker areas was in the ability to express perceptual fine motor skills in such tasks as drawing, block building, puzzle completion, and other coordinated activities; his ability in these skills was comparable to that expected in a child between 24 and 36 months of age. Tracing forms and imitating (as compared with copying) were his primary methods. He had particular difficulty with three-part disjointed puzzles and the reproduction of very basic block patterns.

Exhibit 8-15 presents the prescriptive linkages form detailing Derek's curriculum entry goals on the IATA materials from the TEACH program curriculum.

Exhibit 8–15 Derek's Prescriptive Curriculum Entry Points

PHASE 2.1: Curriculum Linkage

Child: **Derek Webster**   Date: **87-3-6**   CA: **74 months**

Developmental Scale: **BDI; ASIEP**   Curriculum: **IATA; PEP**

PRESCRIPTIVE LINKAGES

DEVELOPMENTAL TRANSITIONS (±)	LINK CODES	CURRICULUM TARGETS
DA = 4B(28-52)	Cognitive	
Matches O, ☐, △ shapes	CG7/CPS	Shape recognition
Recalls familiar objects	CG17/0	Recalls missing object(s)
Responds to one & one more	CG23/0	Aware of amount & number
Gives 3 objects on request	CG25/2B	Gives named objects
DA = 37(21-40)	Language	
Responds to positional concepts	CMB/RL7	Understands prepositions
Responds to "wh" questions	CM13/RLID	Understand questions
Uses 2-3 word phrases ⊚ meaning	CM3B/ELb	Increase word usage
Responds yes-no appropriately	CM4D/RL5	Responds to commands
DA = 22(18-24)	Social-Emotional	
Attends to one activity 3⁺ minutes	AB/VP3	Shifts visual attention
Follows simple game rules	PS63/SS9	Follows game rules
Shares with others & turntaking	PS56/SS4	Enjoys turn-taking
Responds to social contact	PS14/SS3	Increase affectionate contact
DA = 4B(30-50)	Perceptual/Fine Motor	
Holds paper while drawing	MS5/4C	Hold & position paper/cut or draw
Copies ⏐ — O + forms	M6B-7D/2C	Makes strokes ⊚ crayon
Cuts with scissors	M71/1H	Open & shut scissors
Opens padlock with key	MS9/3C	Turn doorknob - place key
DA = 70(54-72)	Gross Motor	
Balances on foot alternately	M24/2B	Balances on 1 foot
Standing broad jump	M25/1E	Strengthening - jump
Alternates feet downstairs	M43/3C	Directional movements
Catches ball	M23/1A	Run to catch a ball
DA = 55(48-60)	Self-Care	
Wash-dries hands assisted	A56/0	Washes-dries supervised
Buttons without assistance	A32/SH3	Button & zip
Serves self food –assisted	A23/0	Get drink unaided
Puts on shoes unassisted	A31/SH2	Sock+ shoes

Phase 3: Program/Intervene

Based upon the prescriptive assessment, the early-intervention team wanted Derek to have as many normalizing experiences as possible. Appropriate social and language models would be crucial. In addition, he would need to learn such prerequisite behaviors as attending during conversation and using language to initiate social exchanges, waiting, sharing, and turn taking. The team planned to promote the selective use of a computer as a learning aid for Derek so that he could be reinforced immediately for his learning and become a somewhat more independent worker on preacademic tasks. The individual dimensions of Derek's program are shown in the Early Childhood Program Prescription form presented in Exhibit 8-16.

Phase 4: Evaluate/Monitor

After 12 months in the school district preschool-kindergarten diagnostic program, Derek demonstrated some important functional gains. Analysis of the progress data showed that, in three of six areas, the structured intervention program designed for Derek was responsible for his dramatically exceeding the rate expected due to maturation. Gains in the perceptual, fine motor, and self-care areas were notable, but the greatest generalizable gains were evident in the socio-emotional competencies, as shown in Exhibit 8-17.

Affective, Social, and Behavioral Characteristics

The areas in which Derek demonstrated the most dramatic changes were in his style of behavior with peers and adults and his orientation to structured tasks. It was clear that the program and Derek's parents deserved much credit for promoting these gains, which had made his behavior more normalized. Quantitatively, on the Childhood Autism Rating Scale (CARS), Derek's atypical behavior previously met criteria for a moderate autistic disorder; in this progress evaluation, his atypical behavior was indicative of a mild autistic disorder.

Derek had clearly learned to adapt and respond to a structured routine. He smiled at success, was motivated by novel activities, and indicated that he wanted to continue rather than end activities. He stayed at table tasks for long periods of time, listened and followed directions, and took cues, prompts, and redirections, such as "look at all the pictures with your eyes," "look before pointing," and "wait until I am done saying all the words."

Derek's performance on the attention subtest of the BDI suggested significant gains in duration and selection when completing activities. He took longer to compare pictures on receptive language and concept tasks and made fewer errors. Socially, Derek now initiated verbal exchanges with others by asking questions (e.g., "Is that your tie?"). He called people by name. Similarly, he showed a much wider and more appropriate range of emotions. He smiled at his success, showed frustration with harder tasks, and openly laughed at funny situations. Yet, there were

Exhibit 8–16 Derek's Program Dimensions

PHASE 3.0: Intervention
EARLY CHILDHOOD PROGRAM PRESCRIPTIONS

Child: **Derek Webster**   CA: **74 mo.**   Date: **87-3-15**

DEVELOPMENTAL ASSESSMENT SUMMARY: Derek's overall performance on play, conceptual, and fine motor tasks was most like that of a 48 month old child. His greatest needs are apparent on prerequisites such as attention, task orientation, social interaction, and purposeful use of language. Derek shows less severe atypical behaviors than reported in the past. Language acquisition & social competence will be the best predictors for the future.

DEVELOPMENTAL PROGRAM GUIDELINES:

FEATURES	OPTIONS	COMMENTS
Instructional Setting	☐ Home-based ☒ Center-based ☐ Combo ☐ Hospital-based	Consider specialized SED or Autism class @ mainstreaming for non-academics
Instructional Methods	☒ Verbal prompts ☒ Physical prompts ☐ Shaping	Focus on behavioral prerequisites; pair, then fade manipulues
Grouping Pattern	☐ 1:1 ☒ 1:1 & small group ☐ 1:1, small/large groups	Start @ 1-1 on focused tasks; pair @ peer; groups of b only
Adaptive Arrangements	☒ Special toys ☒ Communication system ☐ Wheelchair ☐ Room arrangement	Response-contingent toys; computer leisure Word skill program + pictures
Auxiliary Therapies	☒ Speech ☐ PT/OT ☒ Psychologist ☐ Pediatrician ☐ Sensory	1-1 speech/language therapy & classroom teacher consultation. Structured behavior plan
Behavioral Strategies	☐ Primary reinforcement ☒ Token economy ☐ Behavioral contract ☒ Social praise ☒ Time out ☐ Planned ignoring	Stickers, tokens Timers for start-stop activities Social praise paired with other reinforcers
Parent Participation	☐ Conference only ☒ Parent education/training ☒ Counseling/therapy	Parent participation in class; support groups

times when his laughing became silly and too loud and escalated, as if he were still learning to regulate his own behavior and emotions. Simple directions to "use your little voice" and "we have to stop laughing before we can work some more" were, however, usually sufficient to help him manage himself.

Exhibit 8-17 Program/Progress Evaluation for Derek

PHASE 4.0: Evaluation

SUMMATIVE CHILD PROGRESS/PROGRAM EVALUATION SHEET

Child: **Derek Webster**   C.A. **86 months**   Date: **88-4-30**

Developmental/ Curricular Domain	1ST Quarter			4th Quarter			DA Gain	IEI	CEI	M%	P%
	DA	DA Range	DQ	DA	DA Range	DQ					
COGNITIVE	48	(28-52)	65	40	(48-66)	70	12 mo.	1.00	.89	65%	35%
LANGUAGE	37	(21-40)	52	48	(36-52)	56	11 mo.	.92	.96	57%	43%
SOCIAL-EMOTIONAL	22	(18-24)	30	52	(48-54)	60	30 mo.	2.50	1.89	12%	88%
PERCEPTUAL/ FINE MOTOR	48	(30-50)	65	66	(52-68)	77	18 mo.	1.50	1.45	43%	51%
GROSS MOTOR	70	(54-72)	95	80	(78-85)	93	10 mo.	.83	.75	100%	0
SELF-CARE	55	(48-60)	74	64	(52-66)	77	19 mo.	1.58	1.36	47%	53%
DEVELOPMENTAL AVERAGE	46.7		63	62.0		72	15.3 mo.	1.28	1.18	49%	51%

Cognitive and Conceptual Abilities

Derek had made gains on individual skills in the cognitive domain, yet these were not as apparent as his behavioral progress. While he had gained in important language skills, his rate of progress had remained the same in overall cognitive skills since the last evaluation.

As noted, Derek was more competent individually in solving problems non-verbally and less so when verbal reasoning was required. Preacademically, he recognized letters (e.g., D, C, K, R, and I), counted with one-to-one correspondence, recognized some colors more consistently, and had begun to print the letters of his name. The team recommended that Derek be involved the following year in a primary program for autistic children, with regular mainstream experiences for nonacademic subjects.

CASE VIGNETTE 4: VISUAL IMPAIRMENT

Although it ran in their family, no one suspected that Sara had also been affected. Sara's older brother was born with Leber's optic atrophy, a hereditary disorder that causes cortical blindness and is often associated with mental retardation and neuromotor deficits. When Sara was born, the doctors and the family believed that she was fine because pregnancy, labor, and delivery were uncomplicated. Sara was an easy baby, sleeping often and showing no upset, even when hungry. However, during the second month, the mother began to worry because Sara's eyes were beginning to show roving, jerky movements; Sara seemed uninterested in faces and toys; and she was floppy. A visit to the pediatrician confirmed the parents' worst fears; neurophysiological examination and Visually Evoked Response assessment showed that Sara was blind. Despite this, the pediatrician indicated that he believed Sara was too young to be involved in any programming. The parents became worried and contacted the local MH/MR center, which provided only home-based services to Sara, beginning at 8 months of age, since the family lived in a rural area.

Sara was now almost 3½ years old. She had shown slow but important progress in gross motor, social communication, and play skills. However, she seemed to be increasingly frustrated and moody; she often threw tantrums when she did not get her way or when demands were made upon her, especially during physical therapy. Since Sara was still being educated at home, her mother would have liked her to go to a center and be involved with other children and adults. The mother was beginning to feel overwhelmed by Sara's problems and the needs of her older son. A recent divorce had left her alone and very stressed. After an initial home visit, the early-intervention team from the local school district met to discuss Sara's and her mother's involvement in a center-based program.

Phase 1: Screen/Identify

The team members completed the LINK personal data form on Sara (see Exhibit 8-18). Based on a consensus of their judgments and assessments derived from Sara's previous home-based program and their own initial observations, they converted their initial impressions and screening information into data on the PODS profile sheet (see Exhibit 8-19). On the basis of these functional ratings, the team began to make some decisions about Sara's assessment and possible programming needs. The profile demonstrated that Sara displayed significant deficits, despite her progress during home-based treatment in numerous areas, especially sensory, gross motor, communication, self-regulation, cognitive, and social. It was clear that adaptive assessment strategies would be necessary to determine specific levels in these areas and the purposeful goals that could integrate therapies for Sara in her new preschool program.

Phase 2: Assess/LINK

The team decided that use of a battery of specialized scales for visually impaired infants and preschoolers, with norms for blind children as well, would be the best initial approach. Table 8-4 lists the norm, curricular, judgment, and ecological measures that were selected for Sara. The *Reynell-Zinkin Developmental Scales* and the Project Oregon Curriculum offered the most effective basis for program planning. The *Maxfield-Buccholz Social Maturity Scale* enabled the mother to contribute to the assessment process by gauging her reports of Sara's attained competencies. Finally, the Parenting Stress Index allowed the team to determine the degree of stress that the mother was experiencing and to tailor counseling and therapy so that they targeted the dynamics of the interaction between Sara and her mother.

The Early Intervention Progress Profile (see Exhibit 8-20) shows Sara's performance in the major developmental domains. The results generally confirmed the screening indications; however, it was apparent that Sara had made substantial progress since her last evaluation in the home-based program 3 months previously at 37 months of age. Gains in the cognitive and social areas were most evident. Her

Table 8–4 Sara's Prescriptive Developmental Assessment Battery

Type	Scale
Norm-based	Reynell-Zinkin Developmental Scales
Curriculum-based	Project Oregon Curriculum
Judgment-based	Maxfield-Buccholz Social Maturity Scale
Ecological	Parenting Stress Index (PSI)

Exhibit 8–18 Sara's Personal Data Form

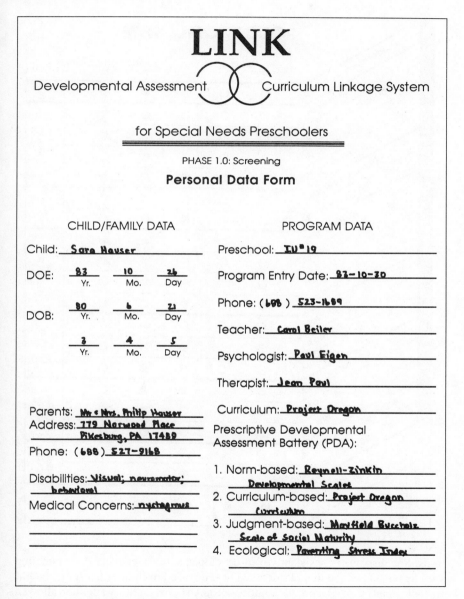

LINK

Developmental Assessment ⬭⬭ Curriculum Linkage System

for Special Needs Preschoolers

PHASE 1.0: Screening

Personal Data Form

CHILD/FAMILY DATA

Child: **Sara Hauser**

DOE: **83** Yr. **10** Mo. **26** Day

DOB: **80** Yr. **6** Mo. **21** Day

3 Yr. **4** Mo. **5** Day

Parents: **Mr & Mrs. Philip Hauser**
Address: **779 Norwood Place**
Pikesburg, PA 17489
Phone: (**688**) **527-9168**

Disabilities: **Visual; neuromotor;**
behavioral
Medical Concerns: **nystagmus**

PROGRAM DATA

Preschool: **IU #19**

Program Entry Date: **83-10-30**

Phone: (**688**) **523-1689**

Teacher: **Carol Beiler**

Psychologist: **Paul Eigen**

Therapist: **Jean Paul**

Curriculum: **Project Oregon**

Prescriptive Developmental
Assessment Battery (PDA):

1. Norm-based: **Reynell-Zinkin**
   Developmental Scales
2. Curriculum-based: **Project Oregon**
   Curriculum
3. Judgment-based: **Mayfield Buccholz**
   Scale of Social Maturity
4. Ecological: **Parenting Stress Index**

residual vision and increasingly functional play and social skills were most responsible for the functional gains.

Sara's strongest skills on the Reynell-Zinkin scales were shown in a variety of tasks requiring her to search for and identify objects tactilely and to follow direc-

Exhibit 8–19 PODS Ratings for Sara

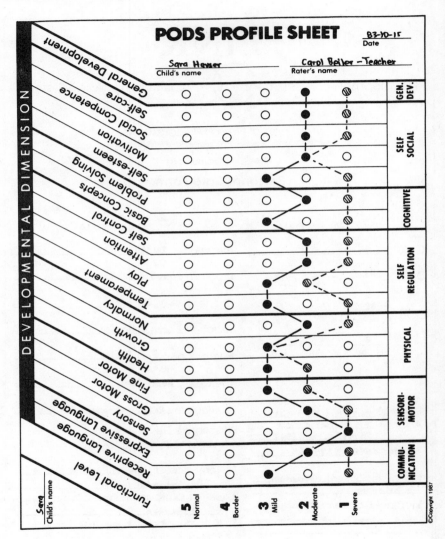

tions. She displayed consistently well-developed skills in tactilely discriminating various objects mixed in a plastic bowl or sequenced in front of her (e.g., rabbit, fish, elephant, shoe, spoon, ball, rattle, bell). Also, her auditory attention allowed her to hold a sample object in her hand and then "find one just like this one" from an array of three to four objects (e.g., spoon/spoon, cup, shoe, bell, ball). Similarly, she followed one- and two-part directions, even those that had a novel aspect (e.g., "put the block in your ear," "sit on the spoon"). She was beginning to recog-

Exhibit 8–20 Sara's Progress Profile

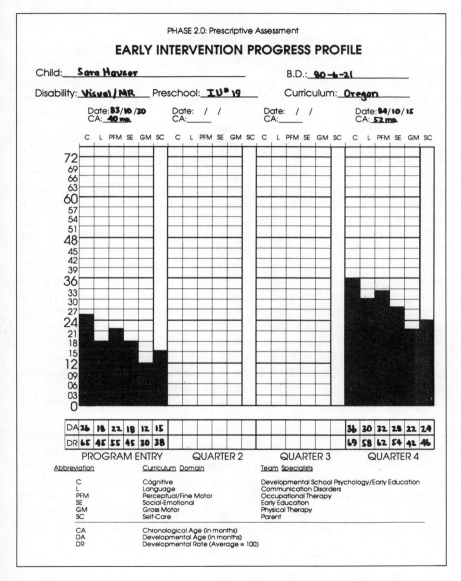

PHASE 2.0: Prescriptive Assessment

EARLY INTERVENTION PROGRESS PROFILE

Child: **Sara Hauser**　　　　　　　　B.D.: **80-6-21**

Disability: **Visual/MR**　Preschool: **IU# 19**　　　Curriculum: **Oregon**

Date: **83/10/30**　Date: / /　　Date: / /　　Date: **84/10/15**
CA: **40 mo.**　　CA:____　　CA:____　　CA: **52 mo.**

DA	26	18	22	18	12	15												36	30	32	28	22	24
DR	65	45	55	45	30	38												69	58	62	54	42	46

PROGRAM ENTRY　　　QUARTER 2　　　QUARTER 3　　　QUARTER 4

Abbreviation	Curriculum Domain	Team Specialists
C	Cognitive	Developmental School Psychology/Early Education
L	Language	Communication Disorders
PFM	Perceptual/Fine Motor	Occupational Therapy
SE	Social-Emotional	Early Education
GM	Gross Motor	Physical Therapy
SC	Self-Care	Parent
CA	Chronological Age (in months)	
DA	Developmental Age (in months)	
DR	Developmental Rate (Average = 100)	

nize big-little object concepts and also position concepts, such as on, in, and under. She identified body parts on herself, on dolls, and on adults and also engaged in reciprocal doll play with adults (e.g., "hug Kermit," "kiss Kermit").

In problem-solving tasks, Sara was capable of completing basic activities involving object searching. She located noise-maker toys hidden in containers and under cloths and could build two-block towers using oversized blocks. Finally, she showed emerging skills in completing basic three-hole, form board, shape-matching tasks; yet, she used a very haphazard, trial-and-error approach, which allowed her to match only the circle with its recess.

Three major deficits appeared to have a significant impact on Sara's cognitive problem-solving skills in terms of entry into the program: (1) her inability consistently to use single words for communication and object labeling; (2) her inability to use, and the resistance she displayed to the use of, her right hand as a tactile exploratory guide in object manipulation; and (3) her haphazard, trial-and-error style of completing structured problem-solving tasks.

Sara had a style of behavior that was generally typical of 1½- to 2-year-old children. She showed definite preferences for toys and situations. Abrupt changes in situations or physical demands placed upon her, such as those involved in physical and occupational therapy, often resulted in tantrums and screaming in order to end the therapy. In addition, she often stubbornly shook her head "no" in the middle of an activity to assert her independence.

The best approach to working with Sara, in view of her temperament and visual deficits, appeared to be a flexible play approach that placed a premium on using novel tasks and toys and on giving her definite verbal and physical cues and preparatory statements (e.g., "Now, we're going to find toys in a bowl"). She understood contingencies and could respond to some limits, such as, "First we will play with the puzzle, then we can play with your toy." It was thought that a clock with a timer might serve to give Sara a better sense of the beginning and end of different segments of the therapy session or of a structured task; it might also serve to structure a sense of time and reduce her tantrums to some degree. Finally, Sara was very sensitive to position changes; she had to be seated in a wedge seat that stabilized her at the trunk, facing a table elevated to her hand level, to allow more efficient manipulation of objects; otherwise she would become afraid and irritable and begin to throw tantrums.

The Prescriptive Linkages form in Exhibit 8-21 matches Sara's developmental competencies with objectives in the Oregon Curriculum that was used for interdisciplinary instruction and therapy. For example, Sara was beginning to show greater selective attention and memory skills in searching for hidden objects, with noise-maker toys as cues. Also, her functional communication skills were targeted in the use of words and other means to convey her wants and to initiate interactions with adults and peers. A parallel goal was to promote a wider range of emotional reactions.

Phase 3: Program/Intervene

The Early Childhood Program Prescriptions form in Exhibit 8-22 presents an outline of the essential features that the team believed should be included in Sara's center-based developmental program. Increased time in center-based program-

Exhibit 8–21 Prescriptive Linkages for Sara

PHASE 2.1: Curriculum Linkage

Child: _Sara Hauser_	Date: _83–10–31_	CA: _40months_
Developmental Scale: _Reynell–Zinkin_	Curriculum:	_Oregon_

PRESCRIPTIVE LINKAGES

DEVELOPMENTAL TRANSITIONS (±)	LINK CODES	CURRICULUM TARGETS
DA = 26 (20–34)	Cognitive	
Adaptive use of objects	MU1/C25	Brings object to self beyond reach
Retrieves object in box @ lid	SM12/C13	Finds hidden noisemaker toys
Sorts big–small objects	SM18/C27	Matches same size objects
Meaningful object relations	MU3/C36	Nests cups
DA = 18 (12–21)	Language	
Gives object on request	Cb/L13	"Give it to me"
Uses "more" appropriately	EL7/L19	Requests by words
Selects named objects & labels	VC10/L35	Feels & finds toys named
Recognition of familiar sounds	VCb/L22	Anticipates event ē sound cue
DA = 18 (15–24)	Social-Emotional	
Attends to communication	C3/S12	Attends with smile & recognition
Demands personal attention	SA/S1b	Pulls at adult to show something
Seeks close personal contact	EC2/S18	Affection shown to others
Responds to signs & gestures/play	C7/S27	Participates in reciprocal games
DA = 22 (18–30)	Perceptual/Fine Motor	
Takes objects from container	SM9/FM27	Removes objects from container
Adaptive use of objects	MU2/FM31	Turns handle/lever on toy
Relates 2 objects : stage II	SM10/FM29	Removes circle from puzzle
Explores moving parts	SM11/FM22	Manipulates moving parts
DA = 12 (9–14)	Gross Motor	
Reach—move to sound cues	VC6/L22	Anticipates events via sounds
Directed locomotion to voice	EE3/L22	" known " " "
Directed personal movement	EE9/6M22	Crawls on hands–knees
Finds door of room – stands	EE5/6M21	Pulls self to standing
DA = 15 (12–16)	Self-Care	
Holds cup when drinking	SA9/SH15	Holds cup, drinks – 2 hands
Attempts self feed via spoon	SA11/SH1b	Filled spoon to mouth
Pulls off socks – shoes	SA12/SB24	Pulls off socks

ming (versus home-based programming) was necessary to give Sara opportunities to learn more naturally about real-life events (e.g., play and conflicts with peers, field trips to zoos and parks). In addition, the programming would target the mother's needs to reduce her stress and adjust her interactions with Sara. Behavior management programming would concentrate on methods of rewarding and disciplining Sara in her responses to rules and limits and the demands of others. It was

Exhibit 8–22 Program Considerations for Sara

PHASE 3.0: Intervention
EARLY CHILDHOOD PROGRAM PRESCRIPTIONS

Child: _Sara Hauser_   CA: _40 months_   Date: _83-10-30_

DEVELOPMENTAL ASSESSMENT SUMMARY: Sara has shown progress since her involvement in home-based programming, yet, important additional areas must be emphasized, particularly social, language, and behavioral. She has begun to "make sense" out of her world since learning to move out to sound sources. Her play with toys is more purposeful. Yet, she shows little emotional reactions to success on tasks and is often irritable with tantrums. She typically uses her body and behavior rather than language to communicate. Give-and-take social games are beginning.

DEVELOPMENTAL PROGRAM GUIDELINES:

FEATURES	OPTIONS	COMMENTS
Instructional Setting	☐ Home-based ☒ Center-based ☐ Combo ☐ Hospital-based	Learning about real life events in natural settings (parks, etc.) Low distraction settings
Instructional Methods	☒ Verbal prompts ☒ Physical prompts ☒ Shaping	Needs physical cues Stress direction following Stress facial orientation
Grouping Pattern	☒ 1:1 ☒ 1:1 & small group ☐ 1:1, small/large groups	One-one for instruction Peer-pairing for games not large groups
Adaptive Arrangements	☒ Special toys ☐ Communication system ☐ Wheelchair ☒ Room arrangement	Toys with levers; tactile & auditory cues Corner chair for support Setting: high pile rug
Auxiliary Therapies	☒ Speech ☒ PT/OT ☒ Psychologist ☐ Pediatrician ☒ Sensory	Integrated goals thru consultation, not separate sessions Behavior plan
Behavioral Strategies	☐ Primary reinforcement ☐ Token economy ☐ Behavioral contract ☒ Social praise ☒ Time out ☒ Planned ignoring	Thrives on adult attention Loves physical play Discipline by withd. attention
Parent Participation	☐ Conference only ☒ Parent education/training ☒ Counseling/therapy	Vision specialist with mother; reduce stress respite care

agreed that respite care would be made available to the mother to ease her separation from Sara, foster her independence, and allow her time to cope emotionally. Finally, it was decided that special response-contingent toys and computer programs would be tried with Sara in an effort to increase her ability to be a responsive learner, to teach her task orientation and attention without constant adult guidance, and to provide immediate reinforcement for her problem-solving behaviors and communication skills.

Phase 4: Evaluate/Monitor

At the end of the year, program personnel evaluated Sara's progress on the curricular goals highlighted during her prescriptive assessment at entry into the program. Exhibit 8-23 summarizes the progress data. A comparison with the PODS profile sheet in Exhibit 8-19 reveals how consistent Sara's gains were across various dimensions. In general, she demonstrated very significant functional gains in the center-based program—an overall rate of 10 months' gain over a 12-month period. All progress indexes suggested that the individualized program designed for her had had a significant impact on her rate of gain, which was generally higher than that observed at program entry.

Sara had begun to use words, instead of misbehavior or global gestures, for communication. Her tantrums had stopped, both at home and at preschool. She responded better to directions and faced the person speaking. Socially and emotionally, she was much more expressive and smiled and clapped her hands at her success on tasks. She actively initiated social games with others and had started to tease in play. She showed particular gains in using her hands more precisely to explore and play with toys; she also used her hands to guide her in attending to the parts or features of objects in order to identify them.

The mother had become a true "partner" in Sara's classroom programming; she felt much more confident and comfortable in separating from Sara, in disciplining her when necessary, and in encouraging her to be more independent in work and play. The mother reported that, because of Sara's gains and because she had recognized the benefits of using respite care and "refueling" herself emotionally, she felt much less stress. She had joined a parents' group and had begun to socialize with several friends. Since her son was presently being educated in a partly residential school in the state, she felt that she had much more control over her life and now could better help Sara with new-found energy.

CASE VIGNETTE 5: HEARING IMPAIRMENT

Andrea was a healthy 5 lb, 8 oz baby; no complications or risks were evident during pregnancy or delivery except a mild episode of jaundice, which did not require treatment. Andrea was discharged after only 3 days in the hospital. She slept and nursed well during her first few months and seemed generally content and interested. Yet, Mrs. Hughes was worried; her friends and relatives tried to reassure her and suggested that such fears were typical of first-time mothers. Even her pediatrician discounted her doubts and indicated that her baby most probably was a "visual learner."

Exhibit 8–23 Sara's Progress Evaluation

PHASE 4.0: Evaluation

SUMMATIVE CHILD PROGRESS/PROGRAM EVALUATION SHEET

Child: __Sara Hauser__   C.A. __52 months__   Date: __84-10-18__

Developmental/ Curricular Domain	1st Quarter			4th Quarter			DA Gain	IEI	CEI	M%	P%
	DA	DA Range	DQ	DA	DA Range	DQ					
COGNITIVE	26	(20-34)	65	36	(28-40)	69	10 mo.	.83	.75	70%	22%
LANGUAGE	18	(12-21)	45	30	(18-22)	58	12 mo.	1.00	.95	45%	55%
SOCIAL-EMOTIONAL	18	(15-24)	45	28	(21-30)	54	10 mo.	.83	.80	54%	46%
PERCEPTUAL/FINE MOTOR	22	(18-30)	55	32	(24-36)	62	10 mo.	.83	.82	66%	34%
GROSS MOTOR	12	(9-14)	30	22	(15-26)	42	10 mo.	.83	.74	36%	64%
SELF-CARE	15	(12-16)	38	24	(18-28)	46	9 mo.	.75	.75	51%	49%
DEVELOPMENTAL AVERAGE	18.5		46	28.7		55	10.2 mo.	.85	.82	54%	46%

However, when Andrea was 13 months old, Mrs. Hughes became convinced that Andrea had a hearing problem, since she did not turn to sounds and was unusually interested in vibrations of the washing machine on the floor. Also, Andrea seemed to stop "talking" and never learned any words after learning to babble and coo. To add to her worries, Mrs. Hughes remembered that her mother's father, his two sisters, and a cousin were either deaf or hard-of-hearing.

From this point, Mrs. Hughes insisted that her pediatrician refer her to the local speech and audiology clinic at the hospital in her city. After a series of tests, it was determined that Mrs. Hughes had been correct all along; Andrea was diagnosed as having a severe congenital sensorineural hearing loss in both ears. The clinic counseled Mrs. Hughes about Andrea's needs and referred her to a specialized school for the deaf that operated a center-based early-intervention program for children from birth to 5 years of age. Mrs. Hughes had feelings of relief mixed with anger and confusion over the fact that her doubts had not been taken more seriously and that the problem had not been diagnosed earlier. She worried whether it was too late for Andrea.

Phase 1: Screen/Identify

The home visit by the speech/language therapist from the school reduced Mrs. Hughes's anxieties considerably. Andrea warmed up to the therapist immediately and was able to play well with the toys she had brought with her. This provided the team and Mrs. Hughes with some estimate of Andrea's relative strengths and weaknesses.

The therapist's impressions as presented to the team are profiled on the PODS graph in Exhibit 8-24. It was clear that Andrea had many strong capabilities despite her hearing impairment, especially in the play, motor, and social areas. Based on this screening, the team decided to phase Andrea directly into the classroom-based program (see Exhibit 8-25).

Phase 2: Assess/LINK

The team selected the diagnostic battery in Table 8-5 to prescribe initial goals for Andrea's individualized educational and therapeutic program, based on her current age of 18 months. The scales were chosen because they included adaptations (EIDP) or accommodations for children with hearing impairments (SECS) and because they identified goals important in the development of social orientation, gestural language, and total communication for young deaf children (DCC).

Affective and Behavioral Characteristics

Andrea was an extremely socially responsive girl. Her activity level was typical for her age. She was engaging, playful, and cooperative throughout the evaluation and truly a joy to work with. In the evaluation setting, she explored her environ-

Exhibit 8–24 PODS Screening Profile for Andrea

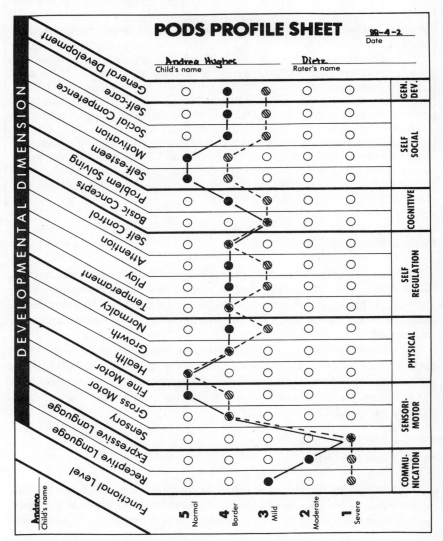

ment and was interested in the toys and new people. Her attention to tasks and to people was fairly age-appropriate. It was easy to get her interested in new items and fairly easy to get her to relinquish objects no longer needed in the assessment. She was fairly persistent in her efforts and aware of her successes. At times, she would clap for herself when she successfully completed a task. She would then look to the adults in the room for added positive reinforcement.

Exhibit 8–25 Andrea's Personal Data Form

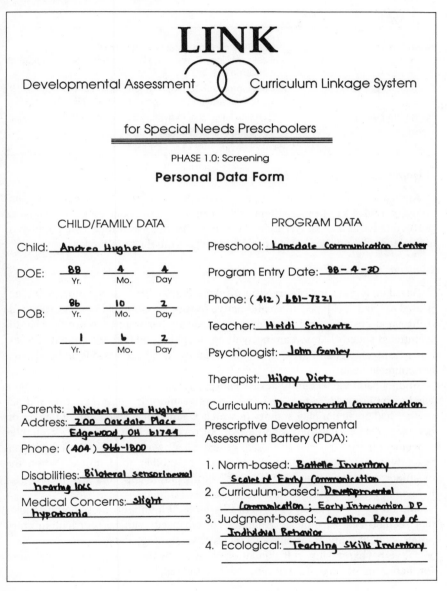

LINK

Developmental Assessment ◯◯ Curriculum Linkage System

for Special Needs Preschoolers

PHASE 1.0: Screening

Personal Data Form

CHILD/FAMILY DATA

Child: **Andrea Hughes**

DOE: **88** Yr. **4** Mo. **4** Day

DOB: **86** Yr. **10** Mo. **2** Day

1 Yr. **6** Mo. **2** Day

Parents: **Michael e Lara Hughes**
Address: **200 Oakdale Place**
Edgewood, OH 61744
Phone: (**404**) **966-1800**

Disabilities: **Bilateral sensorineual**
hearing loss
Medical Concerns: **slight**
hypotonia

PROGRAM DATA

Preschool: **Lansdale Communication Center**

Program Entry Date: **88 - 4 - 20**

Phone: (**412**) **601-7321**

Teacher: **Heidi Schwartz**

Psychologist: **John Ganley**

Therapist: **Hilary Dietz**

Curriculum: **Developmental Communication**

Prescriptive Developmental
Assessment Battery (PDA):

1. Norm-based: **Battelle Inventory**
   Scales of Early Communication
2. Curriculum-based: **Developmental**
   Communication ; Early Intervention DP
3. Judgment-based: **Carolina Record of**
   Individual Behavior
4. Ecological: **Teaching Skills Inventory**

Table 8–5   Andrea's Prescriptive Developmental Assessment Battery

Type	Scale
Norm-based	Battelle Developmental Inventory (BDI)
	Scales of Early Communication Skills for Hearing Impaired Children (SECS)
Curriculum-based	Developmental Communication Curriculum (DCC)
	Early Intervention Developmental Profile (EIDP)
Judgment-based	Carolina Record of Individual Behavior (CRIB)
Ecological	Teaching Skills Inventory (TSI)

Cognitive and Adaptive Skills

Andrea's cognitive performance on various developmental tasks, excluding language, revealed a rather consistent performance level of about 16 to 20 months, as profiled in Exhibit 8-26. Her style of playing with toys was primarily manipulative and relational, and she showed some emerging symbolic play capacity.

Communication Skills

Based on reports and observation, Andrea, despite her hearing impairment, appeared to have developed some alternative forms of communication. She pointed, using hand gestures, and made noises to indicate her wants and needs. She differentiated sounds like screaming, yelling, laughing, and other "excited" noises. She readily engaged in eye contact and used her facial expressions and body in a communicative fashion.

Andrea had independently developed specific gestures for activities; she had a hand-to-mouth gesture for "eat" and a hand gesture for "give me." She and her mother had created a play activity in which the mother would gently blow air on her face. Andrea had developed a symbol for this activity—making a circular movement in the air with her hand to generate her own breeze—and used this consistently to demonstrate that she wanted her mother to continue. When the examiner showed her the sign for "more" during play, it appeared to be meaningful to her and was incorporated into play with the examiner.

The Prescriptive Linkages form in Exhibit 8-27 highlights those competencies that seemed best to indicate Andrea's current needs and her curriculum entry points. Note the emphases on social interaction, signing, and gesturing responses. Vocal/verbal expression, self-regulation for attention, and occupying self on a task for increasing periods of time were also highlighted.

Phase 3: Program/Intervene

A total communication program was judged by the team to be the best approach to promote Andrea's development and learning (see Exhibit 8-28). Given her near-

Exhibit 8–26 Andrea's Current Developmental Levels

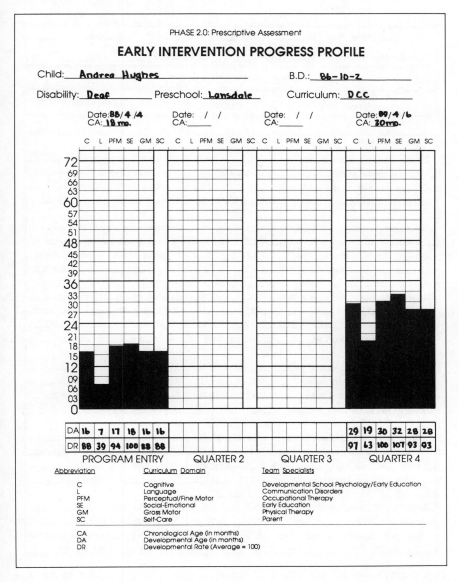

PHASE 2.0: Prescriptive Assessment

EARLY INTERVENTION PROGRESS PROFILE

Child: **Andrea Hughes**   B.D.: **86-10-2**

Disability: **Deaf**   Preschool: **Lansdale**   Curriculum: **DCC**

Date: **88/4/4**   Date: / /   Date: / /   Date: **89/4/6**
CA: **18 mo.**   CA:_____   CA:_____   CA: **30mo.**

	DA	DR
PROGRAM ENTRY	16 7 17 18 16 16	88 39 94 100 88 88
QUARTER 4	29 19 30 32 28 28	97 63 100 107 93 93

Abbreviation	Curriculum Domain	Team Specialists
C	Cognitive	Developmental School Psychology/Early Education
L	Language	Communication Disorders
PFM	Perceptual/Fine Motor	Occupational Therapy
SE	Social-Emotional	Early Education
GM	Gross Motor	Physical Therapy
SC	Self-Care	Parent
CA	Chronological Age (in months)	
DA	Developmental Age (in months)	
DR	Developmental Rate (Average = 100)	

average cognitive abilities, it was thought that signing paired with words would prove to be the best option. The team believed strongly that Andrea must be integrated at her early age with nonhandicapped toddlers and preschoolers so that she would readily model appropriate social, communication, and self-regulatory behaviors. The program would also stress Mrs. Hughes's close involvement in the

Exhibit 8–27 Prescriptive Linkages for Andrea

PHASE 2.1: Curriculum Linkage

Child: __Andrea Hughes__ Date: __88-4-6__ CA: __18 months__

Developmental Scale: __BDI; SECS__ Curriculum: __DCC; EIDP__

PRESCRIPTIVE LINKAGES

DEVELOPMENTAL TRANSITIONS (±)	LINK CODES	CURRICULUM TARGETS
DA = 16 (12-20)	Cognitive	
Places circle & square in frmbrd	CG5 / EIDP	Matches shapes / puzzles
Reaches around barrier for toy	CG22 / Dcc 29	Uses novel measures to get obj.
Recognizes self as cause of events	CG37 / DCC V13	Repeats action intentionally
Knows objects by use/function	SECS RLI/ EIDP 41	Gestures re: object use (DCC)
DA = 7 (6-10)	Language	
Associates words @ objs./actions	SECS RLI / C. 20	Demonstrates use of play obj.
Responds to different voice tones	CM 4 / C 2	Attends to sound experiences
Uses gestures to indicate needs	CM32 / F2	Performs action to express desire
Produces single-syllable c-v sounds	CM31 / F6	Gestures/Vocalizes in context
DA = 18 (16-24)	Social-Emotional	
Responds to social praise-rewards	PS 11 / C 20	Responds to reprimand/praise
Enjoys play @ other children	PS 23 / C 19	Child plays @ peer "sharing" toys
Follows directions re: daily routine	PS 62 / C 48	Child follows agent-action-obj.
Identifies self in mirror	PS 34 / EIDP 169	Identifies self in mirror
DA = 17 (15-19)	Perceptual/Fine Motor	
Places rings on post in any order	M 66 / EIDP 32	Places pegs
Neat pincer @ small objects	M 51 / EIPP 19	Uses neat pincer @ raisin
Removes raisin from bottle	M 67 / EIDP 75	Retrieves raisin from bottle
Extends toy to person & releases	M 50 / EIDP 155	Gives toy to adult
DA = 16 (15-18)	Gross Motor	
Stands upright for 30 secs-no spp.	M 6 / EIDP 267	Stands alone
Stoops, squats, stands back up	M 12 / EIDP 275	Squats in play, resumes standing
Kicks ball - no falling	M 14 / EIDP 288	Kicks ball
Walks up four stairs @ support	M 38 / EIDP 278	Walks upstairs 1 hand held
DA = 16 (12-17)	Self-Care	
Asks for food-drink @ gestures	A 18 / F2	Performs action re: desire
Feeds self @ utensil-no assist	A 20 / EIDP 192	Feeds self @ spoon
Helps with dressing - arms/legs up	A 26 / EIDP 212	Cooperates in dressing - moves limbs
Occupies self 10⁺ min. w/o attent.	A 6 / EIDP 165	Chooses toy & plays by self

classroom as a means of learning effective behavior management techniques and teaching behaviors.

Phase 4: Evaluate/Monitor

After 12 months in the center-based program, Andrea showed important functional gains in several developmental and behavioral areas (see Exhibit 8-29). At

Exhibit 8–28 Andrea's Program Guidelines

PHASE 3.0: Intervention
EARLY CHILDHOOD PROGRAM PRESCRIPTIONS

Child: __Andrea Hughes__ CA: __18 months__ Date: __98-4-6__

DEVELOPMENTAL ASSESSMENT SUMMARY: Andrea has many well-developed play, social, motor, and symbolic skills despite her severe hearing impairment. Unlike some other such young children, she has acquired a sense of the value of communicating and has even developed some creative signs on their own. A Total Communication program is vital to foster her range of competencies with mother as a "partner" in the classroom.

DEVELOPMENTAL PROGRAM GUIDELINES:

FEATURES	OPTIONS	COMMENTS
Instructional Setting	☐ Home-based ☒ Center-based ☐ Combo ☐ Hospital-based	Arrange opportunities with normal toddlers regularly
Instructional Methods	☒ Verbal prompts ☒ Physical prompts ☐ Shaping	Andrea already attends expecting manual cues & signs
Grouping Pattern	☐ 1:1 ☒ 1:1 & small group ☐ 1:1, small/large groups	Couple some 1-1 language therapy (@) class routines
Adaptive Arrangements	☐ Special toys ☒ Communication system ☐ Wheelchair ☐ Room arrangement	Total communication approach
Auxiliary Therapies	☒ Speech ☐ PT/OT ☒ Psychologist ☐ Pediatrician ☒ Sensory	Integrate in classroom Focus on preventing behavior problems Consultant on materials
Behavioral Strategies	☐ Primary reinforcement ☐ Token economy ☐ Behavioral contract ☒ Social praise ☐ Time out ☐ Planned ignoring	Highly motivated by activities themselves Is motivated by stickers on harder tasks despite young age; great attention
Parent Participation	☐ Conference only ☒ Parent education/training ☐ Counseling/therapy	Use TSI to promote mom's skills

---

the same time, Mrs. Hughes had become a much more effective teacher and manager of Andrea's behavior; she was strongly motivated to create learning opportunities for Andrea that were highly interactive. The staff were very impressed with Mrs. Hughes's quick ability to understand and use the strategies demonstrated.

A review of Andrea's progress chart showed that the total communication program appeared to have been well-matched with Andrea's needs; her language prog-

Exhibit 8-29 Program/Progress Data for Andrea

PHASE 4.0: Evaluation

SUMMATIVE CHILD PROGRESS/PROGRAM EVALUATION SHEET

Child: **Andrea Hughes**   C.A. **30 months**   Date: **89-4-6**

Developmental/ Curricular Domain	1st Quarter			4th Quarter				IEI	CEI	M%	%
	DA	DA Range	DQ	DA	DA Range	DQ	DA Gain				
COGNITIVE	16	(12-20)	88	29	(24-32)	97	13 mo.	1.06	1.00	81%	19%
LANGUAGE	7	(6-10)	39	19	(12-21)	63	12 mo.	1.00	1.02	39%	61%
SOCIAL-EMOTIONAL	18	(16-24)	100	22	(24-34)	107	14 mo.	1.17	1.08	86%	14%
PERCEPTUAL/ FINE MOTOR	17	(15-19)	94	30	(27-32)	100	13 mo.	1.08	1.00	87%	13%
GROSS MOTOR	16	(15-18)	88	28	(24-30)	93	12 mo.	1.00	1.00	88%	12%
SELF-CARE	16	(12-17)	88	28	(21-28)	93	12 mo.	1.00	.96	88%	12%
DEVELOPMENTAL AVERAGE	15	(6-24)	83	27.7	(12-34)	92	12.7 mo.	1.06	1.02	78%	22%

ress had increased from 39 percent to 63 percent of the expected rate. In fact, during the 1-year program in the communication area, her language gain was maintained at a normal rate, that is, 1 month of gain for each month of programming. It was decided that Andrea would be integrated increasingly with her normal peers as she continued to thrive in the program.

CASE VIGNETTE 6: TRAUMATIC BRAIN INJURY

Nicki was having so much fun with her friends in the yard that she never saw the car coming. The driver of the car swerved just as Nicki bolted into the driveway. Nicki, age 33 months, was admitted to the university children's hospital for a closed head injury. In addition, she suffered numerous fractures, contusions, and lacerations, since she was dragged 50 feet by the car that had hit her. Upon arrival in the emergency department, she was comatose with evidence of head trauma, fractures, and possible abdominal injuries. As a result, a shunt was placed in her brain to relieve the pressure of the cerebral spinal fluid. She had sustained a subdural hematoma to the right parietal area of her brain.

Nicki's next 2 months in the acute care hospital were filled with further complications. Her shunt became infected, resulting in encephalitis, a brain inflammation. Recurrent bouts of encephalitis necessitated two other brain operations to revise her shunt. During her first 3 weeks of acute care hospitalization, she was responsive only to pain. Ophthalmological evaluation revealed bilateral optic atrophy. As Nicki emerged from coma, she was functionally blind in her left eye and showed significant visual impairment in the right. A CT scan revealed evidence of pressure on her brain as well as some cortical atrophy. Clinically, she showed a left hemiparesis.

After about 3 months in the acute care hospital, Nicki was well enough medically to be transferred to a pediatric rehabilitation facility for intensive interdisciplinary intervention. At first, she was mostly responsive only to specific tactile and auditory stimulation. Gradually, over the first month in the rehabilitation hospital, Nicki began to recover. She began to use her right hand to reach toward people in a halting manner; her vision in the right eye also began to resolve. However, the staff began to observe recurrent seizures and minor episodes of sensitivity to sights, sounds, and position changes and some staring or "tuning out" behavior. Nicki's mother, who was only 17 years old, was encouraged by these changes but was afraid and overwhelmed by what had happened to her daughter.

Phase 1: Screen/Identify

The rehabilitation team decided that Nicki's recent gains indicated that she was ready for a full program of hospital-based services to support her developmental progress and recovery (see Exhibit 8-30). The team consisted of specialists in occupational therapy, physical therapy, speech/language therapy, early childhood spe-

Exhibit 8–30 Nicki's Personal Data Form

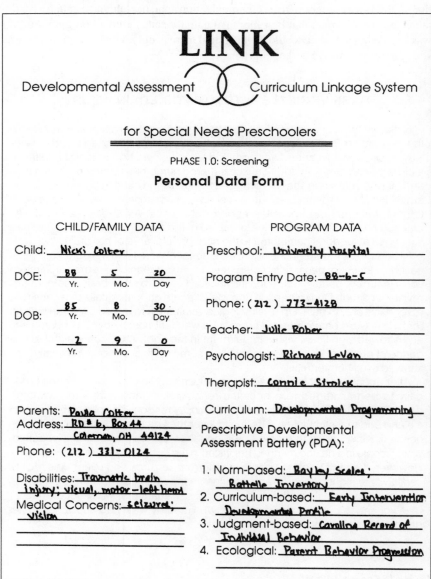

LINK

Developmental Assessment ⟨⟨ Curriculum Linkage System

for Special Needs Preschoolers

PHASE 1.0: Screening

Personal Data Form

CHILD/FAMILY DATA

Child: **Nicki Colter**

DOE: **88** Yr. **5** Mo. **20** Day

DOB: **85** Yr. **8** Mo. **30** Day

2 Yr. **9** Mo. **0** Day

Parents: **Paula Colter**
Address: **RD # 6, Box 44**
Coleman, OH 44124
Phone: (**212**) **331-0124**

Disabilities: **Traumatic brain
injury; visual, motor - left hemi**
Medical Concerns: **seizures;
vision**

PROGRAM DATA

Preschool: **University Hospital**

Program Entry Date: **88-6-5**

Phone: (**212**) **273-4128**

Teacher: **Julie Rober**

Psychologist: **Richard LeVan**

Therapist: **Connie Simlck**

Curriculum: **Developmental Programming**

Prescriptive Developmental
Assessment Battery (PDA):

1. Norm-based: **Bayley Scales;
Battelle Inventory**
2. Curriculum-based: **Early Intervention
Developmental Profile**
3. Judgment-based: **Carolina Record of
Individual Behavior**
4. Ecological: **Parent Behavior Progression**

cial education, developmental school psychology, pediatrics, social work, nursing, and therapeutic recreation. The team had experience in planning services that would be sensitive to Nicki's temperamental/behavioral style, sensorimotor limitations, and neurophysiological status. After observing Nicki in several situations

Exhibit 8–31 PODS Ratings for Nicki

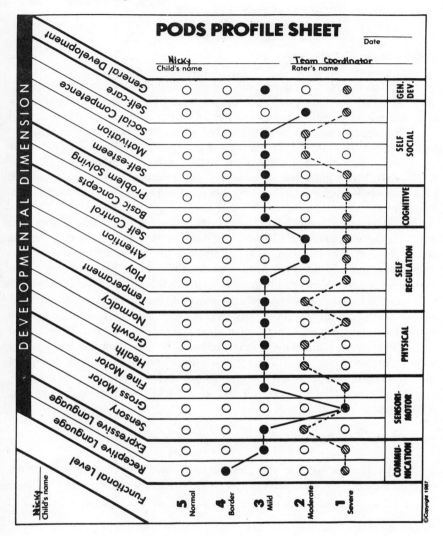

on the brain injury unit, the team members independently completed the PODS rating scales and then met to reach a consensus about her functional needs.

Exhibit 8-31 profiles Nicki's degree of functional deficits as judged by the team. Her deficits in most areas were severe; yet, the team members consistently agreed that her social interaction skills and affective responses, such as smiling and vocalizing to gain adult attention, were her strongest capabilities and must be fostered early. It was decided that Nicki's mother would be the focal point of the therapies;

she would be counseled regarding her own needs and would receive practical coaching on how best to encourage Nicki's recovery.

Phase 2: Assess/LINK

It was clear that Nicki would remain in the rehabilitation hospital for some time, until she could be transitioned to a community early-intervention program. For now, her chronic medical needs and her emerging recovery of skills dictated hospital-based services. The team decided on a prescriptive developmental assessment battery that would guide them in more comprehensively assessing her status and progress. Exhibit 8-30 and Table 8-6 indicate the battery chosen for Nicki. The BSID, BDI, EIDP, and CRIB scales were selected because they were all sensitive to Nicki's neurodevelopmental and neurobehavioral patterns and included adaptations for her visual and neuromotor impairments.

The Progress Profile for Nicki showed that many of her adaptive behaviors were much like those observed for a 1-month-old infant, even though she was 33 months of age at the time of the accident (see Exhibit 8-32). However, her social interactions were much better developed, approximating those at 3 months of age. The team observed that Nicki had begun to "spurt" developmentally in the 2 weeks following the initial evaluation, probably reflecting the phenomenon of spontaneous recovery characteristic of the early stages of a head injury. Thus, they decided to wait to design a detailed intervention plan. The next month, at a chronological age of 35 months, Nicki showed dramatic gains, to the extent that many of her social, play, and language skills were much like those expected at 18 months of age. At this point the team re-evaluated her and then began to plan her program. Exhibit 8-33 shows the Prescriptive Linkages in Nicki's program for the 2 months at the hospital.

Phase 3: Program/Intervene

The team planned specific strategies that would enable them to implement their classroom-based and individual therapies with Nicki, as shown on the Early Child-

---

Table 8–6   Nicki's Prescriptive Developmental Assessment Battery

Type	Scale
Norm-based	Battelle Developmental Inventory (BDI)
Curriculum-based	Early Intervention Developmental Profile (EIDP)
Judgment-based	Carolina Record of Individual Behavior (CRIB)
Ecological	Parent Behavior Progression (PBP)
	Parenting Stress Index (PSI)
	Family Needs Survey (FNS)

Exhibit 8–32 Nicki's Developmental Levels Graphed on the Early Intervention Progress Profile

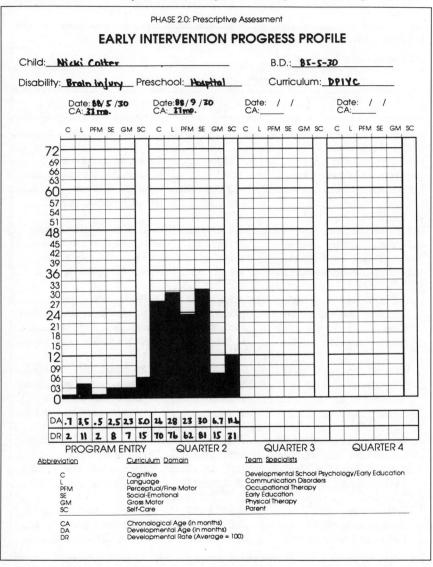

PHASE 2.0: Prescriptive Assessment

EARLY INTERVENTION PROGRESS PROFILE

Child: **Nicki Colter**   B.D.: **85-5-30**

Disability: **Brain injury**   Preschool: **Hospital**   Curriculum: **DPIYC**

| Date: **88/5/30**
CA: **32 mo.** | Date: **88/9/30**
CA: **37 mo.** | Date: / /
CA: | Date: / /
CA: |

	DA	DR
C	.7	2
L	3.5	11
PFM	.5	2
SE	2.5	8
GM	23	7
SC	5.0	15
C	24	70
L	28	76
PFM	23	62
SE	30	81
GM	6.7	15
SC	11.4	31

PROGRAM ENTRY   QUARTER 2   QUARTER 3   QUARTER 4

Abbreviation	Curriculum Domain	Team Specialists
C	Cognitive	Developmental School Psychology/Early Education
L	Language	Communication Disorders
PFM	Perceptual/Fine Motor	Occupational Therapy
SE	Social-Emotional	Early Education
GM	Gross Motor	Physical Therapy
SC	Self-Care	Parent
CA	Chronological Age (in months)	
DA	Developmental Age (in months)	
DR	Developmental Rate (Average = 100)	

hood Program Prescriptions form in Exhibit 8-34. Note the emphasis on the use of technology, such as response-contingent toys, computers, and the use of peer-pairing during instructional sessions. The team placed special emphasis on the mother's pressing demands as a single adolescent mother who was depressed, anxious, and unsure of her ability to care for Nicki's chronic multiple impairments. The possibility of foster care was an issue that needed to be explored.

Exhibit 8–33 Nicki's Curriculum Entry Points on the Prescriptive Linkages Form

PHASE 2.1: Curriculum Linkage

Child: __Nicki Colter__   Date: __88-b-1__   CA: __35months__

Developmental Scale: __BDI__   Curriculum: __DPIYc__

PRESCRIPTIVE LINKAGES

DEVELOPMENTAL TRANSITIONS (±)	LINK CODES	CURRICULUM TARGETS
DA = 18 (12–30)	Cognitive	
Reaches around barrier	CG 22/b4	Knows toy screened
Selects hand hiding toy	CG 1b/77	Deduces toy location
Matches forms	CG 7/92	Matches 4 shapes
Recalls objects	CG 17/94	Names missing object
DA = 18 (9–21)	Language	
Associates spoken words & objs.	CM 5/L110	Looks at named objs & people
Follows 3+ verbal commands	CM b/ L118	Follows familiar directions
Gives objects on request	CB 25/L123	Selects 2 of 3 objects
Associates spoken words & pictures	CN 19/ L124	Points to 4 pictures
DA = 21 (15–24)	Social-Emotional	
Initiates social contacts	PS 45/SE15b	Initiates social games
Separates easily from parent	PS 15/ SE158	Plays apart from familiar person
Plays independently	PS 47/SE159	Varies play with toys
Plays alongside child	PS 48/ SE161	Plays near other children
DA = 12 (9–16)	Perceptual/Fine Motor	
Releases toy from grasp	M 50/ PFM 18	Drops block with release
Pulls open drawers	M 49/PFM 23	Removes cover from box
Reproduces lines	M 68/PFM 31	Imitates crayon stroke
Places rings on post	M Lb/PFM 24	Places pegs – objs. in holes
DA = 3 (1–b)	Gross Motor	
Turns head in supported sitting	M 3/ GM 24D	Supine–integrates ATNR
Sits without support – 5 secs.	M 4/ GM 241	Sits trunk erect
Moves lying to sitting	M 10/ GM 236	Prone– rolls to supine to sit
Lifts head on stomach	M 2/ GM 231	Prone– head chest 90°
DA = 6 (3–8)	Self-Care	
Feeds with spoon	A 20/ SC183	Picks up spoon
Drinks from cup assisted	A15 / SC 182	Drinks from cup with help
Feeds self bite-sized pieces	A1b/ SC185	Finger feeds

The mother reported great stress on the PSI; she felt the need for more social support and counseling, as indicated in interviews with the social worker and her responses on the FNS. The team observed that the mother's ability to interact with Nicki, as documented on the PBP, was strained and anxious. Unfortunately, the mother felt incapable of interacting with Nicki; Nicki's irritability with her, contrasted with her calm organized behavior with other team members, had exacer-

Exhibit 8–34 Capsule Summary of Nicki's Programming Needs on the Early Childhood Program Prescriptions Form

PHASE 3.0: Intervention
EARLY CHILDHOOD PROGRAM PRESCRIPTIONS

Child: **Nicki Colter** _____ CA: **35 months** _____ Date: **88-6-5** _____

DEVELOPMENTAL ASSESSMENT SUMMARY: Nicki has shown remarkable gains in play, language, and social skills. Her revised program must capitalize on these gains to help her use the skills functionally across people and situations. We must pair her with 1-2 other children to model social and language behaviors; use electromechanical toys to prompt attention & cause-effect play. Mother needs our help to decide on the foster care issue.

DEVELOPMENTAL PROGRAM GUIDELINES:

FEATURES	OPTIONS	COMMENTS
Instructional Setting	☐ Home-based ☒ Center-based ☐ Combo ☐ Hospital-based	5-1/2 days/week to increase endurance Integrated therapies
Instructional Methods	☒ Verbal prompts ☒ Physical prompts ☐ Shaping	Must learn to respond to verbal cues only
Grouping Pattern	☐ 1:1 ☒ 1:1 & small group ☐ 1:1, small/large groups	1-1 for therapy Peer-pairing to practice skills
Adaptive Arrangements	☒ Special toys ☒ Communication system ☒ Wheelchair ☐ Room arrangement	Switch toys Computer - light pointer Adapted pogon buggy
Auxiliary Therapies	☒ Speech ☒ PT/OT ☒ Psychologist ☒ Pediatrician ☒ Sensory	Integrate PT/OT, speech @ preschool Behavior plan Seizures Check left eye vision
Behavioral Strategies	☐ Primary reinforcement ☐ Token economy ☐ Behavioral contract ☒ Social praise ☒ Time out ☒ Planned ignoring	Social praise & preferred activities as reinforcers Time-out & ignoring
Parent Participation	☐ Conference only ☒ Parent education/training ☒ Counseling/therapy	Help for mother's anxiety & depression; check foster care

bated the problem. Individual counseling with the mother had been only slightly successful.

Phase 4: Evaluate/Monitor

After 4 months of intensive rehabilitation, Nicki was ready to be transferred to a community-based Easter Seal's program. At this point, the mother had firmly decided to transfer Nicki to a specialized foster care family. Nicki had demonstrated significant developmental and behavioral gains as the result of a combination of factors, including her resolving medical conditions, her body's and brain's "spontaneous recovery" to some extent, and the impact of intensive team instruction and therapy (see Exhibit 8-35). Overall, she had progressed at the accelerated rate of a 6-months' average developmental gain for each month of treatment/therapy, or six times the expected rate in normal child development. Yet, while significant intervention gains exceeding 90 percent were apparent, these were somewhat inflated, due to the element of spontaneous recovery.

Nicki's strongest functional gains were in the acquisition of language, social, and cognitive skills. She also showed strong increases in perceptual/fine motor skills, but these were tempered by her visual deficits and left-sided hemiparesis, which appeared to be a permanent disability. Her least well-developed skills were observed in the gross motor and self-care domains.

Nicki showed marked improvements in various behavioral areas involving social communication skills; however, on the CRIB she continued to show enduring deficits in various self-regulatory areas, such as hyperactivity, inattention, memory deficits, low tolerance for frustration, widely changeable moods, and high sensitivity to changes in stimulation. Overall, in 4 months Nicki had progressed from a severe to a moderate/mild level of developmental disability in cognitive, language and social areas, as shown in her DR of 70 and her PODS ratings of 3 and 4. It was decided that the hospital team would work with the Easter Seal personnel in transferring Nicki's program, in consultation with the pediatrician and nurses regarding care for her chronic health problems, particularly her seizures.

APPLIED CASE EXERCISE: LANGUAGE/LEARNING DISABILITIES

Chris's developmental history was typical of children born prematurely. He was delivered by cesarean section at 38 weeks' gestation because of an abrupted placenta, renal failure, and respiratory distress, which required oxygen. Seizures occurred within 24 hours, requiring treatment with phenobarbital. Chris was hospitalized for 2 weeks, after which time Mrs. Norman was told that her son was "at risk" for developing minor to moderate handicaps, due to the complications associated with his prematurity.

Chris's parents were worried that little help would be available to them after they left the hospital. Fortunately, the services of a high-risk infant program were

Exhibit 8-35 Nicki's Progress Data

PHASE 4.0: Evaluation

SUMMATIVE CHILD PROGRESS/PROGRAM EVALUATION SHEET

Child: __Nicki Cotter__   C.A. __21 months__   Date: __88-9-30__

Developmental/ Curricular Domain	1st Quarter			2nd Quarter			DA Gain	IEI	CEI	M%	P%
	DA	DA Range	DQ	DA	DA Range	DQ					
COGNITIVE	.7	Newborn	2	26.0	(21-32)	70	25.3	6.0	5.8	1%	99%
LANGUAGE	3.5	(0-3.5)	11	28.0	(12-28)	76	24.5	6.0	6.8	2%	98%
SOCIAL-EMOTIONAL	2.5	(0-3.5)	8	30.0	(24-34)	91	27.5	7.0	4.6	1%	99%
PERCEPTUAL/ FINE MOTOR	.5	Newborn	2	23.0	(18-26)	62	22.5	6.0	5.5	1%	99%
GROSS MOTOR	2.3	(0-2.5)	7	6.7	(3-8)	15	4.4	1.0	1.9	7%	93%
SELF-CARE	5.0	(0-5.0)	15	11.6	(7-12)	31	6.6	2.0	3.4	9%	91%
DEVELOPMENTAL AVERAGE	2.4		7	20.9		56	18.5	4.5	2.4	4%	96%

available for Chris. A follow-up evaluation was conducted by the clinic every 3 months to aid the parents and pediatricians in tracking the course of Chris's development and his need for treatment. Chris showed steady physical growth during his first 2 years. However, two problems were observed consistently: several middle ear infections, and low muscle tone in the shoulder, neck, and trunk areas.

The Bayley Scales of Infant Development were administered on each 3-month visit. At 3 months, Chris performed in the normal or average range (DR = 102); however, with each successive evaluation, his performance deteriorated to a rate of 75 at 18 months. The BSID from his final evaluation at 24 months was merely descriptive, due to his uncooperative behavior, inattention, and poor communication skills. Chris's skills on the BSID were significantly affected by his language deficits. Specifically, the deficits were identified in expressive language development. At 2 years of age, Chris preferred to point or gesture to communicate and had only a ten-word vocabulary. When Chris did speak, many basic sounds were unintelligible. It was suspected that his chronic ear infections interfered with his language development. He was referred to a speech and language program for evaluation and individual therapy.

Chris participated in individual therapy for 6 months, beginning when he was 3½ years of age. During this time, he made more attempts to communicate verbally and increased his expressive vocabulary; however, his overall communication skills were still significantly delayed. He would communicate with his peers only when prompted. Chris struggled to remember concepts and even the shortest directions. As demands were placed on him to learn more complex concepts and follow more directions, he seemed frustrated, often refused to cooperate, displayed occasional tantrums, and repeatedly said, "I don't know." He preferred easy activities or played with toys appropriate for younger children. Mrs. Norman and the language therapist were painfully aware of his limited language, memory problems, and trouble relating to peers. Chris also seemed increasingly sad. His parents became increasingly concerned about his future success or failure in school as he neared kindergarten entrance. When Chris was 4 years, 3 months old, they requested a complete psychological evaluation to make sense of his problems and to get help for them.

Phase 1: Screen/Identify

At Mrs. Norman's request, a speech therapist, the preschool teacher, and a social worker from the local special education service unit visited the home to talk to her about her concerns and to observe Chris's behavior informally, using a variety of structured and unstructured tasks.

Cognitive Abilities

Chris was evaluated in the living room with his mother present. He was shy and quiet, needing time to warm and adjust to the unfamiliar situation. Although compliant, he needed and responded well to a gentle, low-demand approach with directions given softly and his performance regularly reinforced by social praise. When tasks were presented in a game-like form, his behavior became considerably more spontaneous and emotionally expressive, with smiles and laughs.

At this point, Chris seemed sensitized to success and failure in situations and appeared to view himself as different from his peers. He preferred activities that were easier, such as those that were nonverbal. Since he was often impulsive and distractible, he needed a pairing of verbal and physical prompts to focus his attention and maintain his performance on more difficult tasks. Such directions as "Look before we point" or "Let's listen with our ears" (holding ears as a visual cue) were very helpful as aids.

Chris's behavior on various tasks seemed to indicate specific learning difficulties. His most apparent deficits were observed in tasks that required short-term memory in processing both auditorially (e.g., directions, numbers, and stories) and visually (e.g., pictures, sequencing motor acts) presented material and in gross motor activities. He showed widely scattered abilities in the age range from 2½- to 4½ years. For example, he had considerable difficulty processing and remembering the details of short stories read aloud to him; yet, he showed well-developed skills in verbally naming concepts that fell in generic categories (e.g., things to ride, eat, and wear and animals).

Language Learning, and Neurodevelopmental Skills

Chris's language learning and neurodevelopmental skills were much like those of a 36-month-old child, for example, in spatial relations, auditory memory, sound blending, knowledge of numbers, and general factual information. In the area of language processing, he showed a latency in responding to verbal directions. He was most comfortable with directions or sentences that contained only one or two concepts or parts; beyond this he had great difficulty. His speech was apraxic, and he showed some word-finding difficulties, such as in identifying scissors as "cut things." He also showed some verbal substitutions, such as "pock sickle" for popsicle, and "busgetti" for spaghetti. In the gross motor area, he had difficulties in coordination, precision, spatial awareness, and balance and trunk control.

Socioemotional Characteristics

The fact that Chris was beginning to react emotionally to his difficulties was a matter of concern. His mother reported that he had begun to make comparisons with other children regarding his lack of success; he had begun to cope by lightly stalling or refusing on certain tasks, for example, by saying "I don't know" rather than attempting the task. He needed strong encouragement to risk performance on tasks that he perceived as only slightly more difficult. He displayed a tendency to play with toddler toys and younger children. At home, his desire to sleep with his parents and his difficulty in adjusting to having his own room appeared to be stress-related.

In the context of the local preschool program, a child study team met to discuss its impressions of Chris's needs (see Exhibit 8-36). The three early-intervention team members independently rated their judgments about Chris on the PODS profile sheet (see Exhibit 8-37). They reached a consensus about Chris's difficulties in understanding concepts, using language with others, attending to and following directions, and complying with rules and limits. They also decided that he had problems in gross motor activities and eye-hand coordination, particularly in drawing and writing. The team members concluded that a more comprehensive assessment of Chris's strengths and weaknesses was needed to determine his specific programming needs, and they decided that he was in need of some form of special programming.

Phases 2 and 3: Assess/LINK and Program/Intervene

The information on the case exercise presented thus far depicts the kind of problems typically presented by children who are referred to special needs preschool programs. Using this information, the reader is now in a position to practice the steps in the LINK model.

First, based on the screening information in Phase 1, select a prescriptive assessment battery for Chris that would most effectively allow you to identify curriculum goals for individualized programming. Consider Chris's age and developmental deficits as described. Then, choose a curriculum-compatible norm-referenced measure from Chapter 4 that would enable you both to determine his current levels of functioning and to establish curriculum entry points. Next, review Chapter 6 and select a curriculum that contains goals that match Chris's cognitive, neuromotor, social, language, and behavioral needs and his pre-K program. Complete the sections in Exhibit 8-36 that refer to the curriculum and the prescriptive assessment battery.

Once you have done this, based on your assessment of Chris's range of competencies, complete the Prescriptive Linkages form in Exhibit 8-38. Now, based on the curriculum you have chosen, find linkages for each of the scale or test items listed in each developmental domain. Finally, complete the Early Childhood Program Prescriptions form in Exhibit 8-39, indicating your appraisal of the program characteristics that should be considered in programming and teaching Chris.

Phase 4: Evaluate/Monitor

Assume that Chris has participated in your program for a 12-month period and has shown measurable developmental gains since his entry into preschool. He is now 63 months of age and eligible for transition to a type of kindergarten setting. Is he ready? How much progress has he demonstrated? Has the program been effective? In order to begin to answer these questions, complete the Summative Evaluation Form in Exhibit 8-40 and calculate Chris's progress in the columns for DA, Gain, IEI, M%, and I%.

Exhibit 8–36 Personal Data Form for Chris

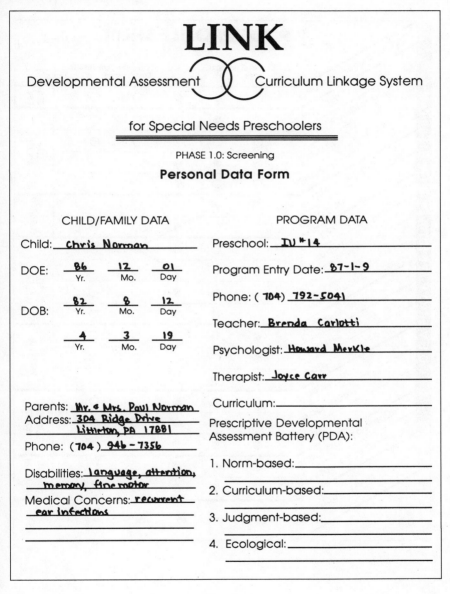

LINK

Developmental Assessment ⬭⬭ Curriculum Linkage System

for Special Needs Preschoolers

PHASE 1.0: Screening

Personal Data Form

CHILD/FAMILY DATA

Child: **Chris Norman**

DOE: **86** Yr. **12** Mo. **01** Day

DOB: **82** Yr. **8** Mo. **12** Day

4 Yr. **3** Mo. **19** Day

Parents: **Mr. & Mrs. Paul Norman**
Address: **304 Ridge Drive**
Littleton, PA 17881
Phone: (**704**) **946-7356**

Disabilities: **language, attention, memory, fine motor**
Medical Concerns: **recurrent ear infections**

PROGRAM DATA

Preschool: **IU #14**

Program Entry Date: **87-1-9**

Phone: (**704**) **792-5041**

Teacher: **Brenda Carlotti**

Psychologist: **Howard Merkle**

Therapist: **Joyce Carr**

Curriculum: _____

Prescriptive Developmental
Assessment Battery (PDA):

1. Norm-based: _____

2. Curriculum-based: _____

3. Judgment-based: _____

4. Ecological: _____

Exhibit 8–37 Team PODS Ratings for Chris

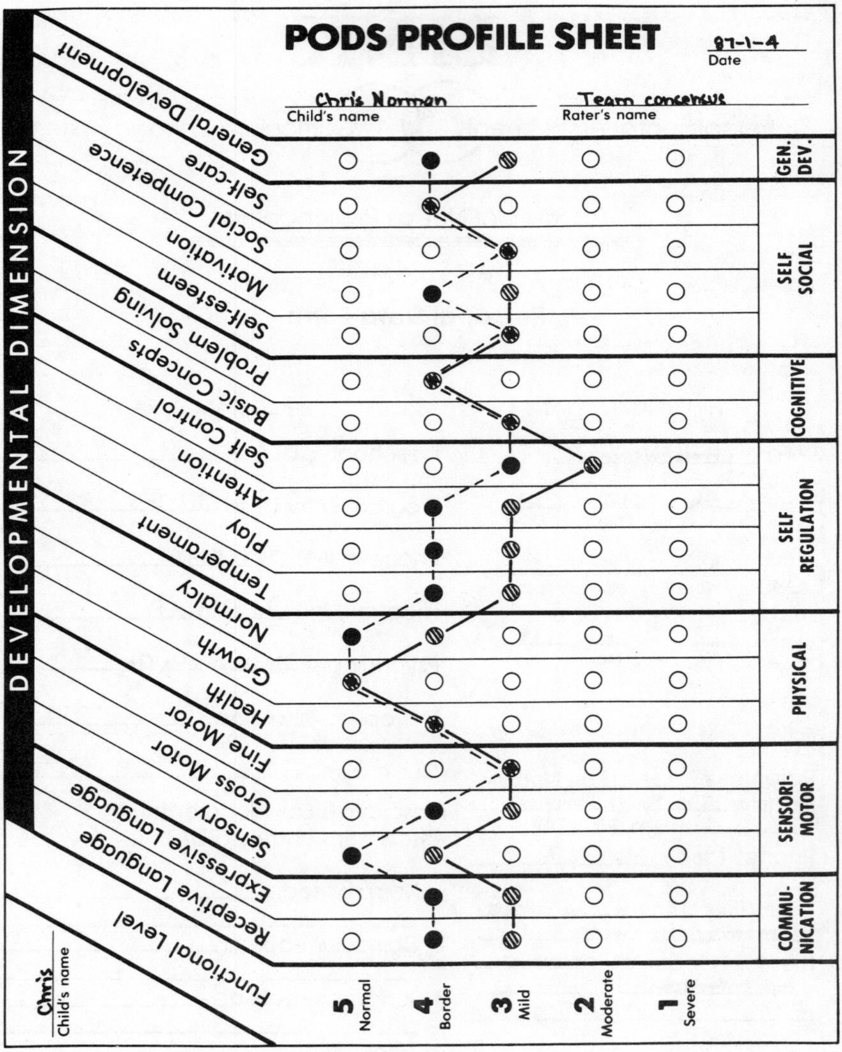

Exhibit 8–38 Chris's Prescriptive Linkages Exercise

PHASE 2.1: Curriculum Linkage

Child: _Chris Norman_   Date: _86-12-18_   CA: _51 months_

Developmental Scale: _____   Curriculum: _____

PRESCRIPTIVE LINKAGES

DEVELOPMENTAL TRANSITIONS (±)	LINK CODES	CURRICULUM TARGETS
DA = 42 (30–45)	Cognitive	
Knows opposite analogy concepts		
Recalls phrase & story details		
Counting & number problems		
Defines vocabulary words		
DA = 42 (24–45)	Language	
Groups concepts in generic sets		
Follows directions re: concepts		
Remembers hidden pictures		
Identifies letters, words, numbers		
DA = 40 (24–40)	Social-Emotional	
Attends for longer periods		
Stays with difficult task		
Cooperative play with friends		
Responds to success & rewards		
DA = 45 (36–45)	Perceptual/Fine Motor	
Solves 3-5 piece puzzles		
Draws human & geometric forms		
Writes letters & numbers		
Writes name		
DA = 40 (30–42)	Gross Motor	
Balances on either leg		
Coordinates movements - running		
Right-left orientation		
DA = 40 (30–42)	Self-Care	
Dresses with V, M prompts		
Uses fork, spoon & knife		
Adjusts to new people & settings		

Exhibit 8–39 Chris's Program Prescriptions Exercise

PHASE 3.0: Intervention
EARLY CHILDHOOD PROGRAM PRESCRIPTIONS

Child: __Chris Norman__   CA: __51 months__   Date: __06-12-18__

DEVELOPMENTAL ASSESSMENT SUMMARY:

DEVELOPMENTAL PROGRAM GUIDELINES:

FEATURES	OPTIONS	COMMENTS
Instructional Setting	☐ Home-based ☐ Center-based ☐ Combo ☐ Hospital-based	
Instructional Methods	☐ Verbal prompts ☐ Physical prompts ☐ Shaping	
Grouping Pattern	☐ 1 : 1 ☐ 1 : 1 & small group ☐ 1 : 1, small/large groups	
Adaptive Arrangements	☐ Special toys ☐ Communication system ☐ Wheelchair ☐ Room arrangement	
Auxiliary Therapies	☐ Speech ☐ PT/OT ☐ Psychologist ☐ Pediatrician ☐ Sensory	
Behavioral Strategies	☐ Primary reinforcement ☐ Token economy ☐ Behavioral contract ☐ Social praise ☐ Time out ☐ Planned ignoring	
Parent Participation	☐ Conference only ☐ Parent education/training ☐ Counseling/therapy	

Exhibit 8–40 Chris's Progress Data and Exercise

PHASE 4.0: Evaluation

SUMMATIVE CHILD PROGRESS/PROGRAM EVALUATION SHEET

Child: __Chris Norman__   C.A. __63 months__   Date: __87-12-5__

Developmental/ Curricular Domain	1ST Quarter			4th Quarter			DA Gain	IEI	CEI	M%	P%
	DA	DA Range	DQ	DA	DA Range	DQ					
COGNITIVE	42	(30-45)	82	54	(42-60)	86	—	—	.96	—	—
LANGUAGE	42	(24-45)	82	52	(42-60)	83	—	—	.80	—	—
SOCIAL-EMOTIONAL	40	(24-40)	77	50	(40-54)	79	—	—	.80	—	—
PERCEPTUAL/ FINE MOTOR	45	(36-45)	81	52	(48-54)	83	—	—	.64	—	—
GROSS MOTOR	40	(30-42)	77	50	(42-54)	79	—	—	.80	—	—
SELF-CARE	40	(30-42)	77	52	(45-52)	83	—	—	1.00	—	—
DEVELOPMENTAL AVERAGE	—		—			—		—			

Appendix A

Snapshot Outlines of Developmental Scales

Attachment Indicators During Stress (AIDS)

Author(s): H. Massie, S. Campbell
Year: 1983
Publisher: Authors
Address: B. K. Campbell, Children's Hospital and Medical Center
            PO Box 3805, San Francisco, CA 94119

Assessment type: Judgment-based/clinical observation and rating of infant-mother interactive patterns to "screen" pathology or dysfunctions.
Age range: Birth to 18 months.
Domains/Contexts: Infant's behavior/mother's response in the behavior patterns of both partners in gazing, vocalizing, touching, holding, affect, and proximity; assesses behavior during a pediatric physical exam and after; used in any other interactive context.
Handicap options: Observation rating of normal and atypical interaction patterns via operational ratings and "pictograms."
Curricular links: Offers general goals for counseling and interactive therapy in a program.
Scoring/Sample: 5-point rating scale based on delayed observations.
Technical support: $N = 228$ mother-infant pairs ($\overline{x}$ = SD by age and sex); few technical studies.
Training needed: Thorough knowledge of scale definitions and good observation skills.

Critique:
- Unique assessment of a complex interplay.
- As yet, unvalidated.
- Use only with other measures.

Citation:
Massie, H. N., & Campbell, B. K. (1983). M-C Scale of Mother-Infant Attachment Indicators During Stress. In J. D. Call, E. Galenson, & R. L. Tyson (Eds.), *Frontiers of infant psychiatry* (pp. 394–412). New York: Basic Books.

Bayley Scales of Infant Development (BSID)

Author(s):	N. Bayley
Year:	1969 (Revision underway, expected publication in 1990)
Publisher:	Psychological Corporation
Address:	555 Academic Court, San Antonio, TX 78204-0952
Phone:	1 (800) 233-5682

Assessment type: Norm-based; developmental diagnosis and assessment of current functional levels.

Age range: 2-30 months.

Domains/Contexts: Mental scale (163 items), motor scale (81 items), infant behavior record (clinical rating of 30 dimensions).

Handicap options: Clinical adaptations in scoring and administration by changing objects, regrouping items, and scoring DRs<50.

Curricular links: Empirical matches with curricula by domains and tasks.

Scoring/Sample: Developmental standard scores (PDI, MDI, DA) and percentages for the IBR scale; behavior sample by performance, observation, interview, and report; using P, F, or R; Norms =1,262, national sample 1960 census.

Technical support: Excellent reliability and validity, but dated item placements particularly for motor items.

Training needed: Supervised training in administration, scoring, interpretation by a psychologist or other qualified diagnostician.

Critique:
- Represents still the most technically adequate developmental scale.
- Needs reorganization into several domains.
- Requires adaptations for handicap administration.
- Must incorporate novel tasks from recent developmental research.

Citations:

Reuter, J. (1982). *Kent Scoring Adaptations for the Bayley Scales of Infant Development.* Kent, OH: Developmental Metrics.

Hoffman, H. (1982). *Bayley Scales: Modifications for Youngsters with Handicapping Conditions.* Commack, NY: United Cerebral Palsy.

Naglieri, J.A. (1981). Extrapolated developmental indices for the Bayley. *American Journal of Mental Deficiency, 85*(5), 548–550.

Bagnato, S.J., & Lewellyn, E. (1982). Developmental assessment/curriculum linkages. In S. Willoughby-Herb & J.T. Neisworth (Eds.), *HICOMP preschool curriculum,* (pp. 43–62). San Antonio, TX: Psychological Corporation.

Campbell, S. (1986). Evidence for the need to renorm the BSID. *Topics in Early Childhood Special Education, 6*(2), 83–96.

Whiteley, J.R., & Krenn, W.A. (1986). Uses of the Bayley Mental Scale with nonambulatory profoundly retarded children. *American Journal of Mental Deficiency, 40*(4), 425–431.

Callier-Azusa Scale (CAS): Assessment of Deaf-Blind Children

Author(s):   R. Stillman
Year: 1974
Publisher: The Council for Exceptional Children
Address: 1920 Association Drive, Reston, VA 22091
Phone: 1 (800) 731-6000

Assessment type: Judgment-based; observation and ratings of increasingly adaptive functional skills.
Age range: Birth to 98 months.
Domains/Contexts: 5 subscales: socialization, daily living skills, motor development, perceptual abilities, and language development.
Handicap options: Ratings based on functional skills; rough task analyses highlight tactile modes of experiencing.
Curricular links: Developmental task analyses generate functional treatment goals, and examples provide instructional suggestions.
Scoring/Sample: Numbers in ascending order are circled to identify current functional capabilities by rough DA estimates.
Technical support: Construction of the scale in field-test settings with deaf-blind children.
Training needed: Minimal; direct observation experience and knowledge of consequences and examples.

Critique:
- Functional sequences offer instructional objectives.
- Tasks provide adaptive options.
- Can be completed by professionals and paraprofessionals.
- Criterion-referenced, but not an effective curriculum.

Citation:
Diebold, L.T. (1978). Developmental scales versus observational measures for deaf-blind children. *Exceptional Children, 44*(4), 275–279.

Cognitive Abilities Scale (CAS)

Author(s):   S. Bradley-Johnson
Year: 1986
Publisher: PRO-ED
Address: 8700 Shoal Creek Boulevard, Austin, TX 78758
Phone: (512) 451-3246

Assessment type: Norm-based; identifies deficits in prerequisite cognitive and preacademic skills.

Age range: 2- and 3-year-olds.

Domains/Contexts: 88 items in 6 domains: language, imitation, reading, memory, mathematics, and handwriting.

Handicap options: Appropriate for nonverbal and communication-disordered toddlers and preschoolers; using motivating toys.

Curricular links: Focuses upon important preacademic concepts for planning instructional programs.

Scoring/Sample: Standard scores and percentiles.

Technical support: Norms = 536 children in 27 states (1985 statistics); adequate data on interval consistency, test-retest reliabilities/criterion construct, and predictive validity.

Training needed: Thorough knowledge of manual and idiosyncrasies of assessing nonverbal children.

Critique:
- Evaluates prerequisite conceptual skills.
- A simple, effective nonverbal measure.
- Narrow age range seriously limits general program use.

Coping Inventory (CI)

Author(s):   S. Zeitlin
Year: 1985
Publisher: Scholastic Testing Service, Inc.
Address: 480 Meyer Road, PO Box 1056, Bensenville, IL 60106
Phone: 1 (800) 642-6787

Assessment type: Judgment-based/norm-based; clinical rating of adaptation and coping in the early-middle childhood years.

Age range: 2½ to 16½ years.

Domains/Contexts: 2 categories: self and environment; 3 coping styles: productive, active, flexible; 48 items in 6 subsections.

Handicap options: Natural or contrived observation of interactive coping behaviors rated for quality and effectiveness; handicap norms.

Curricular links: Enhances decisions about arranging the instructional environment to foster adaptive behaviors.

Scoring/Sample: 5-point Likert rating with item definitions; 1 = not effective, 5 = effective most of the time.

Technical support: Norms = 1,116 children/454 normal, 600 handicapped; adequate reliability and validity; norms by handicap group $\bar{x}$ and SD.

Training needed: Minimal; direct observation experience and thorough knowledge of item definitions.

Critique:
- A creative interactive measure.
- Facilitates team and program decision making.
- Handicap norms are its most valuable feature.
- Item definitions lack consistent clarity and operationalization.

Citation:
Zeitlin, S. (1981). Learning through coping: An effective preschool program. *Journal of the Division of Early Childhood, 4*, 53–61.

Developmental Activities Screening Inventory II (DASI-II)

Author(s):   R. Fewell, B. Langley
Year: 1984
Publisher: PRO-ED
Address: 8700 Shoal Creek Boulevard, Austin, TX 78758
Phone: (512) 451-3246

Assessment type: Adaptive curriculum-based; interim "clinical" screening of performance on landmark tasks to accommodate the frequent lag between problem identification and programming.
Age range: 0-60 months.
Domains/Contexts: 55 unclustered developmental competencies, including fine-motor coordination, cause-effect, means-end, association, number concepts, size discrimination, seriation.
Handicap options: Screening tasks translate to instructional objectives, which include standardized modifications for nonverbal and visually impaired preschoolers.
Curricular links: Assessment tasks are converted into instructional goals with suggested teaching strategies.
Scoring/Sample: Pass (P), fail (F) scoring with comments section for qualitative scoring of emerging skills; total passes added to basal age level results in rough DA and ratio DR equivalents.
Technical support: Best as a clinical instrument; concurrent validity data available.
Training needed: Minimal testing experience required; thorough reading of manual and practice with items.

Critique:
- Excellent interim link between screening and instructional planning.
- Unclustered nature of tasks is a weakness.
- Excellent adaptive testing/teaching options.

Citation:
Fewell, R. R. (1986). Some new directions in the assessment and education of young handicapped children. In J. M. Berg (Ed.), *Science and service in mental retardation* (pp. 179–188). London: Methuen.

Gesell Developmental Schedules (GDS) (Two Versions)

Author(s):   1-H. Knobloch, H. Stevens, S. Malone, 1980
             2-N. Ames, S. Gillespie, J. Haines, N. Ilg, 1979
Year: 1980
Publisher: 1-Harper and Row
             2-Programs for Education, Inc. Publishers
Address: 1-2350 Virginia Avenue, Hagerstown, MD 21740
             2-Dept. 182, Rosemont, NJ 08556
Phone: 1-(203) 776-8125
             2-(609) 397-2214

Assessment type: Norm-based; diagnosis of degree of developmental deficit.
Age range: 1: fetal to 36 months; 2: 24 to 72 months.
Domains/Contexts: Adaptive, language, personal-social, gross motor, fine motor.
Handicap options: Multidomain organization facilitates profile analysis; predominance of cognitive/motor items limits use as adaptive measure of intellectual status.
Curricular links: Behaviors and multidomain profile are the bases for the design of most developmental curricula.
Scoring/Sample: Fully acquired (+), emerging (±), and absent (−); DA ranges and DRs for each domain with the adaptive DR indicative of intellectual level; full examination contains neurological exam and parent developmental ratings.
Technical support: Norms vary widely, depending on the version; $N = 927$ examinations from infants in the Albany, NY, area (volunteers); adequate inter-rater reliability data reported.
Training needed: Strong developmental and neurological background; extensive assessment experience needed to promote accurate interpretation of results and diminish the effects of the qualitative scoring system.

Critique:
- Comprehensive clinical measure of neurodevelopmental status.
- Most curricula use GDS tasks as their content base and, thus, link.
- Qualitative scoring procedures limit reliability.
- Norms are inadequate.
- Manual is *must* reading for all developmentalists.

Citations:
Knobloch, H., & Pasamanick, B. (1974). *Developmental diagnosis*. New York: Harper & Row.
Ames, N., Gillespie, S., Haines, J., & Ilg, N. (1979). *Gesell Institutes child from one to six: Evaluating the behavior of the preschool child*. New York: Harper & Row.
Knobloch, et al. (1980). *Manual of developmental diagnosis*. New York: Harper & Row.
Bagnato, S.J. (1981a). Developmental scales and developmental curricula: Forging a linkage for early intervention. *Topics in Early Childhood Special Education, 1*(2), 1–8.

Haessermann Educational Evaluation (HEE):
Psychoeducational Evaluation of the Preschool Child (PEP-C)

Author(s):   E. Haessermann, J. Jedrysek, E. Pope, J. Wortis
Year: 1958, 1972
Publisher: Grune & Stratton
Address: 111 Fifth Avenue, New York, NY 10003
Phone: 1 (800) 393-6500

Assessment type: Norm-based/criterion-referenced; offers a functional and adaptive assessment of various neurodevelopmental processes for at-risk and cerebral-palsied preschoolers.

Age range: 24 to 72 months.

Domains/Contexts: Language understanding and use; recognition of pictorial symbols, color discrimination, numbers and relationships, memory and recall, visual-spatial orientation; PEP-C has 31 developmental tasks for ages 3-6.

Handicap options: Provides perhaps the oldest and most detailed description of standardized stimulus-response modifications for each item to accommodate cerebral-palsied children; manual provides practical decisions on how to assess "hard-to-test" children (autistic, cp, sensorially impaired).

Curricular links: Systematic sampling strategy probes upper-to-lower limits of functioning under adapted and nonadapted conditions to detect individualized developmental objectives and effective instructional/therapeutic strategies.

Scoring/Sample: Combines quantitative and qualitative ratings of current functioning (P, F, PF); strives to detect intact motor, sensory, language capabilities.

Technical support: Clinical strategy with a 25-year experimental base; newly marketed scales have built upon and incorporated Haessermann procedures.

Training needed: Thorough reading of the manual and supervised assessment of young neurologically impaired children; physical therapist should be a partner in the assessment sessions.

Critique:
- Indispensable reading for all psychologists and early interventionists.
- Superior adaptive assessment options.
- Samples important prerequisite psychological and neurodevelopmental processes.
- Publisher should promote updating and a new edition in view of PL 99-457.

Citation:
Haessermann, E. (1958). *Developmental potential of preschool children: An evaluation in intellectual, sensory, and emotional functioning.* New York: Grune & Stratton.

Hiskey-Nebraska Test of Learning Aptitude (HNTLA)

Author(s):   M. Hiskey
Year: 1966
Publisher: Author
Address: 5640 Baldwin, Lincoln, NB 68508

Assessment type: Norm-based; adapted for hearing impaired children; designed for use with both hearing and deaf children.

Age range: 3-16 years.

Domains/Contexts: Behavior samplings in the areas of memory, picture identification, and picture association for use with the deaf have demonstrated relevance to the school-learning potential of deaf children.

Handicap options: Pantomime directions for hearing impaired.

Curricular links: Identifies general cognitive needs of hearing-impaired children.

Scoring/Sample: Instructions for pantomime administration.

Technical support: In the standardization samples, there were more deaf than hearing children at each age level. Parental occupational level for the hearing population corresponds closely to U.S. census data. There are no comparable data for the deaf population. However, since it uses deaf students in the sample, it is superior to many nonverbal tests standardized in hearing children but used with the deaf. Split-half reliability for the deaf is reported to be .95, and for the hearing .93, in groups having an age range of 3-10; .92 and .90 respectively for age range 11-17. There is no other information reported for these groups. Subtest intercorrelations for the deaf range from .33 to .74 for age range 3-10 and .31 to .43 for ages 11-17. For the hearing, the intercorrelations range from .32 to .78 for 3-10 age group and .25 to .46 for 11-17 age group. A correlation of .86 is reported for IQ comparisons with the S-B, and .82 for the WISC.

Training needed: Administrator must be skilled when presenting the test to a deaf student; experienced psychometricians should give the test; each of the subtests yields a separate score that converts to a learning age and a learning quotient for deaf students; for hearing children, grade equivalents are given.

Maxfield-Bucchholz Social Maturity Scale (M-B)

Author(s): J. Maxfield, B. Bucchholz
Year: 1957
Publisher: American Printing House for the Blind
Address: 1839 Frankfort Avenue, Louisville, KY 40206

Assessment type: Judgment-based measures with norms; designed to measure the personal and social development of blind children.

Age range: Birth to 6 years.

Domains/Contexts: Scale consists of 95 items divided into seven categories: self-help general (G), self-help dressing (D), self-help eating (E), communication (C), socialization (S), locomotion (L), and occupation (O); scale generates a social (SA) and social quotient (SQ).

Handicap options: Vineland adapted for the young blind child.

Curricular links: Develop mental reference to most blind curricula.

Scoring/Sample: Five scoring levels are presented: (+) if the child clearly demonstrates the skill; (+F) if the subject has formerly demonstrated the skill but did not do so during the session; (+No) if there has been no opportunity for the child to learn the skill due to the restraints of his blindness, but skill could be easily learned if the child were not blind; (±) if the skill is in an emergent state; and (−) if the skill is clearly not evident. Full credit is given to +, +F, and + No scores; half-credit to ± ; and no credit for minus. The number of correct items is added to determine SA and SQ scores.

Technical support: Standardization sample was based on 605 ratings on 398 children who were considered "legally blind" from birth. The manual reports the statistical data on the parents, aside from age, were not available. The children tested were from New York City, New Jersey, Boston, Connecticut, Chicago, and Minneapolis. The manual reports difficulty in reliability and validity. Difficulties in validity-testing due to the small size of the population, the diversity in the types of blindness, and the difficulty of diagnosis with very young children. The authors feel that some degree of validity was established by the procedures employed in setting up the scale, such as the percentage-passing technique and the refinements that served to distribute the items by category.

Training needed: Good rapport with both the child and the informer is considered essential to proper administration; experience with the testing and interviewing of children and parents and familiarity with the scale and the specific items are suggested.

Critique:
- The M-B scale seems to be well designed and set up.
- Clearly, there is a need for such a scale for use with blind children.
- A need for further study on its validity and reliability is indicated.

Play Assessment Scale (PAS) (Research Edition)

Author(s):   R.R. Fewell
Year: 1986
Publisher: Author
Address: Tulane University, New Orleans, LA

Assessment type: Norm-based; description of the infant's object and social play acts that exemplify perceptual and conceptual skills.

Age range: 2-36 months.

Domains/Contexts: Play behaviors under two conditions: spontaneous non-directed, and verbal prompting followed by physical and combined verbal and physical prompts.

Handicap options: Relies on naturalistic observation of the infant's typical play behavior repertoire; toys selected according to developmental level; scoring is quantitative and qualitative; good for hard-to-assess children (autistic).

Curricular links: Developmentally sequenced play routines and assessed need for instructional strategies (e.g., verbal and physical prompts).

Scoring/Sample: +/- scoring with detailed, behaviorally specific exemplars for each play task; qualitative scoring of prompts V, M, V + M; $N = 30$ children; norms generate "play age."

Technical support: Field testing ongoing; technical adequacy undetermined; some concern with interassessor reliability.

Training needed: Supervised training in observation, scoring, and interpretation through *in situ* assessment and videotape exercises.

Critique:
- Unique device to assess a vital developmental process.
- Provides a vehicle to appraise multiple areas systematically through structured play routines.
- Shows adaptive qualities and relevance for intervention planning.

Citation:

Fewell, R. R., & Rich, J. S. (1987). Play assessment as a procedure for examining cognitive, communication, and social skills in multihandicapped children. *Journal of Psychoeducational Assessment, 5,* 107–118.

Preschool Language Scale (PLS)

Author(s):	E. Zimmerman, P. Steiner, T. Pond
Year:	1979
Publisher:	Psychological Corporation
Address:	555 Academic Court, San Antonio, TX 78204
Phone:	1 (800) 228-0752
Cost:	$60+

Assessment type: Norm-based/curriculum-referenced; comprehensive diagnostic appraisal of receptive and expressive language skills.

Age range: 12-84 months.

Domains/Contexts: 2 clusters: auditory comprehension and verbal ability; tasks measure sensory discrimination, logical thinking, grammar and vocabulary, memory and attention span, temperal/spatial relations, and self-image.

Handicap options: Comprehension items facilitate assessment of nonverbal preschoolers; Mexican-American transition version.

Curricular links: Developmental tasks are compatible with items in most infant-preschool curricula.

Scoring/Sample: Language age scores for both auditory comprehension and verbal clusters.

Technical support: Field-test use in nursery schools, Head Start, and Follow Through programs and clinic settings; no national norms.

Training needed: Thorough familiarity with manual, materials, and procedures.

Critique:
- Most widely used preschool language scale.
- Developmental tasks are highly curriculum-compatible.
- Manual provides valuable rationale and research references for each item and age placement.
- Wide diagnostic use demands national standardization.

Sequenced Inventory of Communication Development (SICD)

Author(s):   E. Hedrick, J. Prather, B. Tobin
Year: 1975
Publisher: University of Washington Press
Address: Seattle, WA 98195

Assessment type: Receptive and expressive language.
Age range: 4 to 48 months
Domains/Contexts: Receptive scale: speech awareness, discrimination, understanding of speech; expressive scale: motor response, vocal response, verbal response.
Handicap options:
Curricular links: Authors suggest that categories that contain errors should be assessed in more depth and this should be used to establish therapy goals.
Scoring/Sample: 252 children, 12 at each of 12 age levels (every 3 months from 4 months to 48 months). Only Caucasian children were samples. Children were eliminated from sample if any known physical or mental abnormality was noted or if a hearing loss >30 dB at 2000 HL was present. Children were all from middle-class families.
Technical support: Not available.
Training needed: No specialized training necessary.

Critique:
- Quick and easy to administer.
- Test items include toys that are attractive and maintain the interest of the children.
- Although the test assesses a number of expressive and receptive language skills, only a limited number of items is provided for each ability; this suggests the tool is a good screening device but may not provide definitive information as to the presence or absence of a receptive or expressive language deficit.

Symbolic Play Test (SPT)

Author(s):	T. Lowe, E. Costello
Year:	1976
Publisher:	NFER Publishing Company, LTD
Address:	2 Jennings Building, Thames Avenue, Windsor, Berks SL4 1QS ENGLAND

Assessment type: Norm-based; description of symbolic play skills and understanding of semantic concepts when language is impaired.

Age range: 0 to 36 months.

Domains/Contexts: Spontaneous nonverbal play tasks in four independently structured play situations with various toys.

Handicap options: Nonverbal format adjusted to child's state and level of responsiveness and motor deficits.

Curricular links: Play situations and demands are developmentally sequenced.

Scoring/Sample: +/− scoring (DA and standard scores) based on understanding intent of play task (clear examples of passes in manual) independent of motor difficulties; norms $N = 137$ children 12-36 months in inner-city London.

Technical support: Moderate test-retest reliability, .71-.82; concurrent validity low.

Training needed: Knowledge of child development, play skills, and thorough reading of manual and scoring key.

Critique:
- Useful, short, motivating nonverbal measure.
- Some adaptive qualities.
- Reveals implications for play goals in treatment.
- Limited norms; best for qualitative use only.

System To Plan Early Childhood Services (SPECS)

Author(s):   S. J. Bagnato, J. T. Neisworth
Year: 1989
Publisher: American Guidance Service
Address: Publisher's Building, PO Box 99, Circle Pines, MN 55014
Phone: 1 (800) 328-2560
Cost: $75

Assessment type: Judgment-based; synthesizes child/family data from multiple sources to guide team decision making and planning of service delivery mode and specific program dimensions.

Age range: 24-72 months.

Domains/Contexts: Consists of 5 instruments that survey characteristics of the child, family, and program: PODS, POFS, TREAT, and Child and Family Services Indicators.

Handicap options: Uses a diagnosis-free, functional approach to clarify capabilities, deficits, and needs of handicapped children and their families.

Curricular links: Synchronizes team (professionals, paraprofessionals, and parents) assessment, treatment, and progress/program evaluation; translates team functional assessment data into goals and strategies for child and family intervention.

Scoring/Sample: 5-point functional rating scales, ranking of service delivery needs, program intensity scores; integrates diagnostic data from multi-measures and several people for a broad sample.

Technical support: Field-test data with $N = 300$ normal and handicapped preschoolers across special education, hospital, day care, agency, and day treatment settings.

Training needed: Experience with team procedures; good observational skills; practice with SPECS components.

Critique:
- Provides the only commercially available assessment/intervention linkage model.
- Enables an early intervention team to design a congruent treatment plan.
- Used to integrate the perspectives of medical and educational professionals.
- Presents a nonthreatening, productive way to obtain reliable parent perceptions.
- Care must be taken in using SPECS; should be used only in conjunction with formal performance measures and with several people.

Infant Temperament Scale (ITS), Toddler Temperament Scale (TTS), Behavioral Style Questionnaire (BSQ)

Author(s):	W. Carey, S. McDevitt, W. Fullard
Year:	1977 (1); 1978 (2); 1975 (3)
Publisher:	W. B. Carey
Address:	319 West Front Street, Media, PA 19063
Phone:	(215) 566-6641
Cost:	$20 +

Assessment type: Judgment-based/normed; assesses clusters of behavior associated with temperament or behavioral style.

Age range: 4-8 months (1); 12-36 months (2); 36-84 months (3)

Domains/Contexts: Activity, approach, rhythmicity; adaptability, intensity; mood, persistence, distractibility, threshold.

Handicap options: Assesses qualitative dimensions of individual mood and behavioral characteristics.

Curricular links: Provides guidelines regarding the child's typical response to environmental stimulation and allows translation to arranging the instructional/therapeutic setting.

Scoring/Sample: 90 + questions; 6-point Likert rating scale, 20-30 minutes completion time.

Technical support: Adequate reliability studies; norms.

Training needed: Knowledge of norms and parent interview skills.

Critique:
- ITS assesses important behavior characteristics, possibly partly constitutional.
- TTS enhances other measures.
- BSQ is too lengthy for parents.

Citation:
Carey, W. B. (1985). Clinical use of temperament data in pediatrics. *Journal of Developmental and Behavioral Pediatrics, 6*(3), 137–142.

Wisconsin Behavior Rating Scale (WBRS)

Author(s):   A. Song, J. Jones
Year: 1980
Publisher: Central Wisconsin Center for the Developmentally Disabled
Address: 317 Knutson Drive, Madison, WI 53704

Assessment type: Judgment-based; interview-informant appraisals of functional skills.

Age range: 0-36 months.

Domains/Contexts: 11 subscales: gross motor, fine motor, expressive and receptive language, play, socialization, domestic activity, eating, toileting, dressing, grooming.

Handicap options: Includes alternative items to permit approximate assessment of blind and deaf-blind children.

Curricular links: Items within domains are compatible with objectives in many developmental curricula for the severely handicapped.

Scoring/Sample: 0,1,2 N.O ratings: 0 = no response/total assistance, 1 = emergent <50%, 2 = independence >50%; total "behavioral age" and age equivalents for each subdomain.

Technical support: Norms = 184 normal and 325 institutionalized, retarded individuals.

Training needed: Firm knowledge of task requirements.

Critique:
- Creative blending of norm, criterion, judgment, and adaptive features.
- Promising reliability and validity studies.
- Clinically underestimates normal developmental levels; norms may need revision.

Citation:
Song, A., Jones, S., Lippert, J., Metzger, K., Miller, J., Borreca, C. (1984). Wisconsin BRS: Measure of adaptive behavior for the developmental levels of 0-3 years. *American Journal of Mental Deficiency, 88*(4), 401–410.

Appendix B

Snapshot Outlines of Developmental Curricula

Adaptive Play for Special Needs Children: Strategies To Enhance Communication and Learning

Author(s):	C.R. Musselwhite
Date:	1986
Publisher:	College Hill Press, Inc.
Address:	4284 41st Street, San Diego, CA 92105
Phone:	(800) 343-9204

Focus: Handicap-sensitive.

Target population: Children with disabilities.

Program type: Resource book; could be used for home- or center-based program.

Content area: Advances in play as a learning tool; development of adaptive play material; specific teaching skills and support system.

Materials/Cost: Book: $20.50.

Training needed: Professionals, parents, paraprofessionals who have a knowledge of children with disabilities.

Quality of materials: Soft-bound book; well organized; material clearly presented.

Family involvement: Parents can use this as a source book for home.

Comment:
- Well-organized, clearly presented material.
- Mainstreaming ideas, resources and support groups identified.
- Family involvement.

347

Arizona Basic Assessment and
Curriculum Utilization System (ABACUS)

Author(s): J. McCarthy, K. Lund, C. Bos, S. Vaughn, J. Glatke
Date: 1988
Publisher: Love Publishing Company
Address: 1777 South Bellaire Street, Denver, CO 80222
Phone: (303) 757-2579

Focus: Developmental milestones.
Target population: Children 2 to 5½ with special needs.
Program type: Individual or small-group center-based.
Content area: Body management, self-care, communication, preacademic, and socialization.
Data system: Individual and group record sheets.
Materials/Cost: Complete program: $195.
Training needed: Knowledge and experience with the target population; careful study of manual.
Quality of materials: Series of ten soft-bound books.
Family involvement: Home/parent teaching component for maintenance and generalization.

Comment:
- Family involvement.
- Cognitive-behavioral model.
- IEP or IFSP correlation.
- Cross-referenced with the assessment.
- Complete record system.

Clark Early Language Program (CELP)

Author(s): C.R. Clark, D.F. Moore
Date: 1981
Publisher: DLM/Teaching Resources
Address: One DLM Park, Allen, TX 75002
Phone: (800) 527-4747, TX (800) 442-4711

Focus: Handicap-sensitive.

Target population: Ages 2½ to adult; hearing-impaired, learning-disabled, mentally retarded, aphasic and English-as-a-second-language students.

Program type: Individual and small group settings in center-, home-based, and clinical settings.

Content area: Language (rebus, oral, and optional sign language).

Data system: Program evaluation sheet for formative evaluation.

Materials/Cost: Complete kit $92.50.

Training needed: No training needed for teacher skilled in working with target population other than a careful study of the manual.

Quality of materials: Materials contained in a sturdy carton; organized for ease of use; individual cards of durable design.

Family involvement: Worksheets offer opportunity for parents to reinforce content; rebus cards can be used at home.

Comment:
- Opportunity for parent involvement.
- Well-organized, durable materials.
- Developmental areas are not identified; no way to "fit into the program."

Developmental Communication Curriculum (DCC)

Author(s):	R.P. Hanna, E.A. Lippert, A.B. Harris
Date:	1982
Publisher:	Charles E. Merrill Publishing Company
Address:	1300 Alum Creek Drive, Columbus, OH 48106
Phone:	(800) 233-5682, Ohio call collect (614) 258-8441

Focus: Handicap-sensitive.

Target population: Developmental ages 1 to 5.

Program type: Individual center- or home-based.

Content area: Communication skills taught in the context of play.

Data system: Curriculum guide contains probes that provide a means to monitor and organize records of progress objectively.

Materials/Cost: Complete program includes: curriculum guide, activities handbook, 12 copies each of development communication inventory, and the Parent News ($85); additional DCI 12 for $20, Parent News 12 for $20.

Training needed: Training in working with the target population in speech and language development.

Quality of materials: Material presented in spiral notebook.

Family involvement: Parent News offers description of communication development.

Comment:
- Organized by categories rather than objectives.
- Makes use of augmentative communication.
- Parent communication through Parent News.
- Means to verify teacher and parent observation of child's ability to communicate.

Education for Multihandicapped Infants (EMI)

Author(s): P.B. Wallens, W.B. Elder, S.N. Hastings
Date: 1979
Publisher: Children's Rehabilitation Center
Address: 2270 Ivy Road, Charlottesville, VA 22901
Phone: (804) 924-5730

Focus: Handicap-sensitive.
Target population: Handicapped infants or infants at risk in a newborn intensive care nursery.
Program type: Individual in a hospital setting.
Content area: Kinesthetic stimulation, visual stimulation, auditory stimulation, and parent involvement activities.
Data system: Standardized care plan: cognitive-affective development in the hospitalized infant.
Materials/Cost: EMI infant learning packets: $6.00; EMI curriculum pool materials: $9.25.
Training needed: Program is designed to be used by medical personnel and parents.
Quality of materials: Materials are published in soft-bound books.
Family involvement: Activities to promote parent involvement are included and stressed.

Comment:
- Well-defined and clearly presented activities.
- Plan for consistency among those caring for the infant.
- Parent involvement encouraged and supported.

Infant Learning (IL): A Cognitive-Linguistic Intervention Strategy

Author(s): C.J. Dunst
Date: 1981
Publisher: DLM/Teaching Resources Corp.
Address: One DLM Park, Allen, TX 75002
Phone: (800) 527-4747, TX (800) 442-4711

Focus: Handicap-sensitive.

Target population: Prelinguistic children who are developmentally delayed, severely handicapped, or at risk for learning disabilities.

Program type: Individual home- or center-based.

Content area: Cognition, social and linguistic development.

Data system: Tie in with Uzgiris and Hunt Scale of Infant-Psychological Development; no formative system.

Materials/Cost: Book: $25.

Training needed: Knowledge of the target population and a careful study of the material.

Quality of materials: Soft-bound book.

Family involvement: Ideas for parent/caregiver-infant interaction; everyday activities used as facilitators of learning.

Comment:
- Framework for intervention.
- Phase-intervention model.
- Variety of activity ideas.
- Transposing material into actual program requires careful reading of material.

Infants and Toddlers with Neuromotor
and Other Developmental Delays

Author(s):   F. Connors, G. Williamson , J. Siepp
Date: 1978
Publisher: Teachers College Press
Address: Columbia University, New York, New York
Phone: (212) 678-3929

Focus: Handicap-sensitive.
Target population: Atypical children, birth to 3 years of age.
Program type: Resource book for agencies providing center- and home-based programs; individual and small-group activities.
Content area: Program foundations, developmental program (movement, pre-speech, language, cognition, socioemotional), curriculum in action.
Data system: Sample forms used by participating centers.
Materials/Cost: Book: $17.95.
Training needed: Guide for those with training and experience with the target population; careful study of the text.
Quality of materials: Well-illustrated soft-bound book.
Family involvement: The parent is viewed as the primary programmer.

Comment:
- Additional information on assessment, adaptive equipment, health, programming and delivery services.
- Inexpensive.
- Resource book that needs to be "translated" to individual programs and plans.

Learning Through Play (LTP):
A Resource Manual for Teachers and Parents

Author(s):	R. Fewell, P. Vadasy
Date:	1983
Publisher:	DLM/Teaching Resource Company
Address:	One DLM Park, Allen, TX 75002
Phone:	(800) 527-4747, TX (800) 442-4711

Focus: Cognitive development.

Target population: Birth to 3 years of age.

Program type: Individual, home-based; can be used with center-based program.

Content area: Sensory, perception/fine motor, movement in space, cognitive, language, and social.

Data system: Screening checklist provided to give starting point and a means to monitor progress; permission given to reproduce.

Materials/Cost: Book: $21; materials needed are available in most homes or could be provided readily by an agency.

Training needed: Basic knowledge of target population and study of the text.

Quality of materials: Well-organized binder; material clearly presented.

Family involvement: Activities are designed for parent and child.

Comment:
- Family involvement.
- Adaptations for handicapped.
- Mainstreaming ideas; notes simple ways to accommodate special-needs children.
- Permission to copy activities.

Peabody Developmental Motor Scales (PDMS) and Activity Cards

Author(s):	M.R. Folio, R. Fewell
Date:	1974
Publisher:	DLM/Teaching Resources
Address:	One DLM Park, P.O. Box 4000, Allen, TX 75002
Phone:	(800) 527-4747, Texas (800) 442-4711

Focus: Handicap-sensitive.

Target population: Birth to 83 months.

Program type: Individual center- or home-based.

Content area: Gross and fine motor.

Data system: Scoring book for motor scale; no formative record system.

Materials/Cost: Complete program $175; additional scoring booklets, 15 for $20.

Training needed: Skill in administration of educational or psychological tests to children birth to 7; professional aides and volunteers can learn to administer PDMS.

Quality of materials: Material is organized in a sturdy box; material clearly printed for easy reading.

Family involvement: Activities can be used by parents; cards make it possible to share between different parents at the same time.

Comment:
- Suggestions for use with handicapped children.
- Understanding of spoken language not necessary (tasks are demonstrated).
- Activities can be done with parent at home.
- Well-organized material; easy to use.
- Additional equipment needed for administration (balance beam, tricycles, etc.).

Portage Guide to Early Education (PGEE)

Author(s):   S.M. Bluma, M.S. Shearer, A.H. Frohman, J.M. Hillard
Date: 1976
Publisher: CESA 5
Address: Box 564, Portage, WI 53901
Phone: (608) 742-8811

Focus: Developmental milestones.

Target population: Handicapped and nonhandicapped children, birth to 6 years of age.

Program type: Designed for home-based individual programs; can be adapted for small-group or center-based programs.

Content area: Infant stimulation, cognitive, language, self-help, motor, and socialization.

Data system: Checklist provided for summative evaluation, frequency charts for formative evaluation.

Materials/Cost: Kit including manual and 15 checklists: $50; additional checklists: 15 for $10; portage parent program—Instructor's Set $12, parent reading set $20; A Parent's Guide to Early Education: $15.

Training needed: Knowledge of the target population and a review of the manual; parents can be trained to use the program with support; training workshops available; contact Portage Project Training Coordinator.

Quality of materials: Kit is contained in a sturdy, easily portable case; color-coded cards contain the activities, presented in an easily understood manner.

Family involvement: Parent involvement is the focal point of the program.

Comment:
- Materials are inexpensive, easily portable, and easy to use.
- Adaptation needed for handicaps.
- "Cookbook" format hinders true individualization.

Teaching the Infant with Down Syndrome:
A Guide for Parents and Professionals

Author(s):   M.J. Hanson
Date: 1986
Publisher: PRO-ED
Address: 5341 Industrial Oaks Blvd., Austin, TX 78735
Phone: (512) 892-3142

Focus: Handicap-sensitive.

Target population: Parents and professionals who work with Down syndrome infants.

Program type: Parent-centered, home-based individual program; ideas adaptable to center-based program.

Content area: Gross and fine motor, communication, cognitive, social, and self-help.

Data system: Baby record section allows for formative records.

Materials/Cost: Book: $19; materials needed are generally available; no set list given.

Training needed: Knowledge of normal child development is helpful; material presented in the book enables parent to present the program effectively; consultation with professionals enhances the program.

Quality of materials: Material is presented in one soft-bound, well-organized volume.

Family involvement: Program is intended for parent use in the home.

Comment:
- Practical, clearly stated information for parents.
- Excellent basis for home-based program.
- Emphasis on parental concerns.
- Suggestions for prompts and reinforcers.
- Inexpensive.

Appendix C

Alternative Developmentally Based Assessment Reports

CHILD: Nickolette
PSYCHOLOGIST: J. Johnson

DOT: 83-11-7
DOB: 81-8-5
CCA: 24.5 months
(corrected for 2.5 months prematurity)

DIAGNOSTIC DEVELOPMENTAL ASSESSMENT
AND PROGRESS SUMMARY

Referral Reason

Nickolette, age 24.5 months, corrected for 2½ months prematurity, was admitted to the hospital and rehabilitation center for continuous developmental assessment and therapies following episodes of meningitis and encephalitis, due to complications of her premature birth and numerous shunt malfunctions. Psychological services during Nicky's rehabilitation focused upon the following functions: (1) assessing developmental status and progress as an outcome of her individualized therapy, (2) establishing continuous cognitive goals for curriculum planning, and (3) counseling her mother regarding her own emotional adjustment and her developmental stimulation and behavior management of Nicky.

Background Information

Birth, Developmental, and Medical History

Nickolette was born 2½ months premature (30 weeks' gestation), weighing 2 lb, 14 oz. Delivery was vaginal, but breech. She was born at the hospital and transferred to a medical center, where she received a shunt and remained in acute care for 4 months. Following this stay, Nicky returned to the hospital approximately every 3 months because of numerous shunt malfunctions and revisions. In

May 1983, she contracted pneumococcal meningitis and encephalitis, was hospitalized again, and later transferred to the center for rehabilitation on 7/14/83.

Results from the infant stimulation program and the mother's report indicated that Nickolette exhibited significant motor and language developmental deficits during her early course before her latest illness. However, she used some single words, occasionally naming people and objects, cruising about furniture, and socializing well with adults. It is important to note that her frequent swings between making progress and then relapsing with shunt malfunctions and illnesses stressed both her mother and her mother's parents, to such a degree that they were very ambivalent about Nicky and afraid to attach to her emotionally. The mother's own emotional needs as an adolescent/young adult wanting independence complicated her sense of responsibility in committing to Nicky.

Previous Evaluations and Interventions

Beginning in October 1982, the intermediate unit (IU) provided home-based intervention services to Nickolette and her mother. This consisted of once/week physical therapy, developmental play, and language therapy. Visiting community nurse services were also provided.

A preinjury, curriculum-based developmental progress assessment was conducted by the IU. This revealed Nicky's developmental gains between 1/26/83 and 5/4/83, as shown on the Early Learning Accomplishment Profile (E-LAP). The following developmental ages and levels of functioning were noted:

Area	*1/83 (CCA = 15 mo.)*	*5/83 (CCA = 18.5 mo.)*
Social	12 mo.	17 mo.
Gross motor	9 mo.	9 mo.
Fine motor	14 mo.	16 mo.
Language	12 mo.	13 mo.
Cognitive	14 mo.	18 mo.
Self-help	13 mo.	17 mo.

Discharge Medical Status

Nickolette made significant medical and developmental progress during her 4-month hospital stay. At admission, she showed significant left hemiparesis, affecting both upper and lower extremities, as well as left-eye visual impairment. At discharge, she was using her left hand much better in functional midline play and showed good use of both eyes. Seizures were suspected during her early hospital course but were never documented, although she had some episodes of "tuning out" and staring, which appeared most prominent when she was fatigued.

Developmental Diagnosis and Progress Summary

Throughout Nicky's course of therapy and recovery, the following interdisciplinary battery of team diagnostic scales was employed to monitor her developmental progress and to provide a guide for intervention planning:

- Bayley Scales of Infant Development (BSID)
- Early Intervention Developmental Profile (EIDP)
  (Team Adaptive Curriculum Scale)
- Brazelton Neonatal Behavioral Assessment Scale (BNBAS)
  (Behavioral measure of early recovery)
- Carolina Record of Individual Behavior (CRIB)
  (Clinical judgments of behavioral gains)

General Analysis

During Nicky's 4-month rehabilitation, multiple developmental therapies focused upon specific aspects of her recovery on at least a once-a-day basis: nursing, physical therapy, occupational therapy, speech-language therapy, psychology, recreational therapy, and preschool programming. Monthly re-evaluations of her range and rate of developmental gains were conducted by the interdisciplinary team from July to November 1983.

In general, Nicky demonstrated significant gains within and across all major developmental and behavioral processes. Overall, during her 4-month rehabilitation she made progress at the rate of 2.4 months of developmental gain for each month of therapy, or 2½ times the normal expected rate. Her strongest gains were observed in cognitive, language, and socioemotional processes (3.3 to 1), with significant but much slower rates (reflecting her areas of greatest disability) in gross motor, fine motor, and self-care functions (1.5 to 1). Similarly, Nicky reacquired important behavioral skills in object and social play, goal-directed responses, endurance, and social communication. Despite these important functional gains, Nicky's most enduring and prominent problem in learning was her inability to transfer or generalize skills she had acquired to new but similar problem-solving tasks. Her style of play was predominantly sensorimotor in nature, as she banged, threw, and manipulated objects with only an emerging understanding of the form and function of toys.

Dramatic gains in cognitive developmental skills were observed in Nicky's performance on various structured cognitive measures. Upon admission, her developmental and behavioral skills were so dysfunctional and disorganized that her responses were most accurately monitored by using a scale for premature infants (the Brazelton Neonatal Behavioral Assessment Scale). In July 1983, her responses in such areas as habituating to sights, sounds, and touch, her orientation to objects, and her regulation of her own state and temperament were most comparable with those of neonates at 36 weeks' gestation. Yet, within a 2-week period, she made rapid progress in her use of vision in focusing and tracking and in reaching with her right hand, so that her skills were comparable to those of a 1½-month-old infant.

Nickolette's responses to tasks on the Bayley Scales of Infant Development (BSID) (with motor adaptations) reflected her overall rate of cognitive developmental progress. In July, her developmental age on the BSID was 1.3 months, indicating functioning consistent with a profound level of developmental retardation (DR = 6). In strong contrast, her developmental age at discharge (11/15) was comparable to that of a 12½-month-old infant. This level indicated current cognitive abilities within the high-moderate range of developmental retardation (DR = 50).

Currently, continuing cognitive, language, and social gains are anticipated, although Nicky's rate of gain appeared to slow considerably prior to discharge. These gains will be promoted most effectively by regular structured developmental play activities through the family and Nicky's preschool program. Without such activities, regressions can be expected. In any case, significant developmental and learning deficits will persist and be permanent, requiring continuous special education services.

Specific Analysis

Table C-1 depicts Nicky's baseline (7/15/83) and current (11/15/83) developmental levels within major functional processes, as assessed by the interdisciplinary team.

Table C–1 Nicky's Baseline and Developmental Levels

Process	Baseline Level	Current Level
Cognitive	1.3 mo.	12.5 mo.
Language	1.8 mo.	16.1 mo.
Perceptual/fine motor	.8 mo.	8.0 mo.
Socioemotional	2.8 mo.	15.5 mo.
Gross motor	1.0 mo.	7.1 mo.
Self-care	3.5 mo.	7.1 mo.
Developmental	1.9 mo.	11.1 mo.

Social and Object Play

Nicky's strongest individual skills have always been apparent in her social response to adults and other children. Her pattern of play is predominantly isolated, although she clearly prefers the attention of others and tries to engage them in play by smiling, laughing, and vocalizing. Nevertheless, her style of play is changing, as she more frequently manipulates and inspects the parts of toys and plays with them with some emerging understanding of form and function (e.g., seats a doll in a chair, throws ball, rolls car). Nicky still resorts to infant play patterns of mouthing, banging, throwing, and dropping when she is irritable and fatigued or when she wants to end an activity or gain the attention of others. She also tends to repeat play patterns in a perseverative manner, which needs to be interrupted and directed to more purposeful actions. Finally, Nicky is beginning to engage in some appropriate social play with dolls; she will kiss and hug a "Kermit" puppet, put a spoon in its mouth, and vocalize with jargon-like intonations at a mirror.

Cognitive and Language Processes

Nicky's range of cognitive and language capabilities is most like that of a 12- to 16-month-old infant. Her problem-solving skills and task orientation have shown recent strong increases. Yet, she needs consistent verbal and physical cues to help her sustain attention and performance on a task (e.g., "Nicky, look at me," while briefly restraining her hands on her tray). Nicky has gained in her ability to search for hidden objects in sequence (e.g., 2 cloths), to obtain objects beyond her reach on cloths or with sticks, and to obtain preferred toys that are hidden behind a clear barrier.

Nicky demonstrates increased skills in both imitation and language comprehension. While she has no understanding of pictured objects, she can select the correct object in a two-choice discrimination task with 70 percent accuracy (e.g., ball, cup; bunny, car; shoe, spoon). However, her expressive communication mostly involves gestures and the use of beginning sounds to indicate her wants. She has shown a much greater use of jargon-like intonations and the ability to follow simple directions. Finally, Nicky more consistently imitates fine motor actions (e.g., tapping her head) and initial sounds for basic words.

Offsetting Nicky's recent significant gains in language comprehension and problem solving, her most prominent deficit involves her difficulty in coordinating individual skills and in generalizing them in new situations with similar toys.

Perceptual/Fine Motor Processes

Nicky still shows a significant left hemiparesis, which affects her left field vision and hand use in object play. Her skills in exploring and manipulating objects are most comparable with those of an 8-month-old infant. Currently, she shows much less resistance in using her left hand, although her tendency to become frustrated is greater; generally, she transfers objects from left to right in play. She uses a radial-palmar grasp to obtain toys in a box or clear fishbowl containers; however, she has great difficulty in voluntarily releasing toys into containers because of her motor difficulties, even on her right side. Her skills are most evident functionally in pulling pegs from a pegboard, raking small objects, turning the pages of a cardboard book, and taking the tops from plastic boxes.

Guidelines for Developmental Intervention

The following recommendations are offered as guides for planning home- and preschool-based goals and activities:

- Nicky's strong developmental and behavioral gains during her rehabilitation indicate the impact that structured programming can have for her. It is important that such programming occur on a daily basis to support her recovery. Discharge planning has been arranged with the intermediate unit so that physical therapy, occupational therapy, speech/language therapy, and developmental programming will be integrated into her regular plan. Both the mother and the grandparents (or specialized foster parents, if that occurs) should be involved as regular partners in learning her therapies. The interdisciplinary team's current estimates of developmental/behavioral goals and activities that should be helpful in designing Nicky's IEP are presented in Exhibit C-1. These estimates were based upon suggested strategies in the curriculum Developmental Programming for Infants and Young Children (Schafer and Moersch, 1981).
- During Nicky's hospitalization, specific behavior management strategies were found to be effective in limiting her inappropriate behaviors during therapy and increasing her attention, task orientation, and compliance. Nicky's cognitive developmental stage is now in transition; she is less passive in interactions with toys and adults and more active, teasing, and somewhat resistant in her response to the demands of tasks. In general, this noncompliance (throwing of toys, laughing at her impact on others) is typical of a 6- to 8-month level of understanding. However, she is showing more perseveration in toy play, vocalizations ("raspberries"), and stereotyped patterns of interaction, raising concerns as to whether these patterns may inhibit her ability to use her skills functionally and to progress.

Goals

The following two behavioral goals are projected:

1. to decrease instances of noncompliance (throwing toys, whining, grimacing, and extending legs)
2. to increase instances of more functional toy play and the production of specific sounds to indicate what she wants

Strategies

To decrease the frequency of noncompliant patterns, the following strategies are recommended:

Exhibit C-1 Nicky's Developmental Intervention Linkages

DEVELOPMENTAL INTERVENTION LINKAGES

CHILD **Nicky**   CA **27mo.**   DA **Encephalitis**

±	COGNITIVE PROCESS DA · **12.5 mo.**	DEVELOPMENTAL TASK
+	REPEATED SOUNDS & ACTIONS	
±	MEANS-END RELATIONS	Uses stick to obtain toy beyond reach / Pull cloth to retrieve toy
+	COMBINING ACTIONS	
±	OBJECT PERMANENCE	Object searching under 2 covers: cup and hidden toy under washcloth
—	SPATIALITY	
±	CAUSALITY	Turn handle of Jack-in-box toy
±	IMITATION (SOUND-MOTOR)	Vocal imitation of up-down intonations / Imitate actions; tap head - pat doll
—	OBJECT MANIPULATION & PLAY	Inspecting details of toy parts / Pegboards and rings & spindles
—	FUNCTIONAL RELATIONSHIPS	
	REPRESENTATIONAL THOUGHT	Doll play: feed, drink, mirror, kiss-hug
	FORM DISCRIMINATION	
	MATCHING (OBJECT-PICTURE)	
	NUMBER-SIZE-TIME RELATIONS	
	CLASSIFICATION & SORTING	
	SEQUENCING	
	AUDITORY-VISUAL MEMORY	
	SYMBOLIC THOUGHT	

±	SOCIAL PLAY PROCESS DA · **15.5 mo.**	DEVELOPMENTAL TASK
±	SELECTIVE ATTENTION	Needs physical & verbal cues to attend
±	MANIPULATION & EXPLORATION	Changed style: mouth, bang, throw to functional - exploration in play
+	ATTACHMENT BEHAVIORS	
—	DIFFERENTIATES SELF-OTHERS	Playful response to pictures of self and mirror
+	RELATIONAL OBJECT PLAY	
—	FUNCTIONAL OBJECT PLAY	Container play & voluntary releasing / Functional doll play
—	SYMBOLIC OBJECT PLAY	
+	ISOLATE PLAY	
±	PARALLEL PLAY	Accepts groups of 1-3 other children
—	ASSOCIATIVE PLAY	Reciprocal play in giving toys to others
—	COOPERATIVE PLAY	

Exhibit C–1 continued

DEVELOPMENTAL INTERVENTION LINKAGES

CHILD **Nicky**   CA **27mo.**   DA **Encephalitis**

±	PERCEPTUAL-MOTOR PROCESS DA = **8.0 mo.**	DEVELOPMENTAL TASK
+	VISUAL FOCUSING	
±	VISUAL TRACKING	Finding & obtaining toys out of left visual field
±	DIRECTED REACHING (VISUAL & AUDITORY)	Attends to coordinate vision, reaching and midline toy play
+	HAND MIDLINE SKILLS	
±	GRASPING	Refines voluntary release patterns
—	TRANSFER	Transfers toys right to left Stabilizes with left hand
±	PREHENSION	Picks up small objects with
	CONSTRUCTION	thumb & finger
	TRACING	
	DRAWING	
	WRITING	

±	LANGUAGE PROCESS DA = **16.1 mo.**	DEVELOPMENTAL TASK
+	ORIENTATION & LOCALIZATION	
±	SELECTIVE ATTENTION	Attends with verbal cue only
±	ELICITED SOUNDS	Vocalizes into clear fish bowl
±	IMITATION (SOUND-MOTOR)	Imitates initial sounds Models unseen movements
±	DIRECTION FOLLOWING	"Put rabbit in box" "Give the ball to ____"
±	OBJECT IDENTIFICATION	Cup, baby, ball, spoon, shoe, rabbit
—	OBJECT NAMING	"ball", "cup", "baby".
	PICTURE IDENTIFICATION	
	PICTURE NAMING	
	TWO WORD FORMS	
	SVO FORM	
	AGENT-ACTION RELATIONS	
	SVO & MODIFIERS	
	REFINED STRUCTURES	

COMMENTS: Suggested tasks are based on curriculum stimulation activities in Developmental Programming for Infants and Young Children (1981). Nicky is just beginning to change her play style from mouth, throw, bang to more relational and functional play. Attention is distractible requiring prompts and high-interest toys.

- Initially, attempt to interrupt the throwing pattern before it is completed and gently guide it into more purposeful patterns. Example: gently move Nicky's arm toward the container and tap her hand as a cue to release the toy into the container; immediately reinforce the functional container play with smiling and verbal praise.
- Use "exaggerated" cues when Nicky has tantrums and misbehaves in order to aid her ability to distinguish feelings and acceptable behaviors. This may involve "holding" a frown for a longer period of time and making sure Nicky attends to it. Also, the sound of the therapist's angry voice should be somewhat louder, lower, and more distinct, with a firm reprimand ("No! "No throwing"). This will increase her attention to behavioral cues and compensate for any visual limitations.
- These cues should be followed by a timeout procedure, consisting of three elements:
  1. Removing all toys from her tray and verbalizing a brief contingency, such as, "First, we stop crying, then we can play."
  2. Turning her chair to the wall for 15 seconds and gently restraining her arms
  3. Reforming the position of the chair, reinforcing her noncrying, and replacing the toys

To increase Nicky's functional toy play and communicative vocalizations, the following strategies are recommended:

- Immediately reinforce approximations or specific instances of functional toy play with hand clapping, stroking, and social praise.
- Use a variety of toys that are visually and auditorially stimulating to reduce perseveration and distractibility.

CHILD: Derek   DOE: 87-03-06
PSYCHOLOGIST: J. Probocis   DOE: 81-01-03
                                   CA: 06-02-03

DIAGNOSTIC DEVELOPMENTAL ASSESSMENT

Referral Reason and Background Information

Derek, age 6, was evaluated at the parent's request by Dr. _____, who has been coordinating the provision of home-based early-intervention and behavior management services for the past year. The purpose of the present evaluation is to guide decision making about the most appropriate placement and program planning for Derek within the intermediate unit system.

Derek has been evaluated previously on several occasions, most notably at the _____ Institute for Handicapped Children. The results of this evaluation are more fully discussed in a previous report by Dr. _____. In general, the results indicated that Derek was diagnosed as a child with early infantile autism. Since that time, Derek has been given a general language assessment in the home, using the Preschool Language Scale (PLS). At a chronological age of 5½ years, Derek demonstrated significant deficits in language understanding and use. He achieved a basal level at 33 months and an overall age equivalent of 39 months.

Diagnostic Assessment and Analysis

Derek, age 74 months, was given a comprehensive developmental assessment in the home over a 3-hour period in both structured and spontaneous play situations. Interviews concerning early developmental history and a follow-up of results were also conducted with the parents.

General Analysis

The comprehensive assessment of Derek's capabilities and needs provides strong evidence that he should be viewed and treated as a young multihandicapped child with a pattern of skills and deficits in conceptual, motor, language, and attention areas that is suggestive of some neurological difficulties. Derek's multiple handicaps are evident in four distinct diagnostic areas: (1) He should be appropriately viewed as a child displaying the behavioral characteristics associated with autism. However, his atypical patterns are mild and have decreased markedly in the past 18 months, particularly since his last major evaluation. (2) His cognitive and language deficits, especially, provide evidence of a high-moderate-to-low-mild level of cognitive developmental retardation. (3) Despite his recent increases in language behaviors, he shows a distinct language disorder that is prominent in comprehension and expression, especially in the areas of auditory memory, word retrieval, and processing. Finally, (4) he shows evidence of an attention deficit disorder with hyperactivity.

Given his multihandicaps, if progress is to continue, Derek must receive programming that targets each of these areas simultaneously. It must be emphasized that he has shown significant gains over the past 12 months in two of the most crucial areas: (1) language understanding and use, and (2) social and affective responses (e.g., eye contact, interpersonal relations, and emotions). These gains appear to enhance his potential for progress with structured educational programming and behavior management.

Specific Analysis

The following battery of diagnostic measures was employed in the current evaluation:

- Battelle Developmental Inventory (BDI) (cognitive and communication sub-domains only)
- Individualized Assessment and Treatment for Autistic Children (IATA)
- Childhood Autism Rating Scale (CARS)
- McCarthy Scales of Children's Abilities (MSCA)
- Leiter International Performance Scale (LIPS)

Social and behavioral observations The structured portions of the evaluation were conducted at a child-sized table in a bedroom free of distractions. Derek's attention difficulties and overactivity required that he be contained in his seat with an arm gently about his shoulders as the psychologist kneeled beside him until he became engaged in activities. Then, the structure was reduced somewhat. In order to maintain attention, motivation, and performance on tasks, it was necessary to intersperse the more focused high-demand tasks with active toys as reinforcers. Without this approach, Derek's attention deteriorated quickly. He also needed constant physical and verbal-visual prompts to maintain his performance, since he showed poor visual scanning skills on discrimination tasks; this deficit affected his performance, particularly on the LIPS. On discrimination tasks, Derek's limit was a two- to three-choice task; yet, his eye contact and sustained attention were dramatically different from those observed when home intervention began approximately 1 year ago.

Derek now shows longer periods of face-to-face gazing with smiling and laughing. He often hugs on command and seeks out greater emotional contact with others. He also shows greater participation in verbal and fine motor imitation games. Derek shows some echolalic behavior, but this has decreased considerably over the past 12 to 18 months. He exhibits few ritualistic behaviors typically associated with autism.

General developmental skills. Overall, Derek shows a complex pattern of very widely scattered skills that span the levels from 24 to 54 months. Such variations are often associated with evidence of neurological difficulties. Derek displays his most prominent deficits in such neurodevelopmental areas as perceptual fine motor skills, auditory memory, word retrieval, and language processing.

Similar deficits are evident in cognitive and conceptual areas. Overall, Derek's cognitive skills are much like those expected of a 4-year-old child, suggesting a rate of progress that is approximately two-thirds of that normally expected. Despite Derek's recent functional gains in language, social, and cognitive areas, he has individual skills and concepts that are displayed regularly under selected conditions (repeated cues, situations, toys). However, he has not generalized these to new people, circumstances, and materials. Similarly, Derek has much difficulty applying concepts to solve problems.

Cognitive. Table C-2 profiles Derek's current levels of functioning in several developmental areas, as determined from his performance on the MSCA and LIPS measures. As can be seen, his levels of performance vary from 37 to 48 months in

Table C–2 Derek's Levels of Functioning

Developmental Domain	DA	DR*
McCarthy Scales of Children's Abilities (MSCA)		
Verbal	48 months	65
Perceptual-Performance	37 months	52
Quantitative	37 months	52
Memory	40 months	55
Leiter International Performance Scale (LIPS)		
Nonverbal/Conceptual	41 months	55

*MSCA indexes transposed to a scale with a mean of 100 and standard deviation of 15.

specific cognitive, conceptual, language, nonverbal, and perceptual areas. With indexes from the MSCA transposed to scores with a mean of 100 and standard deviation of 15, Derek shows his most capable individual skills on the verbal subtests of the MSCA, consistent with performance at the 48-month level. Thus, his current rate of cognitive skill development is progressing at a rate that is approximately 65 percent of that expected for his age. This current rate is indicative of a high-moderate to low-mild degree of developmental retardation (DR = 65).

Derek's strongest cognitive skills are evident in remembering and recalling pictures presented visually, in defining basic words (coat, towel, car), in grouping words into generic categories ("things to eat"), and in identifying missing details in pictures. In nonverbal problem solving on the LIPS, Derek's performance is limited by poor visual scanning and attention, although he shows conceptual knowledge into the 5-year level. For example, he is able to match clothes to appropriate persons on a discrimination task. When his attention is focused, he is capable of showing good visual problem solving, as evident in his completion of the Gesell missing parts task (wagon—"the wheel broke off").

Conceptual. Derek's least-developed cognitive skills are apparent in the conceptual area. He knows some colors, shapes, and positional and size concepts. However, he shows limitations in understanding opposites, number concepts and spatial concepts and in memory tasks requiring attention.

Attention. Derek's selective and sustained attention skills are much like those expected at the 18- to 24-month levels. His impulsivity and distractibility are hindrances to his understanding and performance on tasks. He appears to be quite capable of learning through visual tasks, modeling, and guided performance with physical prompts; in these cases, he can repeat actions. In contrast, his attention to auditorially presented material is significantly limited; he has difficulty remembering numbers and unrelated words presented in a series and has considerable difficulty attending to a story and recalling details, even in short eight-word forms or descriptive sentences. He needs much work in careful visual scanning and comparing on tasks that have three to four choices.

Language. Derek's pattern of capabilities shows a large discrepancy between language understanding and use. He has great difficulty expressing definitions beyond objects and functions; even though he may understand the concept, he cannot express his thoughts in coherent sentences or phrases. He shows many of the word retrieval deficits shown by children with neurologically based language disorders. For example, when he has difficulty recalling a particular word for a concept, he will often give associative responses, such as identifying a horn as "a tune" or a lock as "a key." Finally, he has difficulty remembering more than two to three words or elements presented in a direction. Typically, he will quickly give the last word that was presented before it disintegrates in memory. With more meaningful forms (short sentences) he will try to repeat the details in telegraphic fashion before he forgets. Derek shows strong increases in his ability to imitate fine motor actions and gestures.

Perceptual fine motor. In one of his weaker areas, Derek's perceptual fine motor skills—expressed in such tasks as drawing, block building, puzzle completion, and other coordinated activities—are comparable with those expected between 24 and 36 months of age. Tracing forms and imitating (in contrast to copying) are his primary methods. He has particular difficulty with three-part disjointed puzzles and the reproduction of very basic block patterns. He has little understanding of sequencing according to size or of reproducing designs visually, weaknesses that are compounded by his attention deficits.

Guidelines for Intervention

The following recommendations are offered as guides for decision making about classroom placement and program planning:

- Several class options may be available to Derek, depending upon their match with his developmental and behavioral needs. It is very important that cooperative relations between the family and school be maintained and that both parents have opportunities to view each class option in operation to aid their decisions. It is recommended that a multidisciplinary team meeting be arranged so that the most appropriate placement decision for Derek can be negotiated.
- Several factors need to be considered in selecting a class option for Derek. Derek's complex developmental, behavioral, and temperamental needs must be considered in matching him with a teacher who has experience teaching and managing children with autistic characteristics, cognitive/language deficits, and neurological difficulties. His multihandicaps must be considered simultaneously, since he exhibits diagnostic characteristics of several groups. The relationship between Derek and the teacher and the "mix" of children in the classroom should be the primary deciding factors, rather than merely diag-

nostic labels applied to a particular classroom. A low child-teacher ratio (six to eight children) is suggested in order for Derek to benefit from programming. Opportunities for pairing Derek with certain children at slightly higher developmental levels should be available, since he needs appropriate models to increase his skills in language and social areas. Programming must emphasize specific behavioral prerequisites: consistent eye contact, visual attention, and such social skills as waiting, sharing, and turn taking. Finally, the programming must focus on helping Derek learn the value and use of language to communicate his needs and preferences to both adults and children in a social context. Thus, language programming in the classroom must be viewed as a major requirement of his IEP. Derek's potential for progress at higher levels of functioning depends upon distinct increases in both social and language skills.

- It is strongly recommended that computer aids be used in the classroom to help Derek become a more responsive, attentive, and eventually more independent learner. For example, computer-based instruction in concept development could capitalize on his stronger visual skills and provide him with more immediate feedback regarding the appropriateness of his responses; the commercially available *Word Skills* program might be used for this purpose.

- Because of Derek's neuromotor and language deficits, it is recommended that both occupational and speech/language therapy consults be arranged to add important dimensions to his educational program.

- Finally, it is recommended that the parents be afforded the opportunity to become involved in parent support groups through the IU or cooperating agencies; this would help them to understand Derek in similar ways, to learn alternative ways of managing him at home, and to respond to him in a consistent way within the family. The individual emotional needs of both the father and the mother are also important in this context.

Appendix D

Prescriptive Linkages of Selected Scales with the HICOMP Preschool Curriculum

Prescriptive linkages of the following scales with the HICOMP Preschool Curriculum (1982) are detailed in Tables D-1, D-2, D-3, D-4, and D-5.

- Early Intervention Developmental Profile (EIDP)
- Learning Accomplishment Profile (LAP)
- Gesell Developmental Schedules (GDS)
- Bayley Scales of Infant Development (BSID)
- Uniform Performance Assessment System (UPAS)

Table D–1 HICOMP—EIDP Linkages

HICOMP	EIDP	HICOMP	EIDP	HICOMP	EIDP	HICOMP	EIDP	HICOMP	EIDP	HICOMP	EIDP
P4	1	—	53	C44	105	O52	157	—	209	M74	261
M33	2	P20	54	P48	106	—	158	M9	210	M72	262
M29	3	C20	55	—	107	O49	159	—	211	M50	263
M27	4	P20	56	O2	108	O51	160	—	212	M73	264
M28	5	—	57	O3	109	O72	161	—	213	M70	265
—	6	C20	58	O3	110	O116	162	—	214	M113	266
—	7	—	59	O3	111	O111	163	—	215	M107	267
M38	8	—	60	O3	112	O112	164	—	216	—	268
—	9	M64	61	C4	113	O118	165	—	217	M76	269
M39	10	—	62	O9	114	O120	166	—	218	M74	270
M34	11	C20	63	O8	115	—	167	M6	219	M77	271
M36	12	—	64	O11	116	O121	168	—	220	—	272
M37	13	M32	65	O4	117	—	169	—	221	—	273
—	14	P27	66	O3	118	—	170	—	222	M85	274
—	15	P16	67	O5	119	O120	171	—	223		
M40	16	P53	68	—	120	O70	172	—	224		
M38	17	C34	69	C4	121	O93	173	M10	225		
—	18	—	70	P17	122	—	174	M14	226		
M65	19	P111	71	O9	123	O98	175	M11	227		
M69	20	P88	72	O5	124	O98	176	M7	228		
M63	21	P1	73	O9	125	O136	177	M9	229		
—	22	C1	74	C10	126	O101	178	M9	230		
—	23	P1	75	C7	127	O124	179	M11	231		
M64	24	C3	76	M27	128	O65	180	M15	232		
M61	25	—	77	—	129	O141	181	—	233		
M65	26	—	78	C32	130	O95	182	M16	234		
M99	27	—	79	—	131	O124	183	M12	235		
M66	28	C5	80	O44	132	—	184	—	236		
M99	29	C6	81	—	133	O129	185	M9	237		
M69	30	P12	82	—	134	O124	186	M15	238		
M99	31	P12	83	O83	135	O95	187	—	239		
M93	32	C18	84	O31	136	O171	188	M16	240		
M99	33	C9	85	—	137	O166	189	M17	241		
M66	34	C23	86	O34	138	O162	190	—	242		
M69	35	C44	87	—	139	M1	191	M18	243		
M105	36	C36	88	—	140	M1	192	M19	244		
M93	37	C45	89	—	141	M2	193	M45	245		
—	38	C42	90	O78	142	—	194	—	246		
M66	39	P78	91	O51	143	—	195	M42	247		
M92	40	C40	92	—	144	—	196	—	248		
M100	41	C45	93	—	145	M1	197	M47	249		
M1	42	—	94	O48	146	—	198	M44	250		
M30	43	C45	95	O51	147	—	199	M47	251		
M38	44	C44	96	O52	148	M7	200	M46	252		
M33	45	—	97	O52	149	M6	201	—	253		
M38	46	C69	98	O49	150	M3	202	—	254		
—	47	C22	99	O61	151	M15	203	M43	255		
—	48	C49	100	O54	152	M5	204	M52	256		
—	49	C45	101	O53	153	—	205	—	257		
C7	50	C43	102	O50	154	—	206	M49	258		
C10	51	C45	103	O59	155	—	207	M48	259		
—	52	C43	104	O59	156	—	208	M51	260		

Table D–2 HICOMP–LAP Linkages

HICOMP	LAP	HICOMP	LAP	HICOMP	LAP	HICOMP	LAP	HICOMP	LAP	HICOMP	LAP	HICOMP	LAP
M29	FM1	—	FW11	—	CM24	—	LN19	M52	GB11	—	GO15	O185	SG5
M32	FM2	M92	FW12	—	CM25	—	LN20	M45	GB12	M112	GO16	O185	SG6
M33	FM3	M97	FW13	—	CM26	—	LN21	M43	GB13	—	GO17	O227	SG7
M37	FM4	M97	FW14	—	CM27	—	LN22	M43	GB14	—	GO18	M9	ST1
M34	FM5	—	FW15	—	CM28	—	LN23	M46	GB15	—	GO19	O77	ST2
M38	FM6	—	FW16	—	CC1	—	LN24	M51	GB16	M120	GO20	P40	ST3
M61	FM7	—	FW17	—	CC2	P116	LN25	M49	GB17	—	GO21	O166	ST4
M63	FM10	M139	FW18	P125	CC3	—	LN26	M70	GB18	M144	GO22	O135	ST5
M66	FM12	M160	FW19	P125	CC4	P161	LN27	M108	GB19	M146	GO23	O102	ST6
—	FM13	—	FW20	P124	CC5	P158.	LN28	M73	GB20	—	GO24	O205	ST7
M66	FM14	—	FW21	P125	CC6	C133	LN29	—	GB21	—	GO25	O128	ST8
—	FM15	M134	FW22	P125	CC7	C18	LC1	M75	GB22	—	GO26	O166	ST9
M66	FM16	—	FW23	—	CC8	C18	LC2	M48	GB23	M147	GO27	—	SS1
M99	FM17	M133	FW24	—	CC9	C19	LC3	—	GB24	—	GO28	O83	SS2
M66	FM18	—	FW25	P125	CC10	—	LC4	M74	GB25	—	GO29	O104	SS3
M129	FM19	—	FW26	—	CC11	C45	LC5	—	GB26	—	GO30	—	SS4
M96	FM20	—	FW27	—	CC12	—	LC6	—	GB27	—	GO31	M104	SS5
M102	FM21	M171	FW28	P165	CC13	C47	LC7	M85	GB28	O49	SE1	—	SS6
M95	FM22	M160	FW29	P166	CC14	—	LC8	—	GB29	O51	SE2		
M96	FM23	—	FW30	P116	CC15	—	LC9	—	GB30	O61	SE3		
M127	FM24	M166	FW31	P116	CC16	—	LC10	—	GB31	O59	SE4		
M128	FM25	M160	FW32	—	CC17	C78	LC11	—	GB32	O54	SE5		
—	FM26	—	FW33	—	CC18	—	LC12	M114	GB33	O111	SE6		
M99	FM27	M160	FW34	P154	CC19	C86	LC13	—	GB34	O116	SE7		
M100	FM28	—	FW35	P154	CC20	—	LC14	M142	GB35	O118	SE8		
M128	FM29	M159	FW36	—	CC21	C72	LC15	—	GB36	O124	SD1		
M95	FM30	M160	FW37	—	CC22	—	LC16	—	GB37	O124	SD2		
M103	FM31	—	CM1	—	CC23	—	LC17	M119	GB38	O123	SD3		
M127	FM32	M66	CM2	—	CC24	—	LC18	M141	GB39	O162	SD4		
M103	FM33	—	CM3	—	CC25	—	LC19	M151	GB40	O124	SD5		
—	FM34	—	CM4	—	CC26	—	LC20	M109	GB41	O162	SD6		
M165	FM35	—	CM5	—	CC27	P116	LC21	M116	GB42	O125	SD7		
—	FM36	P58	CM6	—	CC28	—	LC22	M145	GB43	O129	SD8		
—	FM37	M95	CM7	C15	LN1	P126	LC23	—	GB44	O168	SD9		
—	FM38	P53	CM8	C39	LN2	—	LC24	—	GB45	O207	SD10		
—	FM39	P84	CM9	C39	LN3	—	LC25	—	GB46	O207	SD11		
M162	FM40	P58	CM10	C39	LN4	P157	LC26	—	GB47	O207	SD12		
—	FM41	P111	CM11	C44	LN5	—	LC27	—	GB48	O207	SD13		
—	FM42	P58	CM12	C72	LN6	M5	GB1	M27	GO1	O206	SD14		
O209	FW1	M127	CM13	C72	LN7	M6	GB2	—	GO2	O206	SD15		
O246	FW2	M103	CM14	C75	LN8	—	GB3	—	GO3	O206	SD16		
M65	FW3	—	CM15	—	LN9	M12	GB4	M32	GO4	O241	SD17		
M65	FW4	P111	CM16	C75	LN10	M32	GB5	—	GO5	O247	SD18		
M65	FW5	M165	CM17	C102	LN11	—	GB6	M78	GO6	—	SD19		
M65	FW6	P113	CM18	C107	LN12	M18	GB7	—	GO7	O244	SD20		
M67	FW7	—	CM19	—	LN13	M16	GB8	—	GO8	O249	SD21		
M67	FW8	P116	CM20	—	LN14	M19	GB9	—	GO9	O246	SD22		
—	FW9	—	CM21	—	LN15	M41	GB10	—	GO10	O92	SD23		
M69	FW10	—	CM22	—	LN16			—	GO11	—	SG1		
		—	CM23	—	LN17			M50	GO12	—	SG2		
				—	LN18			M113	GO13	—	SG3		
								—	GO14	—	SG4		

Table D-3   HICOMP—GESELL Linkages

Age	Motor	Adaptive	Language	Personal-Social
2	M44 M49 M50 M66	M66 M67	C39 C48 C49 P55	O101 O71 O78 O120 O124 — O107
2½	M52 M96 M65	M96 — M67 M92 M94 — M99	C46 — —	— O83 — O127 O133
3	M70 M77 M114 M76 M74 M73 M79 —	— M95 M92 M97 M94 M99 M99 —	C81 — — — — — — —	O160 O163 O162 P132 O145 C80
3½	M108 M79 M118 M73 M109 —	M95 M97 M94 M94	C76 C71 — — —	O138 O134 — C100 O136 —

Age	Motor	Adaptive	Language	Personal-Social
4	M108 M74 M114 M119 M118	M103 M134 M139 M139	C76 C122	O206 O185 O206 O209 O211 O193 — —
4½	M109 M118 M120 —	M103 M134 M133 M139 M171 —	C71 C76 C122 —	C97 C91 —
5	M145 M141 M142 M154 —	— M166 M166 M171 P125 —	— — —	O246 O211 — O206 —

Table D-4 HICOMP—BAYLEY Linkages

HICOMP	Bayley Mental (Yellow)	HICOMP	Bayley Mental (Yellow)	HICOMP	Bayley Mental (Yellow)	HICOMP	Bayley Mental (Yellow)	HICOMP	Bayley Motor (Blue)	HICOMP	Bayley Motor (Blue)
C15	1	P4	52	P12	104	—	155	—	1	M46	53
O10	2	O5	53	—	105	M105	156	—	2	M46	54
P1	3	M32	54	C24	106	P115	157	—	3	M72	55
C15	4	C11	55	M36	107	—	158	—	4	—	56
P4	5	M34	56	M36	108	—	159	—	5	—	57
P3	6	—	57	M64	109	M66	160	—	6	M77	58
P8	7	O12	58	—	110	P116	161	—	7	M51	59
P4	8	M32	59	M61	111	P115	162	M1	8	M52	60
C29	9	O39	60	M65	112	—	163	M10	9	M75	61
P4	10	C4	61	C39	113			—	10	M72	62
P5	11	P1	62	M68	114			M4	11	M73	63
—	12	M39	63	—	115			M2	12	M49	64
C1	13	O5	64	C36	116			M2	13	M70	65
—	14	M35	65	C31	117			—	14	M49	66
—	15	P21	66	—	118			M27	15	—	67
—	16	P21	67	M66	119			M6	16	—	68
O4	17	M34	68	—	120			M3	17	—	69
O3	18	M37	69	—	121			—	18	M74	70
P4	19	M33	70	—	122			M6	19	M70	71
—	20	C3	71	C39	123			M32	20	M107	72
C2	21	—	72	M67	124			M3	21	M75	73
C19	22	P4	73	P42	125			M9	22	M118	74
—	23	P1	74	P63	126			M30	23	M79	75
—	24	O5	75	P42	127			M36	24	—	76
—	25	M34	76	—	128			—	25	—	77
C11	26	M33	77	P55	129			M9	26	M108	78
C11	27	C3	78	C47	130			M5	27	M117	79
C12	28	M31	79	C45	131			M9	28	M119	80
P5	29	C10	80	P57	132			M36	29	—	81
C2	30	—	81	—	133			M9	30		
C2	31	P12	82	M69	134			M37	31		
O9	32T	C17	83	C44	135			M7	32		
O4	33	C14	84	—	136			M7	33		
O9	34	P20	85	C39	137			M36	34		
O4	35	M40	86	C45	138			M9	35		
C19	36	M39	87	—	139			M15	36		
M27	37	C18	88	C43	140			M35	37		
M30	38T	C21	89	—	141			M16	38		
P4	39	P20	90	M66	142			—	39		
M28	40T	P11	91	C45	143			M17	40		
M30	41T	C30	92	—	144			—	41		
P4	42	O13	93	—	145			M35	42		
O12	43T	—	94	C78	146			M18	43		
—	44	P50	95	M67	147			M19	44		
M28	45	C7	96	M86	148			—	45		
M30	46	M65	97	C86	149			M47	46		
C15	47	M62	98	C86	150			M47	47		
C15	48	C3	99	C86	151			—	48		
M29	49	P20	100	—	152			—	49		
—	50	M63	101	—	153			M52	50		
M27	51	—	102	—	154			M52	51		
		—	103					—	52		

Table D-5　HICOMP—UPAS Linkages

HICOMP	UPAS
—	PA 1
0-3	PA 2
0-4	PA 3
M31	PA 4
M27	PA 5
M29	PA 6
M37	PA 7
M39	PA 8
M38	PA 9
M66	PA 10
—	PA 11
M99	PA 12
M63	PA 13
M102	PA 14
—	PA 15
M100	PA 16
M130	PA 17
M95	PA 18
M99	PA 19
M134	PA 20
M139	PA 21
C62	PA 22
P162	PA 23
P142	PA 24
P121	PA 25
—	PA 26
—	PA 27
M165	PA 28
M165	PA 29
M65	PA 30
—	PA 31
—	PA 32
M92	PA 33
M97	PA 34
—	PA 35
M134	PA 36
—	PA 37
M171	PA 38
—	PA 39
—	PA 40
—	PA 41
—	PA 42
P58	PA 43
P53	PA 44
P58	PA 45
P159	PA 46
P53	PA 47
	PA 48
	PA 49
	PA 50

HICOMP	UPAS
—	PA 51
P84	PA 52
—	PA 53
P106	PA 54
P111	PA 55
—	PA 56
—	PA 57
—	PA 58
—	PA 59
—	PA 60
—	PA 61
—	PA 62
C133	PA 63
P124	PA 64
—	PA 65
—	PA 66
P165	PA 67
P116	PA 68
—	PA 69
—	PA 70
—	PA 71
—	PA 72
—	PA 73
—	PA 74
—	PA 75
—	PA 76
C5	C 1
C11	C 2
C15	C 3
C18	C 4
C20	C 5
C18	C 6
C18	C 7
—	C 8
C20	C 9
—	C 10
C18	C 11
—	C 12
C105	C 13
C105	C 14
C105	C 15
C105	C 16
C105	C 17
C78	C 18
C78	C 19
—	C 20
C130	C 21
	C 22
	C 23
	C 24

HICOMP	UPAS
—	C 25
—	C 26
C131	C 27
C131	C 28
C131	C 28a
C131	C 28b
C131	C 28c
C2	C 28d
C1	C 29
C2	C 30
C23	C 31
C8	C 32
C23	C 33
C23	C 34
C23	C 35
—	C 36
—	C 37
C25	C 38
C39	C 39
C40	C 40
—	C 41
—	C 42
C43	C 43
C44	C 44
C54	C 45
—	C 46
C49	C 47
C43	C 48
C48	C 49
C72	C 50
C74	C 51
C84	C 52
C97	C 53
C81	C 54
—	C 55
—	C 56
C106	C 57
C98	C 58
C97	C 59
C109	C 60
C128	C 61
—	C 62
C122	C 63
C122	C 64
C107	C 65
—	C 66
C122	C 67
C122	C 68
—	C 69

HICOMP	UPAS
O46	S 1
O52	S 2
O61	S 3
O111	S 4
O114	S 5
O112	S 6
—	S 7
—	S 8
O231	S 9
O62	S 10
O124	S 11
O125	S 12
O166	S 13
O128	S 14
O167	S 15
O162	S 16
—	S 17
O206	S 18
O207	S 19
O207	S 20
—	S 21
O77	S 22
O102	S 23
O98	S 24
O136	S 25
O138	S 26
O138	S 27
O140	S 28
O141	S 29
O41	S 30
O78	S 31
—	S 32
O146	S 33
O145	S 34
—	S 35
—	S 36
C91	S 37
C93	S 38
O217	S 39
C106	S 40
C106	S 41
C106	S 42
C106	S 43
C93	S 44
M160	S 45
—	GM 1
M1	GM 2
M28	GM 3
—	GM 4
M6	GM 5

HICOMP	UPAS
M5	GM 6
—	GM 7
M3	GM 8
M8	GM 9
M9	GM 10
M10	GM 11
M12	GM 12
M15	GM 13
M16	GM 14
M12	GM 15
M15	GM 16
M15	GM 17
—	GM 18
M16	GM 19
M17	GM 20
M18	GM 21
M19	GM 22
M41	GM 23
—	GM 24
M10	GM 25
M48	GM 26
M41	GM 27
M84	GM 28
M47	GM 29
M70	GM 30
M85	GM 31
—	GM 32
M82	GM 33
M46	GM 34
M46	GM 35
M74	GM 36

HICOMP	UPAS
M74	GM 37
M51	GM 38
M73	GM 39
—	GM 40
M77	GM 41
M151	GM 42
—	GM 43
M71	GM 44
M118	GM 45
M154	GM 46
—	GM 47
M75	GM 48
M143	GM 49
—	GM 50
—	GM 51
M143	GM 52
M80	GM 53
M80	GM 54
—	GM 55
M76	GM 56
M111	GM 57
M148	GM 58
—	GM 59
M50	GM 60
—	GM 61
M78	GM 62
M113	GM 63
M112	GM 64
C62	GM 65
—	GM 66

Appendix E

An Alternative Prescriptive Linkages Form

An alternative prescriptive linkages form, based on the attainment of developmental stages, is presented in Exhibit E-1.

Exhibit E–1 Alternative Prescriptive Linkages Form

DEVELOPMENTAL INTERVENTION LINKAGES

CHILD _____ CA _____ DA _____

±	COGNITIVE PROCESS DA =	DEVELOPMENTAL TASK
	REPEATED SOUNDS & ACTIONS	
	MEANS-END RELATIONS	
	COMBINING ACTIONS	
	OBJECT PERMANENCE	
	SPATIALITY	
	CAUSALITY	
	IMITATION (SOUND-MOTOR)	
	OBJECT MANIPULATION & PLAY	
	FUNCTIONAL RELATIONSHIPS	
	REPRESENTATIONAL THOUGHT	
	FORM DISCRIMINATION	
	MATCHING (OBJECT-PICTURE)	
	NUMBER-SIZE-TIME RELATIONS	
	CLASSIFICATION & SORTING	
	SEQUENCING	
	AUDITORY-VISUAL MEMORY	
	SYMBOLIC THOUGHT	

±	SOCIAL PLAY PROCESS DA =	DEVELOPMENTAL TASK
	SELECTIVE ATTENTION	
	MANIPULATION & EXPLORATION	
	ATTACHMENT BEHAVIORS	
	DIFFERENTIATES SELF-OTHERS	
	RELATIONAL OBJECT PLAY	
	FUNCTIONAL OBJECT PLAY	
	SYMBOLIC OBJECT PLAY	
	ISOLATE PLAY	
	PARALLEL PLAY	
	ASSOCIATIVE PLAY	
	COOPERATIVE PLAY	

Exhibit E–1 continued

DEVELOPMENTAL INTERVENTION LINKAGES

CHILD _____ CA _____ DA _____

±	PERCEPTUAL-MOTOR PROCESS DA =	DEVELOPMENTAL TASK
	VISUAL FOCUSING	
	VISUAL TRACKING	
	DIRECTED REACHING (VISUAL & AUDITORY)	
	HAND MIDLINE SKILLS	
	GRASPING	
	TRANSFER	
	PREHENSION	
	CONSTRUCTION	
	TRACING	
	DRAWING	
	WRITING	

±	LANGUAGE PROCESS DA =	DEVELOPMENTAL TASK
	ORIENTATION & LOCALIZATION	
	SELECTIVE ATTENTION	
	ELICITED SOUNDS	
	IMITATION (SOUND-MOTOR)	
	DIRECTION FOLLOWING	
	OBJECT IDENTIFICATION	
	OBJECT NAMING	
	PICTURE IDENTIFICATION	
	PICTURE NAMING	
	TWO WORD FORMS	
	SVO FORM	
	AGENT-ACTION RELATIONS	
	SVO & MODIFIERS	
	REFINED STRUCTURES	

COMMENTS:

Appendix F

Curricular Assessment Forms for:

LINK: A Developmental Assessment/Curriculum Linkage System for Special-Needs Preschoolers

Stephen J. Bagnato ◆ John T. Neisworth

Name: _____

Address: _____

_____

Affiliation: _____

_____

City/State: _____

Zip: _____

Phone: (   ) _____

Pack of 25 LINK forms (4-phase foldout) $18.75

- Phase 1.0: Screening—Personal Data Form
- Phase 2.0: Prescriptive Assessment— Early Intervention Progress Profile
- Phase 2.1: Curriculum Linkage—Prescriptive Linkages
- Phase 3.0: Intervention— Early Childhood Program Prescriptions

Tablet of 50 Phase 4.0: Program Evaluation Forms . . . . $ 4.50
Postage and Handling . . . . $ 5.25
Total Cost $28.50

Send personal check, money order, or agency purchase form to:
     Developmental Innovations
     Julian Woods
     Julian, PA 16844

For additional information, phone Stephen J. Bagnato, Ed.D., (412) 692-5560

Note: Rates are subject to change with increases in the cost of paper, printing, and postage.

Appendix G

Ordering Information To Obtain Relevant Products and Materials

The following products and materials offer practical solutions for assessment and intervention problems in early intervention. They are available from their publishers or authors. Place a check mark beside the product(s) on which you would like more information and an order form, complete the personal information section, and send to this address:

Stephen J. Bagnato, Ed.D.
Coordinator, Toddler/Preschool Program
Child Development Unit
Children's Hospital of Pittsburgh
3705 Fifth Avenue
Pittsburgh, PA 15213
(412) 692-5560

NAME: _____

ADDRESS: _____

_____

CITY/STATE: _____

ZIP: _____

PHONE: _____

_____ Bagnato, S.J., & Neisworth, J.T. (1989). *System to Plan Early Child-hood Services* (SPECS). Circle Pines, MN: American Guidance Service Publishers.

A team early-intervention decision-making system that synchronizes professional, parent, and paraprofessional assessment, treatment planning, and progress/program evaluation operations for handicapped preschool children and families.

_____ Bagnato, S.J., & Neisworth, J.T. (in press). *Developmental assessment: A guide for the preschool psychologist*. New York: Guilford Press.

A "how-to" guidebook for conducting intervention-based assessment for young exceptional children to meet the mandates of PL 99-457.

_____ Bagnato, S.J., & Neisworth, J.T. (in progress). *Diagnostic assessment reports for special-needs preschoolers:* A developmental alternative.

Sample case studies and three proven styles of assessment reports to facilitate effective communication of functional diagnostic data on infants and preschoolers with various handicaps.

_____ Capone, A., Neisworth, J.T., & Bagnato, S.J. (1988). *Developmental toys: A consumer's guide for teachers and parents*. Dubuque, IA: Kendall-Hunt Publishing Co.

A buyer's guide for evaluating and choosing toys for infants and preschoolers, ages birth to 6 years.

_____ Neisworth, J.T., & Bagnato, S.J. (1988). *The young exceptional child: Early development and education*. New York: Macmillan.

An introductory text in early childhood special education.

References

Abidin, R.R. (1983). *Parenting Stress Index*. Charlottesville, VA: Pediatric Psychology Press.

Adams, J. (1972). The contributions of the psychological evaluation to psychiatric diagnosis. *Journal of Personality Assessment, 36*, 561-566.

Alpern, G.D., Boll, T.J., & Shearer, M.S. (1984). *Developmental Profile II manual*. Los Angeles, CA: Western Psychological Services.

Ames, N., Gillespie, S., Haines, J., & Ilg, N. (1979). *Gesell Developmental Schedules*. Rosemont, NJ: Programs for Education, Inc.

Bagnato, S.J. (1980). The efficacy of diagnostic reports as individualized guides to prescriptive goal-planning. *Exceptional Children, 46*(4), 554-557.

Bagnato, S.J. (1981a). Developmental scales and developmental curricula: Forging a linkage for early intervention. *Topics in Early Childhood Education, 1*(2), 1-8.

Bagnato, S.J. (1981b). Developmental diagnostic reports: Reliable and effective alternatives to guide individualized intervention. *Journal of Special Education, 15*(1), 65-76.

Bagnato, S.J. (1984). Team congruence in developmental diagnosis and intervention: Comparing clinical judgment and child performance measures. *School Psychology Review, 13*, 7-16.

Bagnato, S.J. (1985). Critical review of the BRIGANCE BDIED (invited test review). In J.V. Mitchell, *Ninth mental measurements yearbook* (pp. 1109–1121). Buros Institute, Omaha, NE: University of Nebraska Press.

Bagnato, S.J., Kontos, S., & Neisworth, J.T. (1987). Integrated day care as special education: Profiles of programs and children. *Topics in Early Childhood Education, 7*(1), 28-47.

Bagnato, S.J., & Llewellyn, E. (1982). Developmental assessment/curriculum linkages. In S. Willoughby-Herb & J.T. Neisworth (Eds.), *HICOMP Preschool Curriculum*. San Antonio, TX: Psychological Corporation.

Bagnato, S.J., & Mayes, S.D. (1986). Patterns of developmental and behavioral progress for young brain-injured children during interdisciplinary intervention. *Developmental Neuropsychology, 2*(3), 213-240.

Bagnato, S.J., Mayes, S.D., & Nichter, C. (1988). An interdisciplinary neurodevelopmental assessment model for brain-injured infants and preschool children. *Journal of Head Trauma Rehabilitation, 3*(2), 75-86.

Bagnato, S.J., & Murphy, J.P. (1989). The validity of curriculum-based scales with young neurodevelopmentally disabled children: Implications for team assessment. *Early Education and Development, 1*(1), 19-29.

Bagnato, S.J., & Neisworth, J.T. (1979). Between assessment and intervention: Forging a linkage for the handicapped preschooler. *Child Care Quarterly, 8*(3), 179-195.

Bagnato, S.J., & Neisworth, J.T. (1980). Intervention Efficiency Index (IEI): An approach to preschool program accountability. *Exceptional Children, 46*(4), 264-269.

Bagnato, S.J., & Neisworth, J.T. (1981). *Linking developmental assessment and curricula: Prescriptions for early intervention.* Rockville, MD: Aspen Publishers, Inc.

Bagnato, S.J., & Neisworth, J.T. (1983). Monitoring developmental progress of young exceptional children: Curricular Efficiency Index (CEI). *Journal of Special Education, 17*(2), 189-193.

Bagnato, S.J., & Neisworth, J.T. (1985a). Efficacy of interdisciplinary assessment and treatment for infants and preschoolers with congenital and acquired brain injury. *Analysis and Intervention in Developmental Disabilities, 5*(1/2), 107-128.

Bagnato, S.J., & Neisworth, J.T. (1985b). Assessing young handicapped children: Clinical judgment versus developmental performance scales. *International Journal of Partial Hospitalization, 3*(1), 13-21.

Bagnato, S.J., & Neisworth, J.T. (1987). *Perceptions of Developmental Status: A system for planning early intervention.* University Park: Pennsylvania State University.

Bagnato, S.J., & Neisworth, J.T. (1989a). *Perceptions of Developmental Status (PODS).* Circle Pines, MN: American Guidance Service.

Bagnato, S.J., & Neisworth, J.T. (1989b). *System to Plan Early Childhood Services (SPECS).* Circle Pines, MN: American Guidance Service.

Bagnato, S.J., Neisworth, J.T., & Capone, A. (1987). Curriculum-based assessment for the young exceptional child: Rationale and review. *Topics in Early Childhood Special Education, 6*(2), 97-110.

Bagnato, S.J., Neisworth, J.T., & DeSaunier, D.M. (in press). *Report writing for the developmental school psychologist.* Julian, PA: Developmental Innovations.

Bagnato, S.J., Neisworth, J.T., & Eaves, R. (1977). *Perceptions of Developmental Skills.* University Park: Pennsylvania State University.

Bagnato, S.J., Neisworth, J.T., & Eaves, R. (1978). A profile of perceived capabilities for the preschool child. *Child Care Quarterly, 7*(4), 327-335.

Bagnato, S.J., Neisworth, J.T., Paget, K., & Kovaleski, J. (1987). The developmental school psychologist: Professional profile of an emerging early childhood specialist. *Topics in Early Childhood Special Education, 7*(3), 75-89.

Bailey, D.B., Clifford, R.M., & Harms, T. (1982). Comparison of preschool environments for handicapped and nonhandicapped children. *Topics in Early Childhood Special Education, 2*(1), 9–20.

Bailey, D.B., Jens, K.G., & Johnson, N. (1983). Curricula for handicapped infants. In S.G. Garwood & R.R. Fewell (Eds.), *Educating handicapped infants* (pp. 387-415). Rockville, MD: Aspen Publishers, Inc.

Bailey, D.B. & Simeonsson, R.J. (1985). *Family Needs Survey* (FNS). Chapel Hill, N.C.: Families Project, University of North Carolina.

Bailey, D.B., & Simeonsson, R.J. (1988). Assessing needs of families with handicapped infants. *Journal of Special Education, 22*(1), 117-127.

Bailey, D.B., & Simeonsson, R.J. (1988). *Family assessment in early intervention.* Columbus, OH: Charles E. Merrill Publishing Co.

Bailey, D.B., & Simeonsson, R.J. (in press). Assessing needs of families with handicapped infants. *Topics in Early Childhood Special Education.*

Bailey, D., Vandivieve, L., Dellinger, T.B., & Munn, G.A. (1987). The Battelle Developmental Inventory: Teacher perceptions and implementation data. *Journal of Psychoeducational Assessment, 3*, 217-226.

Bailey, D.B., & Woolery, M. (1984). *Teaching infants and preschoolers with handicaps*. Columbus, OH: Charles E. Merrill Publishing Co.

Bailey, E.J., & Bricker, D. (1985). Evaluation of a three-year early intervention demonstration project. *Topics in Early Childhood Special Education, 5,* 130-138.

Bayley, N. (1969). *Bayley Scales of Infant Development*. New York: Psychological Corporation.

Bell, R.Q. (1979). Parent, child, and reciprocal influences. *American Psychologist, 34,* 821-826.

Bell, R.Q., & Harper, L.V. (1977). *Child effects on adults*. Hillsdale, NJ: Lawrence Erlbaum.

Blacher-Dixon, J. & Simeonsson, R.J. (1981). Consistency and correspondence of mother's and teacher's assessments of young handicapped children. *Journal of the Division for Early Childhood, 3,* 64-71.

Bloom, B.S. (Ed.) (1956). *Taxonomy of educational objectives: The classification of educational goals*. New York: Longsman, Green.

Boehm, A.M., & Slater, B.S. (1974). *Cognitive Skills Assessment Battery*. New York: Columbia University, Teachers College Press.

Bracken, B.A. (1984). *Bracken Basic Concept Scale*. San Antonio, TX: Psychological Corporation.

Bracken, B.A. (1987). Limitations of preschool instruments and standards for minimal levels of technical adequacy. *Journal of Psychoeducational Assessment, 4,* 313-326.

Bradley-Johnson, C. (1986). *Cognitive Abilities Scale*. Austin, TX: PRO-ED.

Brazelton, T.B. (1973). *Neonatal Behavioral Assessment Scale*. London, England: Spastics International Medical Publications.

Brazelton, T.B. (1982). Assessment as a method for enhancing infant development. *Zero to Three, 2*(1), 1-8.

Brazelton, T.B. (1984). *Brazelton neonatal behavior assessment scale—Revised*. London, England: Spastics International Medical Publications.

Bricker, D.D. (1987). *Early intervention with at-risk and handicapped infants*. Glenview, IL: Scott-Foresman & Co.

Bricker, D.D. (in press). *Evaluation and programming for infants and young children*. Eugene, OR: Human Development, University of Oregon.

Bricker, D.D., Bailey, E.J., Gunnerlock, G., Buhl, M., & Slentz, K. (in press). *Evaluation and programming for infants and young children*. Eugene, OR: University of Oregon, Special Education and Human Development.

Bricker, D.D., & Dow, M. (1980). Early intervention with the young severely handicapped child. *Journal of the Association for the Severely Handicapped, 5*(2), 66-77.

Bricker, D.D., Sheehan, R., & Littman, D. (1981). *Early intervention: A plan for evaluating program impact* (WESTAR Series Paper No. 10). Eugene, OR: WESTAR.

Brigance, A.H. (1978). *BRIGANCE diagnostic inventory of early development*. North Billerica, MA: Curriculum Associates.

Brigance, A.H. (1985). *BRIGANCE prescriptive readiness: Strategies and practice*. North Billerica, MA: Curriculum Associates.

Brinker, R.P., & Lewis, M. (1982). Discovering the competent infant: A process approach to assessment and intervention. *Topics in Early Childhood Special Education, 2*(2), 1-16.

Bromwich, A.J. (1981). *Working with parents and infants: An interactional approach*. Baltimore: University Park Press.

Bromwich, R. (1978). *Working with parents and infants*. Austin, TX: PRO-ED.

Brooks-Gunn, J., & Lewis, M. (1981). Assessing young handicapped children: Issues and solutions. *Journal of the Division for Early Childhood, 8*(4), 84-95.

Brooks-Gunn, J., & Lewis, M. (1982). Affective exchanges between normal and handicapped infants and their mothers. In T.M. Fields & A. Fogel (Eds.), *Emotion and early interaction* (pp. 161-188). Hillsdale, NJ: Lawrence Earlbaum.

Brown, D., Simmons, V., & Mehtvin, J. (1979). *Oregon project curriculum for visually impaired and blind preschoolers.* Medford, OR: Jackson County Education Service District.

Brown, L., Nietupski, J., & Hamre-Nietupski, S. (1976). Criterion of ultimate functioning. In M.A. Thomas (Ed.), *Hey don't you forget about me!* (pp. 37-45). Reston, VA: Council for Exceptional Children.

Brown, S., & Donovan, C.M. (1985). *Developmental programming for infants and young children.* Ann Arbor: University of Michigan Press.

Caldwell, B. & Bradley, R. (1978). *Home Observations for Measurement of the Environment.* Little Rock, AR: University of Arkansas, Human Development.

Campbell, D.T., & Fiske, D.W. (1959). Convergent and discriminant validation by the multitrait-multimethod matrix. *Psychological Bulletin, 56,* 81-105.

Campbell, S.Z., Seigel, E., Parr, C.A., & Ramey, C.T. (1986). Evidence for the need to renorm the BSID. *Topics in Early Childhood Special Education, 6(2),* 83-96.

Capone, A., Neisworth, J.T., Bagnato, S.J., & Neisworth, R. (1988). *Developmental toys: A guide for parents and teachers.* Dubuque, IA: Kendall-Hunt.

Carey, W.B. (1985). Clinical use of temperament data in pediatrics. *Journal of Developmental and Behavioral Pediatrics, 6(3),* 137-142.

Carey, McDevitt, & Fullard (1975). *Behavioral Style Questionnaire.* Media, PA: W.B. Carey.

Carey, McDevitt, & Fullard (1977). *Infant Temperament Scale.* Media, PA: W.B. Carey.

Carey, McDevitt, & Fullard (1978). *Toddler Temperament Scale.* Media, PA: W.B. Carey.

Chinn, P.C., Drew, D.J., & Logan, D.R. (1975). *Mental retardation: A life cycle approach.* St. Louis, MO: C.V. Mosby Co.

Cole, K.N., Swisher, M.V., Thompson, M.D., & Fewell, R.R. (1985). Enhancing sensitivity of assessment instruments for children: Graded multidimensional scoring. *Journal of the Association for Persons with Severe Handicaps, 10(4),* 209-213.

Cronbach, L.J., & Gleser, G.C. (1965). *Psychological tests and personnel decisions* (2nd ed). Urbana: University of Illinois Press.

Devenney, S. (1983). Curriculum and effective instruction: Challenges for early childhood special educators. *Topics in Early Childhood Special Education, 2(4),* 67-83.

Diebold, T. (1978). Developmental scales versus observational measures for deaf-blind children. *Exceptional Children, 44(4),* 275-279.

Dubose, R.F., & Langley, M.B. (1982). *Developmental Activities Screening Inventory II* (revised). New York: Teaching Resources.

Duffy, J., & Fedner, M. (1977). Educational diagnosis with instructional use. *Exceptional Children, 44,* 246-251.

Dunst, C.J. (1980). *Uzgiris and Hunt Scales of Infant Psychological Development: Dunst's clinical and educational manual.* Austin, TX: PRO-ED.

Dunst, C.J. (1981). *Infant learning a cognitive-linguistic intervention strategy.* Austin, TX: PRO-ED.

Dunst, C.J. (1985). Rethinking early intervention. *Analysis and Intervention in Developmental Disabilities, 5,* 165-201.

Dunst, C.J. (1986). *Parent and child scale.* Unpublished scale. Family, Infant, and Preschool Program, Western Carolina Center, Morganton, NC.

Dunst, C.J., Brassell, R.R., & Rheingrover, R.M. (1981). Structural and organizational features of sensorimotor intelligence among retarded infants and toddlers. *British Journal of Educational Psychology, 51,* 133-143.

Dunst, C.J., Jenkins, V., & Trivette, C.M. (1984). Family support scale: Reliability and validity. *Journal of Individual, Family, and Community Wellness, 1*(4), 45-52.

Dunst, C.J., & Rheingrover, R.M. (1981). Analysis of the efficacy of infant intervention programs for handicapped children. *Evaluation and Program Planning, 4,* 287-323.

Dunst, C.J., & Rheingrover, R.M. (1983). Structural characteristics of sensorimotor development among Downs Syndrome infants. *Journal of Mental Deficiency Research, 27,* 11-22.

Dunst, C.J., & Trivette, C.M. (in press). Helping, helplessness and harm. In J. Witt, L.S. Elliot, & F. Gresham (Eds.), *Handbook of behavior therapy in education.* New York: Plenum Press.

Dunst, C.J., Trivette, C.M., McWilliams, R.A., & Galant, K. (in press). Toward experimental evaluations of the family, infant, and preschool programs. In H. Weiss & F. Jacob (Eds.), *Evaluating family programs.* New York: Aldine.

Feiring, L. (1985). Review of the Kent Infant Development Scale. In J.V. Mitchell (Ed.), *Ninth mental measurements yearbook* (Vol. 1) (pp. 786–787). Buros Institute, Omaha, NE: University of Nebraska Press.

Fewell, R.R. (1981). Assessment of severely impaired young children: Problems and recommendations. *Topics in Early Childhood Special Education, 1*(2), 9-21.

Fewell, R.R. (1986). Some new directions in the assessment and education of young handicapped children. In J.M. Berg (Ed.), *Science and service in mental retardation* (pp. 179-188). London: Methuen.

Fewell, R.R. (1987). *Play Assessment Scale.* Seattle, WA: University of Washington.

Fewell, R.R., & Langley, B. (1984). *Developmental Activities Screening Inventory II.* Austin, TX: PRO-ED.

Fewell, R.R., & Rich, J.S. (1987). Play assessment as a procedure for examining cognitive, communication, and social skills in multihandicapped children. *Journal of Psychoeducational Assessment, 5,* 107-118.

Fewell, R.R., & Sandal, S. (1987). Seattle early learning inventory assessment. Seattle, WA: Specialty Software.

Field, T.M., Sostek, A.M., Goldberg, S., & Shuman, H.H. (Eds.) (1979). *Infants born at risk.* New York: Spectrum Publications.

Fraiberg, S., Siegal, B., & Gibson, R. (1966). The role of sound in the search behavior of a blind infant. *Psychoanalytic Study of a Child, 71,* 327-357.

French, J.L. (1964). *Pictorial Test of Intelligence,* Chicago, IL: Riverside Publishing Co.

Furuno, S., O'Reilly, A., Hosaka, C.M., Inatsuda, T.T., Allman, T.L., & Zeisloft, B. (1979). *Hawaii early learning profile.* Palo Alto, CA: VORT Corp.

Garwood, _._., Fewell, R.R., & Neisworth, J. (1988). (1987). Public law 94-142: You can get there from here! *Topics in Early Childhood Education, 8*(11), 1-11.

Gesell, A. (1923). *The preschool child: From the standpoint of public hygiene and education.* Boston: Houghton Mifflin.

Gesell, A. (1949). *Gesell Developmental Schedules.* New York: Psychological Corporation.

Glover, E.M., Preminger, J., & Sanford, A. (1979). *The early learning accomplishment profile.* Lewisville, NC: Kaplan School Supply.

Green, M., & Straugh, T. (1979). *Final evaluation report—Oregon project for visually impaired and blind preschool children.* Portland, OR: Northwest Regional Education Laboratory.

Griffith, R. (1970). *Griffiths Mental Development Scale.* England: The Test Agency.

Guidubaldi, J., Newborg, J., Stock, J.R., & Wnek, L. (1984). *Battelle developmental inventory.* Allen, TX: DLM/Teaching Resources.

Haeussermann, E. (1958). *Developmental potential of preschool children: An evaluation in intellectual, sensory and emotional functioning.* New York: Grune & Stratton.

Haessermann, E., Jedrysek, E., Pope, E., & Wortis, J. (1972). *Haessermann Educational Evaluation: Psychoeducational evaluation of the preschool child*. New York: Grune & Stratton. (Original work published 1958.)

Haley, S.M. (1989). Functional assessment in young children with neurological impairments. *Topics in Early Childhood Special Education*.

Hanna, R.P., Lippert, E.A., & Harris, A.B. (1982). *Developmental communication curriculum*. Columbus, OH: Charles E. Merrill Publishing Co.

Hanson, M.J. (1984). (Ed.). *Atypical infant development*. Austin, TX: PRO-ED.

Hanson, M.J. (1985). Analysis of the effects of early intervention services for infants and toddlers with moderate to severe handicaps. *Topics in Early Childhood Special Education, 5*(2), 36-51.

Haring, N.G., White, D.R., Edgar, E.B., Affleck, J.Q., & Hayden, A.H. (1981). *Uniform Performance Assessment System*. San Antonio, TX: Psychological Corporation.

Harms, T., & Clifford, R. (1980). *Early Childhood Environment Rating Scale*. Columbia University: Teachers College Press.

Harris, S.L., & Fagley, N.S. (1987). The Developmental Profile as a predictor of status for autistic children: Four to seven year follow-up. *School Psychology Review, 16*(1), 89-93.

Havinghurst, R.J. (1956, May). Research on the developmental task concept. *School Review*, pp. 215-223.

Hayes, S.C., Nelson, R.O., & Jarrett, R.B. (1987). The treatment utility of assessment: A functional approach to evaluating assessment quality. *American Psychologist, 42*. 963-974.

Hedrick, D.L., Prather, E.M., & Tobin, A.R. (1975). *Sequenced Inventory of Communication Development*. Seattle: University of Washington Press.

Hindley, C.B. (1965). The GMDS. In O. Buros (Ed.), *The Sixth Mental Measurements Yearbook* (pp. 523-524). Highland Park, N.J.: Gryphon Press.

Hiskey, M. (1966) *Hiskey-Nebraska Test of Learning Aptitude*. Lincoln, NE: Author.

Hoffman, H. (1982). *Bayley Scales of Infant Development: Modifications for youngsters with handicapping conditions* (revised). Commack, NY: Suffolk Rehabilitation Center, United Cerebral Palsy.

Hoyson, M., Jamieson, B., & Strain, P.S. (1984). Individualized group instruction of normally developing and autistic-like children: The LEAP curriculum model. *Journal of the Division for Early Childhood, 8*(2), 157-172.

Ireton, H., & Thwing, E. (1979). *Minnesota Child Development Inventory*. Minneapolis, MN: Behavior Systems.

Irwin, J.V., & Wong, S.P. (1974). Compensation of maturity in long-range intervention studies. *Acta Symbolica, 5*(4), 33-45.

Jedrysek, E., Klapper, Z., Pope, L., & Wortis, J. (1972). *Psychoeducational evaluation of the preschool child*. New York: Grune & Stratton.

Jellnek, J.A. (1985). Documentation of child progress revisited: An analysis method for outreach or local programs: *Journal of Division for Early Childhood, 9*(2), 175-182.

Jennings, K.S., Connors, R.E., Stegman, C.E., Sankaranarayan, P., & Mendelsohn, S. (1985). Mastery motivation in young preschoolers: Effect of a physical handicap and implications for educational programming. *Journal of the Division for Early Childhood, 9*(2), 162-169.

Johnson & Johnson Baby Products, Inc. (1982). *Child development products*. Lawrenceville, NJ: Johnson & Johnson Baby Products, Inc.

Johnson, L.J., & Beauchamp, K.D. (1987). Preschool assessment measures: What are teachers using? *Journal of the Division for Early Childhood, 12*(1), 70-76.

Johnson-Martin, N., Jens, K.G., & Attermeir, S. (1986). *The Carolina curriculum for handicapped infants and infants at risk*. Baltimore: Paul H. Brookes.

Jordan, J.B., Hayden, A.H., Karnes, M.B., & Wood, M.N. (1977). *Early childhood education for exceptional children*. Reston, VA: Council for Exceptional Children.

Kanor, S. (1988). *Toys for special children* (revised). Hastings-on-Hudson, NY: Author

Karnes, M.B. (1981). *Small wonder*. Circle Pines, MN: American Guidance Service.

Kearsley, R.B. (1981). Cognitive assessment of the handicapped infant: The need for an alternative approach. *American Journal of Orthopsychiatry, 51*(1), 43-54.

Kiernan, D.W., & Dubose, R.F. (1974). Assessing the cognitive development of preschool deaf-blind children. *Education of the Visually Handicapped, 6*(4), 103-105.

Knobloch, H., & Pasamanick, B. (1974). *Developmental diagnosis*. New York: Harper & Row.

Knobloch, H., Stevens, F., & Malone, A.F. (1980). *Gesell Developmental Schedules: Manual of developmental diagnosis* (rev. ed.). New York: Harper & Row.

Korchin, S.J., & Schuldberg, D. (1981). The future of clinical assessment. *American Psychologist, 36*, 1147-1158.

Krug, D.P., Arick, A.G., & Almond, P. (1980). *Autism Screening Instrument for Educational Planning (ASIEP)*. Austin, TX: PRO-ED.

Langley, B. (1980). *The teachable moment and the handicapped infant*. Reston, VA: Council for Exceptional Children.

Langley, M.B. (1985). Selecting, adapting, and applying toys as learning tools for handicapped children. *Topics in Early Childhood Special Education, 5*(3), 101-118.

Leijon, E.A. (1982). Assessment of behavior on the Brazelton scale in healthy preterm infants from 32 conceptional weeks until full-term age. *Early Human Development, 7*, 109-118.

LeLaurin, K. (1985). The experimental analysis of the effects of early intervention with normal, at-risk, and handicapped children under three. *Analysis and Intervention in Developmental Disabilities, 5*, 129-150.

LeMay, D., Griffin, G., & Sanford, A. (1981). *Learning Accomplishment Profile-Diagnostic Edition (LAP-D)*. Winston-Salem, NC: Kaplan School Supply.

Lowe, M., & Costello, A.J. (1976). *Symbolic Play Test*. Windsor, Berks, England: NFER Publishing.

MacTurk, R.H., & Neisworth, J.T. (1978). Norm- and criterion-based measures with handicapped and nonhandicapped preschoolers. *Exceptional Children, 45*(1), 34-39.

Mahoney, G.J., & Powell, A. (1986). *The transactional intervention program: Teacher's guide*. Farmington, CT: Pediatric Research and Training Center, University of Connecticut Health Center.

Massie, H.N., & Campbell, B.K. (1983). M-C Scale of Mother-Infant Attachment Indicators During Stress. In J.D. Call, E. Galenson, & R.L. Tyson (Eds.), *Frontiers of infant psychiatry* (pp. 394-412). New York: Basic Books.

Maxfield, K.E., & Bucchholz, S. (1957). *Maxfield-Bucchholz Social Maturity Scale*. Louisville, KY: American Printing House for the Blind.

McCarthy, D. (1972). *McCarthy Scales of Children's Ability*. San Antonio, TX: Psychological Corporation.

McCarthy, D. (1972). *McCarthy Scales of Children's Ability Manual*. Cleveland, OH: Psychological Corporation.

McGrew, K. (1986). *Clinical interpretation of the WJ Tests of Cognitive Ability*. Orlando, FL: Grune & Stratton.

McLean, M.A., McCormick, P.A., Bruder, M.B., & Burdg, L.D. (1987). An investigation of the validity and reliability of the Battelle with a population of children younger than 30 months with identified handicapping conditions. *Journal of the Division for Early Childhood, 11*(3), 238-246.

McReynolds, P. (1985). Psychological assessment and clinical practice: Problems and prospects. In J.N. Butcher & C.D. Spielberger (Eds.), *Advances in personality assessment* (Vol. 4, pp. 1-30). Hillsdale, NJ: Lawrence Erlbaum.

Meehl, P.E. (1959). Some ruminations on the validation of clinical procedures. *Canadian Journal of Psychology, 13,* 102-128.

Meier, J. (1976). Screening, assessment, and intervention for young children at developmental risk. In N. Hobbs (Ed.), *Issues in the classification of children* (Vol. 2). San Francisco: Jossey-Bass, Inc.

Mittler, P. (Ed.) (1981). *Frontiers of knowledge in mental retardation* (Vol. 1, pp. 293–301). Baltimore, MD: University Park Press.

Moersch, M., & Schafer, D.S., (1981). *Developmental Programming for Infants and Young Children.* Ann Arbor, MI: University of Michigan Press.

Moog, J.S., & Geers, A.V. (1975). *Scales of Early Communication Skills for Hearing Impaired Children.* St. Louis: Central Institute for the Deaf.

Mori, A.A., & Neisworth, J.T. (1983). Curricula in early childhood education: Some generic and special considerations. *Topics in Early Childhood Special Education, 2*(4), 1-8.

Mott, S.E., Fewell, R.R., Lewis, M., Meisels, S.J., Shonkoff, J.P., & Simeonsson, R.J. (1986). Methods for assessing child and family outcomes in early childhood special education programs: Some views from the field. *Topics in Early Childhood Special Education, 6*(2), 1-15.

Naglieri, J.A. (1980). Comparison of McCarthy General Cognitive Index and WISC-R IQ for educable mentally retarded, learning disabled, and normal children. *Psychological Reports, 47,* 591-596.

Naglieri, J.A. (1981). Extrapolated developmental indices for the Bayley. *American Journal of Mental Deficiency, 85*(5), 548-550.

Naglieri, J.A. (1985). Normal children's performance on the McCarthy Scales, Kaufman Assessment Battery, and Peabody Individual Achievement Test. *Journal of Psychoeducational Assessment, 3,* 123-129.

NASP/APA Special Interest Preschool Group. (1987). Preschool practices, problems, and issues. *Preschool Interests, 2*(3), 1-11.

Neisworth, J.T. (Ed.) (1982). *Assessment in special education.* Rockville, MD: Aspen Publishers, Inc.

Neisworth, J.T., & Bagnato, S.J. (1986). Curriculum-based developmental assessment: Congruence of testing and teaching. *School Psychology Review, 15*(2), 180-199.

Neisworth, J.T., & Bagnato, S.J. (1988). Assessment in early childhood special education: A typology of dependent measures. In S.L. Odom & M.B. Karnes (Eds.), *Early intervention for infants and children with handicaps.* Baltimore, MD: Paul H. Brookes.

Neisworth, J.T., & Madle, R.A. (1975). Normalized care: A philosophy and approach to integrate exceptional and normal children. *Child Care Quarterly, 4*(3), 93-104.

Newborg, J., Stock, J., Wnek, L., Guildubaldi, J., & Svinicki, J.S. (1984). *Battelle developmental inventory (BDI).* Allen, TX: DLM/Teaching Resources.

Oelwein, P.L., Fewell, R.R., & Pruess, J.B. (1985). The efficacy of intervention at outreach sites of the program for children with Down syndrome and other developmental delays. *Topics in Early Childhood Special Education, 5*(2), 78-87.

Peters, D.L., Neisworth, J.T., & Yawkey, T.D. (1986). *Early childhood education: From theory to practice.* Monterey, CA: Brookes/Cole.

Piaget, J. (1952). *The origins of intelligence in children.* New York: International Universities Press.

Prus, J.S., & Prus, A.S. (1988). *Early Childhood Assessment: Developmentally-based Psychological Reports,* paper presented at NASP Conference, Chicago, IL.

Ramsay, C., & Fitzhardinge, P.M. (1977). A comparative study of two developmental scales: The Bayley and the Griffiths. *Early Human Development, 1*(2), 151–157.

Reiber, J.L., & Embry, L.H. (1983). Working and communicating with parents. In E.M. Goetz & K.E. Allen (Eds.), *Early childhood education: Special environmental, policy and legal considerations* (pp. 153-184). Rockville, MD: Aspen Publishers, Inc.

Reuter, J. (1982). *Kent Scoring Adaptations for the Bayley Scales of Infant Development*. Kent, OH: Developmental Metrics.

Reuter, J., & Bickett, L. (1985). *Kent infant development scale* (2nd ed.). Kent, OH: Developmental Metrics.

Reynell, J., & Zinkin, K. (1975). New procedures for the developmental assessment of young children with severe visual handicaps. *Child Care, Health and Development, 1,* 61-69.

Reynell, J., & Zinkin, K. (1979). *Reynell-Zinkin scales: Developmental scales for young visually handicapped.* Chicago: Stoelting.

Robinson, C., & Rosenberg, S. (1985). Teaching Skills Inventory. Omaha, NE: University of Nebraska.

Rosenberg, S., & Robinson, C. (1984). Teaching Skills Inventory: A measure of parent performance. *Journal of the Division for Early Childhood, 8*(2), 107-113.

Safford, P.L. (1978). *Teaching young children with special needs*. St. Louis: C.V. Mosby Co.

Salvia, J., & Ysseldyke, J.E. (1978). *Assessment in special and remedial education*. Boston: Houghton Mifflin.

Salvia, J., & Ysseldyke, J.E. (1987). *Assessment in special and remedial education* (3rd ed.). Boston: Houghton Mifflin.

Sameroff, A.J., & Chandler, M. (1975). Reproductive risk and the continuum of caretaking casualty. In F.D. Horowitz, M. Hetherington, S. Scarr-Salapatek, & G. Siegel (Eds.), *Review of child development research* (Vol. 4). Chicago: University of Chicago Press.

Sanford, A. (1978). *Learning Accomplishment Profile*. Lewisville, NC: Kaplan School Supply.

Sattler, J.M. (1982). *Assessment of children's intelligence and special abilities* (2nd ed.). Boston: Allyn & Bacon.

Sawyer, R.N. (1974). A factor analytic study of the PTI. *Journal of Educational and Psychological Measurement, 39,* 613-623.

Schafer, D.S., & Moersch, M. (1981). *Developmental programming for infants and young children*. Ann Arbor: University of Michigan Press.

Schakel, J.A. (1987, August). *Supporting paper for position statement on early intervention services in the schools*. Paper presented at the meeting of the National Association of School Psychologists, Washington, D.C.

Schlater, A. (1987). *Seattle inventory of early learning software*. Seattle: Specialty Software.

Schopler, E., & Reichler, R. (1979). *Individualized assessment and treatment for autistic and developmentally disabled children*. Austin, TX: PRO-ED.

Sexton, D., Hall, J., & Thomas, J.P. (1984). Multisource assessment of young handicapped children: A comparison. *Exceptional Children, 50,* 556-558.

Sexton, D., Hall, J., & Thomas, J.D. (1984b). Correlates of parent-professional congruency scores in the assessment of young handicapped children. *Journal of the Division for Early Childhood, 8*(2), 99-106.

Shearer, D.E., Billingsley, J., Froham, A., Hilliard, J., Johnson, F., & Shearer, M. (1976). *Portage guide to early education* (rev. ed.). Portage, WI: Portage Project.

Sheridan, S., Murphy, D., Black, J., Puckett, M., & Allie, E.C. (1986). *Beginning milestones*. Allen, TX: DLM/Teaching Resources.

Shonkoff, J.P. (1981). The limitations of normative assessments of high-risk infants. *Topics in Early Childhood Special Education, 3*(1), 29-41.

Sigman, M., & Pamelee, A.H. (1979). Longitudinal evaluation of the preterm infant. In T.M. Field, A.M. Sostele, S. Goldberg, & H.H. Shuman (Eds.), *Infants born at risk* (pp. 336-409). New York: Spectrum Publications.

Simeonson, R.J., & Bailey, D.B. (1988). *Family assessment in early intervention.* Columbus, OH: Charles Merrill.

Simeonsson, R.J., Huntington, E.S., & Parse, S.A. (1980). Expanding the developmental assessment of young exceptional children. In J. Gallagher (Ed.), *New directions for exceptional children* (pp. 51-74). San Francisco: Jossey-Bass, Inc.

Simeonsson, R.J., Huntington, G.S., Short, R., & Ware, T. (1982). The Carolina Record of Individual Behavior: Characteristics of handicapped infants and children. *Topics in Early Childhood Special Education, 2*(2), 43-55.

Simeonsson, R.J. & Weigerink, R. (1975). Accountability: A dilemma in infant intervention. *Exceptional Children,* April, 474-480.

Song, A., & Jones, S. (1980). *Wisconsin Behavior Rating Scale.* Madison, WI: Central Wisconsin Center for the Developmentally Disabled.

Song, A., Jones, S., Lippert, J., Metzger, K., Miller, J., & Borreca, C. (1984). Wisconsin BRS: Measure of adaptive behavior for the developmental levels of 0-3 years. *American Journal of Mental Deficiency, 88*(4), 401-410.

Sparling, J.J. (in press). Narrow- and broad-spectrum curricula. *Infants and Young Children.*

Stancin, P., Reuter, J., & Bickett, T. (1984). Validity of caregiver information on the developmental status of severely brain-damaged young children. *American Journal of Mental Deficiency, 88*(4), 388-395.

Stillman, R.D. (1974). *The Callier-Azusa scale: Assessment of deaf/blind children.* Reston, VA: Council for Exceptional Children.

Tlucak, M.M., Ernhart, C.B., & Liddie, C.L. (1987). The Kent Infant Development Scale: Concurrent and predictive validity of a modified administration. *Psychological Reports, 60,* 887-894.

Uzgiris, I., & Hunt, J. (1975a). *Assessment in infancy: Ordinal scales of psychological development.* Urbana: University of Illinois Press.

Volkmar, F.R., Cicchetti, D.V., Dykens, E., Sparrow, S.S., Leckman, J.F., & Cohen, D.J. (1988). An evaluation of the Autism Behavior Checklist. *Journal of Autism and Developmental Disorders, 18*(1), 81-97.

Wachs, T.D., & Sheehan, R. (1988). Issues in the linkage of assessment to intervention. In T.D. Wachs & R. Sheehan (Eds.), *Assessment of young developmentally disabled children* (pp. 397-406). New York: Plenum Press.

Wallens, P.B., Elder, W.A., & Hastings, S.N. (1979). *From the beginning: The EMI high risk nursery intervention program manual.* Charlottesville, VA: Children's Medical Center of the University of Virginia.

Warren, S.F., Alpert, C.L., & Kaiser, A.P. (1986). An optimal learning environment for infants and toddlers with severe handicaps. *Focus on Exceptional Children, 18*(8), 1-12.

Watson, J.S., Hayes, L.A., & Vietze, P. (1982). Response-contingent stimulation as a treatment for developmental failure in infancy. *Journal of Applied Developmental Psychology, 3,* 191-203.

Whiteley, J.R., & Krenn, W.A. (1986). Uses of the Bayley Mental Scale with nonambulatory profoundly retarded children. *American Journal of Mental Deficiency, 40*(4), 425-431.

Willoughby-Herb, S.J., & Neisworth, J.T. (1980). *The HICOMP curriculum.* San Antonio, TX: Psychological Corporation.

Wolf, M.M. (1978). Social validity: The case for subjective measurement or how applied behavior analysis is finding its heart. *Journal of Applied Behavior Analysis, 11*(2), 203-214.

Wood, K.M., & Hurley, O.L. (1977). Curriculum and instruction. In J. Hordan, A. Hayden, M. Karnes, & M. Woods (Eds.), *Early childhood education for exceptional children.* Reston, VA: Council for Exceptional Children.

Woodcock, R.W., & Johnson, M.B. (1977). *Woodcock-Johnson psychoeducational battery-preschool cluster*. Allen, TX: DLM/Teaching Resources.

Woodruff, G., & McGonigel, M.J. (1988). Early intervention team approaches: The transition model. In J.B. Jordan et al. (Eds.), Early childhood special education: Birth to three (pp. 163–181). Reston, VA: Council for Exceptional Children.

Worobey, J., & Belsky, J. (1982). Employing the Brazelton Scale to influence mothering: An experimental comparison of three strategies. *Developmental Psychology, 18,* 736-743.

Ysseldyke, J.E., & Salvia, J. (1974). Diagnostic-prescriptive teaching: Two models. *Exceptional Children, 41,* 181-186.

Zeitlin, S. (1981). Learning through coping: An effective preschool program. *Journal of the Division of Early Childhood, 4,* 53-61.

Zeitlin, S., & Williamson, G. (in press). Coping behaviors characteristic of handicapped and non-handicapped young children, unpublished manuscript.

Zeitlin, S., Williamson, G.G., & Szczepanski, M. (1988). *Early Coping Inventory: A measure of adaptive behavior*. Bensenville, IL: Scholastic Testing Service.

Zimmerman, I.L., Steiner, V.G., & Pond, R.E. (1979). *Preschool Language Scale*. San Antonio, TX: Psychological Corporation.

Zuromski, E.S. (1984). Active stimulation programming: An alternative to "learned helplessness." *Overview* (Washington State Department of Social and Health Services), *12,* 1-5.

Index

A

Abidin, R.R., *65*, 122, *123*
Ability training, 16
ABS. *See* Assessment of Basic Skills
Absent skills, 24, 34, 40
Acquired skills, 23, 34, 40
Adams, J., 3
Adaptive curriculum model, 137
Adaptive Play for Special Needs
    Children, *155*, 347
Adaptive process assessment, 27
Adaptive-to-handicap assessment, 45, 52
Administrative appraisal, 240, 259
Affleck, J.Q., *63*, 99
Allie, E.C., 145, *155*, 228
Allman, T.L., *154*, 195
Almond, P.J., *63*, 101, 102
Alpern, G.D., *63*, 88, 89, 90, 106, 207
Alpern-Boll Developmental Profile. *See*
    Developmental Profile II
Alpert, C.L., 57
Ames, N., 336
Arick, J.R., *63*, 101, 102
Arizona Basic Assessment and Curriculum
    Utilization System, *155*, 348
ASIEP. *See* Autism Screening Instrument
    for Educational Planning

Assessment
    See also Multidimensional assessment,
        prescriptive developmental
        assessment, specific categories and
        measures, typology of assessment
    adaptive, 9-10, 42, *50*
    attributes of effective, 9-10, 47
    categorical approach to, 5, 12-13
    common preschool measures of, 35-36
    comprehensive, 14
    contemporary, 12-18
    curriculum linkage with, *238*
    developmental, 14-15
    diagnostic, 5, 13, 14
    formative, 9, 21, 24-25, 35, 147, 255
    infant, 26
    limitations of early childhood, 37-38
    longitudinal, 24
    multidisciplinary, 5-6
    outcomes of, 21, 51-52
    parent participation in, 18
    philosophical base for, 17-18, 38, 40
    psychometric, 14-15
    purpose of, 2-3, 21
    selection of measures for, 36
    summative, 21, 24, 35, 147, 240, 255
    technical support for, 43
    "testing" compared to, 13

NOTE: Page numbers in italics indicate entries found in figures or tables.

About the Authors

Stephen J. Bagnato, Ed.D., is a developmental school psychologist and Assistant Professor of Pediatrics and School Psychology at the University of Pittsburgh School of Medicine. He is also Coordinator of the Toddler/Preschool Program of the Child Development Unit, Children's Hospital of Pittsburgh. Dr. Bagnato specializes in adaptive assessment and intervention with neurodevelopmentally disabled infants and preschoolers and their parents. He has held positions previously at Penn State University, University of Maryland, and John F. Kennedy Institute for Handicapped Children, Johns Hopkins Hospital.

Dr. Bagnato is a member of the editorial boards of *Topics in Early Childhood Special Education, The School Psychology Review, Special Services Digest,* and the *Journal of Psychoeducational Assessment.* He has published numerous research studies and applied materials for developmental specialists on early development, assessment, and intervention. He has published nearly 50 clinical and research studies in school psychology, early childhood special education, and developmental disabilities. He has coauthored three other textbooks on early intervention: *Individualized Education for Preschool Exceptional Children* (Aspen Publishers, 1980), *The Young Exceptional Child: Early Development and Education* (Macmillan, 1987), and *Developmental Assessment: A Guide for the Preschool Psychologist* (Guilford, 1989). He is the coauthor of a System to Plan Early Childhood Services (SPECS) (1989), a preschool team assessment system with American Guidance Service.

In 1986, Dr. Bagnato was recipient of the seventh annual National Braintree Hospital Award for Outstanding Research in Traumatic Brain Injury from the Braintree Hospital and Rehabilitation Center in Massachusetts for his studies on treatment impact and patterns of progress in infants and preschoolers with congenital and acquired brain injuries. He is currently codirector of a federally funded, 3-year HCEEP demonstration project, Developmental Support for Medically Handicapped Infants. His current research interests involve interdisciplinary team decision making; clinical, judgment, and other adaptive assessment procedures; early brain injury; curriculum-based developmental assessment; and program efficacy evaluations.

John T. Neisworth, Ph.D, is Professor and senior graduate faculty member in the Department of Special Education and Director of the Early Childhood Special Education Program at Pennsylvania State University. Dr. Neisworth has extensive research experience and expertise in early intervention curricula and assessment. He is coauthor of the *HICOMP Preschool Curriculum* (Psychological Corporation, 1982), the assessment text *Linking Developmental Assessment and Curricula: Prescriptions for Early Intervention* (Aspen Publishers, 1981), and the introductory text *The Young Exceptional Child* (Macmillan, 1988). He is coeditor for the journal *Topics in Early Childhood Special Education* (TECSE) and is an editorial board member of the *Journal for the Division of Early Childhood, Child and Family Behavior Therapy,* the *Child Care Quarterly,* and the *Journal of Psychoeducational Assessment.*

Susan M. Munson, Ph.D., is Assistant Professor of Special Education at Duquesne University in Pittsburgh, Pennsylvania. Previously, Dr. Munson has held faculty positions at Penn State University and the University of Georgia. She has served as Assessment and Outreach Training Coordinator for Project CONNECT, the former handicapped preschool technical assistance branch of the Bureau of Special Education, State of Pennsylvania. She has been a teacher for both preschool and school-aged physically handicapped and learning-disabled children and an educational diagnostician for a special education unit diagnostic team. Dr. Munson specializes in integrated teacher training and mainstreaming issues for mildly handicapped children from 3 to 8 years of age. Her current applied research interests include affective and behavior disorders in learning-disabled children and instructional modifications by regular education teachers for mildly handicapped children.

Dr. Munson is a member of the Council for Exceptional Children, Division of Learning Disabilities. She is also a field editor for *Special Services Digest.*